Water Rights Reform: Lessons for Institutional Design

Edited by Bryan Randolph Bruns, Claudia Ringler, and Ruth Meinzen-Dick

International Food Policy Research Institute
2033 K Street, N.W.
Washington, D.C.

International Food Policy Research Institute
2033 K Street, N.W.
Washington, D.C. 20006-1002
U.S.A.
Telephone +1-202-862-5600
www.ifpri.org

Library of Congress Cataloging-in-Publication Data

Water rights reform : lessons for institutional design / edited by Bryan Randolph Bruns, Claudia Ringler, and Ruth Meinzen-Dick.

p. cm.
Includes bibliographical references and index.
ISBN 0-89629-749-7 (alk. paper)
1. Water rights. 2. Law reform. I. Bruns, Bryan Randolph. II. Ringler, Claudia. III. Meinzen-Dick, Ruth Suseela. IV. International Food Policy Research Institute.
K758.W38 2005
346.04'32—dc22 2005030412

Contents

Tables

Figures

Boxes

Foreword

Access to water is essential for improving the lives of poor people. In many parts of the world, growing competition for scarce supplies of freshwater threatens current livelihoods and hopes for the future. Inadequate institutions for water governance contribute to social inequity, economic inefficiency, and environmental degradation. The importance of water rights is increasingly acknowledged, but too little is known about how water rights systems can be improved in practice, and how to avoid the risk that reforms may backfire, worsening insecurity, confusion, and injustice regarding access to water.

In 2003 IFPRI, building on its past work in this area, led a conference of researchers and practitioners focusing on water rights. This book grew out of that conference. It brings together practical lessons from experience in water rights reform, demonstrating how changes in policies, laws, regulations, agency procedures, and other social practices that arrange rights to water can help resolve conflicts, secure access, and enhance benefits from this most vital of natural resources. The volume contributes to a growing body of knowledge about the management of natural resources, and how policy reforms can help improve the lives of the poor. It illustrates ways in which improved water rights and allocation practices can raise water productivity, enhance livelihoods, and increase benefits from existing and new investments in the sector.

Secure water rights for the poor, and governance structures to ensure that their rights are protected, are needed for both equitable and sustainable water use. This volume sets out to clarify strategies and instruments available to safeguard existing water users and customary rights in the context of supporting equitable and efficient water allocation. Leading researchers and practitioners provide new insights into the options that various stakeholders may consider in developing water allocation institutions. They draw on practical experiences with water rights reforms, including eight detailed case studies on six continents, together with broader comparison and synthesis of international experience. It is my hope that the recommendations in this volume will contribute to the process of equitable and productive reforms in water rights systems.

Joachim von Braun
Director General, IFPRI

Preface

Internationally there is growing understanding that water rights are important and that a lack of effective water rights systems creates major problems for the management of increasingly scarce water supplies. However, discussion of water rights has often failed to recognize the range of available institutional options, the rich diversity of lessons from experience, and the need for appropriate flexibility in adapting institutional design to dynamic local conditions. In response to these concerns, the editors and other colleagues organized an international working conference, held in Hanoi, Vietnam, in February 2003, which brought together practitioners and researchers working on water rights reform. To further share ideas on improving water rights reform, this volume presents revised versions of selected papers from the conference. The focus is on experiences with implementing water rights reform. While it was not possible to include cases from every region of the world, the reform cases come from countries in six continents, and many of the authors draw on additional practical experience and research in multiple countries and regions.

The International Food Policy Research Institute (IFPRI) led the conference organization, and supported preparation of this book. INWENT (Capacity Building International, Germany, Ltd., formerly DSE) provided financial support and working conference facilitation. Both the Asian Development Bank (ADB) and the World Bank (through the Bank Netherlands Water Partnership Program) contributed funds to the workshop. The Challenge Program on Water and Food of the Consultative Group on International Agricultural Research provided support, and the Ministry of Agriculture and Rural Development, Hanoi, Vietnam, was the local host. Researchers from IFPRI and other organizations, as well as expert practitioners with experience in developing water rights and allocation systems, contributed empirical and conceptual knowledge to the discussion. Water policymakers and managers from many countries helped keep discussions oriented toward practical concerns in introducing and implementing reforms in water allocation institutions. After the conference, papers were first reformatted and made available via CD-ROM and Web site.

The editors of this volume would like to highlight their appreciation of the efforts of Franz Heim (formerly DSE/INWENT), Wouter Lincklaen Arriens (ADB), Karin Kemper (World Bank), and Mark Rosegrant (IFPRI) to bring together practitioners and experts concerned with water rights reform and make relevant experience more widely available. Sarah Cline helped with editing the first set of papers. Uday Mohan, Chelo Abrenilla, and Evelyn Banda at IFPRI, and Mary-Jane Banks, IFPRI consultant, provided valuable support for manuscript preparation. Comments from three anonymous reviewers were very helpful in improving the manuscript.

Bryan Bruns thanks his family for their patience and support during the editing process. Ruth Meinzen-Dick thanks Carroll, Laura, and Kevin Dick for their understanding about taking editing even on vacation. Claudia Ringler thanks the IFPRI water team for their continued support.

Introduction

Bryan Randolph Bruns, Claudia Ringler, and Ruth Meinzen-Dick

Rights to water are increasingly crucial and increasingly contested across the globe. Urbanization, industrialization, environmental degradation, agricultural intensification, rising per capita water use, increasing population, and other social, political, and economic transformations contribute to growing scarcity and demand for better management of water resources. In responding to these challenges, the world can draw on a rich heritage of institutions for regulating rights to water and resolving disputes, and a diversity of institutional arrangements that demonstrate great ingenuity in designing solutions to fit the conditions and priorities of various river basins. However, policy discussion in water management has often been impoverished by narrow polarization around a few idealized models of centrally integrated management or water commoditization, even though these comprise only a small and very incomplete subset of the institutional options available for effective management. The authors in this book expand the range of reflection and analysis of water rights reforms, offering insights aimed especially at those seeking practical pathways to improve equity, efficiency, and sustainability in access to water.

In many countries around the world, increasing attention is being directed to the need to improve water rights systems. As water becomes scarcer and access more often contested, societies pursue better rules for coordinating water use and settling conflicts. Lack of well-defined and secure water rights increases the vulnerability of poor, politically and economically weaker water users. Improved water rights institutions can raise water productivity, increase benefits from existing and new investments in water use, and enhance rural livelihoods. However, there is a shortage of information on practical ways to develop better institutions for water rights. Much of the literature focuses on technical complications of water allocation and hypothetical advantages of water markets, without adequate attention to institutional frameworks required for any form of water allocation, and the necessary involvement of stakeholders in the design and implementation of reforms.

Moreover, no water rights reform process takes place on a blank slate: in all cases some forms of claims or rights over water have already been established. Many writings on water rights, however, tend to focus on "pure" or idealized institutional models (and critiques of their shortcomings), rather than on the practical challenges of making major transformations in institutional arrangements. The chapters in this volume draw on empirical experience and analysis of specific cases to discuss how development of water rights can be made more effective, by better understanding and responding to the range of existing rights-holders and claimants, the interplay among management organizations, the variety of institutional options available, the implications for social equity, and the practical problems involved in legislating and implementing an effective water rights system. Based on extensive international experience, this book distills pragmatic, institutionally feasible lessons for improving water rights as tools for better water management.

The first part of the book reviews the range of institutional options available for water rights reformers to consider, combine, and adapt in improving water allocation. Authors in the second part of the book build on their experience in Australia, Mexico, and other countries to identify practical lessons for implementing water rights reforms. The chapters in the third part examine equity issues of revising rules that regulate who has access to water, in South Africa, the western United States, and Andean countries of South America, especially potential impacts on rural communities. The chapters in the fourth part analyze implications of recent water laws for water rights reforms in Spain, Indonesia, and China, focusing on security of rights for existing users and potential transferability of water rights. The final chapter offers conclusions concerning patterns, goals, and institutional design of reforms in water rights, emphasizing the advantages of phased reforms in redesigning governance, resolving tenure, and regulating transfers.

In Chapter 1, discussion of institutional options begins by looking at why water rights matter, and why better "rules of the game" for sharing an increasingly contested resource could make a difference for equity, productivity, and sustainability. In this chapter, Bryan Bruns and Ruth Meinzen-Dick introduce one of the key themes of this book, the need to develop suitable combinations of bureaucratic, market, and self-governance institutions for water allocation. The authors outline some of the key strategies available for dealing with institutional complexity in developing water rights, including forming stakeholder forums, recognizing existing rights, adapting the characteristics of water rights to historical experience and local conditions, integrating multiple institutional frameworks, and developing organizational capacity.

Chapter 2 examines problems of devising water property institutions that effectively align relationships among diverse actors. Edella Schlager delineates the multiple bundles of property rights that may govern rights to water. Comparison of the management of water quantity with water quality, regulating abstraction versus regulating pollution, offers insights into the relative advantages of user self-governance and state regulation in overcoming institutional problems of commitment, agency, and decisionmaking costs. The author argues that successful reform requires careful attention to designing the right relationships among rights-holders.

In Chapter 3, Charles Abernethy offers a general perspective on the implementation of new water rights institutions in response to socioeconomic transformations. Urban and industrial growth brings growing scarcity and competition among water uses and users within basins and sub-basins, so that new institutions for water management are needed. The author suggests specific recommendations on implementing a water rights system, including promoting participation in governance, building political support for water law reforms, developing a hierarchy of basin organizations, integrating existing rights and users, measuring water usage, controlling water quality, enforcing compliance, financing basin water management, and creating incentives for transfers between uses.

The second part of the book opens with a review of the practical challenges that Mexico faced in implementing major reforms in water rights. In Chapter 4, Héctor Garduño looks at how existing water use and wastewater discharge were registered, information systems developed, charging introduced, transferability regulated, and enforcement strengthened. This has built the foundation for using water rights as a management tool, combining economic incentives, stakeholder participation, and law enforcement, in reducing excessive groundwater abstraction, for example. Mexico's experience shows the value of applying a gradual approach in the design and operation of water rights administration, making adjustments through trial and error to match implementation with the capacity of users and institutions.

In Chapter 5, Brian Haisman analyzes how water rights in Australia's Murray-Darling Basin have been redefined over time to respond to changes including rising demand, growing concern for environmental flows, and recognition of Aboriginal water rights. Rights to use water have been modified to implement a "cap" limiting total basin water usage, introduce water trading within and between states, and accommodate more careful accounting for water availability. Early establishment of strong water rights and later changes to facilitate water trading have yielded major benefits for economic productivity. Changes in water rights management intended to give higher priority to environmental flows have begun to have significant impacts on water management and ecosystem restoration.

Part 3 opens with a discussion of reforms to reallocate water rights in South Africa, where political transformation and racial inequities in access to water pose major challenges for water management. In Chapter 6, Ashwin Seetal and Gavin Quibell discuss how procedures have been systematically developed to involve stakeholders, building capacity to manage and productively use water, including redistribution from "haves" to "have-nots," as well as providing water for ecological needs. The chapter describes the process of building consensus on principles for reform, and current efforts to design changes in water allocation institutions.

Chapter 7 recounts how water rights based on the prior rights principle of "first-in-time, first-in-right," supported the growth of irrigated agriculture in the western United States. In recent decades, urban expansion has stimulated the development of water markets through which farmers transfer their rights to cities. Growth in water trading raises questions about whether the interests of third parties may be harmed, and what regulatory protection may be needed. Douglas Kenney offers a critical analysis of how pursuit of environmental sustainability and equity may conflict with the prior rights doctrine as a basis for the future development of water rights, in the western United States and elsewhere.

Chapter 8 highlights ways in which the development of water rights can exclude or include stakeholders, particularly communities of rural water users. Rutgerd Boelens, Axel Dourojeanni, and Paul Hoogendam offer examples from Bolivia, Chile, Ecuador, and Peru to depict ways in which development projects and policy reforms have deprived and excluded the peasant majority of water users in Andean nations. They argue that state, market, and consensus approaches need to be supplemented by empowerment of stakeholder platforms. Their chapter concludes by outlining a framework for assessing and building alternative institutions for integrated, multisectoral watershed management.

Part 4 assesses the implications of new water laws for reforms in water rights. Alberto Garrido's analysis in Chapter 9 finds that Spain's 1999 law still has major shortcomings from the perspective of promoting efficiency, allowing flexibility in the entitlement system, increasing the role of users in financing construction, and improving environmental water quality. While the framework for water transfers has been improved, analysis and experimental studies indicate that restrictions on water transfers still inefficiently block opportunities for increasing water productivity through transfers and water banking, as well as reducing the value of users' rights.

In Chapter 10, Suharto Sarwan, Tjoek Walujo Subijanto, and Charles Rodgers describe the institutional framework for water management in Indonesia and potential implications of the 2004 water law, focusing on differences between water rights for basic usage and commercial exploitation, and prohibition of water rights transfers. The Brantas River Basin in East Java illustrates the development of basin water management institutions. The chapter then discusses development of water rights as property rights and human rights, in the context of the new law.

Chapter 11, by Bin Liu, analyzes institutional design issues involved in developing a water rights system based on China's 2002 Water Law. Several cases illustrate emerging institutional innovations to allow water transfers. The chapter offers analysis and makes recommendations regarding how water rights are defined; balancing public interests and the security of private rights; determining who can hold rights; recognizing existing rights; facilitating transferability; ensuring fairness in permitting; and providing compensation if rights are expropriated.

Chapter 12 summarizes common patterns in water rights reform cases in this book, including performance problems, sources of initiative, allocation institutions before and after reform, participation, and further challenges for improving water management. The chapter assesses achievements and limitations of water rights as tools for providing water for basic needs, security for irrigation, urban water supply, and environmental needs. The chapter concludes by presenting major lessons for institutional design, particularly how better timing of different aspects of reform, in a phased approach encompassing multiple levels of institutional change in redesigning governance, resolving tenure, and regulating transfers, could open practical pathways to more equitable, efficient, and sustainable water allocation.

Water Rights Reform

Part 1

Options for Institutional Design

Chapter 1

Frameworks for Water Rights: An Overview of Institutional Options

Bryan Randolph Bruns and Ruth Meinzen-Dick

— This chapter offers an overview of institutional options for water rights. It introduces reasons why water rights are important and are receiving increasing attention, and then presents general principles related to property rights. Various institutional arrangements may regulate socially accepted claims to water, including self-governance, agency administration, and water markets. Methods for improving water rights and water allocation institutions include forming forums, clarifying water rights, developing techniques for planning and modeling, and building capacity of specialized management agencies. Institutional options for improving water rights can be combined into a framework that draws optimally on the strengths of various water allocation institutions.

As long as water is abundant, it is easy to stay ignorant and unconcerned about who else may be sharing the same river, lake, or aquifer. As populations grow, demands for water rise—for household use, agriculture, and industry. People who use water are increasingly affected by each other's actions. Coordination of water use becomes more complex as well as more crucial. In one way or another, water rights institutions, expectations about what claims to water are socially accepted as legitimate, are shaped by such competition, influencing people's ability to obtain water. Similar pressures to define property rights emerge for land and other resources as they become scarcer. However, whereas changes in land tenure institutions are more familiar, studied, and debated, changes in water tenure have received less attention.

The institutional frameworks that structure socially accepted access and entitlements to water take many forms. Sometimes they are easily seen in local agreements, customs, and physical structures. They may be informal, implicit, and embedded in local practices. Legislation and formal permits may explicitly codify rights. Water quantities are defined in many ways: by proportional shares, taking turns, periods of time, measured volumes, or combinations of these principles. Rights may be held by individuals or by organizations. They may last for a limited time or endure in perpetuity, and may vary according to season and water availability. Rights may apply only to a specific use and parcel of land, or may be flexible in use and transferable. Water quality may be specified, or left unstated. Rights inherently bring duties and responsibilities.

This chapter offers an overview of institutional options for water rights, taking a broad perspective that in trying to improve water resources management it is important to understand the many ways in which access to water is currently controlled and influenced by social institutions, and the multiple means available for improving water allocation. Thus, we go beyond the conventional analysis of water rights as deriving only from government law books and regulatory agencies to include a range of other types of water rights that exist in practice.

The chapter is particularly concerned with the "rules of the game" that structure access to water when competition over water expands beyond small face-to-face communities. In these cases, interaction occurs between strangers who may have few other common concerns beyond sharing an increasingly contested resource. The institutions involved include not just formal water rights supported by laws and licenses, but a range of different negotiation arenas through which different stakeholders in water management may seek to increase, defend, or otherwise influence their access to water, for example, by building infrastructure, adjusting gates and other water facilities, negotiating disputes, appealing to bureaucratic agencies, suing in court, or lobbying for legislation.

The second section of this chapter presents some of the reasons why water rights are important and are receiving increasing attention as a means for alleviating poverty, promoting economic growth, and protecting habitats and environmental services. Next, the third section looks at general principles of property rights, after which the fourth section examines three major types of water allocation institutions: agency allocation, user management, and water markets, and how these may be combined and transformed. The fifth section reviews some of the means available for improving water allocation institutions, including ways of clarifying water rights, strengthening forums for interaction among stakeholders, forming specialized agencies, and applying planning and modeling methodologies. The concluding section summarizes some of the main institutional options for water rights and opportunities for improving water allocation.

Why Water Rights?

The institutions that influence access to water matter for many reasons. Life and livelihoods rely on water. Lack of clean water impoverishes people and hinders opportunities while better access to water can be an important tool for alleviating poverty (Lipton, Litchfield, and Faurès 2003). Quality of life is affected not only by physical access to water, but also by the degree of influence people have on decisions about water allocation. Expectations about secure access to water influence investment decisions, by both industrial investors and subsistence farmers.

The unique properties of water complicate the determination of rights, as patterns of water use are dynamic and complex. Changes in water and land use by humans add sediment, fertilizers, and wastes that flow downstream to affect other users. Deforestation, cultivation, reforestation, and other land-use changes reshape how water flows across, into, and out of aquifers and rivers. Shifts in quantity, timing, and quality of water flows create, destroy, and transform aquatic habitats. The impacts of climate are mediated by the institutions that regulate access to water. Attempts to protect water quality, preserve wetlands and other aquatic habitats, and prevent intrusion of saline water into deltas and aquifers are inextricably interlinked with other water management institutions and activities.

Water allocation institutions matter for people's livelihoods, income, and for protection of the environment. Thus water rights help determine if people are included or excluded in the control of a vital resource for their lives. Improvements in water rights institutions can help reduce poverty, improve economic productivity, and protect nature. Efforts to improve water allocations may, however, be ineffective or even produce effects opposite from those intended, unless grounded in a good understanding of social institutions that shape access to water, and a careful assessment of the options available for improving water management. The diversity of culture, environment, economic activities, and other conditions means there is no one best way to improve water rights and water allocation institutions. The best route to better water management depends on where you are starting from, with many pathways available.

Property Rights, Water Rights

Before delving further into the different types of water rights, it is useful to examine some basic concepts related to property rights, and some of the relevant principles from land rights. Property rights can be defined as "the claims, entitlements, and related obligations among people regarding the use and disposition of a scarce resource" (Furubotn and Pejovich 1972). As long as the resource is plentiful, there is little pressure to define or enforce rights. As the resource becomes scarcer, however, there is greater competition for it, and property rights can clarify expectations and thereby reduce conflict over the resource.

Bromley (1992:4) points out that "Rights have no meaning without correlated duties . . . on aspiring users to refrain from use." Property rights are not a relationship between a person and a thing, but are social relationships between people with regard to some object (the property). Property rights are effective (legitimized) only if there are some kind of institutions to stand behind them, and the rights are only as strong as those institutions.

In many cases, the state is a primary institution supporting property rights, but this is not necessarily the case. Customary rights may be backed by local authority and social norms. In the case of land rights in Africa, many customary land tenure arrangements have provided as much tenure security as government-issued title to the resource (Bruce and Migot-Adholla 1994). The same often applies to water rights (Bruns and Meinzen-Dick 2000). Security of property rights—the assurance that one will receive benefits in the future—matters because it affects incentives to invest in and conserve the underlying resource.

Although many people equate property rights with "ownership" of a resource and the ability to do whatever one wants with it, it is more useful to think of bundles of rights that different parties may hold. These bundles of rights can be broadly defined as use rights of access and withdrawal, and control or decision-making rights to manage the resource, exclude others from it, and to alienate, or transfer, rights to the resource to others (see the chapter by Schlager in this volume, and see Schlager and Ostrom 1992; F. and K. von Benda-Beckmann and Spiertz 1996).

Different people, groups, or agencies may hold different and overlapping bundles of rights over the same resource. For example, in the case of water, all women of the community may have rights to draw water from a stream for cooking and washing purposes. Animal owners may have the right to water their herds or flocks at certain places. Farmers who invested in building an irrigation system may have rights to divert water for their crops (all of which are use rights). At the same time, the village community, irrigators' association, or the state may claim rights to decide on the timing of water use, changes to the river, and granting of permission to new users (management or control rights). These overlapping uses and users of water complicate analyses and mean that simplistic models of water rights derived from pure state or private land ownership are unlikely to be appropriate.

Institutional Alternatives for Water Allocation

Property rights regimes can be broadly classified as public, private, and common property, based on who holds rights. In public property, the state holds rights; in private property, individuals (or legal individuals, such as corporations) hold rights; and in common property, rights are held by a group of people. Similarly, institutional arrangements for water allocation, and particularly for reallocation, can be grouped in three broad types (Meinzen-Dick and Mendoza 1996; Meinzen-Dick and Rosegrant 1997):

- In user-based allocation, water users join together to coordinate their actions, managing water resources as a form of common property.
- In agency allocation, water is treated as public property, with government agencies assuming authority for directing who does and does not receive water in accordance with bureaucratic policies and procedures.
- In market allocation, which corresponds with private property held by individuals or organizations, water may be allocated and reallocated through private transactions, with users trading water through short- or long-term agreements, reallocating rights in response to prices.

These three forms of water allocation institutions may be combined in various ways at different locations and levels of water management. For example, within the same river basin or even within an irrigation system, there may be common property management within and between some groups of users, transfers between individual farmers occurring through market-type mechanisms, and agencies administering allocation of water resources. User management and private exchanges may be based solely on local institutions, or take place in the context of licenses and other government regulations. A theme of this chapter is that improving water management will often be a matter of finding an optimal combination of all three forms of allocation institutions, employing multiple frameworks that draw on the different advantages of self-governance among users, bureaucratic agencies, and market mechanisms.

User-Based Allocation

In many places throughout the world, water rights derive from membership in local organizations that manage irrigation or water supply systems. Access to water often depends on contributions to the original investment and on fulfilling continuing obligations for operation and maintenance. Allocation of water may be assigned according to shares of the available flow, periods of time, quantities, turns, and other rules (Maass and Anderson 1978). Such rules become embodied and further modified in the physical shape of division structures and outlets, and in procedures for distributing water during periods of scarcity.

A common source of problems occurs when outside intervention, intended to improve local systems, is carried out without due attention to the existing local rights and obligations. Externally imposed criteria, such as allocation strictly in proportion to land area, may not only increase inequity, but also disrupt local rights and practices with their flexible adaptations to the complexity of local history and conditions, such as detailed adjustments made locally to account for such factors as earlier investments in building the system; variations in soils, slopes, and drainage; and tolerance for minor or temporary violations of local rules (e.g., see Vermillion 2000). External intervention may also ignore or disrupt local sources of knowledge and legitimacy. At the local level, the effectiveness of institutions may derive from longstanding relationships between friends and neighbors; informal or formal organizations; and local values regarding equity, leadership, sanctions, and other matters. These relationships constitute a form of social capital, which provides an essential framework for water rights and allocation at the local level.

In many aspects of natural resources management, including water, the value of local institutions, such as irrigators' organizations, is now more widely appreciated. Rather than ignoring or replacing local organizations, attempts are being made to integrate them into government arrangements, for example, through the establishment of formal water user organizations, transfer of management responsibilities for irrigation or water supply to community-based groups, and increasing stakeholder participation in the planning and management of large water projects and river basins.

As competition over water grows, local organizations face competition from other users, particularly those taking water upstream and downstream users who want to limit upstream abstractions. Typically, such conflicts extend beyond the bounds of face-to-face communities. As mentioned previously, solving such problems requires dealing with strangers who often have few links beyond using the same resource. As in other aspects of social and economic life, governments can play a crucial role in creating institutions, including laws, courts, regulatory bodies, and other public services, which help disputants to resolve their differences peacefully and forge enforceable agreements. Important choices are involved in what role government chooses to play concerning such disputes, whether facilitating negotiations among users, asserting direct control through a government bureaucracy, or establishing conditions that enable users to transfer water among themselves, or some combination of these.

Agency Administration

National constitutions, laws, and regulations usually declare that water is owned by the nation, with the government authorized to control water resources in the national interest. This has typically been interpreted as a mandate authorizing bureaucratic agencies to control water directly (rather than indirect control through establishing and regulating institutional frameworks for self-governance and voluntary exchange). Allocation decisions were often framed primarily in technical terms of engineering procedures such as irrigation schedules and reservoir operation rules. User participation beyond the lowest level of the system was often absent, or officially restricted to submitting requests. Subsequent decisions were typically at the discretion of agency officials, with relatively little communication and accountability to users. Professional norms and bureaucratic procedures thus became a primary basis for water allocation in agency-controlled systems, often with little or no formal specification of water rights of the ultimate users. Moreover, during the twentieth century, governments dramatically expanded their roles in many spheres, including water management. Government agencies built large dams, reservoirs, irrigation networks, and urban water supply systems, and usually continued to operate the projects they had built. The rules and procedures of such agency projects ("project law") thus played a major role in determining who received water. Agencies building and managing reservoirs, irrigation systems, and other projects typically did not just directly deliver water, but also carried out a range of regulatory roles, allocating rights, resolving disputes, and reallocating water. A number of countries have adopted devolution policies or "irrigation management transfer" (IMT) since the 1990s, and this has provided the impetus for reforms to water laws in some cases. But in practice, many countries have not turned over their water allocation function to user groups, or even provided users with significant formal water rights (Vermillion 2001), leaving allocation relatively unclear, uncertain, and unaccountable.

Market Allocation

The holder of a water right, whether an individual, association, municipality, or other entity, may be able to transfer their rights over water to others. In other words, one part of the "bundle" of rights would be alienation rights. A water right might be transferred temporarily as in a lease, or permanently. It might be tied to land or transferable separately. Although individuals often hold use rights to water even under agency- or user-based allocation systems, larger institutions, such as water users' associations or government agencies, may hold decisionmaking rights concerning reallocation or transfer. Rights-holders may be able to arrange transfers among themselves, or the transfers may need to be reviewed and authorized by another body, whether a local irrigators' organization or a government agency.

Short-term water transactions tend to be common within local areas, whether irrigators along a canal swapping turns or pump owners delivering water to adjoining lands. The parties involved in such transactions often know each other quite well as neighbors or relatives, and their agreements tend to be largely self-enforcing. Because they undertake repeated transactions and want to do so in the future, they are usually keen on maintaining a reputation of trustworthiness. Under such conditions, short-term "spot" markets for water can emerge relatively easily (Saleth, Braden, and Ehart 1991; Easter, Rosegrant, and Dinar 1998).

For longer-term or permanent water transfers it is harder to create credible commitments. If water rights are not clearly recognized by local communities and government, and accepted as transferable, then it is difficult to be sure that an agreement will be fulfilled. In the event of disputes, courts may be unwilling to enforce agreements, unless a suitable institutional framework exists for transferable water rights.

An often-cited advantage of transferable water rights and water markets is that voluntary transactions should direct water to economically more valuable uses. This can lead to increased efficiency of water use and create incentives for existing users to conserve water, because they can gain by selling or lending the surplus to others. In Chile, for example, secure and tradable water rights sometimes fostered efficient use of water, facilitated a shift to high-value crops that use less water per unit of output, and induced improved efficiency in urban water supply services. Moreover, construction and operation and maintenance (O&M) subsidies to better-off farmers and urban consumers could be reduced and redirected as targeted subsidies to poor urban water users and small-scale farmers (Gazmuri Schleyer and Rosegrant 1996). However, in some cases when reservoir operators changed the timing of river flows and reduced water availability to farmers downstream, affected farmers were unable to get courts to restore the access to water they had previously enjoyed. Speculative acquisition of rights reduced water availability for current use, and may have fostered monopolistic practices in hydropower production. Such problems can be severe unless there is an adequate and effective regulatory framework for water markets (Bauer 1997, 1998, 2004).

In many cases, the two parties engaging in the transaction are not the only ones affected by water use: others are also often affected by changes in the place and time at which water is used. For water markets to work well, such third parties need

Table 1.1 Types of water allocation institutions

	User group management	Agency allocation	Water markets
Key characteristics	Collective decisionmaking among water users, for example, an irrigators' association	Bureaucratic agency controls directly	Trading among users, temporary or permanent transfers
Advantages	Legitimacy based on custom Local knowledge and experience Adaptable	Standard procedures Technical expertise River basin perspective	Voluntary Prices reveal opportunity costs for users, create incentives to conserve
Disadvantages	More difficult if users do not know each other and lack existing relationships	Information intensive Difficult to customize to particular conditions	Risk of neglecting impacts on third parties If transactions rare or complex, then hard to establish prices

access to mechanisms that inform them about changes that might affect them, and the opportunity to object to or put conditions on transactions and to receive adequate compensation if they are harmed by the water transfers. The potential for water markets to develop is also constrained by other factors, including the frequency of transactions, the physical infrastructure required to implement and measure a transfer, and political objections to water trading.

Each of the three types of allocation institutions has advantages and disadvantages, as summarized in Table 1.1. Typically, water allocation occurs through a combination of institutional arrangements including agency roles, user self-governance, and at least some forms of exchange.

Combinations

As water flows through a basin, it may be governed by a whole range of allocation institutions, from private property to common property to agency-controlled state property to open access public property (Meinzen-Dick 2000). Government control over water abstraction often concentrates on major intakes and relies on local institutions for more detailed distribution and conflict management. From the aspect of reducing transaction costs of time, effort, and other resources required to manage water, such a combination of institutions may be far less costly than reliance on a single type of institution (Guillet 1998). Thus, the typical situation is not one of a single, homogeneous, and consistent regulatory regime, but rather of water flowing through diverse, overlapping sets of rules.

Claims to water can be based on many sources, including community norms, religious values, historic practices, agency regulations, and laws enacted by different levels of government. Instead of a single uniform set of principles and rules, a variety of institutions come into play. Research on legal pluralism has demonstrated not just the continuing strength of "local" or "customary" law, but also how various legal orders, such as customary law, religious law, and project law, continue to evolve and interact (Griffiths 1986; Merry 1988; F. and K. von Benda-Beckmann and Spiertz 1996; Spiertz 2000).

Analysts of legal pluralism point out that rather than a simple duality of state law and local law, there is often a complex interaction that might include local norms and practices, village and district governments, and religious values and leaders, as well as other ideas and principles at the community level. Actions of national and state or provincial governments may be shaped through the procedures of projects, legislation, administrative procedures, and court rulings. Each of these legal orders constitutes a framework for allocating water. Different frameworks may be mutually supporting, or in conflict. Water allocation institutions do not stand alone, and usually depend on other institutions such as courts, legislative bodies, and administrative agencies.

These overlapping definitions of property rights can be seen as problematic and a source of confusion and conflict. They also create space for maneuver, formation of coalitions, and institutional innovation to solve problems. Disputants can employ multiple strategies, "shopping" among different forums and making various arguments to pursue their claims. The interaction of different kinds of rights, and existence of multiple legitimizing frameworks, is part of the context within which "rights" evolve in response to changing pressures on the resource and on society (Meinzen-Dick and Pradhan 2002).

Neglect of customary rights in the formulation of water law and policies can cause serious opposition from those whose rights are ignored (Burchi 2005). Discussions of the interaction between state and local property institutions often perceive these as completely separate systems. However, deeper research often reveals that "local" institutions were established or heavily influenced by external factors such as colonial legal regimes and earlier kingdoms. Similarly, water resources that appear to be fully under state control, such as government-managed irrigation systems, may turn out to overlay preexisting local irrigation systems. Local institutions often handle much of water allocation within their boundaries, with conflicts usually resolved through community processes rather than bureaucratic or legal procedures. As water is increasingly contested, however, local institutions come into greater contact with others, bringing different ideas, opportunities, and dangers.

Transformations

Rules and practices regulating access to water are dynamic. Often they provide principles, guidelines, and precedents, but their application to specific cases is open to further debate and interpretation, which may not occur until forced by a particular problem. Changes in water scarcity shift the value of water to different users, reshaping the incentives to obtain more water or defend current access. New opportunities may arise in which water use can be far more productive, but require moving water from some current use. If there is no flexibility in water allocation, obtaining new supplies can be extremely expensive, for example, through building storage or diverting water from other basins.

As water becomes more contested, asymmetries between stakeholders may also become more pronounced. Typically, urban and industrial users have advantages over rural and agricultural users in terms of wealth, power, and knowledge of bureaucratic procedures. Their interests are often more easily organized than those of the large number of dispersed users in rural areas, and therefore may be more effectively defended. Urban and industrial users are usually willing to pay substantially higher prices than the monetary value of water in agricultural use, but they also demand a higher quality of service and reliability. However, existing users, such as irrigators, may have advantages as well, including the legitimacy that comes from longstanding use, political appeal of sustaining farming lifestyles, and the difficulty outsiders face in trying to control a large number of widely scattered users.

Water rights change, evolve, and adapt. There is no single or inevitable pathway for change in water allocation institutions. Agencies have tended to take on increasing roles in water allocation. This may, however, sometimes be due simply to lack of adequate consideration of the existence or possibility of self-governance among users. Markets may play a valuable role in facilitating the voluntary transfer of water to higher value uses, but this still requires a suitable enabling framework of law and infrastructure, as well as regulatory protection against negative third-party effects. If transactions are too scarce then markets may not develop even when enabling conditions are in place.

Changes in water rights institutions are sometimes discussed as if they would be carefully planned and carried out only after a process of thorough deliberation. In practice, droughts and other crises may precipitate urgent actions that deny some rights and strengthen others, with relatively little discussion or assessment of alternatives. Ideas formulated in calmer circumstances may lie in wait and then be taken up when there is political attention and urgency. Protection of instream flows and aquatic habitats often emerges from a process of environmental debate and regulation very different from the irrigation and municipal water supply interests that have tended to predominate in the water sector, bringing new ideas and legal principles into the process of allocating water. Protection of endangered species and wetlands is based on different objectives and criteria than those used to determine volumes of water to be abstracted for use in irrigation or urban water supply. Concern about the environment and public health, reinforced by better technology for detecting pollutants, has brought increased attention to water quality, and the challenges of controlling point and nonpoint sources of pollution. Changes in the prevailing balance of interests in the water sector and in the broader political economy may open new opportunities for change that had earlier been excluded or not even considered.

Improving Water Allocation Institutions

There are many ways to go about enhancing water allocation institutions. Done well, institutional changes may help to make water use more efficient, equitable, and environmentally sound. However, there are also serious risks of disrupting existing institutions, worsening inequities, or creating perverse incentives that compound problems, despite any good intentions that may lie behind reforms. Improving water rights is sometimes seen as simply a matter of issuing formal licenses. Such formal registration may be neither the first nor the best way to go about improving water management. This section outlines some of the institutional options that may form useful components of a framework for improving water allocation.

Forming Forums

Establishing forums or platforms that bring together representatives of water users may be a faster and more effective approach to solving water allocation problems than immediately attempting to strengthen administrative procedures for formalizing water rights. Participatory forums can provide knowledge and legitimacy in revising rules and resolving conflicts over water allocation. Forums may include basin committees, water parliaments with authority to determine budgets and policy, water courts or other bodies with quasi-judicial authority to resolve disputes, advisory committees, and federations of stakeholder organizations, as well as more informal networks of individuals and organizations. Participatory approaches tend to produce results much more easily acceptable to those involved. Engaging stakeholders also helps to better prioritize efforts and identify measures that will be most effective in solving actual problems in specific locations.

The selection of representatives to take part in forums can be a challenge, and needs to be done carefully so as to obtain representatives who will be trusted and accepted as legitimate. Activities can be carried out through transparent, public processes open to any individuals and groups who are sufficiently interested to take part, rather than artificially restricting or excluding participants. It may be important to be proactive about inviting participation of women and people who live in more isolated areas, have lower incomes, are less well educated, ethnically distinct, or for other reasons might not be as likely to take part even if they could be significantly affected by changes in water allocation institutions. In many cases, forums can be made more democratic and inclusive by means of additional outreach to share information. Facilitators can aid particular groups of stakeholders in understanding issues and preparing themselves to take part in a participatory process.

For forums to be effective, public involvement usually needs to go beyond just dissemination of information through meetings and formal public hearings and instead promote interactive discussion and joint problem-solving. A variety of methodologies are available through which committees, citizen panels, and other groups can learn about technical aspects of issues, consider various views and goals, assess policy options and scenarios, and formulate recommendations for how to deal with various problems (IAP2 2000). However, if forums do not have meaningful tasks or lack a genuine opportunity to influence water management, then they may be a waste of time for those involved. Furthermore, not everyone wants to participate. Those who do usually are already busy and face many competing demands for their attention, so forums and other participatory processes need to be efficient in terms of time, information, and other resources. It is important to respect the views of those who may choose not to take part in a particular process, while still finding ways for those who are interested to proceed.

Governments do not have a monopoly on forming forums to address problems in water allocation. User groups, nongovernment organizations, and others outside of government can also take the initiative, as occurred with the Landcare movement for watershed management in Australia and various watershed conservation initiatives in India, New Zealand, the Philippines, and elsewhere. Such forums may be able to solve problems themselves, or offer recommendations for further discussion and consideration in cooperation with others. Groups may be organized based on a particular river basin or sub-basin. In some cases, a coalition or alliance of existing civic and community groups may provide an effective structure for addressing shared concerns along a river or within a watershed.

Recognizing Rights

Improving water rights is sometimes taken to mean that there must be immediate and comprehensive registration in a central cadastre. However, this is far from the only—or even the best—possibility. In most cases, people's actual water rights are embedded not in certificates, but in the rules governing who can use how much water, for what purposes. A gradual approach allowing clarification of rights in response to specific problems and local conditions can offer one way to efficiently provide an enabling framework for improving basin water management. Imposing comprehensive registration is likely to be difficult and costly. It risks delegitimizing and disrupting existing arrangements, without yielding adequate benefits. Even in the case of land rights, which are easier to establish than water rights, cadastres have proven very expensive and problematic, often increasing conflicts, particularly where preexisting systems of multiple, overlapping rights are replaced by individual rights. Moreover, even after the cadastre is established, landowners frequently do not update the records, especially where state structures are less effective than community institutions in effectively backing types of rights over the resource (see Okoth-Ogendo 1986; Toulmin and Quan 2000). Other approaches, such as strengthening forums for dispute resolution, may do more to protect existing users, and make it easier and less costly to improve water resource management.

In countries such as Indonesia, for example, where farmers have had customary water rights, but have less economic power or access to state agencies than factory owners, hasty or biased formalization of water rights creates a risk that poorer people will lose out (see Sarwan, Subijanto, and Rodgers, this volume). By contrast, in South Africa, where the apartheid system had vested water rights with white farmers with large holdings, the new water law attempts to redress these imbalances by prioritizing water rights for the poor and for the environment (see Seetal and Quibell, this volume).

Many new moves to "establish" water rights act as if there was a blank slate, in which the state holds all water rights and can unilaterally allocate those rights as it wishes. But in almost all cases where water has been in use, existing institutions constitute a system of implicit water rights, based on the ways water is currently being withdrawn, and steps taken or not taken to control withdrawals, particularly during periods of shortage. This is not to say such an existing system is ideal, equitable, or consistent, but it is an important point of reference and the empirical starting point. Current users will usually view their accustomed use as legitimate, and be inclined to challenge anything that they would see as infringing on their rights.

The current system, including its implicit water rights, possesses the institutional inertia that comes from familiarity and acceptance of current practice. It embodies considerable knowledge about how water is currently distributed and the means available for controlling allocations. This knowledge is not limited to written rules and regulations and ideas about how water is controlled, but includes the tacit knowledge embedded in the physical design of intakes and outlets, and in the evolution of practices that have been found to be workable. This implicit system constitutes a valuable resource, built on lessons from experience integrated into local understanding. "Tacit knowledge" is not easily transferable, so there is a comparative advantage for local compared to state control and decisionmaking (see Schlager, this volume). Appropriately using and building on current allocation institutions can make an invaluable contribution to the efficiency and effectiveness of any efforts to improve water allocation institutions.

A crucial first step may be acknowledging existing rights. This does not necessarily require that current rights be registered or formally recorded. Nor does it mean that they must be accepted completely or uncritically, but it is important to ensure that they are not simply ignored, disregarded, or dismissed as illegal. In common law legal systems, recognition of the validity of such existing practices may be a straightforward process. Civil law can also provide ways to recognize customary practices. One example is the way in which the Japanese River Law "deems" that agencies treat existing users as if they have water rights, without requiring any separate process of registration or formalization (Sanbongi 2001).

Adjusting Characteristics of Water Rights

The bundle of rights authorized by association by-laws, an agency-issued permit, or a contractual agreement can be adjusted. Quantity, timing, duration, exclusiveness, transferability, quality, and other specific characteristics and applicable rules may be changed, or made explicit where they were previously ambiguous or unspecified. If such changes are to constitute improvements, and not just an arbitrary imposition of external models that may be inappropriate, ineffective, and even counterproductive, then it will be important to adapt the definition and characteristics of rights in accordance with the history, priorities, and values of a particular country, basin, and set of water users. For example, many African customary water rights systems give priority to "primary" water uses, which includes domestic use, livestock watering, and certain areas of irrigated gardens (Derman, Hellum, and Sithole 2005; Meinzen-Dick and Nkonya 2005). As African countries develop more formalized water rights, it is important that these primary water uses—which go beyond the basic domestic use that is normally recognized—continue to receive priority, without necessarily being required to pay fees or go through difficult registration processes.

Changes in water law may have major implications for equity, efficiency, and other goals, particularly in terms of how they affect the entitlements of existing users and potential access of new water users. Technical analysis and legal drafting can support, but should not neglect or replace, consultation among stakeholders and democratic decisionmaking, which can play an essential role in adapting water rights to fit local conditions and needs.

Integrating Multiple Water Rights Frameworks

Where local customs and practice and national constitutions and laws do operate on different principles and procedures, it may be important to consider ways to improve integration, resolving or reducing conflicts while still trying to maintain the advantages of different institutional frameworks. This need not mean forcing local institutions to fit national mandates, but can involve revising laws and regulations and suggesting practical accommodations in how laws are implemented.

Formal recognition of existing rights does pose potential problems. These include the ways in which any process of formalization may, deliberately or inadvertently, transform rights; questions about ratifying existing inequities in who gets water (and differing views about what is and is not equitable); and risks of manipulation and abuse of the recognition process. These are linked to the capacity of current governance institutions. Problems can be reduced by transparent, accessible administration in a way that is open to the participation of all users, including those who may be poor, illiterate, living in remote areas, or otherwise disadvantaged in dealing with bureaucratic procedures, as exemplified by South Africa's efforts (Seetal and Quibell, this volume).

As with land titling and land reform, there is much scope for debate about the feasibility for promoting more equitable distribution, and how to best pursue equity under such circumstances. A commonly cited example is the Sukhomajri irrigation system in India, in which rights to water under a newly constructed system were assigned to all village members, including landless households, based on labor investment in creating the system (Joshi and Seckler 1982). Rather than simply assigning rights in accordance with landholding, replicating existing patterns of unequal resource tenure, rights were proactively allocated in a way intended to increase the assets of the poor. At a minimum, this shows the scope for creative alternatives in allocating rights, particularly to newly developed water supplies.

A more subtle issue is that any formalization, even a minimalist recognition, may transform rights, for example, if it individualizes rights that have been held by kin groups or other collective entities. Authority to resolve disputes may shift to local governments for matters that had previously been dealt with through inheritance systems framed by local customs, religious values, or other institutions that may differ from formal law in terms of both concepts and the forums and processes used for dealing with conflicts. To minimize these problems and increase the social legitimacy of water rights administration, Nigeria has customary courts that deal with customary land and water rights issues, drawing upon a range of local experts and oral history as evidence (Burchi 2005).

Gradual and Selective Licensing

In clarifying government frameworks for water rights, the existing system of implicit rights deserves due attention. Means of acknowledging existing rights, without requiring immediate or comprehensive registration, can be explored (e.g., see Burchi 2005). In some cases legal requirements for licensing may exist, but may be implemented only for some uses and users. Municipal and industrial users may have to obtain licenses, but not agricultural users. Large-scale uses may require licenses, but not small-scale users. Rather than assuming that comprehensive formal registration is necessary, it may be worthwhile to assess the potential consequences of formalizing rights in the form of licenses or other instruments, considering when and where it may be worth promoting more thorough registration or licensing of water use. This can not only help to economize on scarce budgets and focus government efforts on those problems that deserve highest priority, but can also help avoid activities that disrupt existing water allocation arrangements that may still be functioning relatively effectively.

Inventories

Mapping existing water uses, for example the irrigation systems along a stream, may sometimes be seen primarily as a technical matter. Rather than assuming that inventories can be done only by a government agency, it is worth noting that users themselves may initiate and conduct inventories. For example, an inventory could be compiled by irrigators along a river reach or within a particular sub-basin. Inventories may be important to show the extent of current use, and hence the limits on new rights that can be issued without impairing existing uses. In many countries, inventories of irrigation systems have helped to demonstrate that farmer-managed irrigation systems and other small-scale irrigation cover much larger areas than had previously been shown in official records, important information in terms of understanding how water is currently used (e.g., see Yoder and Upadhyay 1988; Ambler 1994; Tan-Kim-Yong 1995). However, inventories have major implications in terms of which users and uses are recognized by or "visible" to the government (Scott 1998). In this regard, water use inventories are similar to mapping of land use: there is considerable risk that even in recording the uses they are likely to lose their flexibility. The inventories can be used as much to impose controls as to defend the prior rights of customary users (see Peluso 1995; Fox 1998). Irrigation inventories are thus not only a technical procedure, but should be designed with attention to participation, transparency, accountability, accessibility, and other characteristics that may affect not just their accuracy, but how they are perceived and used, and their consequences for the water rights of existing and potential future water users.

Education and Training

Educational activities are important measures for improving water allocation institutions. Information can be communicated through meetings, brochures, newspapers, radio, television, and other media. Educational activities may spread information about current rules and regulations, or promote awareness of problems that need further attention. Farmer-to-farmer exchange and other forms of peer learning may not just help impart skills and knowledge in more easily understood and appropriate ways, but also provide valuable ways to share experience and facilitate networking among water users (Pradhan 1994).

Planning, Modeling, and Scenarios

Formulating plans can provide a good way to bring together available technical information and use expert analysis to assist in assessing problems and exploring potential solutions. A variety of methods are available for analyzing problems such as those in water resource management, where the same resource is used for multiple purposes by many different stakeholders. Biophysical computer models represent the physical relationships involved, for example, the linkages between rainfall, flows into rivers and aquifers, and usage upstream, with water availability downstream. Integrated hydrological–economic models can combine information on flows with economic information about costs and benefits of water in various uses (Rosegrant et al. 2000). Scenarios can be used to present management alternatives, such as changes in how water rights are allocated and allowing greater transferability of rights.

There are important questions to be considered about how planning and modeling are done. Who will be involved? Who defines the problems to be considered? What resources are available? What time frame will be analyzed? How will issues such as environmental impacts and water quality be integrated? However, planning can take up much time and expense only to be ignored or rejected, particularly if it is treated as a narrow technical exercise without stakeholder involvement.

Strengthening Agencies

Much thinking concerning agencies for river basin management is still dominated by the Tennessee Valley Authority model of the 1930s. A large government-established bureaucracy carried out construction and management, focused on reservoir construction and operation, operating in a top-down technocratic way. Although that is one option, and many attempts have been made to repeat it in various parts of the world (with limited success), there are many other ways in which specialized agencies may play a role in supporting basin water allocation and water use rights. Agencies may act as specialized technical advisors. They may work as a technical secretariat, supporting a body of stakeholder representatives, as with French water "parliaments." An agency may have a narrow mandate focused on regulatory activities, or may also take on broader resource management roles. Management activities need not include construction, and various agencies may deal with specific issues, rather than having control concentrated in a single agency.

There is a risk of uncritically, and wastefully, copying examples of water management, including the administration of water rights, from wealthy Westernized countries, whereas tropical countries usually have very different management priorities (Shah, Makin, and Sakthivadivel 2001). Safeguarding and strengthening water management on rainfed lands and microwatersheds in upstream areas may do more to protect livelihoods and prevent poverty than large projects downstream. Bigger may not be better, but instead bring diseconomies of scale that block organizational effectiveness. Unrealistic assumptions about the technical feasibility of new management methods may mean that capabilities of basin organizations fall far short of expectations.

Pathways for Change

As discussed earlier, many means are available for improving water allocation institutions. These can be chosen and applied in accordance with particular circumstances. It is, however, crucial to consider the process that will be used. In many cases, what is needed is not just refining technical analysis or fine-tuning of regulations. Dealing with new problems, or issues where efforts so far have been ineffective, may require not just involving more stakeholders but constituting new institutions, in the form of regulations, organizations, and other institutions, that have the scope, authority, capability, and other characteristics needed to deal with the relevant problems.

Conclusions

For many reasons there is increasing agreement on the need for greater attention to the role of water rights in water resources management. Safeguarding and improving the access of poor people to water is vital for their lives and livelihoods. Clarity and security about water availability is important to poor farmers and others who want to make investments that depend on reliable supplies. Flows of water for aquatic environments need to be ensured because of their importance in sustaining habitats and species, providing recreation, maintaining water quality, and other goals.

Various types of institutional arrangements may be used to regulate socially accepted claims to water, including user self-governance, agency administration, and water markets. In practice, different types of institutions are often combined, and a suitable combination may be more efficient and workable than overemphasis on a single type of allocation. Attempts to improve water allocation institutions can be more effective if they are based on an understanding of existing institutions and the various options available for change. Different river basins have different physical and social conditions, and usually different problems and priorities for improvement. There is no single recipe for improving water rights, but instead a range of options from which to choose.

Methods for improving water rights and water allocation institutions include forming forums, clarifying water rights, planning and modeling techniques, and capacity building for specialized management agencies. These can be used in various sequences and combinations, depending on local problems and priorities, to develop frameworks for water rights that draw optimally on the strengths of various water allocation institutions.

References

Ambler, J. 1994. Small-scale surface irrigation in Asia: Technologies, institutions and emerging issues. *Land Use Policy* 11 (4): 262–274.

Bauer, C. J. 1997. Bringing water markets down to earth: The political economy of water rights in Chile, 1976-95. *World Development* 25 (5): 639–656.

———. 1998. Slippery property rights: Multiple water uses and the neoliberal model in Chile, 1981–1995. *Natural Resources Journal* 38: 109–153.

———. 2004. *Siren song: Chilean water law as a model for international reform.* Washingon, D.C.: Resources for the Future.

Benda-Beckmann, F. von, K. von Benda-Beckmann, and J. Spiertz. 1996. Local law and customary practices in the study of water rights. In *Water rights, conflict and policy,* eds. R. Pradhan, F. von Benda-Beckmann, K. von Benda-Beckmann, H. L. J. Spiertz, S. S. Khadka, and K. Azharul Haq. Colombo, Sri Lanka: IIMI.

Bromley, D. 1992. The commons, property, and common-property regimes. In *Making the commons work,* ed. Daniel Bromley. San Francisco: Institute for Contemporary Studies.

Bruce, J. W., and S. Migot-Adholla, eds. 1994. *Searching for land tenure security in Africa.* Washington, D.C.: World Bank.

Bruns, B. R., and R. S. Meinzen-Dick, eds. 2000. *Negotiating water rights.* London: Intermediate Technology Publications. New Delhi: Vistaar.

Burchi, S. 2005. The interface between customary and statutory water rights—a statutory perspective. Paper presented at the African Water Laws Workshop: Plural Legislative Frameworks for Rural Water Management in Africa. January 26–28, 2005, Johannesburg, South Africa. http://www.nri.org/waterlaw/AWLworkshop/BURCHI-S.pdf.

Derman, B., A. Hellum, and P. Sithole. 2005. Observations on the intersections of human rights and custom: A livelihood perspective on water. Paper presented at the African Water Laws Workshop: Plural Legislative Frameworks for Rural Water Management in Africa. January

26–28, 2005, Johannesburg, South Africa. http://www.nri.org/waterlaw/AWLworkshop/DERMAN-B.pdf.

Easter, K. W., M. W. Rosegrant, and A. Dinar, eds. 1998. *Markets for water: Potential and performance.* Boston: Kluwer.

Fox, J. 1998. Mapping the commons: The social context of spatial information technologies. *The Common Property Resource Digest* 45: 1–4.

Furubotn, E. G., and S. Pejovich. 1972. Property rights and economic theory: A survey of recent literature. *Journal of Economic Literature* 10 (4): 1137–1162.

Gazmuri Schleyer, R., and M. W. Rosegrant. 1996. Chilean water policy: The role of water rights, institutions, and markets. *International Journal of Water Resources Development* 12 (1): 33–48.

Griffiths, J. 1986. What is legal pluralism? *Journal of Legal Pluralism* 24: 1–50.

Guillet, D. 1998. Rethinking legal pluralism: Local law and state law in the evolution of water property rights in northwestern Spain. *Comparative Studies in Society and History* 2: 97–117.

IAP2 (International Association for Public Participation). 2000. *IAP2 Public Participation Spectrum.* International Association for Public Participation. http://www.iap2.org/practitionertools/spectrum.html.

Joshi, D., and D. Seckler. 1982. Sukhomajri: Water management in India. *The Bulletin of Atomic Scientists* 38 (3): 26–30.

Lipton, M. J., J. M. Litchfield, and J. M. Faurès. 2003. The effects of irrigation on poverty: A framework for analysis. *Water Policy* 5 (5): 415–426.

Maass, A., and R. L. Anderson. 1978. *. . . And the desert shall rejoice: Conflict, growth and justice in arid environments.* Cambridge, Mass.: MIT Press.

Meinzen-Dick, R. S. 2000. Public, private, and shared water: Groundwater markets and access in Pakistan. In *Negotiating water rights,* eds. B. R. Bruns and R. Meinzen-Dick. London: Intermediate Technology Publications. New Delhi: Vistaar.

Meinzen-Dick, R. S., and M. S. Mendoza. 1996. Alternative water allocation mechanisms: Indian and international experiences. *Economic and Political Weekly* 31 (13): 25–30.

Meinzen-Dick, R. S., and L. Nkonya. 2005. Understanding legal pluralism in water rights: Lessons from Africa and Asia. Paper presented at the African Water Laws Workshop: Plural Legislative Frameworks for Rural Water Management in Africa. January 26–28, 2005, Johannesburg, South Africa. http://www.nri.org/waterlaw/AWLworkshop/MEINZEN-DICK-R.pdf.

Meinzen-Dick, R. S., and R. Pradhan. 2002. Legal pluralism and dynamic property rights. CAPRi Working Paper No. 22. Washington, D.C.: CGIAR System-Wide Program on Collective Action and Property Rights. http://www.capri.cgiar.org/pdf/capriwp22.pdf.

Meinzen-Dick, R. S., and M. W. Rosegrant. 1997. Alternative allocation mechanisms for intersectoral water management. In *Strategies for intersectoral water management in developing countries:*

Challenges and consequences for agriculture, eds. J. Richter, P. Wolff, H. Franzen, and F. Heim. Feldafing, Germany: Deutsche Stiftung für internationale Entwicklung.

Merry, S. E. 1988. Legal pluralism. *Law and Society Review* 22: 869–896.

Okoth-Ogendo, H. W. O. 1986. The perils of land tenure reform: The case of Kenya. In *Land policy and agriculture in Eastern and Southern Africa,* eds. J. W. Arntzen, L. D. Ngcongco, and S. D. Turner. Tokyo: United Nations University.

Peluso, N. L. 1995. Whose woods are these? Counter-mapping forest territories in Kalimantan, Indonesia. *Antipode* 27 (4): 383–406.

Pradhan, U. 1994. Farmer-to-farmer training as a way of assistance to the farmers on the improvement of irrigation systems. In *From farmers' fields to data fields and back: A synthesis of participatory information systems for irrigation and other resources,* eds. J. Sowerwine, G. Shivakoti, U. Pradhan, A. Shukla, and E. Ostrom. Proceedings of an International Workshop held at the Institute of Agriculture and Animal Science, Rampur, Nepal, March 21–26, 1993. Colombo, Sri Lanka; Kathmandu, International Irrigation Management Institute and Institute of Agriculture and Animal Science, Rampur.

Rosegrant, M. W., C. Ringler, D. C. McKinney, X. Cai, A. Keller, and G. Donoso. 2000. Integrated economic-hydrologic water modeling at the basin scale: The Maipo River Basin. *Agricultural Economics* 24 (1): 33–46.

Saleth, R. M., J. B. Braden, and J. Wayland Ehart. 1991. Bargaining rules for thin spot water markets. *Land Economics* 67 (3): 326–339.

Sanbongi, K. 2001. Formation of case law and principles in watershed management. In *Proceedings of the regional conference on the legal aspects of sustainable water resources management,* Teslic, Bosnia, Herzegovina, May 14–18, 2001, ed. S. Bogdavonic. Novi Sad, FR Yugoslavia: International Association of Water Law.

Schlager, E., and E. Ostrom. 1992. Common property and natural resources: A conceptual analysis. *Land Economics* 68 (3): 249–252.

Scott, J. 1998. *Seeing like a state: How certain schemes to improve the human condition have failed.* New Haven: Yale University Press.

Shah, T., I. Makin, and R. Sakthivadivel. 2001. Limits to leapfrogging: Issues in transposing successful river basin management institutions in the developing world. In *Intersectoral management of river basins,* ed. C. L. Abernethy. Feldafing, Germany: German Foundation for International Development (DSE) and Colombo, Sri Lanka: International Water Management Institute (IWMI).

Spiertz, H. L. J. 2000. Water rights and legal pluralism: Some basics of a legal anthropological approach. In *Negotiating water rights,* eds. B. R. Bruns and R. S. Meinzen-Dick. London: Intermediate Technology Publications and New Delhi: Vistaar.

Tan-Kim-Yong, U. 1995. *Muang-fai communities are for people: Institutional strength and potentials.* Bangkok: Chulalongkorn University Social Research Institute.

Toulmin, C., and J. F. Quan, eds. 2000. *Evolving land rights, policy and tenure in Africa.* London: DFID/IIED/NRI.

Vermillion, D. 2000. Water rights in the state of nature: Emergent expectations in an Indonesian settlement. In *Negotiating water rights,* eds. B. R. Bruns and R. S. Meinzen-Dick. London: Intermediate Technology Publications and New Delhi: Vistaar.

Vermillion, D. 2001. Property rights and collective action in the devolution of irrigation system management. In *Collective action, property rights, and devolution of natural resource management: Exchange of knowledge and implications for policy,* eds. R. S. Meinzen-Dick, A. Knox, and M. Di Gregorio. Feldafing, Germany: Zentralstelle für Ernährung und Landwirtschaft.

Yoder, R., and S. B. Upadhyay. 1988. Reconnaissance/inventory study of irrigation systems in the Indrawati basin of Nepal. In *Irrigation management in Nepal: Research papers from a national seminar,* Bharatpur, Nepal, June 4-6, 1987. Kathmandu, Nepal: IIMI (IIMI pub 88-07).

Chapter 2

Getting the Relationships Right in Water Property Rights

Edella Schlager

— In most places around the world, multiple types of property rights regimes govern water. This chapter outlines various types of property rights and explores institutional design problems concerning commitment, agency, and decisionmaking costs. The implications of these problems for institutional relationships between communities and higher-level government are contrasted for water quantity allocation and water quality regulation. Successful reform must center on getting the relationships right among the actors exercising property rights in relation to water systems.

In any given setting many different individuals, organizations, and governments will be exercising property rights in relation to water sources. For instance, most western U.S. states use several types of property rights systems to govern water, and that is even before taking into account the property rights of the federal government or of Native Americans. In most irrigation systems, farmers, farmer associations, the operator of the system, and perhaps provincial and national governments will be exercising various property rights in relation to the system and its water. All of these instances can be made more complex by including international boundaries and property rights in competing uses of water. Most societies use multiple types of property rights regimes to govern water depending on its type (ground, native surface, project, effluent), its location, and its use.

Given the complex institutional setting of water, the multiple types of property rights systems involved, and the multiple actors concurrently exercising rights in any given setting, better governance is a critical but difficult task. Various observers of current reform efforts urge consideration of different dimensions of institutional reform (Birdsall, Graham, and Sabot 1998; Ramaswamy and Cason 2003). International lenders have begun to emphasize the necessity of comprehensively planning national poverty reduction programs as a precondition for financial assistance. Observers of urban water supply and sanitation system privatization have urged investment in the capacities of governments to regulate private utilities effectively. Nongovernmental organizations have urged attention be given to including communities and citizens in identifying, planning, developing, and operating local water systems. Each group has identified critical aspects of realizing good governance—strengthening the competence and including the active participation of different levels of government and of citizens.

One aspect of realizing good governance that has not received enough attention concerns the interactions and relationships among different levels of government, among different organizations functioning at different levels from the international to the local, and among individuals and organizations functioning at the same social level. Relationships among governments, organizations, and citizens are of central importance to scholars focusing on polycentric governing systems (Ostrom 1987; Oakerson 1999). Polycentric systems are defined as "many overlapping arenas (or centers) of authority or responsibility. These arenas exist at all scales, from local community groups to national governments" (McGuiness 1999:2).

Considerable discussion has been devoted to attempting to identify the appropriate level of government, or the appropriate public or private organization, to assign responsibility for carrying out specific tasks. Young (2002) argues that attention to such issues is somewhat misdirected. Although allocating appropriate tasks to different levels of government and to public and private organizations is certainly important, just as important is devising and supporting cooperative and mutually beneficial relations among diverse actors. Given that property rights consist of bundles of rights and that in every water setting property rights are unbundled with many individuals and organizations concurrently exercising shared rights, just as much if not more attention should be devoted to getting the relationships right among people and organizations (Young 2002). Attending to the interactions among actors and limiting opportunities for opportunism, free riding, and exploitation is critical if effective and efficient water supply and sanitation systems are to be made available to all people (Ostrom 1992).

Relationships among diverse actors in water settings are based on property rights. In the next section, property rights and their importance and complexity are delineated. The third section explores the challenges of devising water property rights that foster credible commitments; control the behavior of agents; and reduce decision costs, particularly in the context of vertical linkages between communities and national governments. The fourth section compares advantages of community governance for water allocation with advantages for government roles in regulation of water quality. The fifth section concludes the chapter by suggesting that reform, if it is to be successful, must center on getting the relationships right among the actors exercising property rights in relation to water systems.

Property Rights

According to J. R. Commons (1957), property rights define relationships among people regarding things. Property rights define differing relationships among persons depending on the bundles of rights that people hold. Schlager and Ostrom (1992) define five types of distinct rights that may be bundled together in a variety of ways:

- access: the authority to enter a resource;
- withdrawal: the authority to remove units from a resource;
- management: the authority to make decisions about how the resource is to be used;
- exclusion: the authority to decide who may enter the resource; and
- transfer: the authority to sell, lease, or bequeath the resource.

The rights of access, withdrawal, management, exclusion, and transfer are roughly cumulative. The right of withdrawal implies a right of access. To make use of a resource one must be able to access it. The right of management implies rights of access and withdrawal. The holder of the right of management has the authority to define rights of withdrawal, that is, how the resource is to be used. A complete set of rights is commonly thought of as ownership. The holder of such a complete set of rights possesses the authority to define rights of access and rights of withdrawal as well as the authority to transfer portions of or all of the rights to someone else.[1]

Even in relation to a single type of water, multiple actors may exercise different bundles of rights in relation to it. For instance, many national governments are considering introducing market-based aspects to the provision and production of potable water in urban areas. Governments may select from a variety of contractual relationships (Johnstone and Wood 2001a:10–12). Each type of contract represents a different bundle of property rights, a different means by which governments may divide and share their rights in water systems. A service contract, in which the government contracts for a specific activity, such as meter reading, involves a government sharing some management rights with a private company. The private company exercises limited (in terms of time and scope) management authority in relation to a water system. This contrasts sharply with a concession whereby the private company not only operates and maintains the system, but also invests in it. The government allows the private company to exercise the complete right of management, within certain constraints as specified in the concession. In addition, the private company exercises the right of exclusion. In its maintenance, investment, and expansion decisions, it decides who will have rights of access and withdrawal, again subject to conditions identified in the concession.

In a setting in which a government has signed a concession with a private consortium to operate, maintain, and expand an urban water system, government agencies, the consortium, and citizens who are customers of the utility all exercise property rights in relation to the water system. The government continues to exercise rights of transfer, exclusion, and management. However, through the concession it shares the rights of exclusion and management with the consortium. Through the concession, the government may have established a variety of performance targets. The private consortium attempts to realize those targets through the management and exclusion choices that it makes, such as how much to invest in maintenance versus expansion of the system. Citizens exercise rights of access and withdrawal. The choices and actions that each actor takes affect all other actors.

Problems of Commitment, Agency, and Decision Costs

Commitment Problems

One issue almost certain to arise in institutional relationships for water governance is that of commitment. How committed is each of the actors to their agreements even in the face of temptations to violate them?[2] For instance, a government may be tempted, in the face of the consortium raising water rates, to renege on its commitment to allow it to realize sufficient revenues to cover the costs of investing in water delivery systems, including reasonable rates of return. A government may violate its commitment by forcing the consortium to lower its rates or by limiting the rate increases allowed.[3] Once a government reneges, however, the consortium faces few incentives to make long-lasting investments in the water system, thereby negating many benefits that could have been realized under a concession (Noll, Shirley, and Cowan 2000).

Commitment problems may also arise between the utility and its customers. Citizens may be tempted, in the face of increasing water rates, to evade their commitment to pay for their rights of access and withdrawal of potable water. Citizens may refuse to tie into the water system or they may tap into the system illegally. The effect of citizens reneging on paying for their rights of access and withdrawal are similar to the government reneging on its commitment to allow the utility to realize adequate revenues—the utility faces fewer or weaker incentives to invest in the development and maintenance of the water system. This problem has emerged in several cities that have signed concessions with private water consortiums, such as Buenos Aires (Mazzucchelli, Pardinas, and Tossi 2001).

Vertical linkages, interactions among groups and organizations that extend across levels of social organization, present particularly difficult commitment problems (Young 2002). National governments can take a larger perspective and attempt to balance the interests and activities of local and regional actors. But national governments can also pursue interests and goals that are at odds with local interests and goals. A national government may hold expanding foreign exchange earnings as a priority and allow industries to extract and pollute water at the expense of other local livelihoods. Or, as Noll, Shirley, and Cowan (2000) argue, some national regimes have been reluctant in reforming and investing in water systems in regions that provide very little electoral support to ruling parties. As Young (2002:267) concludes, national "regimes provide arenas in which the interests of powerful, nonresident players often dominate the interests of small-scale local users." Commitment problems can be especially problematic in vertical relations. National governments are often tempted to violate commitments made to local governments, whether those commitments involved allowing local governments considerable decisionmaking authority, or providing financial support for local undertakings, or national officials overturning the commitments their local representatives have made to local citizens and officials.

From the perspective of local governments, commitment problems in relation to national regimes are especially thorny. Relationships between national and local governments tend to be more asymmetrical, leaving local governments particularly vulnerable to the actions of national governments. For local governments the issue centers on gaining and maintaining the commitment of national governments to relationships that support their ability and capacity to govern well. This may be even more of a problem for water users' associations that do not have government standing.

Commitment problems can be anticipated and, thus, the actors can take steps to attempt to reduce their likelihood. Noll, Shirley, and Cowan (2000) note a variety of ways of "tying the hands" of government to make reneging on a commitment to utilities to recoup their costs much more difficult and costly. For instance, a government agency can be created to oversee and regulate private utilities, which is insulated from short-term political pressures. This may be accomplished by appointing executives to terms that extend across several election cycles, and making removal procedures of executives and managers difficult and time consuming. By insulating the regulatory agency from short-term political pressure, elected officials and their constituents may not as easily manipulate the concession for their own ends. Another solution is for governments to commit financial resources to large projects that would be lost if assets are expropriated (Noll, Shirley, and Cowan 2000:251).

In addition, steps may be taken to ensure that water users tie into the system once it is completed. For instance, the U.S. Bureau of Reclamation, which builds and operates large surface water projects in the western United States, requires water users to sign "take or pay" contracts. Water users commit to paying for their share of the operation and maintenance costs of the water system even if once the system is completed they choose not to tie into and take water from it.

A multitude of mechanisms may be used to discourage national governments from reneging on their commitments to local governments. For instance, constitutional provisions provide greater protection from reneging than does legislation, particularly if national officials cannot easily amend the constitution and if the constitution is interpreted and enforced by an independent judiciary. Commitments to capacity building may be supported through dedicated sources of funding, such as bonds, the authority to levy fees, and earmarking of taxes, that do not pass through an annual budgetary process, but rather require special legislative action to change. Tying the hands of national governments in ways that permit local governments and organizations the authority and capacity to exercise their rights is key to resolving vertical commitment problems.

Ideally, limiting the authority of national governments to impinge on and violate the rights of actors and organizations at lower levels of social organization allows societies to tap into the benefits and strengths of local-level governments. Local communities are, in general, better at identifying, addressing, and resolving local problems than are regional or national governments. Better time and place information and more immediate feedback promote the creation of rules and projects that better fit the circumstances. Furthermore, local participation in rule and project creation can translate into greater legitimacy and consequently higher levels of rule conformance. Limit the authority of local actors, organizations, and governments to exercise authority, or regularly violate such authority, and the benefits of local participation and governance dry up. Locals are much less likely to invest in self-governance if that investment is regularly squandered. Examples abound of national governments acting in ways that discourage local level governance, such as governments seizing control of what had historically been locally owned and governed resources (Alexander 1982; Lansing 1991; Lam 1998; Agrawal 1999).

The institutional mechanisms discussed earlier make it less likely or more costly for the government or for water users to renege on their commitments. As Noll, Shirley, and Cowan (2000) argue, however, in making it much more difficult for the government to renege, utilities are granted increasing leeway to act, even to act in inappropriate ways. For instance, the private utility may capture the regulatory agency and the agency may seek to realize the interests of the utility and not necessarily the interests of water users. In other words, commitment problems are resolved at the expense of agency problems.

Agency Problems

Agency problems arise as property rights holders exercise the authority granted to them by their property rights in ways that undermine, perhaps even subvert, the authority of others to exercise their property rights. For instance, if a utility chooses to siphon off a significant portion of the revenues that it collects from water users and invest those revenues in activities other than the maintenance and operation of the water system, water users' abilities to exercise their rights of access and withdrawal are impaired. Withdrawal of water from the system becomes increasingly problematic as the system crumbles.[4]

That said, local governments and communities can exercise their authority in ways that directly violate national interests and goals, and that can be as heavy handed as their national government counterparts. As Rose (2002: 251–252) argues, American courts have been suspicious of customary law and practices, refusing to allow longstanding practices to "create legal rights that would govern communities." Customary rights were viewed as antidemocratic and courts argued that communities should be governed by open, constitutional practices, and that legislation should be openly discussed and determined.

Numerous case studies of successful local-level governance bear out these concerns. While communities have devised arrangements that support sustainable use of common-pool resources, the practices that they follow in relation to some community and noncommunity members can be alarming. Whether it is Maine lobster gangs destroying each other's equipment (Acheson 1975), or the Berbers and Arabs using the Harantine as indentured labor in the building and maintenance of irrigation systems in numerous communities in the Ziz Valley of Morocco (Ilahiane 2001), communities may exercise their authority in questionable ways. Agency problems are not limited to criminal behavior. Many agency problems involve more mundane issues. For instance, a constant source of tension between the U.S. federal government and state governments revolves around state implementation of federal environmental laws, such as the Clean Air Act and the Clean Water Act. The federal government prefers stricter implementation plans and more active monitoring and enforcement than states are often willing to provide (Landy, Roberts, and Thomas 1994).

Agreements can address agency problems by specifying more completely the actions that agents must take or goals that agents must achieve in exercising their property rights. For instance, in a number of concessions that cities have signed with private water consortiums, specific performance-centered goals are written into the contracts. Common goals include extending coverage to specific areas and rehabilitating existing infrastructure within specified time limits, reducing unaccounted for water, and meeting specified water quality standards, assuming, of course, that the government has the ability and wherewithal to enforce such stipulations against multinational corporations.

More completely specifying the actions of shared property rights holders, or agents, comes with consequences. Decisionmaking costs increase as the shared property rights holders bargain and negotiate over the specific actions and goals that they must agree to meet. The more actions and goals considered, the higher the decisionmaking costs. At some point the decisionmaking costs overwhelm the benefits to be realized by more completely specifying actions. It is neither possible nor desirable to eliminate agents' discretion. The level of conflict among property rights holders directly affects decisionmaking costs. Higher levels of conflict tend to increase decisionmaking costs, thereby limiting the extent to which the actions of agents will be specified. In other words, agency problems are resolved at the expense of decisionmaking costs (Horn 1995).

Decisionmaking Costs and Uncertainty

Decisionmaking costs and agency problems may be exacerbated by uncertainty. If the setting in which agents are to act is not well understood, or if the setting is characterized by legal, economic, or social uncertainty, devising a set of meaningful actions or goals may entail considerable decisionmaking costs, as information gathering and processing activities may need to be extensive and time consuming. For example, many urban poor live in areas far from existing infrastructure, on difficult terrain such as steep and rocky slopes, floodplains, and landfills, in semipermanent housing, with no urban planning and no legal title to their property. Devising workable water systems in such settings may be possible only with considerable field information and experience (Johnstone and Wood 2001b:46–47).

Such decisionmaking costs may be avoided by adopting a set of actions and performance goals with little consideration given to the diverse and uncertain settings that agents are likely to confront; however, decisionmaking costs are then offset by confounding agency problems. Inevitably, even if agents work diligently to achieve agreed upon goals, they will be tripped up by novel circumstances. Again, decisionmaking costs may be reduced at the expense of agency problems and agency problems may be reduced at the expense of increased decisionmaking costs.

One approach suggested for addressing situations characterized by considerable uncertainty is to engage in more open-ended contracts in which actions and performance goals may be revised, either over the course of the bidding process or over the course of the contract, as circumstances change and as actors gain experience and greater knowledge of diverse settings (Johnstone, Hearne, and Wood 2001:40–41). Open-ended contracts provide opportunities to address agency problems by revising actions and goals, but they also provide opportunities for reneging on commitments. For instance, renegotiating the terms of a concession to better fit it to its circumstances will provide opportunities for a government to renege on its commitment to allow the private utility to earn a reasonable return on its investment.

Rose (2002) argues that as settings become increasingly complex and uncertain, market-like relationships become increasingly untenable. If the advantages of a concession—investment in and careful management of a water system—are to be realized, for instance, the concession must be stable and secure so that the concessionaire may rely on it and plan accordingly. Incorporating multiple qualifications and conditions, that is, permitting a certain open-endedness, allows for flexibility in the face of uncertainty and surprise, but it reduces security. Conversely, devising fixed and relatively simple concessions enhances security, but limits the ability to respond to new and unexpected circumstances (Rose 2002:244–245). The point at which complexity and uncertainty overwhelm the benefits of market-based arrangements varies depending on the circumstances. Community-based governance can be a viable alternative if market-based arrangements are inappropriate.

Commitment, agency, and decisionmaking costs are ubiquitous (see Box 2.1). They can arise in any setting in which more than one person is making choices (Miller 1992; Horn 1995). Consequently, they are likely to arise in some form in virtually every water setting because of shared property rights among governments, organizations, and citizens. In choosing how to allocate and share property rights so that appropriate incentives are created that encourage the realization of desired goals, individuals must also pay attention to the trade-offs that must be made among transaction costs. For instance, a single-minded focus on efficiency may lead to unintended consequences if commitment and agency problems are neglected.

Box 2.1 Transaction costs and trade-offs

Commitment

Definition: following an agreed upon course of action even when confronted with the temptation to abandon agreement

Solutions: institutional mechanisms that make abandoning agreements difficult and costly

Examples: dedicated sources of funding, such as bonds or earmarked taxes, making it difficult for legislature to change or seize

However: institutional mechanisms that discourage abandoning agreements open opportunities for agency problems, for example, revenues from dedicated funding may be spent inappropriately

Agency Problems

Definition: acting in ways that undermine an agreement

Solutions: precisely define actions of parties to the agreement; provide opportunities for parties to reconsider agreement

Examples: line item budgets; sunset provisions in agreements

However: precisely defining actions increases decisionmaking costs and opportunities to reconsider agreements allow for commitment problems

Decisionmaking Costs

Definition: costs of bargaining and negotiating an agreement

Solutions: reduce costs by developing relatively vague or open-ended agreements with details to be worked out over time

Examples: cost plus contracts

However: vague or open-ended agreements allow opportunities for both agency problems and commitment problems to emerge

Coordinating the exercise of property rights and attending to the trade-offs among commitment, agency, and decisionmaking costs will be further explored in the next section in relation to two different settings—water allocation and water quality. The means by which a community of roughly co-equal water users may coordinate their actions and address the trade-offs among commitment, agency, and decisionmaking in relation to water allocation and use are explored first. This is contrasted to a situation in which a government and not a community makes the rules that would allow water users to coordinate the exercise of their property rights.

Community-Based Governance of Water

During the past 15 years, considerable attention has been devoted to community or local-level governance of common-pool resources such as water, forests, fisheries, and rangelands. Common-pool resources are defined as natural or man-made resources for which exclusion is difficult and costly to achieve, and use is subtractable (Ostrom and Ostrom 1977). In governing common-pool resources well, problems arising from both lack of exclusion and subtractability must be addressed. Limiting access to a common-pool resource does not ensure its sustainability if those who have access may harvest or otherwise use the resource in unsustainable ways. Conversely, carefully governing the use of a common-pool resource does not guarantee its sustainability if exclusion has not been adequately dealt with.

Considerable attention is being devoted to the study and promotion of community-based governance, in part because of the perceived failure and recognized limitations of state-centered and market-based approaches. State-centered governance of natural resources has produced disappointing results. Deforestation has, in some cases, accelerated. Rich and productive fisheries have disappeared. State-owned water systems have been poorly managed and maintained. Although market-based approaches are recognized as having the potential to overcome some failures of a state-centered approach, there is increasing recognition that market-based approaches are not appropriate in all circumstances (Rose 2002; Tietenberg 2002). For instance, lack of supporting institutional arrangements from governments and communities, thin markets, settings involving considerable externalities and spillovers, and transaction costs that exceed the benefits generated by market arrangements have all been noted.

Community-based governance, in many instances, performs better than government-centered approaches because locals possess superior time and place information about the resource and how their actions affect the resource. Local users, in designing rules of access and of use, can draw on this information as well as their understanding of the social setting to better match rules to circumstances. Also, locally designed rules are viewed as legitimate and are more likely to be followed than rules that are imposed by outsiders. Well-designed rules that are followed produce superior performance (Ostrom 1990; Tang 1992).

Many of these same themes are beginning to emerge in the literature assessing countries' experiences with concessions, leases, and contracts for urban water and sanitation systems. State-owned and -operated utilities have, in general, performed poorly for a variety of technical and political reasons. For instance, public managers of such systems face few incentives to provide effective service because their compensation and employment is not conditioned on performance. In many instances, limits on charging fees for services severely constrain the resources available to reinvest in the system. Political overseers often view public utilities as sources of patronage (Noll, Shirley, and Cowan 2000). Urban settings and urban populations are heterogeneous. Such heterogeneity challenges the ability of a centralized approach to effectively produce and deliver water and sanitation services. State-centered approaches tend to deliver a homogeneous set of services not well suited for such diverse settings.

It is a mistake, however, to assume that citizens are not consuming water and sanitation services if they are not tied into a large-scale water system. Citizens make arrangements for alternative services, and often the provision of alternative services requires citizens to engage in collective action. Citizens actively engage in diverse forms of local governance with the purpose of providing water and sanitation services. Analysts are beginning to recognize and identify examples of workable community-based efforts, whether in relation to collecting bills or providing voluntary labor to build or tie into a system. This recognition of the viability and desirability of community-based efforts has in turn produced calls for actively involving communities and neighborhoods in water system reforms if cost-effective and appropriate water services are to be provided to all residents in a timely manner.

Analysts recognize that private sector participation in the provision and production of water services requires an active government presence and that considerable attention must be devoted to building the capacity of governments to engage in oversight roles. Part of that government capacity building must include attending to and supporting local-level governance even at the neighborhood level. There is considerable potential and possibility for community-based governance to address the numerous challenges of water production and appropriation. The choices are not solely state-centered or market-centered.

Challenges for Community Institutions

Even assuming that a community has considerable management and exclusion rights and that relationships among community members are not severely asymmetrical, communities still confront multiple problems in governing a shared water system. In resolving each problem, communities must also balance transaction costs. Among the most pressing problems that appropriators of a water system face are exclusion, water allocation and use, and maintenance. Exclusion centers on deciding who will be allocated the rights of access and withdrawal and the basis of those rights. Allocation and use issues involve determining how rights of access and withdrawal may be exercised. Maintenance centers on deciding how maintenance activities will be carried out and allocating the burdens of such activities. Each issue is intertwined and thus how well one issue is addressed will affect how well the other issues will be resolved. The failure to adequately limit access will place considerable stress on allocation and use as too little water is allocated among too many water users. That, in turn, will threaten maintenance as water users may feel that the benefits that they receive from the system are so meager that they are reluctant to contribute to its maintenance.

Problems of access, use, exclusion, and maintenance implicate property rights and how they are exercised. The uncoordinated exercise of property rights may lead to disaster. Too many people taking too much water and not contributing to the upkeep of the system can drive it into ruin. The coordinated exercise of property rights can make all water users better off. Coordination requires rules, and rules, to be effective, require commitment to comply with them. Unconditional commitment can never be realized. On multiple occasions water users will be tempted to break the rules; drought, loss of family labor, increasingly attractive alternative income opportunities are among many reasons that will tempt water users to back out of their commitments. Commitment to the rules may quickly unravel as water users come to realize that rule violations are the norm. Thus, coordination of the exercise of property rights requires rules to guide behavior and commitment to following those rules. Commitment problems are reduced to the extent that it becomes difficult and costly to evade the rules.

In a community in which resource users are on roughly equal footing, the distinction between commitment problems and agency problems becomes blurred. Users are committing to one another that they will follow the agreed upon rules. They are not agents for one another. In a number of instances, however, users may choose to delegate authority to some to carry out duties on behalf of all community members. In numerous farmer-managed irrigation systems, farmers select guards to oversee the water allocation process. In addition, these same farmers often select leaders who are to coordinate labor contributions for the maintenance of the water system. Delegating authority to some to act on behalf of all creates the possibility of agency problems. How do water users ensure that their guards and their leaders act in appropriate ways?

Communities of water users face numerous challenges in governing their water systems. They must limit entry, allocate water, and maintain the water system. They must credibly commit to following the rules that they design to address these challenges and they must maintain control over those to whom they delegate authority on behalf of the community. One of the keys to doing all of these things well is in designing rules well matched to the setting and the various challenges that they face.

Designing Rules

Communities devise rules that guide and constrain members' exercise of their shared property rights in relation to one another. Ideally, the rules should provide appropriate incentives for individuals to exercise their rights in ways that sustain the water system, that is, they should serve as incentive generators. This view of rules underlies game theory. Games are solved by identifying the payoffs (or incentives) that rules and strategies produce.

Part of the value of the growing literature on community-based governance of common pool resources is the identification of the hundreds of types of rules designed by communities that in their particular context generate appropriate incentives for community members to exercise their property rights in ways that individually and collectively make themselves better off (Ostrom 1999). For instance, many communities successfully control access to their shared resources against outsiders by adopting rules that establish specific requirements for gaining entry to the shared resource. The most common forms of what Ostrom (1999) calls boundary rules are residency requirements. Additional rules often require membership in a local water users' association, ownership of land in the command area of an irrigation system, payment of fees, and ownership of shares of a local organization or of the resource itself. As Ostrom (1999:513) concludes: "Many of the rich diversity of boundary rules used by appropriators in the field attempt to ensure that the appropriators will relate to others who live nearby and have a long-term interest in sustaining the productivity of the resource."

A rich diversity of rules is also characteristic of community attempts to resolve allocation and use issues. Commonly used water allocation rules include fixed time slots, rotation systems, and a fixed percentage of water available at a given time (Tang 1992). Fixed time slots are among the most commonly used rules, whereas fixed percentage of water is less commonly used. Ostrom (1999) notes that fixed time slots provide irrigators considerable certainty concerning when they will receive water, however, the amount of water that will be available is not certain. For fixed time slots to work well some amount of water must be regularly available. Fixed percentage rules allocate water among irrigators when it is available. Such rules provide considerable certainty over a share of water but not necessarily the timing of when and how much water will be available. In many irrigation systems governed by farmers, different sets of allocation rules are used depending on the availability of water (Tang 1992; Lam 1998). During seasons of plentiful water, all irrigators may be allowed to take as much water as they want. During seasons of limited water supplies, allocation and use rules may be strictly followed, and in seasons during which water supply is very poor, farmers may have in place rules that shut down certain portions of the command area.

In general, these rules closely tie irrigators together, with the welfare of one highly dependent on the actions of the others. Taking water out of turn, or taking water outside of the rotational system, affects the availability of water for other irrigators. Furthermore, these rules provide incentives to farmers to both follow them and monitor them. Failure to take water at the allotted time can be disastrous to an irrigator, as can allowing another to take water at the irrigator's allotted time.

Rules do more, however, than create incentives to act in particular ways. Another dimension of rules that receives somewhat less attention is their ability to generate information about the behavior of others who are also subject to the rules (Runge 1984) and about the effects of people's actions on a water system. Runge (1984) argues that in many common-pool resource settings, appropriators are conditional cooperators. Individuals are more likely to cooperate with one another and follow agreed upon rules that allow them to coordinate their actions if they believe that others are also following the rules. How do they know if others are following the rules? They know if in following the rules they are also able to easily observe the actions of other individuals. Furthermore, they may be much less likely to violate the rules if they know that their actions are easily observed. Ostrom (1999) observes that a defining feature of rules devised by communities is the ease by which rules may be monitored by all appropriators. Rules of allocation and use commonly rely on some form of taking turns, closely tying together the actions of appropriators. Missing a turn or taking a turn out of order is readily observed. Also, commonly understood water rotation systems allow farmers to readily check on the actions of those who are in charge of moving the water from segment to segment of the command system.[5] Thus, well-designed rules that generate information by easing the costs of observation help reduce commitment and agency problems. This is one reason that it has been easier to establish property rights for surface water (where withdrawals are more easily observable) than for groundwater.

Finally, another means by which commitment and agency problems are reduced is by making rule violations, if detected, costly. That is, enforcement and sanctioning also have a key role to play. Since considerable self-monitoring occurs within many community-based arrangements, considerable social pressure is brought to bear on individuals to follow the rules. Appropriators may chide one another and publicly comment on one another's behavior. In many communities, self-monitoring is the only form of rule enforcement.[6] In other communities, appropriators select monitors, or guards, to supplement self-monitoring and enforcement activities. Guards, who are invariably drawn from their own communities, are typically given considerable authority in dealing with minor infractions, and much less authority to deal with major infractions. Guards may impose small fines at the time of the rule infraction that must be paid on the spot. More serious rule infractions often require the rule violator to be brought before some type of group of his peers to be sanctioned. In any case, sanctioning is graduated. Minor offenses are dealt minor punishments and serious offenses are dealt more serious punishments, both with the goal of bringing the violator back into the fold of rule-following appropriators.

Community-devised rules are embedded in dense social networks that support and encourage rule-following behavior. Multiple and personal ties among appropriators encourage rule-following behavior. Violating the trust of a neighbor, friend, or family member is more difficult and costly than violating the trust of a stranger. Community-devised rules, in turn, often support and maintain dense social networks (Ostrom 1999). For instance, the widespread use of local residency requirements as a condition of accessing a shared resource means that local people who know one another and who have ties to the area are going to be using the resource.

Zanjera Example

The *zanjera* system used in parts of the Philippines, as described by Coward (1979), encapsulates the numerous issues covered earlier. To be part of a *zanjera* system, an individual or family must acquire a share in the irrigators' association. The share entitles the holder to land in the irrigation system, a portion of water, and a right to vote for leaders. In turn, the share obligates the holder to abide by the rules of the association and contribute to the maintenance of the system. Thus, access is strictly limited through the acquisition of shares. Each share is associated with several pieces of land dispersed from the head of the canal to the tail of the canal. Using scattered plots of land dampens the severe conflicts that often emerge among head-enders and tail-enders. In addition, farmers face incentives to ensure that water allocation rules are abided by so that water is available to plots located toward the end of the canal. Finally, scattering plots throughout the command area allows farmers to better deal with severe water shortages. During water short periods, entire sections of the command area are shut down to irrigation. Farmers may lose a plot or two of land to such a closure; however, farmers will still have access to land in sections that are still irrigated.

Even though such rules appear to provide adequate incentives for farmers to follow the rules and to generate sufficient information so that farmers can determine whether rules are being followed, farmers select guards from among themselves to implement, monitor, and enforce the rules. Guards are compensated by being allocated additional plots of land located at the tail end of the canal. The compensation scheme provides clear incentives for guards to monitor water allocation rules carefully. But what keeps the guards from exploiting their position and grabbing more water than they are allowed? Who monitors the monitors? The guards are farmers who live and work among those they are monitoring. Farmers can easily monitor one another as well as the guards. Since guards are farmers, they are also embedded in numerous social networks and they are well versed and conditioned by community norms and expectations.

Comparing Community and Central Governance

Community-based governance has the potential to work well for a variety of reasons. First, community members who devise the rules are also subject to them. The rules are likely to carry considerable legitimacy, which enhances commitment to them. Second, community members who devise the rules can draw on critical time and place information to better match the rules to the setting and to the problems that the community confronts. The rules are likely to be designed in ways that provide incentives for people to follow them most of the time, reducing the magnitude of commitment and agency problems. Furthermore, rules are often designed in ways that generate considerable information for community members. In following the rules, water users can easily observe whether others are also following the rules and whether guards are monitoring and enforcing the rules. Finally, social ties and norms can act to reinforce rule-following behavior. It is easier to take advantage of a stranger compared to a neighbor not just because a stranger may have a more difficult time understanding what has occurred, but also because the stranger has little recourse against the person who cheated. Time and place information and social ties and norms are vital mechanisms for addressing resource and relationship problems, mechanisms to which other forms of governance do not have such ready access.

To demonstrate this latter point, imagine a setting in which a provincial or central government rather than the community exercises considerable authority in relation to exclusion and management of a water system. The primary locus of governance and rulemaking is with the higher level of government. Just as with community-based governance, commitment to the rules devised by the central government is problematic. Commitment on the part of the water users to the rules is affected by a variety of factors—perceived legitimacy of the rules, how well

Table 2.1 Characteristics of central governance versus community governance

	Community governance characteristics	Central governance characteristics
Scale	Smaller—within boundaries of communities, unless coordination among communities	Larger—crossing boundaries of communities
Typical resource application	Extraction	Pollution
Information	Specific, time and place	Generalized, technical
Social ties and norms	Powerful	Weak
Rules	Multiple depending on resources and users	Tend to be uniform across resources and users
Monitoring and enforcement	Tend to be more informal, rest heavily on social ties and norms	Tend to be formal and independent of communities

the rules match the interests of water users, and how well matched the rules are to the physical and social circumstances.

Each of these factors favors community-based governance over higher level governance of water abstraction (see Table 2.1). Central government authorities do not have access to the time and place information that would allow a careful matching of the rules to the physical and social circumstances. Also, government authorities will take into account different or multiple interests in devising rules. No longer is it just the interests of water users that will be addressed. For instance, government authorities and water users often part ways on issues of exclusion. Governments often seek to extend the water system to as many users as is possible even if that is likely to exceed the capacity of the system (Tang 1992). This, in turn, places considerable pressure on designing allocation and use rules that extend water to the very edges of the water system and on ensuring the reliability of a stable water supply. Time and place information, which government officials do not have ready access to, would support the development of well-matched rules. However, the more finely tuned the allocation and use rules are, the greater the burden of monitoring such diverse rules. Moreover, water users may be unwilling to follow rules that they believe reveal information about themselves that can be used to their disadvantage by authorities. The most well-known instance of this is the reluctance of consumers of public goods to honestly reveal their demand, understating their demand if they believe they will have to pay, and overstating their demand if they believe that it will be made available to them for free (Oakerson 1999).

Given the numerous information problems that government officials are likely to encounter, often governments adopt a single type of allocation rule and apply it uniformly. A single type of rule applied to all water users is perceived as fair—all water users are treated alike; and a single type of water rule is easier to design, monitor, and enforce by government officials. The multiple resources that water users can draw on to buttress commitment to rules are much less available to government officials. Government officials cannot readily tap legitimacy, time and place information, social ties, and networks. Thus, commitment problems on the part of water users in government-managed systems are likely to be more acute.

Commitment becomes a two-way street in this setting. The issue is not just how committed are the appropriators to following the rules. Just as important is how committed the government is to following, monitoring, and enforcing the rules. The government must implement, monitor, and enforce the rules that it has adopted in a consistent fashion. If government officials repeatedly violate the rules, or refuse to enforce them against certain individuals, commitment among water users is likely to begin to erode. If water users have no means, or very weak means, by which to hold government officials accountable, commitment problems may become that much more severe. Thus, in this situation, it is not just a matter of providing assurances to water users that all water users will follow the rules; it is also a matter of providing assurances that the government will also follow the rules.

As Ostrom (1990) notes, a critical piece to addressing issues of commitment is monitoring and enforcement of the rules. Not only does monitoring and enforcement discourage would-be rule-breakers from following through on their intentions, but effective monitoring and enforcement provides assurances to all water users that rule-following behavior is being encouraged.

Just as with community-based governance, however, appointing guards to monitor and enforce the rules creates agency problems. How does the government ensure that its guards effectively guard? This is a particularly challenging issue. According to Tang (1992), in many government-managed irrigation systems, guards are appointed who are not part of the communities that they are monitoring, nor are they subject to the rules that they are enforcing. Thus, community ties and norms do not act to keep guards in line as they do in community-governed systems. In fact, one of the reasons that outside guards are used in government-owned irrigation systems and are often regularly rotated among water systems is so that communities do not "capture" guards (Tang 1992).

Although the problem of community capture appears to be taken care of, the central issue remains—how to ensure that guards guard well. A delicate balance must be struck between providing too powerful incentives to monitor carefully, such as directly tying compensation to the number of rule violators detected, encouraging guards to prey upon water users, and providing inadequate incentives to monitor carefully so that hardly any monitoring occurs at all. Furthermore, in government-managed systems, enforcement tends to be less immediate than in community systems. The problem is compounded further by the remote location of irrigation systems so that it is difficult for superiors to monitor guards or for guards to have easy access to government conflict resolution mechanisms.

Government officials do not have access to time and place information that would assist them in devising finely tuned rules that would provide appropriate incentives and information to water users. In addition, government officials, through the rules that they adopt, often pursue goals not entirely compatible with the interests of communities. Commitment to the rules in such settings is challenging. One of the most critical tools that governments have available to them to support rule-following behavior is monitoring and enforcement. However, monitoring and enforcement is itself problematic.

When Are Higher Levels of Government Appropriate?

The above argument should not be interpreted as meaning that higher levels of government have no role in governing water. First, governments can support the efforts of locals to govern water systems through a variety of actions. Governments can commit to allowing water users to engage in local governance by recognizing such rights and by making it difficult for government officials to intervene in local affairs. In addition, governments can provide conflict resolution mechanisms for water users to sort out their differences.

In both California and Colorado, state courts of equity provide forums for water users to resolve their conflicts. In California, water users can adjudicate their water rights by allowing a judge to define and allocate rights or by devising their own water allocation and use arrangements that the judge must then approve. Such adjudications are recognized under state law and are enforceable (Blomquist 1992). Judges also appoint water masters to monitor the arrangements and to provide that information to water users.

In Colorado, state water courts help water users settle their conflicts. The initial action in a state water court is to have a water referee work with the conflicting parties to resolve their conflicts. If that fails, the water judge oversees the hearing and renders a judgment. The Colorado State Engineer's Office works closely with the water courts, providing technical information to help resolve the conflict. Finally, states can provide technical and financial assistance to local water users to assist them in better understanding, repairing, and maintaining their water systems. The key is in providing local water users with assistance and not taking over, and in resolving issues to the satisfaction of government officials.

Second, communities are ill equipped to handle some water issues, requiring governments to take the lead in addressing them. In particular, communities may not have the capacity or the incentive to address water quality problems. As Rose (2002:239) argues: "in the case of many environmental resources—for example, wide-ranging fish or animals, or widely dispersed or invisible pollution—community members are unlikely to observe the impacts of behaviors even within the community, much less the environmental impacts of others on an intercommunity basis. Hence communities may not generate resource-related norms with respect to the entire resource, but at most with respect to some aspect of its use."

Water quality issues are significantly different from water allocation and use issues. Applying Ostrom's (2001) resource and appropriator attributes to the issue of water quality helps to clarify the difference. Ostrom (2001) suggests that resource users are much more likely to devise rules to govern their use of a resource if they have access to reliable, low-cost indicators that readily inform them of the condition of the resource; if resource dynamics are relatively predictable so that users can learn and act in meaningful ways; and if the spatial extent of that aspect of the resource that is the focus of concern is sufficiently limited so that the community has some hope of gaining control over it.

Water quality issues do not stack up well against Ostrom's resource attributes. Reliable, low-cost indicators of water quality are unlikely to be available, resource users are unlikely to detect or readily understand the dynamics of water pollution, and water transports pollutants far from their sources, making it difficult for community-based collective action to make a difference. Pollution sources may not originate within the community, and if they do, communities may find it more desirable to simply allow water sources to transport the pollutants elsewhere. Thus, unlike water allocation and use issues in which water users have many mechanisms that allow them to learn, to observe, and to effectively act, such is not the case with water quality issues. Water users cannot easily observe one another's polluting activities. Polluting activities may even be hidden from the polluter. The consequences of polluting activities may be difficult to detect, and even if detected, community members may believe that there is little that they can do that would effectively deal with the issue.[7]

Is it then simply a matter of governments investing in modeling the dynamics of water pollution, and monitoring and detection? Would supplying high-quality information be sufficient to spur community governance efforts to address water quality problems? This would not necessarily be true because of two of Ostrom's (2001) attributes of appropriators—common understanding and salience. Even if a government generates good quality information about pollution levels in water, such information does not readily translate into a common understanding of how water users' actions contribute to water quality problems. Multiple types of pollution introduced in different locations make it challenging to identify the primary causes of pollution and the appropriate actions to take. Also, water quality may not become a salient issue to most water users until the issue is quite severe and the low-cost ways that individuals may use to mitigate the consequences of water pollution are no longer viable. Even then, however, community-based action may not emerge. Individual behavior is difficult to readily and publicly observe, and individual behavior does not immediately and directly affect the welfare of others in any observable fashion.

Although water allocation and use issues, because of the nature of the problem, fit well with the strengths of community-based management, water quality issues do not fit as well (see Table 2.1). The many mechanisms that communities call upon in governing the use of a water source are likely to come into play around water quality issues only, if at all, in weaker forms. Thus, water quality is likely to be an issue better suited to the capacities of higher-level governments. First, one of the strengths of a larger government is to account for regional issues, support coordination among communities, and balance interests among communities. A higher-level government has the ability to prevent or limit communities from disposing of their pollution problems on one another. Second, although higher-level governments do not have access to good time and place information, they can access the technical resources and expertise necessary to identify, measure, and monitor water quality problems. Third, higher-level governments have the authority to devise rules and regulations, and to provide the resources needed to invest in pollution prevention and mitigation.

Although a higher-level government has at its disposal mechanisms better suited to addressing water quality issues than does a community, in deploying those mechanisms commitment, agency, and decisionmaking problems must be addressed. Decisionmaking costs may be quite high if a government attempts to craft relatively detailed rules covering different sources and types of pollution across diverse circumstances. Decisionmaking costs may be lowered by defining less precise regulations; however, that raises agency costs. Those subject to the rules may act in unintended or unanticipated ways and those monitoring and enforcing the rules may be given too much leeway in carrying out their duties.

Commitment, agency, and decisionmaking costs may be mitigated somewhat by the participation of communities in various aspects of water quality issues. As argued earlier, communities may not be well suited for taking a lead role in addressing water quality issues. Nevertheless, actively involving communities in some aspects of water quality can support the efforts of governments to address such issues. For instance, the U.S. Environmental Protection Agency (EPA) is actively reaching out to communities to address nonpoint sources of water pollution. The command-and-control approach of developing and implementing strict regulations appeared to work reasonably well to limit the impacts of major single-point sources of pollution, such as waste water treatment plants, and paper and pulp mills, on water quality. However, such an approach does not work well in addressing the activities of hundreds, if not thousands, of individual farmers and homeowners as they apply insecticides, pesticides, and fertilizers to their fields and lawns. Not only are the individual impacts quite small, although collectively they are significant, but the point of use (where the fertilizer was applied) versus the point of impact (where the fertilizer enters a water source) may be quite different. Rather than attempting to regulate each individual pollution source, the EPA is instead working with local communities to develop local governing arrangements better suited to addressing nonpoint sources of pollution. Through its National Estuary Program the EPA works with coastal communities to mitigate the effects of nonpoint sources of pollution on estuaries and through its watershed partnership program it works with inland communities to protect local watersheds (EPA 2004a, b).

In general, communities have mechanisms available to them that governments do not that allow communities to more readily address the trade-offs in a water allocation and use setting. However, in a water quality setting, governments possess clear advantages over communities for addressing water quality problems while also attending to the trade-offs among commitment, agency, and decisionmaking.

Conclusion

Water allocation and use and water quality problems present different challenges to communities and governments. In many instances communities may be better suited for addressing and resolving water allocation and use issues. Communities of water users can access a variety of mechanisms that allow them to govern such problems while mitigating and developing appropriate trade-offs among commitment, agency, and decisionmaking problems that are inherent in any situation in which multiple actors exercise shared property rights. Governments can strengthen and support communities in their efforts at managing water allocation problems. Such support may act to reduce the transaction costs communities must bear in coordinating the actions of their members, such as when governments provide conflict resolution mechanisms or when governments support community monitoring efforts. Of course, coordinating the actions of governments and communities, that is, ensuring that vertical linkages are mutually supportive, raises additional transaction cost issues. In many instances, governments are better suited for taking the lead in relation to water quality issues. Governments have access to resources and expertise necessary to manage water quality concerns. Involving communities, however, can mitigate the transaction costs that governments face in such undertakings. Community involvement may lead to community commitment and thus ease the burden on government enforcement efforts, for instance.

Attending to commitment, agency, and decisionmaking problems that are likely to arise in a given setting may lead to a reconsideration of who should exercise which rights. For instance, limiting the ability of government officials to use resources for patronage instead of for the operation and expansion of a water system often requires that authority to exercise certain property rights be allocated away from government officials. Engaging in a concession with a private firm allocates management and exclusion rights away from government officials and to private managers. Addressing agency problems that may be encountered by granting greater authority to a private firm to operate and expand a water system may require water users to be allocated limited management and exclusion rights so that they have the authority to ensure that they gain access to water services. Several analysts have noted the need to allow citizens, especially poorer citizens, the authority to explore and possibly provide water services in their neighborhoods, particularly if the concession period means it would be decades before they would receive service.

Appropriately resolving water allocation issues and water quality issues is not simply a matter of assigning the task to the actors best suited to resolving the issue. It is also a matter of attending to the relationships among those who concurrently exercise property rights in a given water allocation or water quality setting. Addressing the interactions that are likely to emerge among actors often provides insight on who should take the lead in resolving a collective problem. Conversely, focusing on the appropriate level of government or appropriate actors to address problems often provides insight and guidance on dealing with structuring appropriate relationships among them.

Getting relationships right among diverse property rights holders is as difficult and technically challenging as it is to build an irrigation system or a water and sanitation system. It is as difficult and technically challenging as developing incentive-compatible market arrangements, which are just a special case of getting relationships right. Focusing on getting relationships right among diverse property rights holders adds considerable, but necessary, complexity to the provision and production of water systems and water quality.

In general, social scientists understand the strengths and the limitations of government-centered approaches to addressing common-pool resources. They are coming to a better understanding of the conditions under which market-based arrangements are likely to work well as well as the limitations and shortcomings of market-based approaches. They have also come to recognize and better understand alternatives to government and market approaches, which has led to a much greater appreciation of the strengths and limitations of local-level, self-governing efforts.

This greater awareness and understanding of many different types of institutional arrangements has increasingly led to the understanding that there is no single best arrangement for solving common-pool resource problems. Rather, in many settings, a combination of approaches is likely the more effective approach. Furthermore, a greater understanding of diverse institutional arrangements has led to an appreciation of the importance of attending to the interactions among the many actors inevitably involved in most water settings.

Notes

1. However, it is important to note that rights of access, withdrawal, management, exclusion, and transfer are not absolute. They are often conditioned by government regulation.

2. The concept of commitment, or credible commitment, is central to game theory and a political economy approach to management and governance. North (1998) suggests that commitment is vital for reducing uncertainty surrounding economic and political interactions. For specific applications of the concept see North and Weingast 1989; Horn 1995; Greif, Milgrom, and Weingast 1998).

3. Noll, Shirley, and Cowan (2000) note that another way in which a government may avoid its commitment to a concessionaire to earn reasonable rates of return on its investment in a water system is through overregulating water quality.

4. A substantial body of work on agency theory exists within economics. See, for instance, Jensen and Meckling (1976); Holmstrom (1982); Baker, Jensen, and Murphy (1988); and Barney and Ouchi (1986).

5. Rose (2002) suggests that irrigation systems may be unique among common pool resources in terms of the ease by which water users may observe one another as they work their fields and wait their turns for water.

6. Tang (1992:241) found that just over half of the farmer-managed irrigation systems that he studied appointed guards from within the communities to monitor rules. The remainder of the systems had no formal guards.

7. As Rose (2002:246) notes: "Whatever difficulties there may be in monitoring extractive activities, they generally pale by comparison to the problems of monitoring the introduction of pollutants into the air or water or groundwater. Not only does the receiving medium disperse the polluting elements, but insofar as pollutants are invisible and intangible, even polluters themselves may not know what they are doing."

References

Acheson, J. 1975. *The lobster gangs of Maine.* Hanover, N.H.: University Press of New England.

Agrawal, A. 1999. *Greener pastures: Politics, markets, and community among a migrant pastoral people.* Durham, N.C.: Duke University Press.

Alexander, P. 1982. Sri Lankan fishermen: Rural capitalism and peasant society. *Australian National University Monographs on South Asia,* No. 7. Canberra: Australian National University.

Baker, G., M. Jensen, and K. Murphy. 1988. Compensation and incentives: Practice versus theory. *Journal of Finance* 43: 593–616.

Barney, J., and W. Ouchi. 1986. Agency theory. In *Organizational economics,* eds. J. Barney and W. Ouchi. San Francisco: Jossey-Bass.

Birdsall, N., K. Graham, and R. H. Sabot, eds. 1988. *Beyond tradeoffs: Market reforms and equitable growth in Latin America.* Washington, D.C.: Inter-American Development Bank.

Blomquist, W. 1992. *Dividing the waters: Governing groundwater in southern California.* San Francisco: ICS Press.

Commons, J. R. 1957. *Legal foundations of capitalism.* Madison: University of Wisconsin Press.

Coward, E. W., Jr. 1979. Principles of social organization in an indigenous irrigation system. *Human Organization* 38: 28–36.

Environmental Protection Agency. 2004a. National Estuary Program. www.epa.gov/owow/estuaries.

———. 2004b. Watersheds. www.epa.gov/owow/watersheds.

Greif, A., P. Milgrom, and B. Weingast. 1998. Coordination, commitment, and enforcement: The case of the merchant guild. In *Explaining social institutions,* eds. J. Knight and I. Sened. Ann Arbor, Mich.: University of Michigan Press.

Holmstrom, B. 1982. Moral hazard in teams. *Bell Journal of Economics* 13: 324–340.

Horn, M. 1995. *The political economy of public administration.* New York: Cambridge University Press.

Ilahiane, H. 2001. The ethnopolitics of irrigation management in the Ziz Oasis, Morocco. In *Communities and the environment: Ethnicity, gender, and the state in community-based conservation,* eds. A. Agrawal and C. Gibson. New Brunswick, N.J.: Rutgers University Press.

Jensen, M., and W. H. Meckling. 1976. Theory of the firm: Managerial behavior, agency costs, and ownership structure. *Journal of Financial Economics* 3: 304–360.

Johnstone, N., and L. Wood. 2001a. Introduction. In *Private firms and public water: Realising social and environmental objectives in developing countries,* eds. N. Johnstone and L. Wood. Cheltenham, U.K.: Edward Elgar.

———. 2001b. Water and sanitation in low income neighbourhoods: The scope for service differentiation and decentralized management. In *Private firms and public water: Realising social and environmental objectives in developing countries,* eds. N. Johnstone and L. Wood. Cheltenham, U.K.: Edward Elgar.

Johnstone, N., R. Hearne, and L. Wood. 2001. Regulation of social and environmental concerns with increased private sector participation in the provision of water and sanitation. In *Private firms and public water: Realising social and environmental objectives in developing countries,* eds. N. Johnstone and L. Wood. Cheltenham, U.K.: Edward Elgar.

Lam, W. F. 1998. *Governing irrigation systems in Nepal: Institutions, infrastructure, and collective action.* San Francisco: ICS Press.

Landy, M. K., M. J. Roberts, and S. R. Thomas. 1994. *The Environmental Protection Agency: Asking the wrong questions: From Nixon to Clinton.* Expanded edition. Oxford: Oxford University Press.

Lansing, S. 1991. *Priests and programmers.* Princeton: Princeton University Press.

Mazzucchelli, S., M. R. Pardinas, and M. G. Tossi. 2001. Private sector participation in water supply and sanitation: Realizing social and environmental objectives in Buenos Aires. In *Private firms and public water: Realising social and environmental objectives in developing countries,* eds. N. Johnstone and L. Wood. Cheltenham, U.K.: Edward Elgar.

McGuiness, M. 1999. Introduction. In *Polycentric governance and development,* ed. M. McGuiness. Ann Arbor, Mich.: University of Michigan Press.

Miller, G. 1992. *Managerial dilemmas.* New York: Cambridge University Press.

Noll, R., M. Shirley, and S. Cowan. 2000. Reforming urban water systems in developing countries. In *Economic policy reform: The second stage,* ed. Anne Krueger. Chicago: University of Chicago Press.

North, D. 1998. Five propositions about institutional change. In *Explaining social institutions,* eds. J. Knight and I. Sened. Ann Arbor, Mich.: University of Michigan Press.

North, D., and B. Weingast. 1989. Constitutions and commitment: The evolution of institutions governing public choice in seventeenth-century England. *The Journal of Economic History* 49: 803–832.

Oakerson, R. 1999. *Governing local public economies.* Oakland, Calif.: ICS Press.

Ostrom, E. 1990. *Governing the commons: The evolution of institutions for collective action.* New York: Cambridge University Press.

———. 1992. *Crafting institutions for self-governing irrigation systems.* San Francisco: ICS Press.

———. 1999. Coping with tragedies of the commons. *Annual Review of Political Science* 2: 493–535.

———. 2001. Reformulating the commons. In *The commons revisited: An American Perspective,* eds. J. Burger, R. Norgaard, E. Ostrom, D. Policansky, and B. Goldstein. Washington, D.C.: Island Press.

Ostrom, V. 1987. *The political theory of a compound republic.* 2nd edition. San Francisco: ICS Press.

Ostrom, V., and E. Ostrom. 1977. Public goods and public choices. In *Alternatives for delivering public services: Toward improved performance,* ed. E. S. Savas. Boulder, Colo.: Westview Press.

Ramaswamy, S., and J. Cason, eds. 2003. *Development and democracy: New perspectives on an old debate.* Hanover, N.H.: Middlebury College Press.

Rose, C. 2002. Common property, regulatory property, and environmental protection: Comparing community-based management to tradable environmental allowances. In *The drama of the commons,* eds. E. Ostrom, T. Dietz, N. Dolsak, P. C. Stern, S. Stonich, and E. U. Weber. Washington, D.C.: National Academy Press.

Runge, C. F. 1984. Institutions and the free rider: The assurance problem in collective action. *Journal of Politics* 46: 154–181.

Schlager, E., and E. Ostrom. 1992. Common property and natural resources: A conceptual analysis. *Land Economics* 68 (3): 249–252.

Tang, S. Y. 1992. *Institutions and collective action: Self-governance in irrigation.* San Francisco: ICS Press.

Tietenberg, T. 2002. The tradable permits approach to protecting the commons: What have we learned? In *The drama of the commons,* eds. E. Ostrom, T. Dietz, N. Dolsak, P. C. Stern, S. Stonich, and E. U. Weber. Washington, D.C.: National Academy Press.

Young, O. 2002. Institutional interplay: The environmental consequences of cross-scale interactions. In *The drama of the commons,* eds. E. Ostrom, T. Dietz, N. Dolsak, P. C. Stern, S. Stonich, and E. U. Weber. Washington, D.C.: National Academy Press.

Chapter 3

Constructing New Institutions for Sharing Water

Charles L. Abernethy

— In recent decades, the socioeconomic contexts within which countries make decisions about allocations of water among users have changed. General economic development, urban expansion, electricity generation, and waste emission have all increased greatly, especially in developing countries. These trends have brought many basins nearer to scarcity, and rendered previous patterns of allocation obsolete. New institutions, based on river basins and sub-basins, must evolve. Allocation among user categories requires political rather than technical decisions. A strong basic water law appropriate to the new pressures should underpin these new institutions. Licenses to abstract should be clearly documented. Procedures, especially for granting new licenses, should be based on principles of disclosure, transparency, and stakeholder consultation. This chapter also discusses requirements for measurement, control of water quality, financing of new institutions, security of rights, and transferability.

The requirements for a sustainable water allocation system have become much more complex. People use water in many more ways, and for many more purposes. The potential for pollution is increasing. Economic activities are diversifying rapidly, and it is not easy to keep pace with the changes that are occurring. Major modern factors that complicate water management are economic development, urbanization, power generation, and waste emission. There are others, but these four stand out as the most difficult to control or manage. Even where robust systems of traditional water rights have existed and have proved themselves to be sustainable, effective, and sufficiently equitable, it is questionable whether it will be possible to build upon these traditional systems, and adapt them so as to integrate these modern forces into the older patterns of social management.

More probably, new management institutions and procedures have to be created. In many countries, not a great deal of time is left for this. From that perspective, the existence of strong traditional systems can become an obstacle, hindering new developments. Those traditional systems may have ardent supporters who oppose the introduction of more complex, multifunctional systems.

This chapter assumes that an institutional system, capable of handling the problem of allocating water among all the multiple types of users in a modern state, has to be built up afresh, not by adaptation of something that existed before. However, in situations in which traditional systems do exist, for certain uses and where those traditional systems are respected by those directly affected by them, it is assumed that such traditional systems will be assimilated into any newer arrangements that aim to facilitate more complex sets of uses. New arrangements should be designed to accept traditional (single- or dual-use) systems of rights with minimal distortion.

This chapter does not specifically consider the problems of transnational river basins, although they are obviously important. They are not essentially different from the problems that appear within a country, except that the concept of national sovereignty means that agreements at the transnational level are usually of a more limited range, covering aspects of quantity sharing, quality control, and perhaps timing, but not extending into issues of policy about different types and locations of use. The first step, however, seems to be to formulate management principles that can be shown to work satisfactorily within countries. Successful multinational, multifunctional basin institutions do exist, but their evolution may take a long time owing to the need for building trust among the participants (e.g., see Hollaender 2001).

This chapter begins with a discussion of traditional water rights systems and multiple uses. It then outlines the major development trends affecting the socio-economic context for water rights systems. After introducing attributes of a water rights system, the following sections analyze specific issues: governance and participation; institutions; laws; licensing and documentation; measurement; quality control; security, compliance, and enforcement; finance; and transferability. The final section summarizes recommendations for water rights administration and implementation.

Traditional Water Rights and Multiple Use

Many systems of traditional water rights exist around the world. Some are ancient. Some, such as the systems of the western United States, are more recent. There can be no doubt about the robustness and sustainability exhibited by some of the older traditional systems. Cardinal features that characterize many of them, such as clear rules, structured stakeholder participation in decisionmaking, use of external arbiters such as priests, and so on, have been described by many authors, notably Ostrom (1992) for the important case of agricultural systems.

Many of these were either single-function systems or two-function systems. They might address water allocation and utilization among users who all wanted it for essentially similar purposes. Irrigated agriculture, domestic use, and livestock watering are the most common of these uses. In environments such as desert margins, dual-use rule-systems often occur, for example, to share scarce water between agriculture and livestock. Often those are uneasy arrangements between groups of people who may be ethnically different, perhaps mutually unfriendly, but who have found some sustainable arrangement that limits conflicts and, through well-understood rules, enables two groups and two lifestyles to coexist.

Such systems often used time of access as a principal basis for rules. Different kinds of access restriction often protect water quality, such as separating sources for domestic users or prohibiting livestock access upstream of points designated for domestic users.

One of the greatest problems in incorporating existing traditional systems of water rights is the concept of equity. The principles of a sharing system can be rather easily understood, in a single- or dual-use situation. In irrigation water, for example, allowing the same time for water delivery to each irrigated hectare (the *warabandi* principle), or the same amount of water to each household, or something of this sort achieves equity (in a simple form). Long-established irrigation systems may have evolved extra layers of complexity, for example, senior and junior rights, without losing the users' perceptions that there is a basic principle of equity that underlies and explains the rules.

It is wrong, of course, to adopt an idealistic view that traditional rule systems for agricultural water were all focused on equity. Power relationships are also highly important. Some traditional systems that seem highly inequitable reflect the outcome of struggles between castes, tribes, families, or other groupings, perhaps centuries ago. People involved may know that, and may think that it is better for them to accept the situation than to challenge it.

Water professionals have begun to seek means of taking multiple uses into their analytical paradigms (e.g., Meinzen-Dick and van der Hoek 2001, and other chapters published in the same volume) but there is a long way to go. Multiple-use systems require allocation among different uses: how much to the cities, how much to industries, how much to food production, and so on.

The concept of equity becomes more difficult to interpret, especially in the case of industrial users. A right to abstract water may be assigned, for example, to a specific industrial company. However, the company is not the sole beneficiary of that right. Benefits flow to others too, in the form of employment and other aspects of economic growth, which developing countries generally seek. The power dimension is inevitably present too, and it is usual to suppose that the power of an industrial company exceeds that of an irrigators' association, although this may not always be the case.

Simple equity concepts have become difficult to sustain in a more complex world. Allocation principles now require value judgments, about what the whole society, urban and rural, wants to achieve, and this in turn implies a political process. A context that is only technological and administrative cannot solve many of the issues. Water engineers and technologists have not, until recently, been accustomed to perceiving themselves as part of the political system, and have not been very good at interacting with it. However, countries that try to implement reforms of water laws without addressing the political dimension will find that they have dysfunctional institutional arrangements. Political manifestations such as street demonstrations may well appear.

Water management, even for single uses such as domestic or agricultural uses, today involves not single organizations, but hierarchies of organizations. In agriculture there may be, above the individual peasant farmer, a field-channel group, a secondary canal organization, an irrigation system organization, and perhaps a river basin organization. Each of these can assign rights effectively only to the next level below. Therefore, the end-user, the individual, depends on the satisfactory functioning of a series of organizations, and a series of linkages between these organizations, to translate a theoretical right into reality. Dysfunctional institutions unfortunately are too prevalent, most of all for the urban poor of modern large cities, and to politically weak rural groups such as villages or smaller user groups such as inland fishermen.

Impacts of Modern Development Trends

If a system of water rights is to be sustainable in the modern context, it will have to respond to these four development trends, each of which has caused vast social changes in the past 40 years:

- economic development;
- urbanization;

- power generation; and
- waste emission.

The ways in which these trends are affecting water users may be summarized briefly. Economic development has brought industrial uses of water to the forefront. Governments encourage and promote establishment of industrial factories in many ways. As industry expands, it draws people in for employment, and they become dependent on it for their livelihood. Not all industrial investors show respect for the needs of the rural poor or the environment, but even those who want to follow high standards of behavior face a practical problem. To be viable, most industrial processes usually need a guaranteed source of water. Investors need to be sure that this will be available for many years. In the absence of a well-ordered system of water rights, such a guarantee of future water availability will be sought through political and bureaucratic channels, which often are not sufficiently transparent. The lack of an ordered system of water rights thus appears likely to lead to gradual deprivation of traditional rights, and very often also to damage of those rights through reductions of water quality.

Urbanization brings a chain of rather similar effects. As cities grow, they require rapidly increasing supplies of domestic water. In some basins where there are already many agricultural users, these supplies may be found only by reducing the agricultural share. There may be an apparent logic to justify these rural-to-urban transfers, if the growth of cities accompanies reductions in rural population. However, in many cases the new entrants to city populations have come from other basins.

In the urban case, the holder of the right to abstract water from the river will not be the end-user. It will be a large public entity, with a great deal of political weight. It may be expected that this kind of organization will have greater access to political decisionmakers than the holders of traditional agricultural rights can achieve.

The urban water-supply organizations then usually proceed to distribute water with a great deal of inequity. Pipes connect directly to the houses of people who are better off. Poorer people may have to collect water at public standpipes, or buy it from vendors at prices far higher than those charged in the residential areas with direct supplies.

The problem of the urban poor, especially in the megacities that characterize much of the development pattern of recent decades, illustrates why we will need new institutional arrangements, rather than evolution from past traditions. The urban poor have virtually no traditional basis for any such evolution. They are largely young, they have mostly come into the cities in the recent decades, from many parts of the country but probably with an emphasis on the poorer provinces. People in this category are a fast growing proportion, already (in some countries) similar to or even exceeding the farmers in numbers. This movement of population should logically be accompanied by some orderly, parallel transfer of rights to water, from rural to urban users; but in general we lack satisfactory mechanisms for bringing this about.

Generation of electricity is in a similar position. People want electricity. As the national economy grows, the demand for electricity generally rises at a much faster rate. Any government that fails to keep pace with this demand is considered inefficient and unsatisfactory. The Philippines and Sri Lanka have experienced this during the past 10 years. From this situation, electricity-generating organizations derive a capacity to acquire water rights and to build dams.

Generation of hydroelectricity does not consume much water, but it affects water resources in a different way. Power demands are relatively uniform through the year, whereas irrigation water demands have strong seasonal variations. Conflicts therefore arise in the dry season, when irrigators need maximum water, but power generators may prefer to keep it in upstream storage. The urban population is likely to support the power generators in this matter. At present, disputes of this sort tend (in many countries) to be resolved in the political arena, rather than through application of rights concepts.

The case of the Pak Mool Dam in northeastern Thailand is an illustration. Fishermen, farmers, and the electricity-generating agency have different views about an appropriate operating rule for this dam. The democratization of politics in the country means that decisions, which in the past were taken largely within the big bureaucracies, seem now more open to challenge. Challenges are based upon assertions of prior user rights, but the validity of such rights in a time of rapid national socioeconomic change is not an easy issue to determine, in the absence of structured laws. The result has, however, been an intractable problem that has confronted a series of governments, and is proving extremely difficult to solve.

Disputes of this kind, when they continue without resolution, attract what Tweeten (2000) calls "alternative agricultural advocates," a type of nongovernmental organization (NGO) with a strong sense of moral commitment, even though they may not themselves be involved in the particular issue. Their presence may prolong disputes and make them more difficult to resolve.

Waste emissions have also grown greatly, and have become more varied and probably more hazardous. This growth is a direct consequence of the first two items above, economic development and urbanization, but in general the state of laws about disposal of wastewater is even weaker than that for abstraction of water.

In almost all modes of water use, most of the water is returned into the natural systems after use. Agriculture returns generally the lowest proportion among the major use types, but even in agriculture the global average return flow is probably more than 50 percent. A right to abstract water therefore implies that disposal of most of that water will occur after use, and it is likely that the quality of that used water will be inferior to the water that was abstracted. Some industries, and some cities (but very few agricultural organizations), ensure adequate treatment of the used water before returning it to the natural system. Many do not, and the consequences of this include reduction of the usable amounts in the rivers and aquifers. Since abstraction implies disposal, the two activities should be treated jointly, in overall basin policies and management.

Industrial plants are often accused of being the source of harmful effluents, and indeed, it is often the case. It should not be forgotten, however, that small-scale agricultural users can also do environmental harm, such as from fertilizers, pesticides, and other agricultural chemicals. A system of water rights must be able to deal with the challenges posed by economic development, urbanization, electric generation, and waste emissions.

Attributes of a System of Water Rights

Before thinking about a system of implementing and governing water rights, it is important to be clear about what a water right is. It can have many characteristics. The number of these dimensions seems to increase as societies grow more complex. The list of these attributes should include (at least) the following:

- Quantity: How much water may the holder of the right receive?
- Timing: Are there restrictions on the time when this quantity may be taken?
- Location: Is there a specific place where this water may be taken?
- Quality: Is the holder of the right entitled to expect the water to be at or better than some specific standard of quality, either chemical or biological?
- Conditionality: Is the right absolute, or is it subject to any conditions or variations? For example, will it be different in a year of drought?
- Duration: Is the right permanent, or will it expire after a specified time?

- Disposal: How and where will the water be disposed of after use? Are there rules about the quality of used water for disposal?

- Ownership and transfer: Can the owner of the right transfer it to another person, or another location? Can it be inherited? Can it be sold?

- Source: From where does this right come? Who awarded the right?

- Security and enforcement: Can anyone guarantee the implementation of the right? If the water in the river decreases or becomes polluted, who will make sure that enough remains available for implementing this right?

There are some significant differences between the kinds of rights systems that are appropriate for surface water, and those for groundwater. The issues of groundwater rights, in developing countries, are rather chaotic at present, as countries vary widely in the degree to which they have brought it into their legislative frameworks. Until the 1970s, in Asia and Africa, groundwater was seen as a significant resource for agricultural users in only a few relatively arid countries; and, where it was used, it was generally extracted by animal or human power, so groundwater users had a strong incentive to limit their abstractions. However, the past 30 years have seen an enormous increase in pumping of groundwater, for both urban and agricultural uses.

In regard to agriculture, much of this sudden expansion has been done by farmers individually, rather than by farmers' groups. Indeed the wish to have personal control over decisions about water application and crop timing (or, in other words, to escape from the constraints of the users' group or dependency on agency deliveries) has been one of the significant factors driving this change. Many governments were ill prepared for this sudden development, and applied policies that lacked coherence; for example, by providing heavy subsidies for installation of pumps and for their energy use, even after the depletion of water tables became clear. In semiarid environments such as Iran or Yemen well-understood traditional rules existed and were an important element of local power structures, but in many less arid places both traditional and official rules were weak, or virtually nonexistent. However, an adequate discussion of these complex issues of groundwater management is beyond the scope of this chapter.

Governance and Participation

In many economic development and infrastructure projects, physical development comes first, management institutions are put in place later within the national bureaucracies, and systems of governance for those institutions come last in time. For water rights systems, that process has to be reversed. Physical facilities and managing organizations are certainly necessary for administering a water allocation system. However, correct decisions may not be made, for example about what facilities are needed, and who will pay for them, unless the process begins by developing a consensus about appropriate governance principles for the whole system. A major problem arises from the vast variation in the size and influence of the various organizations and individuals who abstract water from a river or an aquifer. The primary right to abstract water is given in many cases not to the end-user, but to some much larger body: a large irrigation scheme, a city water supply organization, an electricity generating board, or an industrial company. Beside these, there may be individuals or small groups of farmers or fishermen.

Commonly, during scarcity a bureaucratic process makes all the decisions on sharing, involving only the major participants. They may, for example, send representatives to meet in a committee and determine how to react to the scarcity. The small end-users, depending on these large state or semistate enterprises for their supplies, have rights only to the extent that these representatives can win such a right in the committee debate. The process is not normally transparent, and the end-users may remain uncertain of what has happened and what they should expect.

A solution often advocated for this is some form of stakeholder council, enabling participation and promoting transparency in decisionmaking. The principle has had good success in Western Europe, and to some degree in South America. South Africa is promoting it, but it is uncertain yet whether such councils can become robust enough to deal effectively with great inequalities among the users, and particularly to protect the small users while not impeding economic development.

An obvious difficulty is that everybody holds a stake in water. Everyone uses water, usually in several ways. Therefore, applying the stakeholder concept requires some redefinition. Stakeholder participation can refer not to individuals, but to organizations of similar stakeholders. Thus, a stakeholder council will include representatives of industries, urban centers, irrigators' associations, fishermen, national parks, sports and recreational organizations, and perhaps many more.

Another major problem of governance is the choice of the unit of management. The choice is in general between managing within existing boundaries of local government, or within the physical boundaries of river basins. From a physical aspect, the logical unit is the river basin. The term *water basin,* to include aquifer-based units, may be more appropriate, as in the semiarid countries of west Asia. The basin is the physical unit within which water moves and is contained, and within which water can be quantified statistically for sharing. Evidence indicates that successful systems for managing rights more commonly operate in basin-managed contexts (e.g., see Correia 1998; Abernethy 2001; Svendsen 2005).

However, there are sources of strong opposition. Provincial and district governors resist the creation of entities not based on local government boundaries. The large bureaucracies may already have their own regional management structures. However, it will always be difficult, when conditions of scarcity approach, for any organization to allocate secure rights, if it does not have responsibility over a whole basin or at least sub-basin. The river basin, in any case, is only a concept: there can be long debates about exactly which basins or sub-basins are suitable to be the bases for new management organizations. Some may be too large, others (especially in coastal districts) may be considered too small and amalgamated with neighboring units.

Faced with these likely realities, only some broad principles may guide the establishment of governance mechanisms:

- River basins, or water basins in general, should form the basic units of management.

- All large groups of users should be involved in some way in the making of policy decisions.

- Management decisionmaking should be localized, as much as is practicable.

- Local government authorities should be regarded as stakeholders, and entitled to participate in management.

One need only inspect a short list of such aspects to see that there must be another management level above this, to arbitrate the inevitable disputes. Small basins and sub-basins will want to be independent of their larger neighbors: stakeholder organizations that are not represented in the system will complain that they want to be in it.

An even more potent pressure toward a national-level organization, over all river basin units, is that in modern conditions there will be cases where the national government wants to override local wishes. For example, to supply electricity to urban centers, the government may say it is necessary to build a dam; or to supply water to an impoverished part of the country it may want to construct an inter-basin transfer tunnel. The number of such cases seems to be increasing. Thus the governance system that seems most rational would have an apex body in the national government; a set of river basin organizations; and sub-basin organizations within these, down to levels that can facilitate adequate public participation by users' organizations of many kinds. To avoid the problem of dysfunctional linkages between these different organizational levels, clear definition of the different roles and powers of each is essential.

Basin Management Institutions

Next, one should consider what kinds of organizations, and other institutions, seem necessary in order to implement a water rights policy, and what their functions may be. A separation between water resources management and service provision is a key requirement in developing management that can respond effectively to the coming scarcities of water. There has been a tendency, in some countries, to build the institutions for integrated resource management within an existing major service-providing agency. The argument for this has been that the existing agency possesses necessary professional skills. The opposing argument (more valid, in this writer's view) is that a service-providing agency will not be regarded as neutral, and will not be trusted, by other agencies and other types of user, who are in effect in competition with it for the rights to abstract water.

To summarize, a river basin organization should have several characteristics (Abernethy 2005):

- Its primary goal is to provide a framework of legality and security for all the uses of water, including environmental as well as human uses.

- A river basin organization should have no function of delivering water supplies or services, since one of its tasks will be to monitor and control the activities of service providers.

- Its primary funding should come from licenses for abstraction and disposal of water, supported to some extent by penalties for pollution, excessive use, and other unwanted behavior, and permits for nonabstractive uses such as fishing.

- The charge structure should ensure that basic human needs can be satisfied cheaply, and should reflect the scarcity and quality of the basin's water.

Where scarcity threatens a basin, a river basin organization can organize water sharing. It should have its own hydrological database, so that it can estimate how much water is there, both the reliable discharge in dry years and the excess flows in wet years, and so that it can compare such information with the abstraction rights that already exist. However, assigning rights is only one step: ensuring that these rights are secure requires quite different capabilities, as discussed later in this chapter.

The stakeholder principle means that, to a large degree, clients should govern a river basin organization. Major groups of users will be represented on a council, which may have executive powers, or may be advisory. In this context, service-providing organizations (for agriculture, electricity, domestic, and industrial consumers) are often the major direct abstractors of water from the basin, and need to be considered as users.

Initially, in the establishment of such institutions, the existing water bureaucracies, as well as local administrations, will no doubt argue that the other, smaller stakeholders should only give advice, on the grounds of lack of expertise and so forth. It seems desirable to move quickly toward giving them powers of decision rather than just advice; but it probably should develop gradually, and after some experience has shown that the composition of such a council is satisfactory. Some people may expect that a stakeholders' council will automatically be a means for rectifying imbalances affecting the poor; but there is no certainty that that will happen, since the balance of powers among the many stakeholder groups will affect such outcomes.

Water user organizations are not the only stakeholders. A stakeholder is anyone who feels affected by how water resources are managed. This includes people who receive negative effects, such as those downstream (e.g., fisherfolk on coastal lagoons), or people concerned with aspects of the environment and wildlife. All of these, and others, should be considered as groups from which to select stakeholder representatives.

Basin management organizations may often need to be hierarchies of smaller sub-basin units. It is convenient to imagine integrated management of a large basin from source to sea, but it is not easy to integrate the stakeholder concept with big basins. To enable smaller organizations of stakeholders, such as villages, to exercise their voice, it is necessary to have sub-basin units that are relatively local.

However, as in other fields, the application of the principle of subsidiarity, taking decisions at the lowest, most local level that is practicable, means that the specific functions and powers that can be exercised at each level should be defined and separated as clearly as possible.

Basin organizations should not deliver water or other services to water users. The functions of service provision are different. The basin organization should act as the source of water rights. Service-providing organizations, such as irrigation departments or village water supply bodies, would be its clients.

Financial and budgetary independence is important for the maintenance of the stakeholder principle. If the basin organization is dependent on central-government finance to enable it to do its work, it will soon become in effect a government organ rather than one that responds to its own stakeholders.

The development of basin management institutions, incorporating some of the above principles, has begun in recent years in some African countries (e.g., South Africa and Zimbabwe), and has existed for a long time in some South American countries. In Asia, however, these institutions have appeared relatively slowly or not at all. The cases that have appeared (such as the Brantas River in Indonesia) tend to be of a pilot-project type, rather than clear commitments to new orientations of national policy. River management arrangements in the Asian regions tend to involve some kind of compromise between the large service-providing bureaucracies and (sometimes, but not always) the local government units. These arrangements usually lack transparency to other stakeholder groups.

Reforming Water Laws

Reforms within the water bureaucracies are not enough for establishing a modern system of water rights. A strong basic law seems to be essential, but it may also be difficult to achieve this, especially in the more democratic countries. Political opposition to reform can arise easily, and may be strong enough to prevent enactment of a reform law, especially if the government has other political agendas that it considers more urgent.

Sri Lanka, which has one of the strongest democratic traditions in Asia, may be cited as an example of the practical difficulty of enacting a water reform law. Sri Lanka has invested considerable effort in this since the mid-1990s, but reform proposals have twice had to be withdrawn from the legislative process. The obstacles are complex: they include the high level of national pride in the country's ancient irrigation-based culture (which strengthens the appeal of traditionalism), and the existence of alternative agricultural advocates of the kind mentioned earlier, as well as misjudgments in the policy-formation process, most notably in failure to anticipate resistance and to prepare public opinion adequately concerning the need and rationale for changes. These matters have been discussed well by Gunatilake and Gopalakrishnan (2002). It seems notable that in South Africa and Zimbabwe, two countries that have introduced substantial reforms of their water institutions, the political momentum toward new laws was strong, owing to previous patterns of inequitable, ethnically based water policies.

Agricultural populations are declining, relatively, in almost all developing countries, but they are still generally numerous and have many votes. Water reforms, at the present stage of development, are likely to involve some transfer of water resources from agriculture to other types of users, notably to industry and to large urban units. Reforms may also involve new financial mechanisms. A common component is that agricultural users of water find that they are expected to pay more. Opposition politicians are apt to use both of these aspects as a basis for attacking the policy, and defeating or at least delaying its implementation.

These considerations seem to indicate certain aspects of the reform strategy. First, it is vital that policies are well explained, that politicians at the most senior level are involved in them and support them publicly, and that public explanations of the rationale of reform begin well in advance of the formal introduction of changes.

Second, the benefits of reform, especially for the poor and the agricultural sector, should be identified very clearly. Major benefits, for example, may be that the erosion of traditional rights by modern developments can be curtailed and brought under control, and that rights can be expanded to encompass the water quality dimension, which usually is not dealt with in traditional systems as clearly as water quantity and access rules.

In other words, the reform should be presented to agricultural users and their political representatives as a bargain, or a trade-off. Their rights to water will be more firmly entrenched, and their protection against loss of water and health through industrial and urban pollution will be increased. In return, they accept some new ceiling on the amount they can use.

Third, although a comprehensive reform law may appear to be the logical way of introducing reform, in some countries it may be easier to introduce change by stages. In particular, the question of payments may be quite inflammatory for rural communities, and it may be better to deal with it in a separate law, after legislating first to create the institutional base of reformed management.

In many developing countries, a primary law or a constitutional article declares that water is the property of the state, or is managed by the state on behalf of the people. This may cause difficulty, since some major abstractors of water are state organizations, which are service providers for electricity, irrigation, and domestic water. Compliance procedures, which are an essential part of any system of rights, may be weaker for these major state-controlled users. In that case, the small non-state users are likely to suffer.

Licensing and Documentation

The river basin organization can be the source of legitimate rights to abstract water. It can issue documented evidence of the existence, dimensions, and restrictions, of each right, in some form of license. Such a license should address many of the attributes identified earlier.

Agriculture is by far the largest sector of water use in most developing countries. Agricultural users are the most likely to have some system of traditional water rights. It does not make much sense to introduce a new system based on documented rights unless it fully integrates traditional rights. Otherwise, one set of rights or the other will later prove to be meaningless and unenforceable, causing anger that will be expressed politically.

A basin management system can accommodate traditional group-based rights, especially in relation to agriculture, livestock, and fishing. In these cases, the right of each individual user (e.g., each farmer in a group that shares a common water intake) derives from that group. The group has its own sharing and allocation rules and processes, and those do not need to be disturbed. However, in the context of the socioeconomic trends discussed earlier, there is now a need to define the overall limits of the rights of the group as a whole unit. This has to develop through interaction between each user group and the basin or sub-basin organization.

Integrating traditional rights is easy to state as a goal, but difficult in reality. Traditional rights may not be as clear as one would like to suppose. When local leaders understand that the government wants to replace them by documented, explicit rights, they have an incentive to overstate these traditional rights. The negotiations needed to achieve integration may be long and unsatisfactory. There is no guarantee that traditional agricultural users will accept that a traditional right has been extinguished when they receive a modern documented right. All these difficulties will be augmented, if introduction of a payment system accompanies the transition to a documented right. This easily leads to political and NGO agitation for maintenance of the status quo.

The introduction of documented rights is entirely in the interests of users, and can be especially beneficial to small rural users, provided these new rights are going to be secure. Doubt about security may well be a reason for resistance. However, if the right is really reliable and secure, then a documented system brings a number of benefits to users, especially providing the basis for:

- clarity and transparency about the users' entitlement;
- increasing the accountability of the service-providing organizations;
- developing systems of compensation for defective service; and
- the possibility of making the right transferable and thus increasing its value.

A system of licenses in which the user must make some regular (perhaps annual) payment can also operate beneficially for the farmers, since it may make more water available for genuine farmers. Some cases have shown that many people who hold a free right are not actually using it, and will surrender the right rather than pay for retaining it. In the German state of Hamburg, for example, a relatively high abstraction fee for groundwater licenses caused about a third of the licenses to be renounced, and handed back to the regulatory organization, which could then re-issue them to others (Abernethy 2000, based on Buckland and Zabel 1998).

It may take time to convince those who consider that they have a traditional right that these benefits will be the result of accepting a new system. The benefits themselves may be dependent on changes of attitude within the higher service-providing organizations, so convincing the users will not always be easy. However, it is in everyone's interest. If traditional systems cannot be adapted and integrated into a modern system, then it is likely that the economic and social pressure of large new users will reduce the traditional rights anyway, but in a disorganized and unsatisfactory way.

These considerations indicate the need for some key principles, especially in the allocation of new licenses to abstract water. These principles include:

- transparent procedures;
- prior disclosure of proposed new allocations; and
- opportunities for affected stakeholders to express opinions, before decisions are reached on new licenses.

Measurement

An unmeasurable right is essentially unsatisfactory. As scarcity develops, such a right is likely to be a source of conflict rather than of security. One may think of the analogy of land rights. Maps, boundary marks, fences, and so on define the extent of a users' rights, and exhibit these limits transparently. One would hesitate to buy a piece of land if the present owner could not specify where its boundaries are. In the same way, effective rights to water require some kind of measurement so that the extent of that right is clear, to the holder of that right and to anyone else wanting an adjacent right. Perhaps measurements are not thought necessary in the context of traditional water rights, but when there are multiple uses, it is difficult to avoid conflict without measurements.

Measurement does not necessarily mean measuring cubic meters of water. Sharing of water by measuring time of access is probably the most common type of measurement in the agricultural water sector. It can be argued that this is because the measurement of time is relatively uncontroversial and, in a technical and cost sense, not difficult. Measurement of the quantity of water taken by a user is much more difficult, costly, and open to challenge technically.

The role of different forms of measurement, the importance of transparency in the sharing of water, and the role of this transparency in sustaining organizations, is well illustrated in the proportional division structures used for example in many mountain systems in Nepal. Such structures divide water automatically in (nearly) fixed proportions at open-channel bifurcations, the division being usually based on the relative areas of lands to be irrigated by each channel. Horst (1998) has commented strongly on the tendency to make controls in modern irrigation systems too complicated and thereby to lose this element of transparency, which he correctly regards as vital to institutional processes and therefore more significant than technical precision in irrigation delivery.

These statements do not apply to water taken by industrial users, or the better-off domestic users. These users normally receive water in pipes, to which volumetric meters can be attached. Thus two different situations exist in parallel in many developing countries now: agricultural users receive their water from open channels, and it is not measurable at the point of delivery to the individual user, while urban users become accustomed to receiving a monthly bill based on volumes consumed.

The most common way by which countries are trying to resolve this difficulty is by measuring water delivered, not to individual water users, but to larger groups, designated as water users' associations (WUAs). The WUAs may then be treated as the stakeholders' representative, may be assigned a water right, and may be charged for actual measured consumption. The relationships of the WUA with its own members, in terms of finance and of water shares, are then the business of that organization and its members.

At present, such systems are more likely to be found in pump-based irrigation. There are indications that, in smallholder irrigation systems that depend on pumping, more effective local organizations can be established, or they can be established more readily, than in surface-fed systems. Likely explanations for this are that the need to meet a substantial recurring cost for energy consumption is obvious to all; and that, as in the already-mentioned cases of *warabandi* and proportionally dividing weirs, quantification of water shares can be based, to an acceptable degree of accuracy, on an easily measured surrogate variable, in this case the duration of pump operation. A generally accepted method of assessing water shares is an important factor for reducing the risk of conflict within an organization of water users.

Given the need for measurement, a good hydrological department is just as important, in forming a system of effective water rights, as a survey and mapping department is for the management of lands. The basin organization needs competently measured records of:

- its total available water resource;
- all abstractions; and
- the variability of each of these.

Without this database, it is not possible to assign water rights effectively in a situation that is at or approaching scarcity.

Controlling Water Quality

Pollution of the water source reduces or negates the practical value of a right. This problem has increased rapidly, and does not seem to be coming under control. The organization or organizations managing a river have several kinds of duties concerning pollution:

- setting standards;
- monitoring the state of water in the river;
- monitoring effluents; and
- taking effective action against polluters.

Standards are commonly decided at the national level, and are more likely to refer to domestic water than to agricultural water. The use of generalized standards is beginning to be questioned (e.g., by Jensen et al. 2001), so it seems likely that in the future river basin organizations may be expected to take a role in establishing local standards.

Maintaining the state of river quality is a challenging task. Perhaps the greatest cause of infringement of traditional water rights is the reduction of water quality rather than of quantity. It is relatively easy to identify point sources of pollution, such as factory effluents, but difficult to identify dispersed sources such as irrigation users. Thus, in developing countries where small-scale irrigators are users of most of the water, the problem is hard to address, especially with regard to run-off of agricultural chemicals.

A different water disposal problem occurs where agricultural drainage water disrupts established fisheries, especially prawn fisheries, in lagoons or estuaries. This is not due to chemical pollution, but simply to the reduction of lagoon salinity by the fresher drainage water. Many such cases have occurred. Bakker and Matsuno (2001), for example, describing the impacts of the Kirindi Oya irrigation system in Sri Lanka, comment on "the change in salinity levels for Malala lagoon after upstream irrigation development. The change in salinity levels has decreased the population of water birds as it has affected their food supply. Prawn fishing, which previously sustained 400 families, has also been affected by the change and it has now almost disappeared from the area."

This change took place within less than 10 years after installation of an irrigation system of 2,600 hectares. In terms of water rights, this sort of event implies that the granting of a right to abstract water for irrigation can mean, in effect, removing the livelihood of another, existing set of users, as well as causing damage to wildlife, even though the fishermen and the wildlife are not significant consumers of water.

The most promising way forward seems to involve cooperative efforts among various kinds of organizations, plus clear assignment of the lines of accountability. A river basin organization is accountable for the condition of water in its rivers. It should be able to take action, in courts if necessary, against identified large polluters. Legislatures should enable it to impose penalties that are sufficient to deter the polluting behavior effectively. On the other hand, those affected by reductions of water quality should also be able to sue and claim compensation from the river basin organization for allowing this to happen. An irrigators' organization should be accountable for the state of water flowing from its drains. Departments of agriculture should work together with river basin organizations, irrigators' organizations, and their members, to promote safe and acceptable farming practices. The evaluation of an application for a license to abstract water should take into account the location of disposal, and the effect that disposal could have on existing users of that body of water.

Security, Compliance, and Enforcement

A right is only an illusion if it is not secure. Many people who hold, or believed they held, some traditional right to agricultural water have been discovering in the past decade or two that the right can no longer be fulfilled. Can any reformed approach to water rights do anything about this? Table 3.1 shows an example of the problem, as it can appear in a major basin.

The table shows conditions in the Amu Darya basin, an international basin in Central Asia, during one of the river's worst droughts of recent times. There is a

Table 3.1 Sharing of water in the Amu Darya basin in a drought period, 2001

Section of Amu Darya basin	Percentage of quota used, April–June 2001
Upstream section	113.5
Upper middle section	83.4
Overall average	**76.8**
Lower middle section	56.7
Downstream section	39.1

Source: Amu Darya River Basin Authority.

structured basin organization that sets quotas (annually variable, as this is a highly variable river) and monitors outcomes. As the table shows, even in drought, the upstream users are able to abstract more than their assigned quota, while the tail-enders receive less than half of their entitlement.

This pattern is not extreme or even unusual. The majority of rivers, large or small, probably repeat the pattern. The question is, how can it be addressed, and by whom? The rights of downstream users have no meaning, if upstream users take the water before it reaches those downstream. Upstream users may well include strong state and parastatal organizations, such as electricity generators or urban utilities, abstracting from storage dams in the river-source highlands.

An effective compliance system needs at least the following four components:

- appropriately designed rules;
- a monitoring system;
- a judging procedure; and
- penalties.

Rules must be appropriate, in the sense that it must be possible to find out whether they are being broken, and it must be possible to identify the rule-breaker. Monitoring is expensive. Appropriate design of rules can reduce monitoring costs. For example, if there is a rule that an industrial enterprise can pump a certain volume per month from a river, it may be difficult to know whether that amount is exceeded. But if the rule sets ceiling limits on the capacity of the abstraction plant, and its daily hours of operation, then an occasional sudden check can be sufficient to find out whether the company is complying with its license.

The solution seems to require several kinds of adjustments to the existing situation. A possible pathway may be on these lines:

- A basin organization, with substantial stakeholder influence, issues documented rights to user organizations, including public-sector service providers, industries, and other users or groups with independent abstraction facilities.

- The monitoring division of the basin organization observes actual events, and reports any evidence of rule-breaking.

- A system of graduated penalties applies for breaking the conditions of a license: small penalties for initial offences but escalating for repetitions.

- The basin organization judges and assigns penalties for initial offences (if they are not large), but violations move to the law courts for repeat offences, which attract high, deterrent penalties.

None of this is easy to establish. Strong political support, maintained over some years, seems to be an essential factor. The greatest problem is probably the power of the large existing public water bureaucracies, which tend to have strong links to the political system, and often are averse to change. To produce a result in which these organizations accept and comply with rules made by a relatively new river basin organization is clearly difficult.

However, the argument sometimes made by the old public entities, that they can protect users' rights themselves, seems to be contradicted in many cases by actual events. Lang (2002), describing the new catchment councils in Zimbabwe, says:

> Mistrust between the members has been transformed into trust and mutual respect, and has developed into a sense of common identity and self-confidence which seems to present difficulties only to the sectoral officials of the National Water Authority. . . . It is an inspiring example of how the energy of competition for a scarce resource can be transformed into constructive cooperation, and how entrenched structures for the distribution of power and economic benefits can be overcome.

Finance

There are various approaches to the question of finance. The answer depends very much on the institutional system that each country evolves.

An independent basin management organization can finance itself from license fees. It does not need to charge for water services, as that is the business of service providers, which are a different type of organization. It can charge for issuing water abstraction licenses. These charges can be calibrated in many ways: by quantity, duration, abstraction capacity, type of use, expected proportion of return flow, and so on. Buckland and Zabel (1998) describe the workings of these systems, and report abstraction fees that are typically around the equivalent of US$0.01–0.02 for one cubic meter, but in some cases significantly more. In some countries, the product of abstraction fees is sufficient to cover the cost of all regulatory functions. The use of such a system may reduce or eliminate dependence of the basin organization on a budget allocated by the central government, and thus may make it more truly owned by (and responsive to) its stakeholders.

A problem may appear concerning whether the price of water services should vary according to the kind of use for which the water is required. In many countries, at present, financial arrangements for water are biased heavily in favor of agricultural users, who pay much less (or nothing) per cubic meter, in contrast to the domestic and industrial users who are charged more highly. Multiuse systems often favor agricultural users.

It seems undesirable to extend this practice into the field of abstraction licenses as well. The policy of subsidizing irrigated agriculture through low water charges is explained, sometimes, by the fact that the agricultural products of developing countries have been experiencing low levels of profitability, especially in the past two decades. However, it seems economically strange to allocate the largest share of a scarce resource to a low-profit use. As nonagricultural users of water (including those employed by industries) increase rapidly relative to agricultural users, the maintenance of these differentials may be seen as undesirable. Therefore, it seems appropriate that fees for all abstractions, for whatever use, should follow a single set of financial rules.

Transferability

The rapid rate of socioeconomic change that has been experienced in recent decades, especially in Asia, implies that uses and users of water have also changed. Cities have expanded over land that was formerly irrigated. Industries have replaced agriculture as major employers. Recreational uses of water have increased in importance. These and other changes will continue. This means that uses of water have been transferred, prompting the question, if all the previous users of water had held formal, documented rights, what would have happened? Would formal water rights act as an obstacle to all kinds of development and economic change, whether these changes are desirable or undesirable?

A number of people have written about the positive effects of a system of tradable or transferable water rights (e.g., Holden and Thobani 1996). Their argument is, that if users (especially agricultural users) can sell their rights, they will have an incentive to use water efficiently, perhaps invest in water-efficient technologies, and sell their surplus water right, perhaps to an expanding town or city downstream.

The case seems good, but we should note that the examples most often quoted (Chile especially, and Mexico) are significantly different from Southeast Asia. There are reasons why transferability is more difficult to organize in this region. Chile has short rivers, relatively large farms, and a middle-income economic level. Farmers can hold, and sell, individual rights, and investment capital can be found. This is not the case in Vietnam, or in other countries of the region where landholdings are in the sub-hectare scale.

It is difficult to imagine that, in the foreseeable future, Asian farmers will hold individual, personal rights to water that are secure and saleable. Whatever might be the theoretical case for its advantages, the administrative tasks of creating such a system are prohibitive. In the agricultural sector, the extent of formally documented rights seems unlikely to extend beyond the rights of groups: villages or irrigators' associations. In general, these groups may seem less likely than individuals to want to abandon, sell, or transfer a right.

However, change is inevitable, and if Holden and Thobani, and others, are correct to say that a system of tradable rights promotes efficient use of water, then the converse seems to be that the absence of tradability impedes efficiency. Water policy should not be designed as an obstacle to all change. If it is, that policy will probably fail, in the same ways as traditional rights have been superseded in various contexts in recent times. So how can beneficial water transfers be encouraged and facilitated?

It is clear that, if we want to devise systems of water rights that can accommodate the reality of socioeconomic change, there must be some reason, some incentive, for the holders of existing rights to consider whether they need to retain these rights, or whether it may be more advantageous to let them be transferred to someone else.

A system of tradable rights addresses this. The incentive for surrendering the right is that the holder will receive a payment. However, a market system in which private people interact with each other to trade rights is not the only way of achieving an incentive for change, and it may not be the best way.

The example of schemes such as Chhattis Mauja in Nepal (Yoder 1994) tells us that village groups of farmers do not necessarily insist on retaining water rights when there is a clear compensating benefit from surrendering that right. Chhattis Maujas's farmers have developed a procedure where there is a cost for holding the water right. The cost takes the form of contributing labor or money for the annual maintenance of a shared system. If a village reduces its water share, it also reduces its inputs of labor or money. Under these conditions, villages calculate how much water they really need, and are sometimes willing to release some part of their right. But, it is not sold from one user group to another, as apparently might be the case in Chile. The excess water right is returned to the larger community of users, who then can decide what to do with it.

Something along these lines seems to be likely to happen in a system where there is a regular charge for retaining a right, or a license to abstract water. The way forward may therefore be through a system in which abstraction rights, in agriculture and among other small-group users such as villages, are held by the group, in return for some payment to a larger body (basin or sub-basin management organization) for this privilege. The incentive to consider transfers will come through reduction of the license cost. Such a system, operating through basin organizations where stakeholders have strong influence, or perhaps full control, should mean that the reallocation of rights remains in the domain of the stakeholders.

There are a number of reasons for preferring a transfer system in which unused or unwanted rights revert to a basin management organization, which can then reassign them (using as far as possible principles of stakeholder involvement, discussed earlier). Free markets in tradable rights could lead to concentration of these rights in relatively few hands. Moreover, control over the reassignment of unused rights seems to be a necessary management tool, especially when we recognize that such management of rights is not only about the quantities that may be abstracted, but also about their disposal after use, the seasons at which they may be used, and the numerous other dimensions discussed earlier.

This kind of procedure will not work well, however, unless the fee paid for a license is set at an adequate level, so that any license-holder who intends to cease to use the right will be motivated to return it to the organization that granted it. If license fees are low, we should expect that a black market would appear, and people would illegally sell their rights to others in return for payments that exceed the fee. Black markets seem to be especially likely to develop if fees are set at different levels for different types of use.

Other types of interpersonal transfers, including inheritance of rights (which is significant in regard to agricultural water rights), are likely to be regulated within user groups, rather than by general public policy. Agricultural water rights are said, in many countries, to be "attached to the land," meaning that when a piece of irrigated land is sold, the water right goes with it. Much the same can be said about urban "rights" to domestic supply: when the house is sold, the new occupant expects the same delivery of water.

In the agricultural scene, many other types of transfer are taking place, some within the family, some not. A man who chooses to go abroad for employment may give his land to a brother, with no certainty whether this is temporary or permanent. Another farmer who is in debt may give the cultivation rights of his irrigated land for a year or two to the village merchant, in lieu of debt repayment. There are many other patterns of transfer of land rights. These will in general mean that an interpersonal transfer of water right occurs, permanently or temporarily. The regulation of behavior of these kinds is probably best left under the supervision of a local irrigators' association, which is itself the primary holder of a general water right for the village community.

Conclusion

This chapter analyzed issues involved in administering and implementing water rights and recommended ways to improve basin water allocation in response to changing conditions. Protecting and guaranteeing the rights of individuals to abstract or receive water in river basins where there are large numbers of small users of water requires a hierarchy of river basin organizations in some form, with a national regulatory body at the apex. The river basin organization should be the ultimate source of documented rights.

Organizations that provide water services, for agriculture, electricity generation, industry, or domestic uses, should be required to obtain licenses controlling and limiting their water uses for each of their abstraction locations.

These arrangements can integrate traditional single-use rights, for example, for irrigated agriculture, fishing, or livestock. Groups claiming such rights can continue to allocate within their group, but it is necessary to define the total scope of each group right.

It does not seem practicable that individual users, in agriculture and other rural uses such as fishing and livestock, will relate directly to river basin management, as they are too numerous in most developing countries. Instead, river basins will probably devolve rights to local sub-basins, which will in turn control the abstraction rights of user groups. Individual rural users will continue to depend largely on systems of rules within their own user groups.

The structure of river basin organizations should give significant influence to a wide variety of stakeholder representatives. Whether a stakeholder council should have a direct role in decisionmaking or only an advisory role may depend on local circumstances. However, wherever possible it seems that a role in decisionmaking is desirable.

Institutional procedures for allocating new rights should follow the principles of transparency and disclosure to holders of existing rights.

Allocation between different types of use requires decisions that are political rather than technological, although technical data and advice should guide the process of preparing such decisions.

Users of water usually return more than half of the used water back into the natural system. A right to abstract therefore implies disposal. Rights should be qualified or constrained in some way so that the exercise of an abstraction right does not cause problems for other users downstream, through changes in water quality. This requirement should apply to existing and traditional users as well as to new users.

River basin organizations should be independent, neutral among the different groups of users and of service providers, and (in order to preserve their independence) should if possible obtain their own finance, most probably by abstraction fees paid by rights-holders.

Rights to abstract water should not be transferable by sale to other users. If the holder of a license wishes to cease or to reduce its use, the surrendered right should return to the authority that granted it, thus enabling its reissue to another user. This will succeed only if license fees are set at levels near to a market rate. Otherwise, black markets and unregistered transfers are likely to occur.

References

Abernethy, C. L. 2000. Financing river-basin organizations. In *Intersectoral management of river basins,* ed. C. L. Abernethy. Feldafing, Germany: German Foundation for International Development and Colombo, Sri Lanka: International Water Management Institute.

———. 2005. Financing river basin organizations. In *Irrigation and river basin management: Options for governance and institutions,* ed. M. Svendsen. Wallingford, England: CABI.

Abernethy, C. L., ed. 2001. *Intersectoral management of river basins.* Feldafing, Germany: German Foundation for International Development and Colombo, Sri Lanka: International Water Management Institute.

Bakker, M., and Y. Matsuno. 2001. A framework for valuing ecological services of irrigation water: A case of an irrigation-wetland system in Sri Lanka. *Irrigation and Drainage Systems* 15 (2): 99–115.

Buckland, J., and T. Zabel. 1998. Economic and financial aspects of water management policies. In *Selected issues in water resources management in Europe,* vol. 2, ed. F. N. Correia. Rotterdam: Balkema.

Correia, F. N., ed. 1998. *Selected issues in water resources management in Europe.* Rotterdam: Balkema.

Gunatilake, H. M., and C. Gopalakrishnan. 2002. Proposed water policy for Sri Lanka: The policy versus the policy process. *Water Resources Development* 18 (4): 545–562.

Holden, P., and M. Thobani. 1996. Tradable water rights: A property-rights approach to resolving water shortages and promoting investment. In *Strategies for intersectoral water management in developing countries: Challenges and consequences for agriculture,* eds. J. Richter, P. Wolff, H. Franzen, and F. Heim. Feldafing, Germany: DSE.

Hollaender, R. 2001. German experiences in river basin co-operation. In *Intersectoral management of river basins,* ed. C. L. Abernethy. Feldafing, Germany: Foundation for International Development and Colombo, Sri Lanka: International Water Management Institute.

Horst, L. 1998. *The dilemmas of water division: Considerations and criteria for irrigation system design.* Colombo, Sri Lanka: International Water Management Institute and Wageningen, the Netherlands: Wageningen Agricultural University.

Jensen, P. K., Y. Matsuno, W. van der Hoek, and S. Cairncross. 2001. Limitations of irrigation water quality guidelines from a multiple use perspective. *Irrigation and Drainage Systems* 15 (2): 117–128.

Lang, H. 2002. When people agree on fair access to water. *Agriculture and Rural Development* 9 (2): 48–49.

Meinzen-Dick, R., and W. van der Hoek. 2001. Multiple uses of water in irrigated areas. *Irrigation and Drainage Systems* 15 (2): 93–98.

Ostrom, E. 1992. *Crafting institutions for self-governing irrigation systems.* San Francisco: ICS Press.

Svendsen, M., ed. 2005. *Irrigation and river basin management: Options for governance and institutions.* Wallingford, UK: CABI.

Tweeten, L. 2000. Coexisting with alternative agricultural advocates. *Choices* Q2, p3.

Yoder, R. 1994. *Organization and management by farmers in the Chhattis Mauja irrigation system, Nepal.* Colombo, Sri Lanka: International Irrigation Management Institute.

Part 2

Practical Lessons from Implementation

Chapter 4

Lessons from Implementing Water Rights in Mexico

Héctor Garduño

— During the 1990s, Mexico enacted and began applying new legislation, decrees, and procedures regulating water abstraction and wastewater discharge. The water rights administration faced various challenges in implementing registration and enforcing the law, but also provided a basis for putting the "user pays" and "polluter pays" principles into operation. There is still more to be done to use water rights as a true management tool. The main conclusions of this chapter are that (1) the design of a water rights system must never go beyond the implementation capacity of the users and institutions, and that (2) the implementation of a water rights system must be undertaken within a gradual and realistic time frame, measured not in months, but in decades.

Widespread problems regarding water scarcity, pollution, and conflicts among users have made it mandatory to design and implement a water rights system in Mexico that includes both water abstraction "concessions" and wastewater discharge permits. The water law and regulations that came into effect in December 1992 and January 1994, respectively, recognized this situation. However, the three-year period provided to register existing users was insufficient, so the president of the Republic issued decrees to extend it and pardon the arrears of water charges owed by those who applied for water abstraction and wastewater discharge permits. As a result of the presidential decrees, mass media campaigns, and hundreds of meetings with water users, by December 2000 about 320,000 users had been granted abstraction permits, which were recorded in the

Water Rights Public Register. However, the downside of this success story is that the total volume granted in many river basins and groundwater aquifers exceeds water availability. Moreover, as a result of the hasty process, a substantial portion of the information in the register is not reliable. These pitfalls are being addressed in order to improve the quality and reliability of the register.

The Mexican experience over the last 14 years proves that the "user pays" and "polluter pays" principles can be implemented but also that social and political realities make it very difficult to realize systems that strictly follow economic theory. Water abstraction and wastewater discharge levies have in fact contributed to increased water use efficiencies, more rational decisions regarding the location of economic activities, and improved monetary collection. The levies represent—with the exception of 1998—more than 50 percent of the National Water Commission's annual expenditures of around US$1 billion. The challenge now is to increase annual collection and to align levies better with economic incentives.

To deal with the very difficult implementation aspects of law enforcement, including dealing with criminal activity and corruption, procedures are being streamlined; staff members are being trained; users are being made aware of their rights and duties; and offenders are being penalized in accordance with the law. There is increasing recognition that achieving the goal of making water rights a true management tool requires a fine-tuned balance of economic incentives, regulatory enforcement, and stakeholder participation.

The next sections of this chapter present background information on granting water abstraction and wastewater discharge permits to all users in the country, followed by a discussion of the legal framework. The following section discusses implementation issues including how the registration process evolved, water charges and the application of the "polluter pays" principle, transfers, enforcement, information systems, and the use of water rights as a management tool. The main conclusions are that the design of a water rights system must never go beyond the implementation capacity of users and institutions, and that the implementation of a water rights system must be undertaken with a gradual and realistic approach.[1]

Background

Mexico lies within the tropics and contains many mountainous areas as well as valley and plateau regions. Many of the rivers in Mexico are short, flowing from the central mountains to the Atlantic Ocean in the east and the Pacific Ocean in the west.[2] Seasonal changes are most marked by the summer rainy season from June to October. Figure 4.1 illustrates the temporal and spatial variability in rainfall. The variability in rainfall greatly influences water availability and scarcity throughout the

Figure 4.1 Rainfall variability in Mexico

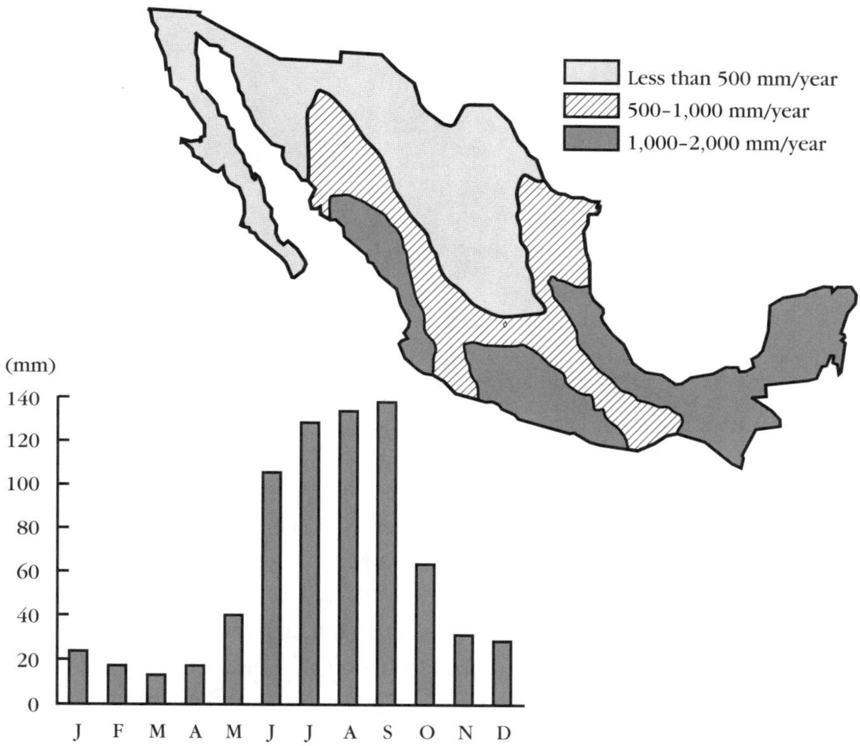

Source: Mexican National Water Commission, "Estadisticas del Agua en México," http://www.cna.gob.mx.

Mexican Republic. The overall annual renewable availability is 450 billion cubic meters (BCM).[3] In spite of the relative abundance of water in some regions, pollution and the need for treatment reduce the actual availability. The total estimated annual water consumption is 72 BCM, with 28 BCM from groundwater sources.

In Table 4.1 the different categories of freshwater use in Mexico in 2002 are shown in terms of annual concessioned volume and number of users in the Water Rights Public Register. The range of water users is very wide; for instance, a user in agriculture can be an individual farmer up to an irrigation system of some 10,000 hectares, and an urban/domestic user can be from a few households sharing one single water source up to Mexico City supplied by hundreds of water wells and transferred surface water from a neighboring river basin. By 1992, the estimated

Table 4.1 Water use concessioned in Mexico, according to the Water Rights Public Register

Category	Volume (billions of cubic meters/year)	Estimated number of users
Hydropower	145.6	88
Agriculture and livestock	56.1	185,856
Urban and domestic[a]	9.6	133,404
Industry[b]	6.9	8,302
Total	218.2	327,650

Source: National Water Commission.

[a]Includes industry supplied by water mains.

[b]Self-supplied industry, including thermal power plants.

number of users was approximately 300,000. However, only 2,000 of those users had a formal concession to use water. Ten years later, 327,650 users had been granted a formal concession.

Out of Mexico's slightly over 100 million inhabitants, more than 20 million live in Mexico City. Average per capita water availability is close to 5,000 cubic meters per year, well above the international scarcity standard of 1,000 cubic meters annually. However, temporal and spatial variability determine actual availability, which does not correspond with water demands. Although the southeast has 72 percent of the total available water resources, it has only 23 percent of the population and 16 percent of the economic activities. The rest of the country has only 28 percent of the available water, but 77 percent of the population and economic activities. This situation gives rise to conflicts among water uses, users, states, and regions. A particularly worrisome situation is that among the 650 identified groundwater aquifers in the country, 100 are subject to excessive exploitation.

Framework

Legal and Institutional Background

Before the Spanish conquest in 1521, the relationship of the Mexican peoples to water was both religious and practical. On the one hand, belief in several water deities was common and, on the other hand, practical realities generated norms defining who could use water, how to resolve conflicts among water users, and how to cope with floods. Inhabitants built water supply aqueducts, irrigation and flood control works, and navigation systems. For 300 years after the conquest, water belonged to the king and a royal grant was required to use it. These rights passed to the state on independence in 1821. The present constitution dates back to 1917, following the 1910 revolution. The following articles of the constitution are relevant to water resources management:

- Article 25. The State shall ensure that all social and economic activities will be undertaken with due care of the environment.

- Article 27. The Nation is owner of all water within its territory, with a few exceptions, and authorizes the government to administer these resources and grant "concessions" for water use.

- Article 31. All Mexicans have the duty to contribute to the public expenditure.

- Article 115. Municipal governments, with assistance from state governments, are responsible for municipal water delivery systems.

Even before the 1917 constitution was enacted, the 1870 Civil Code established that to use water owned by the state, a concession granted by qualified authority was required. From then on, several laws and regulations were issued to regulate a number of water aspects. Three successive laws regarding water owned by the nation were issued in 1910, 1929, and 1934. The government formed the National Irrigation Commission in 1926 and the National Power Commission in 1937. From 1947 to 1976, the Ministry of Water Resources administered water. In addition to building infrastructure and operating irrigation districts, the ministry: (1) created river basin agencies in the main river basins; (2) drafted the Federal Waters Law (FWL) approved by Congress in 1972;[4] and (3) prepared the first National Water Plan in 1975. In 1976, the priority attached to agriculture led to the formation of a combined Agriculture and Water Resources Ministry.

Progress in new construction slowed in the 1980s owing to the financial crisis, which, however, also resulted in the "user pays" and "polluter pays" principles being incorporated into the tax law. The importance of research and development was recognized in 1986 by establishing the Mexican Water Technology Institute. To properly address water management issues, the National Water Commission (NWC) was created in February 1989. The 1972 FWL, along with the Regulations to Prevent and Control Water Pollution issued also in 1972, set up the legal framework for more integrated water resources management, but was insufficient to address all the problems associated with a more intensive water use. Therefore, under the initiative of the Under-Secretary of Hydraulic Infrastructure, the National Waters Law (NWL) was drafted following the guidelines of an updated National Water Plan and international recommendations on integrated water resources management. It was adopted in December 1992 to supersede the 1972 law. The regulations of the new law were issued 13 months afterwards, in January 1994. It should be noted that the regulations for the Water Law of 1972 were never issued.

The 1992 law defined the NWC as "the sole federal water authority in the country." Initially, it remained attached to the Ministry of Agriculture and Water Resources, but in 1995 it moved to the new Ministry of the Environment. The international consensus that water use management should be based on a well-tuned combination of regulatory, economic, and participation instruments is clearly reflected in the main laws that constitute the Mexican water legislation. These are the NWL and those sections of the Federal Tax Law that are related to water, which are referred to in this chapter as the Federal Waters Levy Law (FWLL).

The 1992 NWL calls for an integrated approach to both water quantity and water quality management of surface and groundwater within river basins, which are considered the ideal geographical units for planning, development, and management of water resources. However, when established, the NWC was organized on an administrative boundary basis. Six regional agencies, which grouped several states, were created, along with agencies in each of the 32 states.[5] The regional agencies were later reorganized broadly along river basin boundaries and their number has increased to 13. Their boundaries still follow municipal limits, however, since it was felt that no municipality should have to deal with more than one river basin agency.

In April 2004, the water law was substantially amended;[6] the author is of the opinion that implementation will be even more difficult than it already was with the previous version, owing to some very challenging provisions, such as the mandate to set up river basin agencies throughout the country in only 18 months and excessively high penalties for law offenders—coupled with insufficient institutional enforcement capacity and challenges regarding consolidation of democratic participation for water resources management.

Legal Bases for the Water Rights Administration System

The NWL includes regulatory, economic, and participatory instruments, which are highlighted in Box 4.1. The FWLL defines the tariffs for using water as a public good and for services provided by the state. In addition to setting the rates for concessions and discharge permits, it sets the price for bulk water such as water the NWC supplies to Mexico City.[7] The FWLL complements the definition of economic instruments (in the NWL) by making the "user pays" and "polluter pays" principles operational. Thus, the tariff for abstraction water charges depends on the specific use and the relative scarcity of the water source; and the tariffs for wastewater disposal charges depend on the pollutant load and on the use and vulnerability of the receiving water body. In addition to the constitution, the NWL, and the FWLL, several other legal instruments affect water resources management: international treaties (notably with the United States), the Federal Infrastructure Law, the Federal Environmental Law, and environmental and water supply laws adopted by the legislature of each state.

General Procedure

To fulfill its obligations regarding water rights administration, the NWC carries out the following activities:

- granting, modifying, or canceling concessions pertaining to national waters, federal zones, and the use of gravel and sand from river beds;
- granting, modifying, or canceling wastewater disposal permits;
- operating the Water Rights Public Register;
- monitoring water abstraction, wastewater disposal, and user compliance with legal obligations;
- detecting illegal users;
- determining sanctions against users who violate applicable regulations;
- monitoring payment of water charges and submission of reports to fiscal authorities;
- conciliating or arbitrating disputes between water users; and
- updating of the water user database.

To carry out these activities the Sub-Directorate for Water Administration of the NWC has the following five central units in Mexico City:

- Norms and Procedures;
- Water User Services;
- Water Levy Collection;

Box 4.1 Regulatory, economic, and participatory instruments in the national waters law

Regulatory Instruments

- Water resources planning as the basis for management within river basins.
- Reiteration of the constitutional principle that water can be exploited by individuals or legal associations only by means of a concession granted by the federal executive through the NWC for a period of 5–50 years. The law: (1) defines specific regulations for the principal uses (irrigation; water supply, sewage, and wastewater treatment; power generation; and other productive uses), (2) establishes criteria for the time limit of abstraction concessions, and cancels concessions that are not used within three consecutive years (to avoid speculation and monopoly), and (3) provides for enforcement of efficient water use, with due sanctions on users who apparently waste water.
- Power of the federal executive to limit or prohibit use in the national interest: (1) to prevent or remediate groundwater overdraft, (2) to protect or restore an ecosystem, (3) to preserve sources for water supply or protect them from pollution, (4) to preserve and control water quality, and (5) at times of drought or severe water scarcity.
- Water pollution prevention and control, in that all users who dispose of wastewater must: (1) obtain a discharge permit and comply with the specified discharge standards, and (2) inform the NWC how they will comply with the standards.
- Regulations to manage: (1) the use of federal zones (defined as a strip of land along a river or lake 10 meters wide above the level of the maximum normal flood) and (2) extraction of sand and gravel from a riverbed.
- Users who do not pay the charges specified in the FWLL for water abstraction or wastewater discharge permits are subject to cancellation of their concessions and permits.
- All abstraction concessions, federal zone occupation, discharge permits, and water rights trades must be recorded in the Water Rights Public Register in order to provide users with legal certainty.

- Sanctions on users for not complying with the NWL or its by-laws. Users have the right to appeal against NWC resolutions and to use administrative procedures before resorting to the courts.
- Transitional measures so those users, who have documents other than concessions and permits but are de facto users, can regularize their legal situation.

Economic Instruments

- User obligation to pay the charges established by the FWLL regarding water abstraction, wastewater disposal, use of federal zones, and use of sand and gravel as building materials. Also, concessionaires of hydraulic infrastructure must pay certain charges.
- Tradability of water rights (including abstraction concessions and discharge permits) to promote economically more efficient water allocation.

Participatory Instruments

- Establishment of river basin councils, as coordination and agreement units of federal, state, and municipal authorities, as well as water users and all stakeholders. Their main tasks are to participate in the planning and development of water resources, as well as in the management, particularly to cope with scarcity and pollution problems.
- Establishment of water user organizations, mainly through the divestment of government-run irrigation systems and strengthening of water supply utilities.
- Promotion of social participation in the design, construction, financing, operation, and maintenance of hydraulic infrastructure and services.

Source: National Waters Law.

- Public Water Rights Registry; and
- Monitoring and Control of Users.

The process starts with a person applying for an abstraction concession or a wastewater discharge permit.[8] For the case of water abstractions, Figure 4.2 schematically

Figure 4.2 Relationship between a water user or applicant, the NWC, and the judiciary

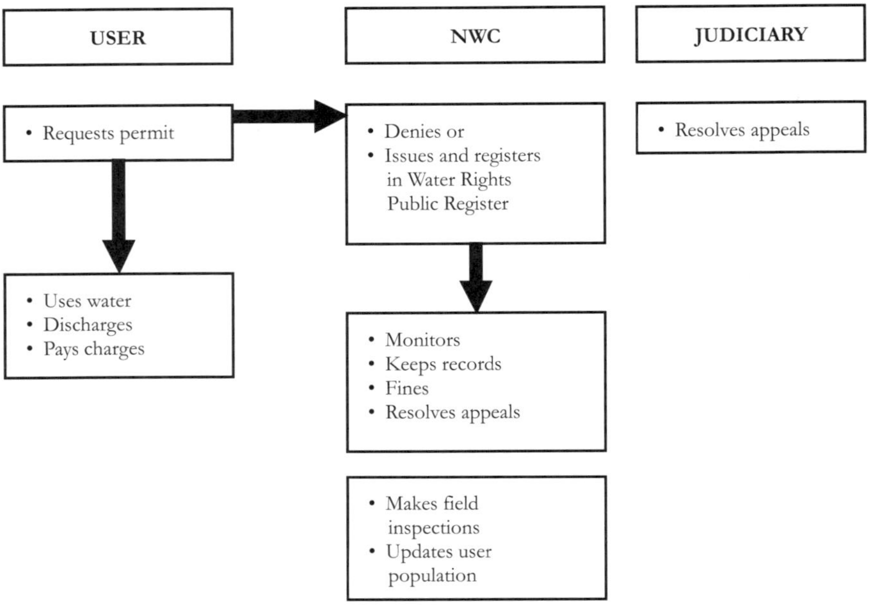

Source: Author.

represents the relationship between a water user or applicant, the NWC, and the judiciary. The applicant usually submits the required information and documents to one of the 32 state agencies of the NWC. Depending on the required abstraction volume and the relative water scarcity, the state manager will decide, or prepare an opinion, and transmit it either to the corresponding regional manager or to the central offices. If there is not enough water or another competing application is judged more beneficial to the public interest, the application is denied. If approved, the agency issues the corresponding entitlement, records it in the register, and presents it to the applicant.

All relevant documents must be properly filed and safeguarded for future consultation, regardless of whether the decision was favorable or not. The process involves several stages and the participation of different offices. It is necessary to keep track of time because the commission has to respond within a maximum of 90 working days after the applicant has provided all required documents. An entitlement is the legal proof of a user's water rights, so it must be recorded in the Water

Rights Public Register, as well as any changes in the status, such as expiration or changes due to rights trading.

Users are required to comply with the terms and conditions of their concession entitlements and wastewater discharge permits. They must prepare quarterly statements of the charges they owe according to the abstracted volume and the polluting load of the wastewater discharge. They fill out payment forms and pay at designated banks. The NWC monitors with a sampling approach to verify if users are complying with the terms and conditions of their entitlements and permits and if they have paid the correct amount of charges. Records are kept for statistical and legal purposes. The NWC has the power to penalize users who do not comply and illegal users detected by the commission.

If the user disagrees with the decision on his application, or the sanctions imposed by the commission, he can lodge an appeal to the commission itself or to the courts of law. The law mandates a close follow-up of each appeal.

Concessions and wastewater discharge permits are issued according to the following criteria:

1. State agencies issue them for relatively small volumes in nonstressed river basins and aquifers.

2. Regional agencies issue them for medium-sized volumes in stressed areas and in areas where there may be conflicts among states.

3. The central level is responsible for the largest volumes, in cases where there may be conflicts among regions, and for transboundary waters.

The work of the five central units is closely interrelated. Together they are responsible for the administration of water rights and thus have a major impact on water use patterns in the country. The personnel in charge of the water rights administration, including those at the central, regional, and state levels, consists of 1,900 persons; of these 40 percent are professionals and 60 percent are support staff.

Implementation and Administration of the Water Rights System

Regularization of Existing Water Users

The benefits of regularizing water rights through a formal concession are twofold. The user would obtain legal certainty and the water authority would obtain the basic information necessary for sound planning and management of resources. Following the passage of the NWL, initially, from 1993 to mid-1995, progress in the regularization of users was slow. It was difficult to comply with the legal and regulatory requirements. Moreover, the NWC lacked capacity to manage the regularization within the transition period provided by the law and its regulations.

The 1992 NWL allowed only one year for all existing users to obtain a concession and registration by December 1993. The regulations under the NWL allowed extending the period for certain users for two more years, until December 1995. Thus, the time constraints were quite stringent. The NWL vested the authority to grant concessions in the director general of the NWC and provided for the delegation of certain functions. From November 1993, even before the regulations were issued, the authority to grant concessions and wastewater discharge permits had been delegated to the sub-director general for water administration, and the regional and state managers. To increase ownership of the new approach and hasten registration, NWC trained its personnel immediately after the law was adopted.

By mid-1994, it was clear that the target to regularize all existing users would not be met. Therefore, application and decision procedures were simplified. The director general of the NWC instructed that no additional requirements beyond those prescribed in the regulations should be imposed on any applicant. However, this was not enough. Therefore in October 1995, the president of Mexico issued three decrees for:

1. agriculture and livestock;

2. industries and services (such as businesses, hotels, sports clubs, and markets); and

3. water supply utilities.

The NWL provides for concessions to last from 5 to 50 years. However, the presidential decrees of October 1995 established that all users who applied would be granted a 10-year concession. The rationale was that in a 10-year period knowledge of water availability and use would be better, and so when users applied for the renewal of their concessions better decisions could be made. Users were given incentives in the form of benefits gained if they adhered promptly to the presidential decrees. They included the partial or total pardoning of unpaid charges and that sanctions would not be applied for the abstraction of water without a concession or for disposing of wastewater without a permit. The result was that in the year

Table 4.2 Comparison of presidential decrees

Points of comparison	First set of decrees: October 1995–October 1996	Second set of decrees: October 1996–December 1998
Users with permit	Preference in subsidies and other benefits	
Administrative regularization	Issuance of concession or permit	User compliance with application requirements
Volume	Availability and third-party effects User must demonstrate effective use	User declares volume under oath NWC can verify
Time frame	Same time frame for all users	More time for domestic and irrigation users
Wastewater quality improvement	Treatment plant NWC approves program	Treatment plant or modified process NWC monitors progress
Fiscal benefits	Pardoning of arrears, partial or total	
Fiscal regularization	Pay charges beginning January 1995	

Source: Adapted from Garduño (2001).

following the adoption of these decrees so many users applied for the benefits of the decrees that the capacity of the NWC turned out to be insufficient to handle all the requests received.

Although the first set of decrees was well received, it imposed bureaucratic burdens both on the user and on the commission. For this reason and because the additional one year granted by the first decrees again proved to be insufficient, a second set of decrees was issued a year later by the federal executive. These were based on even simpler procedures and, more importantly, trusted the user and limited the discretion of the water authority. Both sets of decrees are compared in Table 4.2 and in the following points:

- Only those users using water before October 1995 can apply for the benefits granted by the decrees.

- More benefits and time to apply for these benefits are granted to domestic and irrigation uses than to industry.[9]

- Responsible users who had concessions and permits previously will have preference regarding subsidies and other support programs.

- According to the first set of decrees, a user was considered regularized only after the commission issued the concession or permit, whereas the second set of decrees required only that the user comply with the application requirements.

- According to the first set of decrees, the commission established the authorized volume and duration of the concession or permit through water balances after the applicant demonstrated effective use. However, it was difficult to compute water balances so long as not all uses were known in a particular river basin and the commission did not have enough staff to carry out the task of verifying in the field that every use was in fact a beneficial one. The second set of decrees provided that in all cases the NWC must issue concessions for 10 years and that the user must declare, under oath, the volumes being used. The NWC is then required to verify the truthfulness of a user's claim by checking a statistically representative sample.

- According to the first set of decrees, in order to obtain a wastewater discharge permit and the benefits of the decree, the applicant's treatment project should be approved by the NWC. The second set required only that the applicant present a simplified program to comply with the effluent standard. The same applicant was allowed to improve the quality of the wastewater either by building a treatment plant or by modifying the industrial process. The NWC monitors the progress in wastewater quality improvement programs. Users who do not progress according to their submitted programs will not receive the benefits of the decrees.

- Penal sanctions are imposed on users who are not truthful in their declarations and their water abstraction entitlements may be canceled.

A vigorous information campaign was launched in 1993. Later, the campaign was intensified and hundreds of meetings were held all over the country to induce water users to regularize their administrative and fiscal situation by applying for the benefits of the decrees. The first set of decrees expired in October 1996, and the second in June 1997 for industry and in December 1998 for other users.

Because of the simplification of procedures, the presidential decrees (Table 4.3), and the information campaign, by December 1997 close to 200,000 users had applied for the benefits of the decrees.[10] By December 2000, about 320,000 users had been regularized and their permits recorded in the Water Rights Public Register. Figure 4.3 illustrates the dramatic improvement in issuance of water concessions (compared to the 2,000 concession entitlements issued between 1917 and 1992)

Table 4.3 Water legislation and administration benchmarks

Year	Benchmarks
1992	December: Congress adopts National Waters Law
1993	October: NWC's director general delegates power to issue entitlements and a vigorous communication campaign is launched
1994	January: President issues water law regulations August: NWC's director general simplifies procedures
1995	October: President issues first set of regularization decrees
1996	October: President issues second set of regularization decrees

Source: Author.

with reference to important benchmarks. Nevertheless, the regularization process faced several drawbacks, which are described in the next section.

Regularization of Existing Wastewater Dischargers

For the control of wastewater discharges, probably the most important recent achievement was the adoption in 1996 of a single new standard for all industrial and municipal wastewater disposals. This standard, shown in Figure 4.4, replaced 44 obsolete standards that previously regulated municipal wastewater disposal and

Figure 4.3 Water user regularization

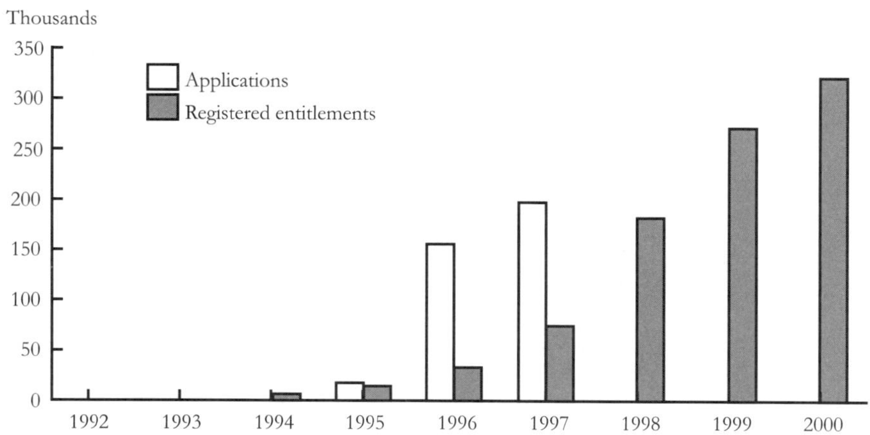

Source: Updated from Garduño (2001) with information from Mexican National Water Commission, "Estadisticas del Agua en México," http://www.cna.gob.mx (2004).

Figure 4.4 The 1996 Wastewater Effluent Standard

Parameters:

- **Basic:** Temperature, pH, oil and grease, floating solids, settleable solids, TSS, BOD, total P, total N
- **Heavy metals:** As, Cd, Cu, Cr, Hg, Ni, Pb, Zn and **cyanides**
- **Pathogens:** Bacteria, viruses, fecal coliforms, and helminth eggs

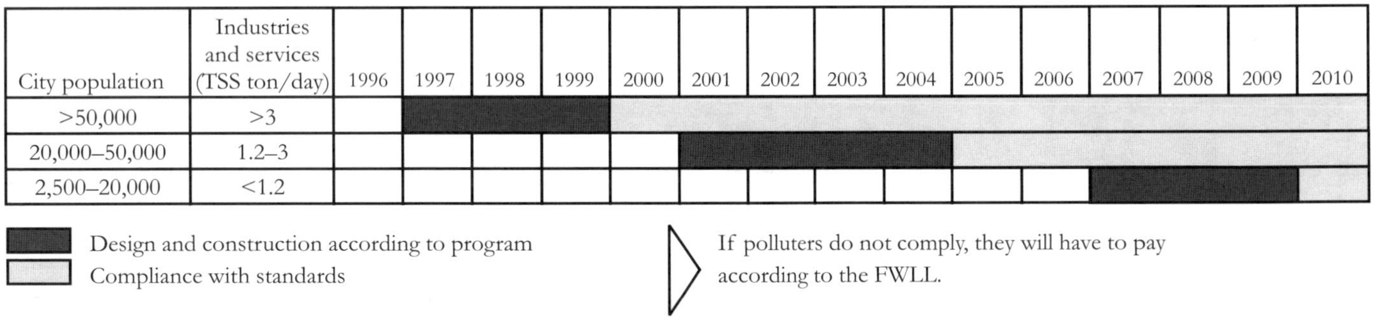

Source: Prepared by author with information from Mexican Standard SEMARNAT 1996-01. (The name was changed from the former one, ECOL 1996-01, in order to include the acronym of the Ministry of Environment and Natural Resources: Secretaría de Medio Ambiente y Recursos Naturales.)

various industrial activities (Jiménez 2005). Moreover, Congress approved reforms to the FWLL regarding wastewater disposal permits that are consistent with the new standard. Users whose disposal does not comply with the standard must pay a corresponding charge, according to the pollution load. A substantial number of new wastewater discharge permits have been issued under the standard now in force.

Users will be required to comply only with the limit values established for those pollutants they produce. The new standard takes into account both the use of the receiving water body as well as its vulnerability. It incorporates gradualism, by stating that major polluters must comply in the year 2000, intermediate ones in 2005, and minor ones in 2010. However, existing plants can continue operating either according to their original discharge permits or following the new standards, depending on the user's choice. If the quality of the discharge exceeds the new standard, the user can apply for a rebate to be applied to the water abstraction charge.

Polluters who exceed more than five times the limit values set for any of the parameters of the new standard had to present, within one year after the standards were adopted, a design and construction program to improve their wastewater quality. The rest have to present a similar program several years before their target compliance date. For example, a medium-size city or industry would have to present its program by December 2000 and start complying with the standard by January 2005. Those users who present their programs on time are exempted from paying discharge charges during the construction period if they progress according to their programs.

Collection of Water Charges

One of the most important economic instruments for water rights administration is the collection of water charges. Charging was introduced in Mexico when the NWC was established with a dual purpose: (1) to increase water use efficiency, promote a gradual shift in water use to higher value priorities, and deter water pollution; and (2) to provide funds for water resources management and development. Figure 4.5 shows the amount of revenues from the collection of water charges from 1989 to 2000 in Mexican pesos. Up to 1993, income (even in real terms) rose year by year. Income (measured in constant values) started to fall in 1994 due to a severe national economic crisis and has not yet recovered from the record 1993 value. Nevertheless, in current Mexican pesos, collection of water charges has consistently increased and it has represented a significant percentage of the NWC expenditure budget, as shown in Figure 4.6.

Table 4.4 shows the sources of income from collection of water charges for 1996. Income from irrigation is small compared to that obtained from industry. In spite of the fact that 80 percent of all water currently used in Mexico is for agriculture,

Figure 4.5 Collection of water charges in Mexican pesos, 1989–2000

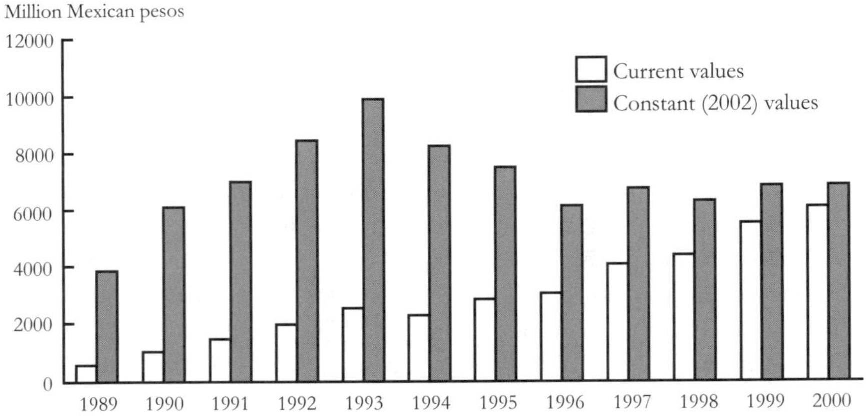

Source: Mexican National Water Commission, "Estadisticas del Agua en México," http://www.cna.gob.mx (2004).

Note: In 2000 one Mexican peso was approximately equivalent to US$0.10.

Figure 4.6 Yearly income as percentage of NWC expenditures

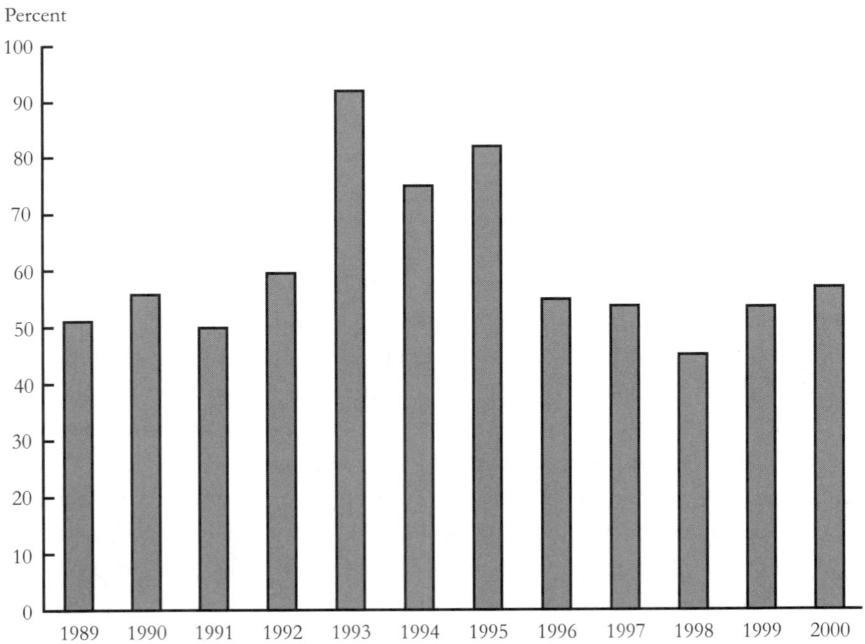

Source: Prepared by author, with information from Mexican National Water Commission, "Estadisticas del Agua en México," http://www.cna.gob.mx (2004).

Table 4.4 Income sources as a percentage of total NWC income in 1996

Sources	Water abstraction	Wastewater discharge	O&M	Others
Industry and services	44	3		
Water supply	6		18	
Hydro- and thermal power	13			
Irrigation	Exempted		4	
Recovery of arrears	2	4		
Miscellaneous				6

Source: National Water Commission Annual Report.

the agricultural sector is exempt from abstraction charges, and pays only fees for operation and maintenance. Hence, it can be argued that industrial water users are subsidizing agriculture and municipal users.

Water subsidies in Mexico have traditionally been used to achieve specific socio-political objectives of food security, providing clean drinking water, and increasing the income and health of the rural poor. Although this in itself is commendable, the total efficiency of water use in the country as a whole needs to be rationalized, in particular with respect to agricultural use. The economic ideal would be to completely remove cross subsidies; however, the NWC needs the money it receives from industry. Most municipal water utilities are financially insolvent and farmers have high social and political standing. Nevertheless, cross subsidies are being removed, but at a very slow pace.

Most water utilities in the country took advantage of the presidential decrees and regularized their water use and wastewater discharge. However, very few kept paying water levies after their concessions and permits were registered. Therefore, a new presidential decree was issued on December 19, 2001, stating that water utilities would be pardoned for unpaid water levies up to December 31, 2001, provided users applied before May 2002 (this deadline was later extended to July 2002) and made timely payments starting in January 2002. Public water utilities should guarantee their payment with their share of federal fiscal participation to which they are entitled and private utilities with any legally acceptable guarantee. A similar decree regarding charges for wastewater discharge was issued. To benefit from this latter decree, applicants should commit themselves to comply with a self-designed program to treat their wastewater in a maximum period of four years. As an additional incentive, the FWLL in 2002 stated that all moneys collected would be applied to improve water supply and sanitation infrastructure.

The response to these decrees was satisfactory. However, a substantial number of water utilities did not apply, either because the time provided was not enough for them to finalize the required financial and infrastructure planning, or because

Table 4.5 Water rights trades in Mexico

Not recorded in WRPR	Recorded in WRPR	
NWC approval not required		NWC approval required
• Within irrigation districts	• Only user changes • Areas designated by NWC	• All other transactions
Probably thousands of permanent and temporary transactions	• 573 groundwater • 7 surface water • 4 wastewater discharges	

Source: Water Rights Public Register, Mexican National Water Commission.

they were not able to obtain from the corresponding municipalities and states a commitment to provide the guarantees described above. Recognizing these difficulties, a new set of presidential decrees issued on December 23, 2002, extended the regularization period until March 2003 and allowed an alternative guarantee from public water utilities.

Water Markets

Several aspects of the 1992 water law address water markets. Users are free to trade their rights within irrigation districts, with no intervention from the commission. Users are also free to transfer their rights when only the user changes or within areas, specially designated by the director general of the commission, although all such transactions must be registered. All other transactions are subject to approval in order to protect the environment and third parties. Table 4.5 summarizes the process for water rights trading in Mexico.

Even before the NWL was adopted in 1992, temporary transactions were common practice within irrigated areas. Up to mid-1998, close to 600 NWC-authorized transactions had been recorded in the Water Rights Public Register, most of them concerning groundwater and the majority from irrigation to industry. This relatively small number may disappoint some economists who believe water markets are the best instrument to achieve optimal water allocation. However, it would have been irresponsible to promote markets before regularizing existing users and improving knowledge regarding water availability. These water rights transfers have provided valuable experience to both the NWC and users, which will be useful when the practice becomes more widespread.

Law Enforcement and Prevention of Criminal Offenses and Corruption

Law enforcement, through intensive monitoring of water abstraction and wastewater discharges, is probably the most difficult task. Nevertheless, now that most users have been regularized, the NWC is in the process of conveying the message to society that the water authority is in fact exercising the power vested in it by the constitution and the laws. This is being achieved by sampling representative users and polluters in the field, and applying severe penalties to those not complying with the conditions of said decrees or that of their respective concessions and permits. Intensive and well-organized actions such as these will increase the credibility of the commission. A sample of news press articles shows that water rights administration has to deal also with criminal offenses;[11] therefore, monitoring and enforcement systems need to be reviewed continually in order to improve them.

Several measures against corruption by NWC personnel, such as the following, have been implemented:

- improved monitoring to detect unethical behavior and severe penalties where appropriate;
- preparation and dissemination to personnel and users of manuals of procedures such as water rights trading, forfeiture, and extension;
- improved monitoring procedures making users aware of procedures and of their related rights and duties; and
- timely response to complaints from users and stakeholders.

Information System

The interactions among the various actors described earlier illustrate the great amount of information involved in the various procedures of the water rights administration system. Given the number of users, the complexity of factors that have to be taken into account to issue a concession or a permit and to monitor compliance, as well as the need to follow up progress at the national, regional, and state levels, the information management needs are quite large and dynamic. Since 1993, after the National Water Law was enacted, four main databases have been developed:

- The user population database is a "learning model" which estimates the number of users and polluters as well as abstraction and wastewater discharge volumes, through available hard data and indirect information and indices. Feedback helps improve the model as monitoring progresses and more hard and reliable data become available.
- The application follow-up database keeps track of all steps required to reply to a user's application.

- The Water Rights Public Register database holds files of concessions, permits, and water rights trades and provides information to the public on request.

- The water taxpayers' database tracks charges paid by users and polluters.

The business procedures related to the water rights administration are quite straightforward and accordingly it should be easy to design a computer system dealing with all its components and the interface among them. However, various factors (hydrological, ecological, economic, social, political, and organizational) determine how and at what pace implementation in the field can be achieved. These factors usually shape the business procedures and in turn impose restrictions on the information systems (hardware and software). Accordingly, the four databases were developed independently. Each has been improved according to the field experience. Consequently, the resulting subsystems are not as dynamic and well integrated as desirable. The following improvements are being carried out:

- Procedures are being simplified to improve the services to the applicant and water user.

- Auditing and training are improving quality control of data, processes, and decisions.

- Desirable improvements for software and hardware as well as telecommunications have been identified, taking into account the best available technology. It has been recognized that they must be gradually introduced and cautiously implemented.

- An executive module with relevant summaries is being developed to aid decisionmakers.

- A Web site is being implemented with information from the Water Rights Public Register.

Making Water Rights a True Management Tool

The current challenge is how to make water rights a true water resource management tool. The answer is a fine-tuned balance of economic incentives, stakeholder participation, and law enforcement. This approach can be illustrated by the case of Guanajuato State, where 17,000 wells are abstracting (mainly for grain production) twice as much water as the natural recharge, causing a yearly drawdown of two meters, severe land subsidence, and water quality deterioration. The government of that state has taken the lead by supporting the establishment of 17 aquifer management organizations (COTAS is the Spanish acronym for Comité Técnico de Aguas Subterráneas).[12] Groundwater users have responded very positively and have participated in many actions such as making sure that the user information in the Water Rights Public Register is reliable. They have shown their willingness to reduce abstraction in order to store the aquifer.

However, economic incentives are required to move from low- to high-value crops. Experience shows that a natural reaction from a poor farmer to subsidies for introducing water-saving technologies for irrigation is increasing the irrigated surface or the number of crops thus abstracting more groundwater. The experience with a rich farmer who reacts to market signals is similar. Therefore, in both cases, in addition to economic incentives, enforced regulations are required to reduce the volume of water in each user's entitlement. Such regulations must result from negotiations between the government and stakeholders; otherwise users will never comply with them and the government does not have the capacity to monitor 17,000 wells.

Outcomes and Lessons from Implementing Water Rights

Mexico's experience offers the following pointers of general validity to the design and operation of water rights administration systems.

A gradual approach to regularizing existing users is preferable. The fact that most existing users have been regularized is not a small achievement. However, the downside of this is that in several river basins and aquifers in dry regions the total volume granted is greater than the water available. Because of the haste in the process imposed by the NWL, a significant amount of information in the Water Rights Public Register is not reliable. A program has been implemented to detect entitlements corresponding to volumes of water not being used, users who—when applying to the benefits of the presidential decrees—declared volumes larger than those that they were actually using, and users who use water for a purpose different from their entitlement.

Water rights systems should never go beyond institutional and user capacity. A water rights system (and water legislation by the same token) does not need to be perfect, but it has to be "implementable," that is, the government should be able to administer and enforce it and users must be able to comply with it.

Adjustment as a result of trial and error is a legitimate feature. Mexico has substantially progressed in the implementation of its water rights administration system. Neither the organizational structure nor the water legislation that support such a system is perfect because it is impossible to anticipate every conceivable implementation issue. Some flaws have been identified through practice and have been dealt with in a dynamic fashion, gradually adjusting the organizational and legal frameworks. The lessons gained in this process may be of benefit to other countries allowing them to anticipate implementation issues while drafting their water legislation, regulations, and implementation tools.

A balance needs to be found between administrative and ecological boundaries and requirements of the water rights administration. The NWC originally set up 32 state agencies and 6 regional agencies that grouped states. Later, the number of regional agencies was increased to 13, whose boundaries follow water divides as closely as possible. This boundary redefinition is consistent with the widely accepted international principle of river basin planning and management, which has been incorporated in the Mexican water legislation. However, to address their water issues, several states have to deal with more than one river basin agency. The following challenges will need to be faced to make the principle operational: (1) developing technical and managerial capacity for the increased number of agencies, (2) modifying procedures and information systems (technical and managerial) in order to fit the new territorial organization, and (3) establishing an adequate communication and negotiation strategy and mechanisms between the NWC and state governments.

Legal obstacles revealed by practice and experience need to be removed. The following legal and administrative provisions have been introduced between 1995 and 1998 to remove some obstacles that hindered implementation:

- Both the NWL and its regulations came into force all over the country the day following their publication in the *Gazette* (*"Diario Oficial de la Federación"*). Therefore, it was necessary to prepare guidelines, procedures, forms, and manuals in parallel with implementation.

- The time frame prescribed by the NWL and its regulations to regularize existing uses and wastewater discharge was too short. Therefore, a set of presidential decrees extended the regularization periods, simplified the requirements for applicants, and pardoned unpaid water charges.

- A presidential decree stipulated causes for not canceling unused concessions.

- Areas where water rights could be transferred separate from land property were prescribed through a presidential decree and a notice in the *Gazette* from the NWC director general.

A fruitful and dynamic bureaucratic–political relationship needs to be built and nurtured. The "ideal" situation (perfect water legislation, perfect organizational structure, enough human–economic–material resources) required for a water rights administration system could neither be conceived nor obtained from the outset. What is required is that those in charge of operating the system make a convincing case for their requirements to be met. But this is not enough; it is also required that the decisionmakers and politicians respond sensibly and support the practitioners. This has happened in Mexico. For instance, political support at the highest level has been evident through several presidential decrees that have helped to implement the system. Another example is the fact that after the overflow of applications from existing users, the director general provided resources (new staff, computers, and vehicles) to deal with the increased workload. Finally and most important: the political will is needed to enforce the law and penalize users who breach it.

Communication plays a critical role in achieving success in the registration of existing users. In addition to the presidential decrees, a vigorous media campaign and contacts with water users through meetings with individuals and their representatives have played an important role.

Functional integration needs to be pursued. Both administrative (issuance of concession entitlements and wastewater discharge permits) and fiscal (water charges collection) functions fall under the same organizational unit. This has been an asset, because a consistent approach has been developed in the relationship between the NWC and its customers in their roles as water users, polluters, and taxpayers. One drawback is that technical functions are carried out by a different unit, which is also in charge of many other tasks such as water quantity and quality monitoring, water resources assessments, the National Weather Service, and dam operation. Therefore, because of its own agenda and priorities, it is difficult for the technical group to provide, within the required time frame, the specific water resources quantity and quality assessments and other inputs required for deciding on each application for a water concession or wastewater discharge permit. This could be overcome by including in the water administration group some minimum technical expertise and charging it with full responsibility in deciding on applications.

The economic value of water needs to be recognized, despite practical difficulties in implementing economic theory. Despite cross subsidies from industry to water supply systems and the fact that irrigation is not charged, the revenue from the collection of charges has been substantial. In 1993, it covered 92 percent of the commission's expenditures. Water abstraction charges have induced water savings and more rational allocation, and wastewater disposal charges have induced the construction of many treatment plants.

The useful role of water markets should be accepted. Water markets in Mexico may play a significant role in the future. Most existing water users have been registered and water quantity and quality databases are being improved. If this trend continues, water markets may be playing an important role in water resources reallocation by the end of the next decade.

Information systems can be a worthy support for water rights administration, provided they are kept simple and improved gradually. The Mexican experience has made it clear that some of the desirable attributes of such a system are:

- The system must be problem-oriented, not technology-oriented.
- The amount of information, the usual complexity of the factors involved, and their interrelatedness justifies the use of the best available information technology in water rights administration. However, it is advisable to develop the system on a gradual basis.
- The implementation stages to improve information technology should be taken into account.
- Available trained human resources as well as existing software, hardware, and telecommunications networks should be considered.
- Institutional restrictions on hiring new employees and buying additional hardware and software should be addressed.
- The system must contain reliable information.
- Protocols for updating information must be strictly followed; otherwise the information system rapidly becomes obsolete.
- The system must be user-friendly.
- The system must be tailored to fit the requirements of decisionmakers at all levels of the institution.
- Particular attention should be given to feeding the processed information to those persons who supply the raw data. Sharing with data providers the analyses carried out with their data motivates them to continue providing data. Providing high-level officials with relevant information from the very beginning helps obtain their support in budgeting further improvements.

Monitoring of performance is to be reckoned as the most difficult, yet critical, task of water rights implementation. Without carrying out this task, law enforcement cannot be achieved. However, it is probably the activity most dependent on proper capacity building. The NWC has started it through periodic visits to water users in the field and is permanently improving its monitoring procedures.

Corruption must be acknowledged and measures taken against it. No water rights administration system is exempt from this problem. It can be reduced by making procedures as simple as possible, making users and stakeholders aware of their rights and duties, and by imposing severe penalties when unethical behavior is disclosed.

Making water rights a true management tool requires a fine-tuned balance of economic incentives, regulations, and stakeholder participation. This is because—particularly in agriculture—users usually do not have the means to move to efficient water use technology, regulations are required to keep abstractions down to a desirable limit, and self-restraint is indispensable because the government does not have the capacity to monitor all uses and users.

Capacity building with a user-oriented approach. Besides improved planning, and a better legal framework, there is a need to achieve a truly enabling working environment and to keep up and increase in quantity and quality human resources training, education, and public communication, for the whole water sector's public and private organizations. A new focus is needed, one that has as its ultimate goal to satisfy not only the water needs and expectations of high-quality service of present users, but also those of all water users of the next generations.

Setting up a water rights administration system, which plays a central role in the sustainable management of water resources, must be regarded as a lengthy process. As a result, the time frame for achieving sustainable water resources management cannot be measured in months, but in decades.

Notes

1. The interested reader is also referred to Garduño (2001) and Cantú-Suárez and Garduño (2003) for more details, and to Garduño et al. (2002) for specific aspects related to groundwater abstraction rights.

2. For three rivers shared with the United States, a treaty allocates the water on an "equitable" basis between the two countries, implemented through the International Boundary and Waters Commission. This commission is also responsible for the joint construction and operation of flood control, diversion, and river channel facilities, and maintains a data collection system.

3. One billion cubic meters is equivalent to 1,000 million cubic meters.

4. The FWL ratified the Ministry of Water Resources to be the only agency with power to grant water permits and dealt with water rights administration in more detail than the former laws.

5. There are 31 states and one Federal District (which is part of Mexico City). For the sake of simplicity they will all be referred to as "states" in this chapter.

6. Given that this chapter was written before the Mexican water law was amended, it is based on the 1992 water law.

7. Among its many responsibilities, the National Water Commission builds, operates, and maintains public hydraulic infrastructure, including dams, supply channels, pumping stations, and other works. However, irrigation infrastructure and other service delivery have been or are being transferred to user-operated irrigation systems.

8. For illustration, only the procedure regarding abstractions is described.

9. In February 2002 an additional presidential decree was issued in order to give a new chance for remaining irregular agricultural users to obtain concessions, setting the application limit up to September 2002. However, most of those who applied have not been able to demonstrate they were using water before October 1995.

10. Yearly application figures from 1998 to 2000 were not available.

11. May 13, 1999, *El Heraldo,* page 2: "False Water Entitlements Are Identified in El Bajio." The NWC reported that it has detected forged water entitlements in several cities of the Bajio region. The commission said it has already presented the cases to penal authorities. It also recommended water users who have bought water rights to go the commission offices and verify that the corresponding entitlements are authentic ones. All application formalities to obtain a water concession or register a water rights transaction should be carried out at the commission's agencies in its regional and state agencies. There is no need to rely on so-called "stockbrokers."

12. The interested reader is also referred to Foster and Garduño (2004) for a description of the achievements and challenges of the COTAS in Guanajuato state.

References

Cantú-Suárez, M., and H. Garduño. 2003. Anexo 2. México. In *Administración de derechos de agua: experiencias, asuntos relevantes y lineamientos,* ed. H. Garduño. FAO Estudio Legislativo 81. Rome: FAO.

Foster, S., and H. Garduño. 2004. The "COTAS": Progress with stakeholder participation in groundwater management in Guanajuato-Mexico. GW-MATE Case Profile 10. Washington, D.C.: World Bank Group and Global Water Partnership.

Garduño, H. 2001. *Water rights administration: Experience, issues, and guidelines.* FAO Legislative Study 70. Rome: FAO.

Garduño, H., S. Foster, C. Dumars, K. Kemper, A. Tuinhof, and M. Nanni. 2002. Groundwater abstraction rights: From theory to practice. GW-MATE Briefing Note 5. Washington, D.C.: World Bank Group and Global Water Partnership.

Jiménez, B. 2005. Treatment technology and standards for agricultural wastewater reuse: A case study in Mexico. *Irrigation and Drainage* 54: 1–11.

Mexican National Water Commission Web site: http://www.cna.gob.mx (accessed August 23, 2005).

Chapter 5

Impacts of Water Rights Reform in Australia

Brian Haisman

— Over time, New South Wales state in Australia's Murray-Darling Basin has adapted its water rights legislation to a more flexible approach to balance large variability in flow, increased withdrawals, and the increased acceptance that instream flow requirements need to be satisfied. Innovative approaches include the definition and trading of water use rights, the separation of the rights to access and extract water from the rights to use water, continuous accounting of water entitlements, quasi-proportional sharing of water shortages, and a strong involvement of local communities in the development of river plans and water allocation rules.

Australia currently faces a series of challenges in water resource management, but the major challenge dominating the public and political agenda is undoubtedly that of addressing the environmental consequences of high levels of water extractions, particularly, but not only, from the country's inland river systems. Behind this specific challenge lies a suite of component issues for water resource management that do not markedly differ in principle from those in many other countries:

- Broad political acceptance of water as a finite resource is relatively recent.
- Debates about the right balance between water extractions and instream needs are a long way from complete.

- Imminent changes resulting from climate change are predicted in stream flows.
- Complex and ever-changing institutional arrangements for water and natural resources management are resulting from current trends in microeconomic and governance reforms.

This chapter focuses on examining water allocations and the accompanying water rights in the context of the inland Murray-Darling Basin where water use is high and the implications of the component issues are nontrivial. The chapter concentrates on the state of New South Wales (NSW), which occupies a major share of the Murray-Darling Basin and accounts for the bulk of water use from the basin. NSW has also recently taken the innovative step of changing its water rights to separate the rights to access and extract water from the rights to use water.

Australia, and the Murray-Darling Basin in particular, has a number of defining characteristics in terms of water rights:

- a federal system of governance with a constitution that leaves water rights as a matter for sovereign state administration;
- some of the world's older systems of administratively granted usufruct rights;
- a semiarid inland climate; and
- a culture of pioneering that drove intense development of water resources.

The chapter examines how water management issues interact with the basin's defining characteristics and draws out broad lessons in water allocations and in water rights administration. The next section provides background on climate, history, and other factors shaping water management in Australia and the Murray-Darling Basin. New South Wales and other states developed their water rights systems within this context, as the third section describes. The fourth section outlines how reforms emerged, starting with a discussion of Aboriginal water rights. The fifth section examines issues of water licensing, river management, equity, and internal arrangements within irrigation schemes. The final section describes some outcomes of water rights reform in increasing water productivity and enhancing the environment.

Country Background

Australia is an ancient island continent that for tens of thousands of years was peopled by hunter-gatherers. Historians continue to debate estimates of original population numbers, but generally agree that populations were in harmony with the landscape capabilities. In the late 1700s, European settlement began, and today Australia is an industrialized nation of some 20 million people. Australia has a high proportion of migrants, initially from Europe but increasingly from Southeast Asia. Currently, 22 percent of the population was born overseas (ABS 2002). The original indigenous peoples, or Aboriginals, presently number some 410,000 or about 2.2 percent of the total population.

Australia is one of the driest continents on earth. Climatic zones vary from outright desert throughout most of the inland, to temperate zones in the southeast and southwest, to wet tropical zones in the north. For the eastern states, the Great Dividing Range—a continuous chain of low mountains extending almost the length of the east coast—separates a sparsely populated semiarid interior dominated by agriculture from a relatively well-watered coastal strip that is strongly urbanized and contains most of the population.

Australia's economy initially built on an agricultural base, but today agriculture generates only some 3 percent of gross domestic product and employs 4.6 percent of the national workforce. Agriculture remains important, however, in Australia's balance of payments and represents up to 20 percent of total exports. The gross value of farm production averaged over the last decade is some A$25 billion, of which 71 percent, A$17.6 billion (US$13.0 billion) is exported (AFFA 2001; Australia 2001).

The Murray-Darling Basin

Approximately 40 percent of this farm production originates in the Murray-Darling Basin in the eastern half of Australia. See Figure 5.1 for a map of the basin. The Basin extends over 1,060,000 square kilometers, covering about one seventh of the land area of Australia. It takes its name from two dominant rivers, the Murray and the Darling, with a combined length of 3,780 kilometers. The rivers are characterized by very flat gradients (most of the basin is less than 200 meters above sea level), highly variable flows, and limited runoff. Because of flat gradients and high evaporation, several of the westward-flowing rivers in the center of the basin virtually terminate in deltaic wetlands systems. All of these wetlands are of significant environmental value and are major considerations in environmental management of the rivers.

The water resources of the basin are now highly developed (Crabb 1997). Annual runoff is some 24 billion cubic meters (BCM) of which around half is lost to evaporation and other natural processes. Total diversions are around 10.6 BCM, of which some 90 percent goes to irrigation. Storage dams in the basin total 34.7 BCM and support some 1,470,000 hectares of irrigation, representing 70 percent

Figure 5.1 Map of Murray-Darling Basin

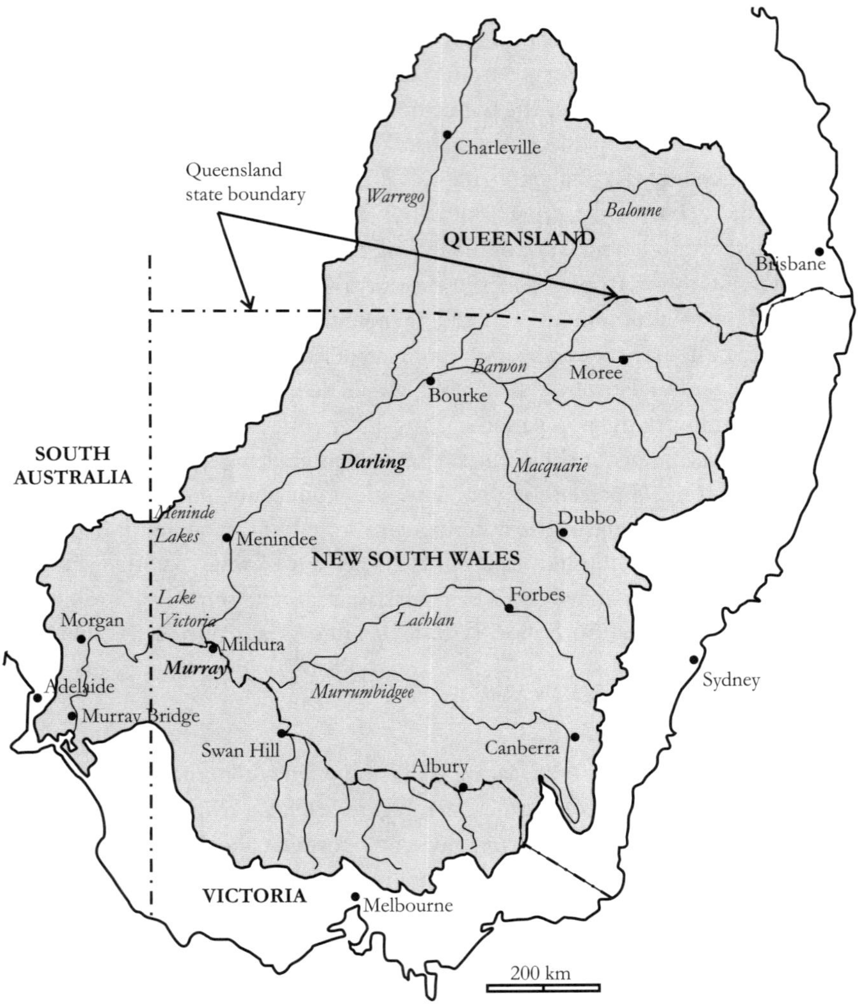

Note: Murray River is the border between Victoria and NSW.

of the Australian total. The basin is now home to nearly 2 million people and boasts a gross domestic product of some A$22 billion.

Frameworks for Defining and Allocating Water Rights

Australia did not exist as a political entity until 1901. Before that time it comprised six sovereign colonies, each governed independently from the United Kingdom. In

1901, the colonies entered into a federation as states of the new Commonwealth of Australia. As initially conceived, the federal level of government dealt primarily with external matters, defense, customs, and the like, leaving natural resources and their management to the newly formed states. While the Australian constitution limits federal government powers, the commonwealth government, by various direct and indirect means, has become steadily more involved in natural resource management.

The constitution continues the rights of the sovereign states to manage their own water resources, but in the last 30 years the subject of possible federal control has been raised more frequently. The water management benefits of this are not especially clear, but the politics proceed apace. The debate has matured in more recent years to one in which the focus for solving interstate issues is more about an oversight of harmonization. This is largely because water management in Australia has moved well beyond consideration of volumes of water to a paradigm that recognizes the multitude of interactions of natural resources, and puts in place an integrated institutional approach. Stand-alone water management agencies no longer exist within basin states. However, this does in turn raise the issue of the role of a basin organization in relation to the role of federal administration in facilitating national policy approaches to water management.

The original agricultural activities of the basin, as elsewhere in Australia, essentially transposed European agriculture, comprising grazing and cropping. The discovery of gold in the second half of the nineteenth century brought an influx of miners and others from the western United States, including the Chaffey brothers, who are credited with the introduction of large-scale irrigation to the Murray Valley. With abundant land, a clear sunny climate, and seemingly plentiful water, the irrigation industry expanded rapidly in the basin.

In an internationally familiar pattern, governments saw a role for themselves in water development, and so built and operated major dams and irrigation areas. There was a prevailing culture of greening the desert or of turning water into gold. Governments built irrigation schemes not as self-contained economic ventures, but rather as part of the development ethic of opening up the inland and promoting the growth of inland "closer" settlements.

The independent activities of the three sovereign states riparian to the Murray River (NSW, Victoria, and South Australia) brought significant conflict and competition for water resources of this transboundary river. In the absence of roads and railways, the Murray River had become a major transport route, but increasing extraction of water for irrigation from this often low-flowing river formed a significant threat to river navigation and trade. The saga of interstate water sharing and the development of the River Murray Commission in 1915 to oversee an interstate agreement on water sharing, joint development infrastructure, and cost sharing is a separate but fascinating study in transboundary water management (Frith and Sawer 1974).

New South Wales and the Murray-Darling Basin

NSW created a Water Conservation and Irrigation Commission in 1912 and gave it responsibility for irrigation development and operations including major dams, plus the administration of water rights. Resource management and environmental protection concepts began to influence changes in NSW public administration in the 1970s. The Irrigation Commission became a Water Resources Commission in 1976 and the state passed its first Environmental Planning and Assessment Act in 1979.

As of early 2003, there was a comprehensive regulatory agency, the Environment Protection Authority, plus a resource management agency—the Department of Land and Water Conservation—responsible for management of soil, water, and vegetation resources, including water rights administration and the administration of integrated catchment (watershed) management. The state has privatized all the former government irrigation schemes and transferred the assets to the new owners. The government's only interaction now with these schemes (totaling around 310,000 hectares) is through single bulk water licenses and various environmental regulations. The government has retained control and ownership of the 16 major rural dams that provide regulated flows for irrigation, towns, and industrial water supply. Table 5.1 shows actual diversions of surface water in the basin.

Table 5.1 shows NSW to be using by far the largest share of the basin's surface water resources at 57.4 percent of total diversions. By comparing NSW water rights (that is, the issued volumetric entitlements) with conservation storage volumes available in major dams and with the actual average diversions, a picture emerges of the key drivers behind water policy in that state. Table 5.2 breaks down water diversions for all regulated river systems (that is, river systems with one or more major dams) for the major component watersheds and river systems of NSW.

The comparative aridity of the Australian continent and the high variability of its stream flows meant that wherever water use development (such as irrigation) was undertaken, it was almost always accompanied and supported by conservation dams. Australia stores more water per hectare of irrigation and more water per head of population for urban water supply than almost any other country. All of the major NSW rivers within the basin now have one or more major conservation dams.

Table 5.1 Average actual diversions in the Murray-Darling Basin, 1988/89–1992/93

State	Diversion for irrigation (MCM)	Domestic, industrial, stock, and town use (MCM)	Total water diversion (MCM)	Diversion as a share of total basin diversion
New South Wales	5,993	146	6,139	57.4
Victoria	3,530	132	3,662	34.3
South Australia	470	104	574	5.4
Queensland	239	7	246	2.3
Canberra	0	63	63	0.6
Total for basin	10,032	452	10,684	100.0

Source: Murray-Darling Basin Ministerial Council (1995).

Although the footnotes indicate that the figures need some interpretation because of complexities of water sharing between the sovereign states of the basin, Table 5.2 nonetheless shows that the capacity of the major dams is around twice that of the annual water entitlements. This is a very high ratio by international standards. Nonetheless, the reliability of irrigation water rights can be as low as a 35 percent probability of having full rights available in any one year because of the high variability of river flows. These factors have strongly influenced water rights concepts and administration in NSW.

Table 5.2 Water use, entitlements, and storage in the NSW portion of the Murray-Darling Basin

River system	Total water diversion (MCM)	Water rights for irrigation (MCM)	All other water rights (MCM)	Total water rights (MCM)	Capacity of major dams (MCM)
Border Rivers	222	1,086	212	1,298	573[a]
Gwydir	300				1,364
Namoi	248				817
Macquarie	471	646	30	676	1,557
Murrumbidgee/Lachlan	2,443	2,995	78	3,073	4,532[b]
Murray/Lower Darling	2,266	2,183	93	2,276	9,323[c]
Total NSW	5,950	6,910	413	7,323	18,166

Source: Murray Darling Basin Commission; Department of Land and Water Conservation NSW.

[a] Includes 261 MCM shared with Queensland.

[b] Augmented by effectively half share of Snowy Mountains Hydroelectric Authority's 4,798-MCM Eucumbene Dam.

[c] Shared with Victoria and South Australia, plus effectively half share of Eucumbene Dam 4,798 MCM.

The Conceptual Basis of NSW Water Rights

Water law in the former Australian colonies originally reflected the common law of the United Kingdom, which in turn derived from Roman and other ancient law. The existence of the underlying public ownership of the resource (*res communis*) was not a concept well known or understood by the settlers. The virtually private and perpetual riparian rights that resulted from colonial application of this common law were quickly perceived to be impractical in Australia's semiarid climate. Apart from this, the riparian doctrine formed a significant constraint on the goldmining industry, which was critically dependent on adequate water supplies.

Toward the end of the nineteenth century, each of the colonies conducted various public inquiries, Royal Commissions of Inquiry, into the management of their water resources. All recommended replacing common law riparian rights with statutory law that would administratively grant usufruct rights to use water. The first NSW Water Rights Act dates from 1896, but the first comprehensive piece of modern water legislation was the Water Act of 1912. This act survived with amendments until 2000, when the current Water Management Act replaced it, but the underlying water rights principles remain to this day.

The Water Act of 1912 specifically vested in the Crown (in effect, the NSW government) the right to the "use, control, and flow" of all surface and groundwater. It established a hierarchy of use or priority in times of water shortage. Users retained some limited riparian rights for livestock watering and for domestic purposes based on home maintenance concepts.[1] The Act required that all other extractions of water be subject to the issue of a license that was, in essence, a license for works to take water from a river, lake, or aquifer. It limited the duration of these licenses, provided for renewal of the licenses, and allowed conditions to be attached to the licenses—such as limiting the size of an area to be irrigated, controlling flow rates and pollution, and so forth. The Act allowed for minor public participation in the licensing process, including the referral of objections to issue of license to a local land board.

Later modernizing amendments provided for the levying of water supply charges where a government work augmented or assured the supply in a river. The amendments also enabled volumetric allocation schemes on rivers and aquifers that set limits on total extractions according to the capacity of the resource, and that shared available water between users on a metered volumetric basis. They also provided for temporary trading of water volumes between holders of licenses, permanent trading of the water licenses themselves, and water planning generally.

Initially, in keeping with the thinking of the times, government irrigation schemes were not part of this water rights system. Irrigation districts, privately owned lands supplied with water by government-owned and operated infrastructure, were included in a special part of the Water Act, but were effectively exempt from licensing. Irrigation areas, government infrastructure servicing government-owned lands leased to farmers, had a separate Irrigation Act, again not part of the licensing process. For both areas and districts, each irrigation farm had a so-called water right that was an annual volume of water more or less guaranteed as a minimum supply. In most years when additional water was available, more water was supplied than specified by this water right and irrigation enterprises began to rely on such additional water.

Although the licensing legislation covered urban water supplies, the government gave scant attention to domestic use until recent years because the Water Act already gave such water the highest priority. As demand for water grew, town water supplies also became subject to volumetric licenses and holders of those licenses were allowed to trade.

Initial allocation of the licensed water rights was essentially on a "first come, first served basis" until the 1970s, when limited resources caused all the main rivers to be closed to further license applications. Note that this is not equivalent to a prior appropriation system—the rights when granted have no seniority attributes and all rights for the same use purpose are treated equally, including in allocation of available water supplies.

The agricultural community in the early years was firmly built around a family farm concept. Irrigation was perceived as something that people undertook in a government irrigation area or district, or undertook as a supplement to traditional farming in the form of a drought-proofing investment. After World War II, the NSW government stepped up construction of headwork dams in the Murray-Darling Basin, but, initially at least, it had to encourage farmers to take up available licenses. These licenses were limited, in area per property on each river, to a figure derived from notions of equitable access and of home maintenance. This was generally 162 hectares on those rivers with flows regulated and augmented by state-owned dams.

Some statistics on Australian farm businesses can help put the Australian experience in perspective with its neighbors in Southeast Asia. The first and foremost thing to note is the contemporary use of the word business. While farming still has strong connotations of a way of life, farming in Australia has never been purely subsistence. It has always been a commercial venture for the production of commodities—despite earlier sociopolitical allocation of lands under closer settlement policies and the like. With Australia now operating in a low- or nil tariff agricultural trade environment, the need for business skills ranks as highly as the need for agronomic skills. Farmers with business degrees are no longer uncommon. This has significant implications for water trading as discussed later.

Figure 5.2 Farm sizes in Australia, 1997

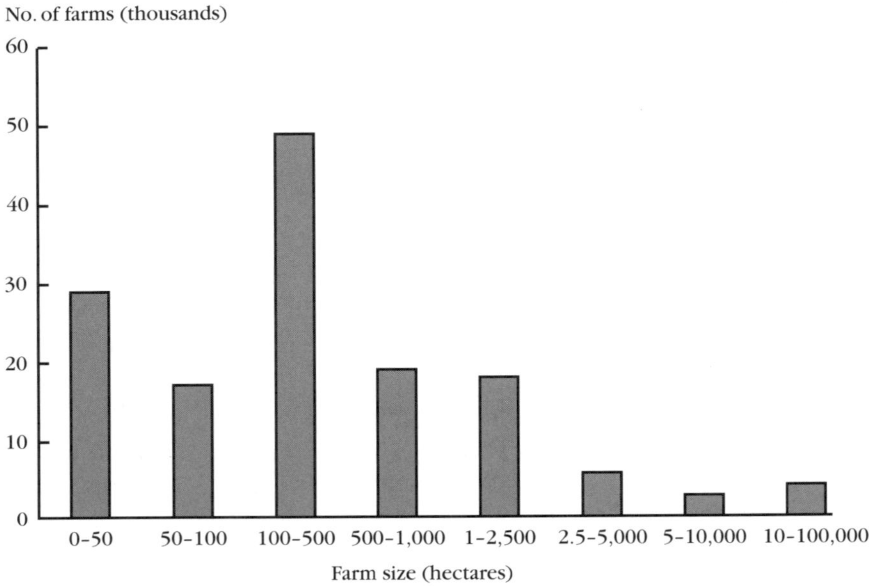

Source: ABS (2002).

Second, flowing from both the commercial factors and geographical factors, farm sizes are generally comparatively large. Farm size ranges from less than 10 hectares for horticulture to more than 10,000 hectares for large grazing properties, with a median size of around 300 hectares, as shown in Figure 5.2.

Irrigation farms in the Murray-Darling Basin have a smaller size range. Horticulture is usually around 10 hectares, although large commercial ventures growing wine grapes range up to 1,000 hectares. A single-family rice farm will typically grow a single crop annually of about 100 hectares. Irrigated cotton farms are larger, with a family-owned farm generally about 400 hectares, although corporate farms can be many times larger (Dunlop and Foran 2001). Individual irrigated farms can therefore be significant in terms of water use. Average applications of irrigation water in the basin (excluding rice) are in the range of 6 to 8 megaliters (ML) per hectare (1 ML = 1,000 cubic meters). Rice (in laser-leveled fields) uses about twice these amounts. Allocation of water to each licensee is covered in more detail later in this chapter.

A key feature of the Water Act of 1912 was that it specifically excluded the payment of compensation for a change in the water volumes allocated to any individual license. Legal issues surrounding this are complex, but the principle was that this was a natural resource, owned by the people collectively, and the rights to use this resource should be attenuated in the public interest. As could be expected, this is the subject of considerable debate as states seek to recover water for instream uses. The new NSW Water Management Act of 2000 has modified this uncompromising approach of the earlier legislation, as discussed later in this chapter in the subsection on recent water rights reforms.

The Political Economy of Creating and Reforming Water Rights Systems

The early adoption of comprehensive water rights, before major water use development, with no riparian rights other than limited livestock and domestic uses, distinguishes Australia from many other countries. Economic considerations drove this early adoption as governments realized in the late 1800s that a riparian rights system placed control of water in the hands of landholders and was a major constraint in the development of a mining industry. This, coupled with the immense variability in runoff, led governments to firmly take up the allocation and management of water rights in the interest of orderly development of the resource.

Aboriginal Water Rights

Traditional use rights have gained close attention only in recent years and are still a matter of debate and resolution through the courts. The Aboriginal peoples of Australia were hunter-gatherers. Water resources formed a natural habitat for food sources. Water has a deep spiritual significance for Aboriginal peoples that is still poorly understood (much is secret) and was certainly not understood at all by the early European settlers. When the British first raised their flag on January 26, 1788, they regarded Australia as *terra nullius*—that is, unoccupied in any sense of land property rights.

Recent court cases have overturned the *terra nullius* doctrine. Subsequent laws now recognize a form of native title that pertains to traditional activities—spiritual, ceremonial, hunting, and the like. While the equivalent position in water is still evolving, modern water legislation such as the NSW Water Management Act of 2000 provides for the holders of native title (to land), without need for a license, to take and use water in exercise of their native title rights. They may not build dams or bores (wells) without approval, and regulations limit the amount of water they can take each year.

The quantities of water currently involved in the exercise of native title rights are generally trivial in the overall management of water rights. They have had limited impact on allocation schemes that were in place before the recognition of native title. There have, however, been some impacts in a number of special cases where umbrella environmental laws required government water agencies to take account of matters of aboriginal significance. One such case in northern NSW involved the Boobera Lagoon, regarded by local aboriginal peoples as the home of the Rainbow Serpent and therefore of critical importance to the Dreamtime (Macintyre 1999).[2] The water agency put special restrictive conditions on water extraction licenses from the lagoon to preserve the Aboriginal heritage values.

The Emergence of a Need for Reforms

Water rights, as created in the first half of the twentieth century, were shaped around strong social concepts of equity. Widespread water sharing was sought by limiting access to a level deemed to be needed for home maintenance. At the same time, for licensed water users, there were no fees or charges for the water used even though public monies funded the major conservation dams. This culture led to a number of unsustainable consequences. Users often did not place a high value on water, and many licenses stayed dormant. In turn, this caused the water agency to suppose that such under-use of available supplies was a permanent feature of NSW irrigation practices. The agency assumed an under-use factor as high as 30 percent on some rivers for purposes of planning the volumetric allocation limits applicable to each river.

With the introduction of irrigated cotton in the 1960s, the era of licensed irrigation farming as a large-scale industry in its own right began, but was severely constrained by the limited water available to any single licensee. Irrigators began circumventing these constraints by elaborate schemes of leasing land in order to accumulate and amalgamate the water volumes needed. Farmers subdivided or leased their land to individuals (often family members) who then each applied for a 162-hectare license. They continued to operate the whole as a single enterprise.

The advent of large-scale irrigation and the flawed assumption of a permanent under-use of licenses, led to an over-allocation of resources with consequences for water supply reliability and for the instream environment. Intense use of water, coupled with agricultural practices in the dry land areas that reflected a European approach rather than Australian realities, has brought a range of natural resource issues into focus. Irrigation-induced salinity appeared more than 30 years ago, but there is now growing evidence of decline in native fish populations, loss of vegetation, degradation of soils, and water quality decline bringing about algal blooms.

The state economy and the community were getting poor value from their water resources as water was locked up in unused or partially used licenses, was frequently used for low-value irrigation, and new enterprises were having difficulty in accessing water. Aging infrastructure requiring refurbishment or renewal was not able to attract public capital funds with the same ease enjoyed by the original construction. In turn, this led to increasing risks and an escalation of operations and maintenance costs with impacts on public recurrent expenditure accounts.

This led to debates about the nature of water management and to conflict between those who favored liberal social goals and those who favored economic goals. Others began to realize the environmental damage resulting from river regulation and high levels of water extraction and campaigned for environmental goals. Discussion about water as a commodity began. The first real questioning of the economic value of irrigation also began—previously the intrinsic worth of irrigation was taken for granted, especially in political circles.

Eventually, the principles of what we now recognize as modern integrated water resources management (IWRM) began to emerge. This paralleled debates elsewhere, although the Australian debate occurred somewhat independently and rather more as a sectoral response to sweeping national microeconomic reforms.

The first genuinely economic response in NSW to modern IWRM was in 1983–84, when the state was in the grip of a severe drought. Water allocations to individual licensees were very low, at about 10–20 percent of licensed water entitlements.[3] In recognition that these volumes were too low for any individual to invest in planting a crop, but could nonetheless generate economic activity if amalgamated, the government announced that irrigators could trade their available water temporarily on an annual basis. After initial apprehension (possibly at the demise of a pervading social view of water resources), irrigators took up the scheme enthusiastically. Twenty years later, water trading forms an integral part of irrigation farm business planning.

The 1980s in fact saw the beginnings of substantial reform. Governments, including that of NSW, began to introduce charges for water taken from the state's rivers and aquifers. This began as a metering fee, but was later augmented by a delivery service charge. This latter charge was calculated as meeting the private good component of the recurrent costs of operations and maintenance of dams and rivers. There are no fees or charges for the water itself by way of royalties or resource rents. The charges are only for value-added services. However, the doctrine of full-cost recovery gained political acceptance and was progressively applied.

Water policy began to reflect environmental studies showing a decline in river health. Some states began to search for ways to halt or reverse the decline. Apart from some localized successes, the decline in the health of inland rivers has continued and has become a significant national political issue. A recent study (CSIRO 2001) of the river condition in the Murray-Darling Basin showed that 40 percent of the river length assessed had biota that was significantly impaired. The study found about 10 percent of the river length to be severely impaired, having lost at least 50 percent of the types of aquatic invertebrates expected to occur there. It found more than 95 percent of the river length assessed in the Murray-Darling Basin has an environmental condition that is degraded, and 30 percent is substantially modified from the original condition.

Furthermore, the basin is geologically and climatically prone to concentrating salt in the landscape. A recent comprehensive salinity audit of the basin showed extensive rising water tables and soil salinization brought about by land-use changes since European settlement (MDBC 1999). Widespread clearing of vegetation accompanied these changes, which has increased the amount of rainfall entering the soil profile. This has gradually filled shallow aquifers, thus bringing natural salt to the land surface and to the rivers. Currently, some 5.1 million tons of salt are mobilized annually. Estimates suggest that the salt-affected area of 350,000 hectares may rise to as much as 9 million hectares before reaching a new hydrologic equilibrium. The effects on river water salinity are equally profound.

The need for environmental flows[4] in the rivers and for the reallocation of water from consumptive use to instream uses is clearly acute. However, as shown later, the increasing capital value of water rights makes purchase of sufficient quantities of the rights to achieve desirable improvements in river health a major imposition on the public purse. It is also well out of the reach of any private institution.

A National Water Reform Agenda

In 1994, the Council of Australian Governments[5] (COAG) agreed on the need for a national water reform program and issued a comprehensive statement of principles and processes. Much of the program relates to institutional reform of the water sector to align with the National Competition Policy, such as the separation of water utilities from resource management agencies. COAG also agreed on the need for environmental flows, although this need was expressed within the context of a major review of water allocation policies, which sought, among other goals, to establish a national framework for the implementation of property rights in water to facilitate the growing trade in water rights. The COAG water reforms contained a number of major elements (AFFA 2003).

All water pricing is to be based on the principles of consumption-based pricing, full cost recovery, and transparency of cross-subsidies with removal of cross-subsidies not consistent with efficient and effective service, use, and provision. For urban water services, charges include an access and usage component. For metropolitan bulk-water suppliers, charges are on a volumetric basis to recover all costs. Any future new investment in irrigation schemes, or extensions to existing schemes, is to be undertaken only after appraisal indicates it is economically viable and ecologically sustainable.

State and territory governments are to implement comprehensive systems of water allocations or entitlements, which are to be backed by the separation of water property rights from land and include clear specification of entitlements in terms of ownership, volume, reliability, transferability, and, if appropriate, quality. The formal determination of water allocations or entitlements includes allocations for the environment as a legitimate user of water. Trading (including across state and territory borders) of water allocations and entitlements is within the social or physical and ecological constraints of catchments.

In addition, states agreed that there should be an integrated catchment management approach to water resources that, as far as possible, separates resource management and regulatory roles of government from water service provision. The integrated approach should give greater local-level responsibility for water resource management, promote greater public education about water use and consultation in implementing water reforms, and provide research into technologies for water use efficiency and related areas.

The COAG Water Reforms were not so much a new policy direction as a consolidation of emerging state policies, but the COAG-endorsed reforms provided the impetus for a consistent national effort. The property rights context caused many in the water industry to see environmental provisions in the simplistic and inadequate light of a volumetric allocation for the environment. It also incidentally caused many irrigators to mistakenly imagine that the property right would be a title to the water itself rather than a usufruct right, and that the rights might be undiminished in perpetuity.

A council of government ministers known as the Agriculture and Resource Management Council of Australia and New Zealand, together with the Australian and New Zealand Environment and Conservation Council, prepared a policy document summarizing and collating state approaches to property rights into a consistent policy statement with a set of agreed principles (ARMCANZ 1995). All consumptive and nonconsumptive water entitlements should be allocated and managed in accordance with comprehensive planning systems and based on full basin-wide hydrologic assessment of the resource. Water entitlements and institutional arrangements should be structured so as not to impede the effective operation of water markets and such that, as far as practicable, trading options associated with property rights in water reside with the individual end-users of water.

Water entitlements should be specified in terms of (1) rights and conditions of ownership tenure, (2) share of natural resource being allocated (including probability of occurrence), (3) details of agreed standards of any commercial services to be delivered, (4) constraints to and rules on transferability, and (5) constraints to resource use or access. Acceptable rules on the holding and trading of environmental flow entitlements should be resolved by jurisdictions at the same time as determining the appropriate balance between consumptive and nonconsumptive uses of water.

Where interstate trading of entitlements is possible, jurisdictions should cooperatively develop, on a catchment by catchment basis, compatible processes for (or at least clear conversion mechanisms between) planning systems and basin-wide hydrologic assessment methods, water entitlement specifications, pricing and asset valuation arrangements, water entitlement trading arrangements, and provisions for environmental and other instream values. In implementing and initializing property rights in water, jurisdictions should call on water users, interest groups, and the general community to be involved as partners in catchment planning processes that affect the future allocation and management of water entitlements. Governments should give urgent priority to establishing the administrative and regulatory arrangements that are necessary to implement and support the strategic framework.

An intergovernmental committee subsequently developed a set of national guidelines (ARMCANZ 1996) for the provision of water for ecosystems that were issued in 1996. All of these represent an agreed on common approach of the various states to water allocation policies and to the formulation of water use rights. Actual implementation, however, shows a number of differences in philosophy.

The Murray-Darling Basin Cap

An audit of water use in the Murray-Darling Basin showed a continued steady growth as users progressively activated unused water rights, as indicated in Figure 5.3 (MDBC 1995). In the light of the evident stress on the basin's river systems, the Murray-Darling Basin Ministerial Council agreed on the need to balance between consumptive and instream uses of water in the basin and, for this purpose, introduced a cap on further increases in diversions or extractions. Cap is the abbreviated term used in the Murray-Darling Basin to describe a limit set on volumes of water extractions. In July 1995, the council agreed to limit the annual levels of water extraction from the basin's rivers to those applicable to the levels of development that existed in 1993–94.

This decision does not refer to the actual volume of water used in 1993–94. Rather, the limit in any year is the volume of water that would have been used with the infrastructure (pumps, dams, channels, areas developed for irrigation, management rules, and so forth) that existed in 1993–94, assuming climatic and hydrologic conditions similar to those experienced in the year in question. That is, the limit in each subcatchment varies year by year in response to climatic conditions.

Figure 5.3 Growth in surface water extractions, Murray-Darling Basin

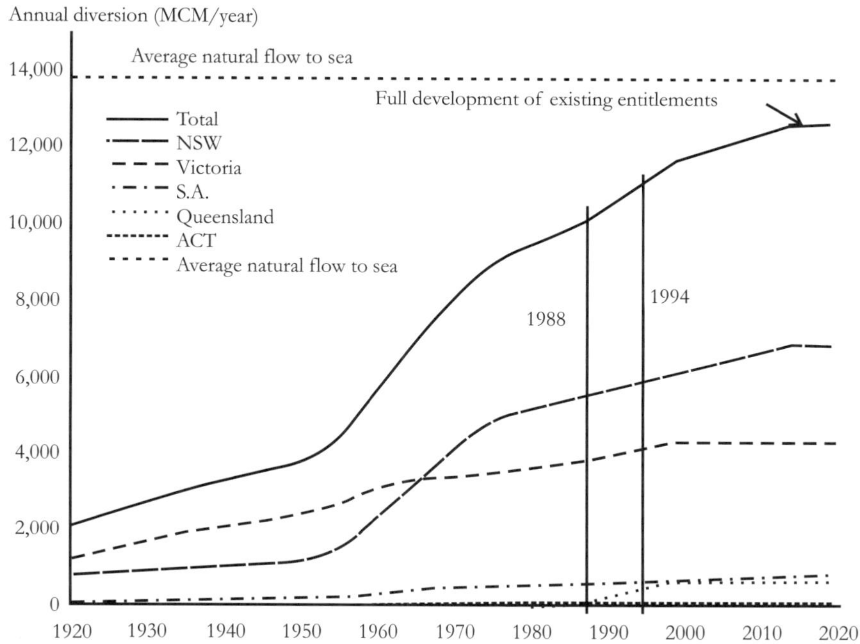

Source: MDBC (1995).

The limit in dry years is higher, for example, than in wet years. The decision is not an attempt to reduce basin water extractions, but is intended simply to prevent them from increasing.

A significant implication of the Cap, as it became known, is that all future growth in water-based economic productivity must come from gains in water use efficiency, or from water trade. As a result, the market value of irrigation water entitlements virtually doubled overnight (Figure 5.4).

With water rights now selling for A$1,000 per ML (A$1 per cubic meter) and basin water use in excess of 10,000 million cubic meters (MCM) per year, to recover 15 percent of this use through purchase would cost in excess of A$1.5 billion. This scale of cost has caused NSW in particular, as the largest water user, to look on the property rights aspects of water rights in a new light.

Recent Water Rights Reforms in NSW

As noted, for many decades NSW has had a comprehensive water rights system governing all extractions of surface and groundwater. The major reform prior to

Figure 5.4 Range of prices for water entitlement transfers in Victoria

Source: MDBC, Planright Australasia Pty Ltd., Victoria.
Note: 1 ML = 1,000 cubic meters.

the 1980s was to convert all rights, except those on small, unregulated streams, into a volumetric basis and to close each river progressively to new license applications. This set up the necessary preconditions for water trading.

Water Trading. As previously described, severe drought in the early 1980s prompted the first limited trading of water quantities. The community had previously expressed apprehension and even opposition to notions of water trading. Many saw it as the end of equitable sharing policies and the substitution of purely economic goals for earlier social goals. Nevertheless, the drought provided the necessary sociopolitical impetus to overcome this reluctance. The temporary trading of water volumes was quickly augmented to include the permanent trading of the water rights themselves. Trade has been buoyant since that time.

Environmental interests were concerned that water rights could migrate in a manner that would further upset the already heavily disturbed river flow patterns in regulated rivers, or would concentrate water use in undesirable ways. However, environmental laws were strong enough for it to be illegal for a water agency to approve anything with significant adverse consequences. There is also a lingering concern among local government authorities that profitable irrigation currently adding value to the local economy could migrate to other local government areas that, for example, had better soils. After 15 years of trading, there is little evidence of this happening. The major issue with the trading of water rights arose because the legislation attached water rights to a particular parcel of land. The capital value of the water right became capitalized into the value of the land. Where the land was collateral for various financial arrangements such as mortgages, the separation of the water right posed a significant issue for both financial institutions and for the landowner. The water agency therefore required a letter of agreement from any party having a financial interest in the property to accompany any application for permanent transfer of water rights.

From a water management aspect, the water agency took a simple approach. It would approve a water transfer if it was operationally possible and there were no adverse environmental impacts. This included approval of temporary (i.e., water volumes, not water rights) transfers between valleys where the rivers or delivery systems have some physical interconnection. Thus, water from the Murrumbidgee River, which is a major tributary of the Murray River, could be sold to the Darling River, which also joins the Murray River, even though the rivers and properties concerned might be 400 kilometers apart.

Environmental Flows—The NSW River Flow Objectives. New South Wales has perhaps the most comprehensive approach to environmental flows. In the early 1990s, it developed a multipart approach to environmental flows (Haisman 1993). Together, these formed a flexible means of attaining environmental goals, which works through a set of merit-based decisions. The following are the key elements:

- minimum flow rules for releases from storages and for pumping from unregulated rivers;
- reservation of water within storage to meet environmental contingencies;
- unregulated flow management to preserve important elements of high flows; and
- specific entitlements for environmental or instream use.

In 1995, the state embarked on a process of determining River Flow Objectives, accompanied by a parallel and complementary set of Water Quality Objectives for every river in the state. The government endorsed these objectives. Broadly speaking, the environmental regulator, the Environment Protection Authority, sets objectives for the resource manager, the Department of Land and Water Conservation, to accomplish. The resource manager achieves this through direct operational management of the dams that it controls on many of the rivers, and through conditioned licensing of the water extractions by private diverters and by public utilities. The important aspect of these environmental flows for water rights is that they diminish the water available for license holders and this has affected water policy. Structural adjustment assistance for changes in water entitlements is an issue for all Murray-Darling Basin states and is the subject of national attention by COAG.

The NSW River Flow Objectives process began by expanding the key elements of environmental flows into a set of principles for the NSW Murray-Darling Basin rivers (Haisman 1999). Reaching agreement on the recommended environmental flow objectives or targets for each river was subject to an initial, wide public consultation process. The negotiation process then passed to River Management Committees set up for the purpose, comprising a range of stakeholders, including water users and environmental interests. The NSW government generally accepted these committees' recommendations for interim flow objectives, but had previously let it be known that it considered a decrease in water availability for consumptive uses of up to 10 percent to be reasonable. This decrease in water availability occurs through a change in reliability, not a change in the nominal volumetric allocations, so in practice its impact varies with climatic conditions.

The adopted packages of interim flow objectives have a heavy emphasis on passing flows for dams, based on principles of so-called translucency. This concept relates to the effect of a dam on flow. If a dam were to pass all inflow, it would be transparent. If a dam were to stop all flow, it would be opaque. In between these hypothetical extremes, the flow is translucent to an extent expressed as a percentage of the inflow released—the higher the figure, the more translucent. Translucent operation of a major dam usually occurs in winter and spring months. Dam operators release a proportion of daily inflow so that downstream river flows mimic natural variability—but with reduced magnitude.

Environmental scientists universally agree on the ecological value of mimicking natural flow variability, particularly for native fish species and macroinvertebrates. The decision support system for the River Flow Objectives models a daily time-step, flow simulation model for each river, directly coupled with a regional economic model for the catchment to evaluate socioeconomic impacts.

An interesting aspect of the NSW approach in relation to water rights is the setting aside of environmental allocations. The first and most studied of these served the critically important Macquarie Marshes. These form a major wetlands system extending over some 1,500 square kilometers near the center of the Murray-Darling Basin. The Ramsar Convention lists them as a wetland of international significance. The marshes are one of the largest semipermanent wetlands in southeastern Australia, and include important breeding sites for water birds. The deltaic wetlands occur near the end of a river system that is regulated by two reservoirs in its upper reaches. Burrendong Dam has a conservation storage of 1,198 MCM plus a further 489 MCM for flood storage, while Windamere Dam has a capacity of 368 MCM. They principally regulate water supplies for irrigation.

Irrigation extractions of some 395 MCM per year had reduced average yearly inflows to the marshes from 525 MCM under natural conditions to around 350 MCM. As with all variable systems, these averages conceal some of the more extreme changes. Growing evidence of substantial decline in both area and ecological function led in 1986 to an Australian first. After much debate, an allocation to the marshes of 50 MCM annually of very high security water was set aside under the control of the NSW National Parks and Wildlife Service. This wildlife allocation was the centerpiece of the 1986 Macquarie Marshes Management Plan that included complex rules for delivery of the allocation, provision for monitoring and research, and an irrigation policy that controlled the nature and extent of irrigation near the marshes.

A major review of the plan in 1994 revealed that decline of the marshes was not likely to cease, and that not only was further water required, but that the plan needed improvement, particularly in the matter of public auditing and community involvement. A new and more sophisticated plan was approved in 1996 with a strong emphasis on adaptive management, and provision for a broad-based Advisory and Audit Committee. A key feature for delivery now of the wetlands allocation is to tie it to rainfall events, thus being able to augment water to the marshes by "piggy-backing" on natural flow events. A community-based Land and Water Management Plan complements the Macquarie Marshes Management Plan.

The most controversial element of the new plan was the provision for a further 75 MCM of environmental allocation, to be supplied at the same reliability as irrigation water in the Macquarie Valley. This new combined allocation to the marshes reduced average diversions for irrigation from 395 MCM per year to 340 MCM per year, a reduction of more than 10 percent. Irrigation interests protested that compensation should accompany this reduction. The NSW government responded by including ongoing socioeconomic studies as part of the plan and setting aside funds for assistance with structural adjustment as part of the statewide water reform agenda. Interestingly, anecdotal evidence from the valley is showing that the irrigation industry has generally risen to the challenge. With a combination of better risk management made possible by flexible water accounting, and through on-farm efficiencies, overall production has not suffered unduly. Again, of course, averages conceal extremes, and weaker enterprises are feeling the strain.

Continuous Accounting. The term *continuous accounting* refers to a flexible system of water accounting coming into use on regulated rivers. The previous system of annual allocation of available water among license holders on regulated rivers remained quite simple for many years. The water management agency allocated available water in each river basin (water in storage plus likely minimum inflows) less losses and commitments as a percentage of each license holder's annual entitlement. This percentage was reviewed monthly and increased in response to any further system inflows until the maximum of 100 percent was reached. The agency delivered water from headworks reservoirs against orders placed by the license holder up to the currently allocated amount, with any unused water forfeited at the end of the year and returned to the common pool. NSW is progressively abandoning annual forfeiture rules in favor of a variety of carryover and quasi-continuous accounting rules.

These rules allow individual water users to carry over some or all of their unused entitlement from one year to the next. They can then use this carryover in addition to any water they receive as part of the annual allocation for the next season. Some systems continuously account for water, with newly available water being continuously shared and added to each water user's account. This enables a license holder to continually assess their available options for use of the allocated water. They can use it (for irrigation or any other authorized use), they can sell it on the temporary transfer market, or they can leave up to one year's additional allocation in the state storage indefinitely. This has revolutionized business planning by irrigators and eliminated potential wastage of water at the end of each season. The system allows each irrigator to apply their own levels of risk management to their enterprise rather than have the state do it for them collectively through allocation announcements under the "use it or lose it" previous system of end-of-year forfeiture. In the Macquarie Valley, where the system is most advanced, there has been an increase in the income per hectare (Dunlop and Foran 2001).

Water Management Act of 2000. By the 1990s, it was clear that the old Water Act of 1912 with its myriad amendments over time was in need of a thorough rewrite to meet modern IWRM goals. Accordingly, after issuance of a White Paper and significant community consultation, the NSW Parliament passed the Water Management Act of 2000. There are many administrative improvements, and several important new elements from a water rights policy perspective.

The Act separated the right to extract or divert surface water or groundwater from the right to use it for a particular purpose at a particular place. The Act distinguishes these rights as *access licenses* and *water use approvals,* respectively. This innovation aims to facilitate water trading. Under NSW environmental laws, the process of gaining approval for a water-using enterprise, whether agricultural or industrial, can be quite protracted and may even involve the full public processes of a statutory environmental impact statement. Formerly, when a landholder acquired additional water by way of trade, it was necessary to go through the entire environmental approval process for each increment of permanent trade. Under the new Water Management Act, an enterprise can now separately acquire environmental and other approvals for the maximum amount of water ever likely to be used at the site, including the maximum expected transfers—whether or nor the applicant has a right to extract water. The approving agency can now rapidly approve water trading, or in other words the acquisition of additional water access rights, without needing to consider the impacts of the use of that water. It considers only operational feasibility (river channel capacity, for example) and instream environmental effects, if any. These provisions also effectively bring to an end the nexus between a parcel of land and any water right used on that land. The Act therefore also contains provisions for the protection of the interests of those who may have financial interests in the land—such as mortgagors and the like.

The Act revised priority of use under conditions of water shortage, to increase the priority of environmental needs. In brief, the priorities are the following:

1. human needs (domestic water);

2. environmental needs;

3. commercial water use (urban) and high security licenses; and

4. normal security licenses (irrigation).

The Act was designed to increase security for entitlement holders (holders of access licenses) through introduction of a common set of license conditions for each valley or river system. A community-based Water Management Committee develops an approved Water Management Plan that sets these license conditions for the particular river. The Water Management Plans take into account a State Water Management Outcomes Plan issued from time to time by the minister that details the outcomes sought from application of the water management principles of the Act. Licenses last for up to 15 years (compared to 5 years under the Water Act 1912) and the applicable Water Management Plan holds for 10 years. The Act allows a license holder to claim compensation if the minister varies a Water Management Plan in a manner that reduces a water allocation.

This approach applies adaptive management. The common Water Management Plan for discrete water resources gives water users common license conditions for a fixed term (10 years) to facilitate investment, while protecting the state's right to amend the license on renewal should environmental or other considerations make this desirable. This is intended to avoid huge public capital costs that might otherwise be involved in purchasing water rights for the public good in the form of environmental flows.

The Act imposed controls on water harvesting by landholders. Water harvesting refers to capture of over-the-ground, run-off flows of water that are not in a recognized watercourse or river. This typically involves building diversion levees or embankments leading to an excavated reservoir. The intensity of water use in NSW is so high that such collection of runoff water on individual properties significantly affects river flows. A landholder may now only harvest up to 10 percent of the surface run-off from their property.

The Act reverses the previous philosophy of developing water projects and then checking their environmental effects. The approach now prioritizes river health and requires that water management and development conform to the needs of the environment. In addition, apart from a significantly more integrated approach to water resource management, the Act strongly increases the role of the community in water planning and management through partnerships with the government.

Implementation, Administration, and Management of Water Rights Systems

Water License Approvals and License Administration

Although the Water Management Act 2000 expressly gives power to the Minister for Land and Water Conservation to grant water licenses, in practice NSW delegates water resource management generally, and specifically for the water license approval and administration process. The Act establishes this power by confirming what amounts in lay terms to the public ownership of water as detailed below in Section 392 of the Act:

(1) *For the purposes of this Act, the rights to the control, use, and flow of:*
   a. *all water in rivers, lakes and aquifers, and*
   b. *all water conserved by any works that are under the control or management of the Minister, and*
   c. *all water occurring naturally on or below the surface of the ground, are the State's water rights.*

(2) *The State's water rights are vested in the Crown, except to the extent to which they are divested from the Crown by or under this or any other Act.*
(3) *The State's water rights prevail over any authority conferred by or under any other Act or law, except to the extent to which this or any other Act expressly so provides.*

The Act then creates a public corporation called the Water Administration Ministerial Corporation as a statutory body representing the Crown and gives it the power to implement the Act. The Act deems anything the minister does in the name of the Ministerial Corporation to be an act of the corporation. The Ministerial Corporation has no staff other than by making use of the staff (public servants) of the Department of Land and Water Conservation (DLWC), and in fact exercises its functions in the name of this department. The Ministerial Corporation can sue and be sued, and can enter into commercial business arrangements (with certain approvals) such as commercial operations in respect of the services provided by its dams and other assets, commercial operations involving its intellectual property, or the formation of commercial partnerships or companies. This legal construct gives continuity and commercial attributes to the management of the state's water that are not readily available under the normal administration of the public service.

The Water Management Act then authorizes the Ministerial Corporation to delegate the exercise of any of its functions (other than this power of delegation) to any person. The Act delegates almost all functions to the director general of the DLWC. In turn, the director general, under terms of other public service legislation, delegates functions to the lowest competent level. DLWC is highly regionalized into eight regions; each managed by a regional director with significant powers and responsibilities. Figure 5.5 shows the functions within a regional office.

The delegation to approve the granting and issuance of a water license extends to the manager of water administration and certain of their staff. Powers of license suspension for breach of conditions, particularly regarding the volumes of water

Figure 5.5 Regional administration

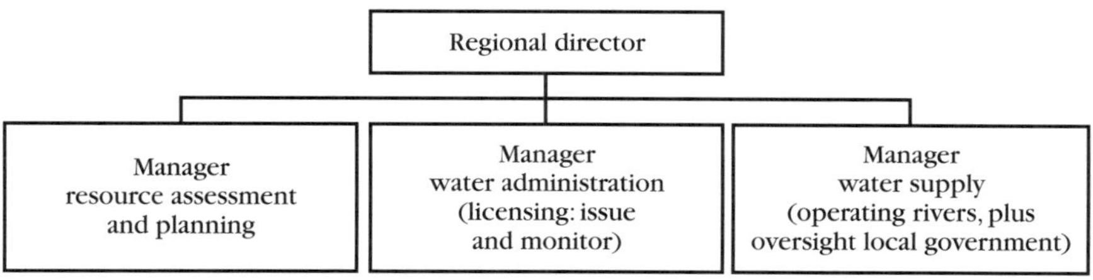

Note: Earlier job titles have been retained in the interests of comprehension.

taken are similarly delegated, including to the metering inspectors who collate and manage water orders on regulated rivers and who oversee the volumes and rates of water withdrawals under both surface and groundwater licenses.

The resources needed for direct water rights administration are consistently underestimated. NSW has issued 130,000 licenses for surface and groundwater (DLWC 1998). About 25 directly involved licensing officers and support staff work in regional offices: a group of about 10 in the Sydney head office manages state-wide systems and administrative matters. In addition, there are some 45 metering officers. Anecdotal evidence indicates that these groups are stretched in coping with both routine license administration and with the additional work of system change to meet reform objectives. Because of policies of full cost recovery, customer groups exert significant pressure to minimize staff numbers.

As already noted, there is strong community participation in the preparation of water management plans that define water sharing rules and water source protection, and in effect define the conditions to be attached to water licenses. A community-based committee develops the draft plan. The draft plan goes on public exhibition for 40 days and the committee may receive comments for consideration. This is a highly simplified description and, in fact, the definition of the contents of water management plans and the rigorous arrangements for their development and implementation are the subject of 17 pages of legislation.

This comprehensive public approach to plan development means that the granting of access licenses (licenses to take water from a water source) that are in accord with the provisions of a water management plan is now a streamlined and almost automatic process. Previous detailed arrangements in the 1912 Water Act for advertising and the hearing of objections and appeals through legal tribunals and the courts are no longer necessary in the majority of cases.

The Water Management Act does retain provisions for the public advertising of license applications and a more streamlined consideration of objections for access license applications in areas that do not have a water management plan in force. The Act also allows appeals to the NSW Land and Environment Court in a number of instances, including by an applicant when the agency refuses a license application or by an objector when it grants a license application.

Accountability and transparency are major principles behind water license administration. The Act requires that a register, publicly available free of charge, record:

a. every application for an access license, and

b. every access license that is granted, renewed, transferred, surrendered, suspended or cancelled under this Act, and

c. *such interests in an access license as the holder of the access license, or the holder of any interest in the access license, requests to be included in the register.*

The provisions at (c) are critically important now that water licenses are no longer tied to any particular parcel of land and are thus quite separate assets in legal and financial terms. For purposes of license administration, DLWC has developed a computer-based management system, which it operates statewide over a wide area network. This system manages every step of the licensing process, and links to water-use databases and the associated water billing systems. The new legislation has required a major and complete overhaul of the management systems to cater to the significant changes in administration.

Water use approvals (the right to use water for a particular purpose at a particular location) are a separate matter. They essentially approve the environmental management associated with any particular water use. This creates the strongest interaction between the Water Management Act 2000 and NSW's primary environmental management legislation, the Environmental Planning and Assessment Act 1979. Because this is not a water rights matter, only a few observations are offered here.

Some applications for a water use approval require submitting a management program for the affected land, and certain classes of use require public advertising. Where applications are advertised and there are objections, the minister must attempt to resolve the issues raised by the objection by means of consultation with the applicant and the objector, with a view to reaching agreement on the matters raised by the objection. This can be dealt with by mediation or neutral evaluation as applicable. At the end of this process, the minister can decide on the application, whether or not agreement has been reached. In some cases, application of the Environmental Planning and Assessment Act may lead to public inquiries through a formal Commission of Inquiry. The Water Management Act requires the minister to have regard for the findings and recommendation of the Commission of Inquiry. As with access license administration, the administration of water use approvals is largely undertaken at the regional office level of DLWC.

Water Rights on Regulated Rivers

The allocation of water to access license holders varies between regulated rivers, those where the flows are augmented and modified by a state-owned dam, and unregulated rivers, those without any state dams. On regulated rivers, the access license confers a right for an annual allocation volume of water expressed in megaliters, but only to the extent that water is actually available. The management of allocations is undertaken by an organization called State Water, which is an internal business unit of DLWC responsible for dam asset management and for the operation of the various weirs and dams.

State Water regularly calculates the percentage of allocation available by adding the water already in storage to minimum expected inflows, then subtracting system losses and environmental requirements. When this percentage is announced, State Water also announces the probabilities of various degrees of improvement within specified times. Thus, a typical allocation announcement might be: "Murrumbidgee irrigators are advised that 65 percent of allocations are currently available. There is a 60 percent chance this will rise to 75 percent by December and a 45 percent chance of 100 percent allocations by the same date."

Regulated water rights in NSW therefore have two key attributes—the allocated volume and the long-term computed probability of availability in any one year. On most regulated rivers in NSW, including all those in the MDB, access licenses are either high security, around 99 percent, or general security, lying in the 35–70 percent security range. Town water supply license-holders, some industries, and irrigators of permanent plantings such as orchards or vines typically use high security licenses. General security licenses are nearly all for irrigation. Today, water trading enables a license holder to alter his security at will by the purchase of additional entitlements.

River operators, who are typically professional engineers, manage the allocated water at the regional level, working with highly trained metering officers. The river operators oversee system hydrology, calculate allocations, and issue operating instructions to the resident staff at the major dams and weirs. Most of the diversion and regulatory weirs are now automated and operated remotely.

The river operators are required to consult continually with water users and other interests and will typically develop annual operating strategies through this process. It is illegal for an access license-holder to take water from a regulated river without first having placed an order for the required volumes and delivery times. It is the task of metering officers to oversee this process, to audit the taking of water, and to oversee regional billing processes.

Water Rights on Unregulated Rivers

Because water use on unregulated rivers is small compared to that on the regulated rivers, DLWC had until fairly recently paid only limited attention to unregulated water rights. The advent of river health concerns, the shortage of water in regulated systems, and favorable commodity prices for wine grapes and for niche fruit and berry crops have now together created a focus on unregulated rivers.

The hydrology behind license allocation is for the most part fairly basic, except for a few of the more significant rivers, because of the earlier focus elsewhere in the river systems. Nonetheless, as with all NSW water licenses, the allocation system provides a basis for sharing available flows rather than the creation of a right to any absolute volumes of water.

Until recently these licenses specified a maximum area to be irrigated, but the need for more intense management has brought about a continuing conversion to a volumetric basis of allocation, plus the associated need for metering. The volumetric conversions create access entitlements with both an annual access limit and three classes of daily access conditions (these conditions include flow trigger levels and daily extraction limits). The classes generally relate to the size (and sometimes purpose) of the access license.

In general, the amount of water available to an access license-holder depends on the following:

1. The annual access volume on their access license. They can divert twice this volume in any one year, provided they do not exceed three times this volume in any three-year period.

2. The amount of water they can extract from available flow each day (determined by their daily flow extraction entitlements).

At times of plentiful flows, the management of rights consists simply of policing access license conditions, and in auditing and monitoring the taking of water. When water shortages become severe, however, the DLWC license administration officers become very busy, as they must progressively suspend rights in accordance with the legislative priority uses, and oversee voluntary rostering or other temporary water sharing strategies. The need to conform to the Murray-Darling Basin Ministerial Council's Cap on extractions has further augmented the requirement for more intense management of unregulated flows.

Virtually all unregulated rivers have longstanding water users' associations. DLWC officers will normally leave the development of rosters to these associations, while providing technical assistance and advice. The advantage of this process, apart from requiring only limited resources from DLWC, is that such associations are not limited in the factors they may consider in allocating roster times. Thus, a landholder who has had their irrigation pump break down at a critical time may receive sympathetic treatment by the community-based association. It is very difficult and quite risky for a public servant to make such social judgments.

Many water users' associations are several decades old and have a great depth of experience in running their rivers under periods of stress. On some major rivers, such as the Barwon-Darling within the Murray-Darling Basin, a representative council of water users' associations, plus local government, indigenous interests, and environmental interests has been formed to oversee major policy development.

Equity Issues Arising from Policy Changes

Policy reforms in water resource management invariably create equity dilemmas associated with the proposed formula for revised water allocations or rights. Should these allocations be granted on the basis of a formal, standard license entitlement (existing or revised) or be based on history of use?[6] This dilemma arises for both the initial allocation scheme for a river or aquifer (if water is already being used, rights exist, whether they are formally recognized or not) and for all subsequent reviews of the allocation scheme.

A simple example can illustrate the equity dilemma. If the new allocation norm for a particular use category is 10 water units, what treatment should be afforded to a user who has a history of consistently using 15 units? To allocate 15 units would diminish reliability for everyone else, but to allocate the norm of 10 units may impose undue financial hardship on the water user. Another equity dilemma arises for an under-user with a history of use of 5 units. To allocate the norm of 10 units would confer a windfall gain on the water user, but to allocate only 5 units would deny the user future growth to levels currently enjoyed by other water users in the allocation scheme.

The NSW approach to this is to undertake intensive public participation in an effort to gain some consensus on the rules. While the consensus naturally varies from community to community, typically the outcome is to (reluctantly) accept the creation of some windfall gains and to either grandfather[7] the overuse or, more commonly, to impose a progressive reduction factor to the overuse over a number of years deemed to be financially absorbable by the water-using enterprise.

The other administrative issue that invariably arises is that, despite well-developed policy and thorough consultation, a few water users do not readily fit the pattern. The NSW approach is to simultaneously deal with such anomalous cases, and with any appeals by water users aggrieved with their revised allocations, by creating an independent Anomalies Committee.

Importantly, this nonstatutory, nonjudicial committee and its operating rules are set up in partnership with the community *ahead* of granting any revised allocations. Typically, the committee will contain an agricultural expert, a water expert, and two or three landholder representatives. Water users with anomalies or appeals will first present their case to the water agency. If dissatisfied with the outcome, water users can then present their case to the Anomalies Committee on the basis that the water agency has previously agreed to accept the judgment of this independent mediator. This approach has enjoyed a very high success rate. The committee disbands at the end of the process.

Water Rights within Irrigation Schemes

As noted, NSW has privatized all of its former government owned and operated irrigation schemes. The new owners are essentially a collective of all the irrigators who now hold shares (in proportion to their former water rights) in a private, limited liability company subject to normal company law. Interestingly, asset transfer from state to the irrigation companies has been accompanied by a substantial 10-year capital annuity from the state in recognition of the backlog of asset maintenance and renewal that had built up during the former public administration. The state treasury was able to demonstrate that this annuity was a positive investment by the state.

Because of the privatization, the state now grants the irrigation companies a single license for bulk water access. Following the complex process of negotiating the form of the irrigation companies and the means for post-privatization protection of the irrigators' interests in both water rights and water supply, the state retained no direct interest in the internal water management and internal allocations (Taylor, McGlynn, and Martin 2001). These activities are now solely the prerogative of the irrigation companies who are free to carry these out in any manner they desire. There is an indirect interest in water operations by the state, however, from an external environmental management perspective—as for any other water-using enterprise.

Outcomes from Reforming Water Rights

Initial Water Rights Implementation 1885–1985

Because Australia adopted comprehensive, administratively granted usufruct water licenses well ahead of major growth during the twentieth century in water-using developments, a key outcome has been relatively ordered water resource management, with a minimum of legal conflict. Water users may take a water agency to court for its alleged failure to issue a license or its heavy-handedness in amending license conditions, but legal disputes between water users in relation to competition for water are rare.

The population has known no other approach to water allocation and generally appreciates that during drought relative water shares are fairly apportioned and reasonably managed. This has been particularly important in a country with highly variable run-off patterns. A key outcome of the comprehensive, unified water rights system is that there is no doubt or confusion about who controls and manages water rights. Everyone knows that this control is vested in government and administered by a single, highly identifiable agency.

More importantly, from a water reform perspective in restoring some environmental balance to the rivers, it is possible for governments to diminish quantity or reliability of supplies to irrigators by at least some degree without compensation. All of the Murray-Darling Basin states are making adjustments in favor of the environment, although governments generally agree that considerations of equity and economics will limit their actions.

The water rights system underpinned the orderly development of a significant irrigation industry that makes a substantial contribution to the rural economy and sustains a number of rural towns and cities. In this regard, it is interesting to compare the water rights systems of NSW and Victoria. While the philosophical and legal basis of the rights is similar, the allocation of water against the rights is not.

Victoria has taken a low-risk approach. Its basic irrigation water rights have an annual security similar to the rights issued in NSW for town water supply. Along the Murray River, for example, Victoria aims to supply full rights in 96 percent of years. NSW takes a much greater chance of shortfall on its general security water rights, and aimed for 70 percent security—defined as a 70 percent chance of getting full allocations by the end of December each year (basically mid-summer).

In fact, most NSW rights have turned out to be less secure because of the flawed assumption that only about three quarters of the rights would ever be activated in any year. Some of the northern rivers in the NSW portion of the Murray-Darling Basin have securities in the 35–45 percent range. Nonetheless, irrigation continues to prosper through on-farm measures such as construction of on-farm water storages to decrease reliability risks and through river operation measures such as continuous accounting.

Two of the outcomes of water allocation and the water rights system in NSW as they applied from 1885 to 1985 have formed major drivers for the water rights reforms previously described:

- a decline in river health aggravated by high levels of water extraction—effectively an over-allocation of water; and

- a barrier to water trading as a means of ensuring continuing economic growth (despite water volumes being limited) arising from a strong nexus between a particular parcel of land and the water rights associated with it.

Water Rights Reform post-1985

The first outcome of note, and perhaps the most significant, has been the creation of a buoyant market in water. The volumes now traded on the temporary[8] market in NSW can exceed 600,000 ML (600 MCM) per year or some 8 percent of the total water rights of 7,323 MCM. Permanent trading of rights has typically been much less, lying in the range 10–50 MCM per year (DLWC 1997).

In fact, the temporary water trade is larger than the figure of 600 MCM as this represents only trade between license holders. To this can be added the trade among the members of the now privatized irrigation schemes covered by a single bulk license for each scheme. In 1997–98, for example, the total trade was some 863 MCM, of which 278 MCM or 32.2 percent occurred within irrigation schemes. Of this total trade, only some 39 MCM involved permanent transfers.

The relatively low percentage of permanent transfers (4.5 percent in 1997–98) is explained by two principal factors. First, water rights are experiencing strong capital growth. Holders of rights are reluctant to sell in such a market. Second, nearly all holders of rights have made significant investments in on-farm infrastructure to make use of their rights. For example, a cotton farm may have water rights worth A$8,000 per hectare, and field development costs in the range A$2–3,000 per hectare. Plant and machinery may be another A$2–3,000 per hectare. These field development assets are almost worthless without water (Table 5.3).

The variation in annual trade volumes is due primarily to climatic variations. If water is plentiful, the temporary transfer price is low and trade is limited. The converse applies in dry climatic sequences and the marginal value of water to an irrigator who has a crop nearing harvest can be very high.

A variety of trading mechanisms exist, ranging from individual deals between neighbors, privately advertised water for trade, the use of water brokers, to water exchanges operating in the former government irrigation districts using a variety of

Table 5.3 Water trade in regulated systems, 1997–98

Category	Traded volume (MCM)	Proportion of trade (%)
Within river system		
Within licenses	278.054	32.2
Between licenses	460.498	53.4
Between river systems	93.597	10.8
Interstate	30.996	3.6
Total	863.145	100.0

Source: Marsden Jacob Associates (1999).

auction techniques. A statewide, Internet-based, water exchange can be found at http://www.waterexchange.com.au.

In some river systems, transfer zones were introduced to assist with environmental and other management issues. These zones limited trade to within the zones or, in some cases, applied reduction factors to allow for trading into zones of rising water tables, or to account for river transmission losses. Such zones also apply on the interstate Murray River, where a pilot interstate water trade is well established.

Few studies have examined the economic outcomes of water trading. However, the studies that have been done indicate a substantial and growing benefit. An early study reported that during the drought of 1987–88 the increase in the value of irrigated agriculture attributable to water transfers was around A$17 million (Sturgess and Wright 1993). In the more typical year of 1988–89, some 280 temporary transfers took place and increased income to irrigation by an estimated A$5.6 million. This increase due to trade was estimated to have risen to A$10 million by 1990–91. Indicative figures for the 1997/98 season estimated that some 824 MCM of temporary trade and the 39 MCM of permanent trade increased the value of irrigated agriculture by around A$30 million and A$35 million respectively (Marsden Jacob Associates 1999).

A High Level Steering Group of the national Standing Committee on Agriculture and Resource Management stated that "trade allows water resources across Australia to be used more productively" (SCARM-HLSG 2000). The group notes however, that much of the potential benefit is yet to be realized. One economic study (AASTE 1999) shows that "there is enough water in the low-to-marginal value end of the irrigation market to supply all the likely long-term growth needs of higher-value intensive irrigation activities in the Murray-Darling Basin." In other words, the Cap is not the end of economic growth.

A significant issue in trade across the transboundary Murray River is the distinct differences in the nature of water allocations to license holders in NSW and in Victoria. As noted previously, the two states have different approaches to the reliability of water allocations. This makes interstate trading by individual water users a more complex affair than trades within states. Minimizing this impediment would add value to water trade in that valley. Other unfinished business is that states generally have still to introduce a full range of more sophisticated transfer vehicles, such as long-term leasing, sale and leaseback arrangements, and possibly even a water futures market.

The second outcome of note has been a strong public perception of the failing health of the rivers of the Murray-Darling Basin associated with high levels of water extraction, and an accompanying and growing political will to take the hard decisions involved in remedial actions. Environmental flow regimes have now reduced the reliability of water available to general security access licenses (primarily irrigation licenses). The environmental allocation of water to the Macquarie Marshes is halting degradation of the wetlands, although it is too early to confidently evaluate recent measures in other rivers such as translucent dam releases and other flow strategies. Evaluation is particularly difficult in Australia's variable climate where conditions drier or wetter than median can persist for a decade or more and completely mask ecological changes resulting from modest flow interventions.

One national study (Cullen, Whittington, and Fraser 2000) has, however, noted, "The emergence of water trading is already allowing water to move from inappropriate areas to places where it can be used to earn a greater return with less environmental impact. This is already providing an environmental benefit."

The third (and associated) outcome of note has been the introduction in the NSW Water Management Act 2000 of an adaptive management approach to the allocations or water entitlements attached to water access licenses. As noted previously, the new Act introduces a common Water Management Plan for discrete water resources that, in effect, freezes the water allocations associated with access licenses for the duration of the plan, but allows the state to amend the license on renewal to meet emerging environmental or other considerations. The state can still amend the access license at any time, but is then obliged to pay compensation. The 10-year license period in the Water Management Plan comes from a fortunate synergy. Investment and finance houses advised that they would readily invest in development with a 10-year resource access right, particularly if the renewal rights were well defined. This matched a generally held belief that meaningful advances in knowledge of ecosystem response to management interventions might take a decade or so to materialize.

In this regard, it is interesting to again compare the reforms in Victoria. Victoria had begun earlier than most states in working toward better-defined water rights as part of a comprehensive plan to create financial sustainability of the water industry. These included a bulk entitlement process for state-owned irrigation areas, which in the Victorian section of the Murray-Darling Basin were by far their largest water users. Bulk entitlements have also been developed for urban water authorities and other public bodies. The entitlements are granted in perpetuity, with limited ability for government to intervene. Entitlement holders can make trade-offs between yield and reliability.

The bulk entitlement process is putting in place a water allocation framework that

- maintains the current environmental values of rivers;
- allows for reallocation of water for environmental purposes through market mechanisms; and
- ensures that future water developments will be assessed so that they adequately meet the environmental requirements of river systems.

The essential difference is that NSW hopes to meet the need for retrieval of water for instream uses largely by uncompensated adaptive management of entitlements whereas Victoria has opted principally for market mechanisms. Not surprisingly, vigorous debate has arisen, and at the end of 2002 the matter of compensation for all retrieved water was taken to COAG for consideration. A Senate Committee has also begun an inquiry into water resource usage. The debate continues, and reveals both a limited understanding by some participants of the modern complexities of water resource management and a strong need for accelerated research into the value of environmental flows.

Toward the end of 2003 COAG agreed on a National Water Initiative, which had "over-allocation" in the Murray-Darling Basin in mind and which was essentially a freshening up of the 1994 water reforms with an emphasis on a national approach to water property rights and the improvement of water market mechanisms. COAG announced that member governments would contribute a total of $A500 million initially. The Murray-Darling Ministerial Council followed up on this and decided that it would concentrate initial efforts on securing the health of six significant ecological assets of the Murray River. The council announced that the necessary additional water "will come from a matrix of options with a priority for on-farm initiatives, efficiency gains, infrastructure improvements and rationalisation, and market-based approaches, and purchase of water from willing sellers, rather than by way of compulsory acquisition."[9]

The fourth and final noteworthy outcome has been the belated recognition by the public, by developers, by irrigators, and by politicians that water is indeed a finite resource. After initial vigorous protests that followed the capping of water extractions in the Murray-Darling Basin, the proponents of new industries no longer question that if they need water supplies they must purchase them from an existing user. Irrigators have also come to realize that halting growth in water use has protected their current reliability of water supply. This is nothing short of a revolution in public thinking in a country with a strong economic development ethic and bodes well for the future evolution of sustainable water management policies in Australia.

Notes

1. The home maintenance concept dominated early rural land and water allocation policies and was centered on providing sufficient land and/or water to allow the self-contained subsistence of an average family, plus adequate water for their livestock.

2. Aboriginal myths and ritual concerning ancestry, natural resources, and sacred and other sites make up the Dreaming, or Dreamtime that brings the past into the present signifying continuity and eternity. The Rainbow Serpent in Aboriginal mythology lives in permanent water holes and is seen as a guardian of water resources, and among other things ensures replenishment of stores of water.

3. "Entitlement" refers to the annual amount of water specified on each license as the limit of water extraction for the licensee. The actual water allocated to that license at any time through the year is a function of current water availability.

4. Environmental flows include water that is left in a river system, or released into it, to manage the health of the channel, banks, wetlands, floodplains, or estuary.

5. COAG comprises the premiers of the various sovereign states, together with the prime minister of the Commonwealth of Australia. It debates matters of national significance.

6. "History of use" refers to a known actual annual sequence of use of water by a particular water user.

7. "Grandfathering" refers to confining the excess allocation to existing users. The excess dies with the existing user and cannot be transferred.

8. "Temporary" water trades are the short-term trading of some or all of the water volumes associated with a water right, not the trade of the right itself which is known as "permanent" water trading.

9. In June 2004, the final version of the National Water Initiative was signed and included a specific agreement that license holders would bear the first 3 percent of any water recovered for in-stream uses, and detailed a sharing between state and commonwealth governments on the remainder. This lays to rest a major debate.

References

AASTE (Australian Academy of Technological Sciences and Engineering). 1999. *Water and the Australian economy.* Victoria, Australia: AASTE, Carlton South.

ABS (Australian Bureau of Statistics). 2002. *Census 2001.* Canberra: Australian Bureau of Statistics.

AFFA (Agriculture Fisheries and Forestry Department, Commonwealth of Australia). 2001. *Australia agriculture assessment 2001.* Canberra, Australia: AFFA.

———. 2003. *Reforming Australia's water resources.* Fact sheets—Natural resource management. Canberra: AFFA.

ARMCANZ (Agriculture and Resource Management Council of Australia and New Zealand—Task Force on COAG Water Reform). 1995. *A national framework for the implementation of property rights in water.* Canberra: ARMCANZ.

———. 1996. *National principles for the provision of water for ecosystems.* ARMCANZ and ANZECC Subcommittee on Water Resources Occasional Paper SWR No 3. Canberra: ARMCANZ.

Australia. 2001. *National land and water resources audit 2001.* Canberra.

Crabb, P. 1997. *Murray-Darling basin resources.* Canberra: Murray-Darling Basin Commission.

CSIRO (Commonwealth Scientific and Industrial Research Organization—Cooperative Research Centre for Freshwater Ecology). 2001. *Snapshot of the Murray-Darling Basin river condition.* Canberra: Murray-Darling Basin Commission.

Cullen, P., J. Whittington, and G. Fraser. 2000. *Likely ecological outcomes of the COAG water reforms.* Canberra: Cooperative Research Centre for Freshwater Ecology, University of Canberra.

DLWC (Department of Land and Water Conservation, Commonwealth of Australia). 1997. *Water markets fact sheet.* Sydney.

———. 1998. *Water sharing in New South Wales—Access and use.* Sydney.

Dunlop, M., and B. Foran. 2001. *Water futures workshop: Issues and drivers.* Canberra: CSIRO Sustainable Ecosystems and Land & Water Australia.

Frith, H. J., and G. Sawer, eds. 1974. *The Murray waters: Man, nature, and a river system.* Sydney: Angus and Robertson.

Haisman, B. 1993. Environmental allocations in river systems. Paper presented at Soil and Water Conservation Association of Australia, Annual Conference, Bathurst, NSW.

———. 1999. Managing the Murray-Darling rivers for environmental uses. Paper presented at "Rosenburg International Forum on Water Policy," March, 1999, Barcelona.

Macintyre, S. 1999. *A concise history of Australia.* Cambridge, U.K.: Cambridge University Press.

Marsden Jacob Associates. 1999. *Water trading development and monitoring.* Sydney: Department of Land and Water Conservation.

MDBC (Murray-Darling Basin Ministerial Council). 1995. *An audit of water use in the Murray-Darling Basin.* Canberra: Murray-Darling Basin Commission.

———. 1999. *The salinity audit of the Murray-Darling Basin.* Canberra: Murray-Darling Basin Commission.

SCARM-HLSG (Standing Committee on Agriculture and Resource Management—High Level Steering Group). 2000. *National approach to water trading—A draft discussion paper.* Canberra: SCARM.

Sturgess, G., and M. Wright. 1993. *Water rights in rural New South Wales: The evolution of a property rights system.* Sydney: Centre for Independent Studies.

Taylor, P., T. McGlynn, and W. Martin. 2001. The influence of privatisation on water rights in NSW. Paper presented at the Regional Conference of the "International Association for the Study of Common Property", September 2001, Brisbane, Australia.

Part 3

Whose Water? Addressing Equity

Chapter 6

Water Rights Reform in South Africa

Ashwin R. Seetal and Gavin Quibell

— South Africa's Water Law Review process and promulgation of the National Water Act and the Water Services Act were intended to address issues of equality and redress past inequities. This chapter presents a framework for a process of transferring both the legal entitlement and the capacity to use water productively from the "haves" to the "have-nots" in South Africa. There are daunting challenges facing water resources managers in South Africa. Progress has been made in many quarters; however, the next test comes with the outcome of implementing the preparatory work in test catchments.

Globally, access to and use of water is highly skewed. It is, however, also increasingly accepted that sustainable development requires improving access to water resources, particularly for the world's poor. Inadequate access to water traps people in a cycle of poverty, poor health, and pollution that they find difficult to escape without active intervention. Poverty and the growing gap between the rich and the poor are also increasingly seen as a major threat to global security and development. These are also some of the prevailing social concerns and scenarios in many parts of South Africa that add to the existing climatic and geographical challenges confronting water resources managers in the country.

Water has become an important element of global politics, and hydropolitics is now offered as a postgraduate course. The potential threat of "water wars" has further highlighted the need for water use reform at both international and national levels. Inevitably, this means taking from the "haves" to give to the "have-nots." Water use reform is therefore inevitable, not only on a global basis but also regionally and within individual countries. Water use reform must go beyond the provision of safe drinking water and include the provision of water for productive uses. However, the manner in which this is done is critical. Although clear arguments exist for taking water away from the "haves" to provide basic drinking and sanitation needs for the poor, taking water from existing productive users to supply emerging users has significant political, economic, and social implications. However, proactive interventions can largely mitigate these implications by not only transferring the legal entitlement to use the water, but also by building the capacity to use the water productively for both the "haves" and the "have-nots." This chapter presents a draft framework for a process of transferring both the legal entitlement and the capacity to use water productively from the "haves" to the "have-nots" in South Africa.

Background

In many respects, South Africa is a microcosm of the global context, with a fair amount of capacity and resources and a constitution generally recognized as one of the most progressive in the world.

The average per capita income in South Africa is one of the highest in the developing world, at US$3,020 per year. However, the distribution of this income is highly unequal, with 11.5 percent of the population below the international poverty line of less than US$1 per day, and 36 percent below US$2 per day. This income distribution is largely a result of the history of apartheid in the country, which not only robbed the black majority of a political voice but also skewed access to the economic and natural resources of the country through a gamut of repressive legislation.

All of this changed with the remarkably peaceful transition to democracy in 1994. The emergence of democracy in South Africa provided the opportunity for the government to revise legislation not only to repeal the old apartheid laws and create equal opportunities, but also to develop legislation aimed at addressing the crippling poverty affecting the lives of the majority of the population. The subsequent 10 years have therefore seen a plethora of new legislation aimed not only at equality, but also at actions to redress past inequities. This was also one of the intentions behind the Water Law Review process, and the promulgation of the Water Services Act (Act 108 of 1997) and the National Water Act (No. 36 of 1998), the latter of which has received international recognition.

Water resources management in the country also presents enormous challenges. The access to, but also availability and distribution of, water is highly skewed. Recently repealed water legislation, which was based on the Roman and Dutch riparian rights principle, gave access to the resource to those who owned land. The minority white population owned approximately 87 percent of the land. A land reform program that commenced several years ago was established to address this issue.

The mean annual rainfall in South Africa is 470 millimeters, which is very low compared to the world average of 857 millimeters; of this, 80 percent falls during the five summer months of the year. Furthermore, the country experiences regular cycles of floods and drought, each lasting approximately 9 years. Even within these larger cycles, there may be annual cycles of flood and drought. The *El Niño* phenomenon further exacerbates the situation. The eastern seaboard of the country is relatively water rich, with average rainfall ranging from 800 to more than 1,000 millimeters per year, while the western parts of the country average approximately 200 millimeters per year. This has led to major investment in infrastructure for large interbasin transfer schemes, both within the country and from neighboring Lesotho, to the economic heartland of the country.

Seventy percent of South Africa's water resources lie in international river basins, shared with two or more countries. Based on data for the year 2000, the annual water requirement of the country is 13,407 million cubic meters (MCM), while availability amounts to 13,878 MCM. Of the available water resources, agriculture uses approximately 60 percent. This sector of the economy contributes approximately 4 percent to the national GDP and provides 11 percent of formal employment. Potential future water availability is approximately 21,000 MCM. Future scenarios for water requirements are based on population growth and economic development. They include a base scenario of approximately 14,500 MCM/year, which is regarded as most probable, and a high scenario as the possible upper limit for planning purposes of approximately 17,000 MCM/year. Strategies to reconcile supply and demand are multipronged and include water demand management and conservation, surface water resource management (operation of dams), management and increased use of groundwater, water reuse, eradication of invasive alien vegetation, reallocation of water, development of surface water resources (building dams, for example), and interbasin water transfers.

Forming the Policy Framework

South Africa's water situation presented a compelling need to review the approach toward water management in the country. A primary consideration of the review was the sociopolitical context of water access for the majority of the population, given the historical and political inequities of apartheid. Past and existing policies and legislation were inadequate and inappropriate for South Africa's water management. Apart from the inequities in access to the resource, or to the benefits from its use by the majority of the population in the country, there was a continuing decline in the quality and quantity of the country's water resources.

The requirement for political leadership and the demonstration of a political will to effect change was a critical starting point in the Water Law review process. The first democratic government of the country recognized and clearly fulfilled this requirement, and the constitution of South Africa provided the foundation for the policy and legislative framework.

It was recognized, very early in the process, that the effectiveness of the review and success of future water management depended on several critical factors:

- Legislation and policy development needed to be an open and consultative process. Unless all members of society felt included in the developmental phases of the process, they would not "buy-in" during the implementation of any new legislation and policy.

- Lessons from international, regional, and local experiences had to be taken into consideration, in order to avoid repeating earlier mistakes or "reinventing the wheel" by duplicating efforts where this was not necessary.

- An integrated approach had to be followed, both within the water sector and with regard to other sociopolitical and socioeconomic developments in the country.

The review process commenced in March 1995 with the publication of a booklet titled *You and Your Water Rights—A Call for Public Response* (DWAF 1995), intended to stimulate public interest and debate on the subject and to solicit comments. These comments were then incorporated into a set of principles developed by a Water Law Review Panel. Following a number of public consultation sessions, these principles to guide the drafting of the new water law were finalized and published as the *Fundamental Principles and Objectives for a New Water Law for South Africa* (DWAF 1997a). The South African government's cabinet approved these principles in November 1996. Technical task teams were then appointed to translate the principles into practical proposals to inform the policy positions of the white paper for a new South African Water Law (DWAF 1997b).

The overall new approach to water management in South Africa is contained in the following source documents that provide succinct syntheses on the subject and collectively incorporate the recommendations mentioned above:

- The *Fundamental Principles and Objectives for a New Water Law for South Africa* defines 28 principles within the categories of Legal Aspects of Water (principles

1–4), The Water Cycle (principles 5–6), Water Resource Management Priorities (principles 7–11), Water Resource Management Approaches (principles 12–21), Water Institutions (principles 22–24), and Water Services (principles 25–28) (DWAF 1997a).

- The *White Paper on a National Water Policy for South Africa* describes the policy framework for water management in South Africa (DWAF 1997b).

- The *Water Services Act No. 108 of 1997* addresses the provision of water services to the citizens of South Africa. This Act will soon be reviewed to realign its appropriateness to the current institutional landscape for service delivery in South Africa, especially in terms of constitutional responsibilities and available capacity and resources for service delivery.

- The *National Water Act No. 36 of 1998* provides framework legislation for the management of the country's water resources. This framework provides for options to be explored and customized for water resource management at local and regional levels because of widely varying circumstances that prevail in different parts of the country. However, all options must be consistent and in harmony with the overall national framework.

The National Water Act includes provisions to ensure equal access to the water resource, but also to take positive action to redress racial and gender imbalances in water use. The Act is founded on public participation. Previously disadvantaged communities can now not only directly influence the way in which water is allocated, but provisions in the Act allow for proactive interventions to provide previously disadvantaged people with the legal entitlement to use water. It is also clear, however, that the legal entitlement to use the water is just the first step in the process and that the sustainability of the water use reform process largely rests on building the capacity to use water productively within rural communities. Developing a toolkit of methodologies for this is the focus of a project funded by the United Kingdom Department for International Development within the Department of Water Affairs and Forestry in South Africa.

Capacity Development

Different projects and agencies define capacity in various ways, but it is generally accepted that capacity and capacity building requires more than just transferring the technical skills to do the job. It requires a range of interventions to ensure that the recipients have not only the technical skills but also the finances and organizational structures to apply these skills. Using a definition of capacity as outlined in another project within the Department of Water Affairs and Forestry in South Africa, this project initially defined capacity as an integrated set of eight aspects that should be addressed:

Mandate. The legal entitlement to water and land comes from the constitution and the National Water Act.

Policy Instruments. Policies provide emerging users with the mandate to use water, but also proactively support capacity building for the productive use of water. Guidelines and procedural references are being developed under the Act. Links are also being created with other planning processes nationally and regionally, including the Integrated Development Plans, the Integrated Sustainable Rural Development Plan, and strategies being adopted by other government departments and agencies including Land Affairs and Trade and Industry.

Organizational Structure. Water management institutions provide the mandate and organize water use. Water management institutions are being established along with closer linkages to other institutions in the spirit of cooperative governance and public–private partnerships (PPP).

Technical Skills. Human resource skills are required to use the water and maintain the equipment. This involves the use of best practices and the development of knowledge management tools, including audiovisual tools, that support the productive use of water.

Procedures. A set of rules should govern water use, including procedures to request water (from impounded reserves) and procedures for paying water user charges. Catchment management agencies (CMAs) make physical plans in their catchment management strategies and water allocation plans.

Planning and Problem-Solving Skills. Skills are required to plan the use of the water in a timely way and to be able to address problems as they arise. As discussed later, such activities build capacity in, and empower rural communities to use water productively.

Financial. Capital is needed to invest in infrastructure to use water, and to operate and maintain the infrastructure. Subsidies assist emerging farmers. The integrated processes focus the resources of all departments on certain development issues.

Networking Skills. These involve the ability to network with other water users in the same catchment or to request extension and technical support. Planning uses participatory approaches, which should lead to consensus. The plans are intended to make use of the capacity of existing users to help emerging farmers.

Enthusiasm. After the initial eight components had been defined, a ninth, and perhaps most critical, component was added concerning willingness or desire to use the water. Peer-to-peer video materials will be developed to show emerging users that it is possible for them to improve the quality of their lives, and to have an economic return from the use of the water. This will be used to both promote participation and to create demand from the rural poor.

The development of procedures and methodologies for water use reform around these nine components is expected to provide a much greater potential for sustainable water use reform.

The Current Water Use Context

According to the National Water Act, "water use" includes the consumptive use of water, the use of water to carry waste, the storage of water, impeding or diverting the flow in a water course, and stream flow reduction activities (such as commercial forestry). Throughout this chapter, the terms "water use" and "water use allocation" refer to water use as defined in Section 21 of the National Water Act. Water use may refer to use of either the surface or groundwater resource. All of these potential uses of water must form part of the process of water use allocation and licensing, and therefore part of the program.

Much of the thinking with respect to allocation planning and compulsory licensing (a specific intervention in which water allocation plans are developed and licenses for water use issued on a catchment-wide scale) has focused on the consumptive use of water, and primarily on water for irrigation. However, the aim will also be to include other uses of the water resource, and to explore the unique challenges that these other uses may pose. In particular, this will include exploring the challenges concerning reallocation of licenses for using water to carry waste.

The emphasis on consumptive use of water for irrigation is understandable, as irrigation uses some 60 percent of the water resource. Although irrigated agriculture contributes only a small portion of South Africa's gross domestic product, it provides socioeconomic stability to rural society. The DWAF therefore intends to introduce measures to ensure the most beneficial use of water, which may entail the reallocation of water among users and sectors. In the long term, the water use allocation process, and the methodologies developed by the program, will strive for the goal of "beneficial use in the public interest."

Much of the socioeconomic stability provided by agriculture in rural areas comes from providing employment to rural communities. National employment in agriculture is 11 percent, and of this only 10–15 percent is in irrigated agriculture. However, agriculture provides much of the country's food security. Market gardening initiatives are one of the most viable ways of securing a better life for the rural poor. Experiences from Southeast Asia have also shown that small intensively farmed plots can be more productive than larger farms. As such, a shift away from large irrigation farms to smaller farms or plots, owned by emerging farmers cultivating high value crops, may hold advantages.

Currently, irrigation water is still primarily in the hands of a few white farmers. Clearly, this pattern must shift. However, many of the existing irrigation water users feel disenfranchised by the new dispensation of water and may not willingly cooperate with the reallocation process, which may slow down reallocation. Willing cooperation from this sector is also important to ensure adequate cost recovery for water use, and will be critical to the sustainability of future CMAs. The manner in which the program will engage these existing water users, and the way it shifts water use patterns, is therefore critical to successful water use reform and for maintaining economic growth and investor confidence.

Current water use patterns in South Africa show not only a racial bias, but also a gender bias. Even though in many rural households women are the primary decisionmakers and have the responsibility for raising crops to feed the family, land ownership is often in the hands of the male members of the household. Gender inequality may therefore be further entrenched by linking water use to property rights over land. The water reform process must recognize and correct these gender inequities in water use.

The Impact of HIV/AIDS

South Africa suffers one of the highest HIV infection rates in the world, particularly among the rural poor. This will have a profound and growing impact on the South African economy. Efforts to reduce poverty will mitigate this impact. The time taken for HIV infection to manifest as AIDS is related to the individual's health and nutritional status. Improved food security and livelihoods among the rural poor (as a result of improved access to water resources) will affect life expectancy in rural areas, with the benefits of reducing health care costs and increasing productivity. In addition, increased mortality among the rural poor, particularly among women in the 20- to 30-year age group, may make it increasingly difficult for rural communities to effectively utilize the water allocated to them. This will be particularly true for labor-intensive community forestry or irrigation schemes. A strategic economic vision for assessing the impacts of water use reallocation must take the impact of HIV/AIDS into account.

The National Water Resources Strategy

Section Five of the National Water Act provides for the development of a National Water Resources Strategy (NWRS). The first edition of the NWRS outlines South Africa's current and future water situation, and outlines reconciliation interventions to balance water availability with water requirements. Where possible the water required for poverty eradication strategies was estimated to determine future water requirements. It should be noted that practical constraints have so far precluded intensive involvement of the rural poor in the process of determining future water requirements. Significantly higher demands may emerge once the poor are engaged. Using this process, the NWRS has highlighted a number of catchments and water management areas that are likely to suffer water stress. The water allocation process in these catchments may require the curtailing of existing lawful water use to achieve greater equity. If so, the compulsory licensing process will be used in these catchments as a tool for reallocation. Accordingly, the NWRS has outlined a program for compulsory licensing in 100 significant surface and groundwater resources based on these reconciliation scenarios.

Water Use Licenses and Compulsory Licensing

The National Water Act makes provision for the authorization of water use in three ways. Schedule 1 use includes relatively small quantities of water mainly for domestic purposes and stock watering. General Authorizations conditionally allow limited water use of larger volumes with some potential for negative impacts on the water resource without a license. Water use licenses control all other water uses. Water use licenses may be required for the abstraction of water (including underground water), storage of water, discharge of waste to water, or the disposal of waste in a manner that may affect the resource, and making physical changes to the structure of rivers and streams.

Water use licensing will be the tool used to ensure equity in water use. In water-stressed catchments, all water use can be reviewed via a compulsory licensing process. Compulsory licensing may be used to

- achieve fair allocation in stressed catchments;
- review prevailing water use to achieve equity;

- promote the beneficial use of water in the public interest; and
- facilitate efficient management of the resource and protect resource quality.

Given that inequities in water use exist in almost every catchment, compulsory licensing could conceivably be considered in any catchment. However, the greatest challenges for reallocation will emerge in situations where there is insufficient water, or where water quality is affecting water use, and existing lawful use of water will have to be curtailed to meet the needs of equity. Cutting back on existing lawful use has complex political, legal, and economic consequences. The manner in which this is done is critical to sustainable development in South Africa.

Several mechanisms can reconcile water requirements, achieving greater equity without significantly curtailing existing lawful water use. In many catchments, a doubling of water use by small-scale irrigation farmers would not require significant reductions by large-scale users. In these cases water conservation and demand management should be used as a first option to reduce water use without affecting economic returns. Similarly, the removal of alien vegetation can increase water availability. Resource management options such as increased storage, regulation of stream flow, or interbasin transfers may also increase water availability. More challenging circumstances could arise in situations in which these interventions will be insufficient to meet demands, and existing lawful water use will have to be reduced to ensure greater equity, to achieve certain water quality objectives, or to shift to more productive water use sectors.

Compensation Where Water Is Reallocated

The National Water Act provides for existing lawful users to claim compensation in cases where they may suffer "severe prejudice to the economic viability of the undertaking" because of water reallocation. However, water users may not claim compensation where the reduction in lawful use is required to

- meet the needs of the reserve (see below);
- rectify an overallocation; or
- rectify an unfair or disproportionate water use.

These provisions were checked for constitutionality when the Act was promulgated. However, the way in which these provisions are used, and the way in which reallocations of water are carried out, may give rise to challenges to the Water Tribunal, or even the High Court, for compensation. It is therefore important for the allocation procedures to be administratively reasonable, fair, and consistent.

Resource-Directed Measures

The National Water Act outlines two complementary approaches toward protecting the water resource: resource-directed measures and source-directed controls. Source-directed controls would take effect through the water use licensing process described earlier. Resource-directed measures focus on the overall health of the water resource and include mechanisms to protect the character and condition of the river and riparian habitats and aquatic biota. Resource-directed measures currently under development by DWAF include

- development of a national classification system for water resources;
- determination of the class of each significant resource;
- determination of the reserve in accordance with the class of the resource; and
- determination of resource quality objectives.

The reserve represents the quality and quantity of water required to protect aquatic ecosystems and to meet basic human needs. It has priority over all other water uses. This portion of the available water is under the direct control of the Minister: Water Affairs and Forestry. The Act specifies that the requirements of the reserve must be met before water can be allocated to other uses. However, where the water is already allocated to other users, the requirements of the reserve may be met progressively over time. The reserve therefore has a significant impact on allocation planning. The NWRS indicates that the determination of the reserve, the resource class, and the resource quality objectives will form part of the compulsory licensing process.

The basic human needs component of the reserve provides water necessary for survival (tentatively set at 25 liters per person per day). Water for domestic use is regarded as a Schedule 1 use, and therefore does not require authorization. All other human uses of the resource would be subject to authorization. However, there is an argument that the human needs reserve should include water required for food security, or for the rural poor to maintain a basic livelihood.

The Role of Catchment Management Agencies

The National Water Act provides for the delegation of water resources management to the lowest possible level. The NWRS has subsequently outlined a framework for water management institutions. Within this framework, the minister retains responsibility for

- specifying the requirements of the reserve;
- specifying the water required for international obligations;
- specifying a contingency to meet future needs;
- authorizing transfers between water management areas; and
- authorizing water use for strategic purposes (e.g., power generation).

DWAF will administer these on behalf of the minister. Management of water resources outside of these functions may be delegated to CMAs—when they have the required capacity. As such, CMAs will ultimately be responsible for water use allocation in unstressed catchments. However, the powers and functions retained at a national level specify the water that will be available for reallocation, and can therefore have a profound impact on the allocation process by the CMA. The way in which the national department interacts with the CMA in this respect is therefore critical. Methodologies for water use allocation must resolve these institutional interactions.

Monitoring

Chapter 14 of the National Water Act places a duty on the minister to develop national monitoring systems. The purpose of these systems is to facilitate the monitoring of water resources and water resources management processes, so as to provide information to water users, water management institutions, and the public. This information is critical not only for the effective and efficient management of water resources, but also to demonstrate that management of the water resource is realizing benefits for all. This is particularly important given the sensitivities about the water reallocation process, and because the ultimate success of the process will largely be determined by the extent of willing participation by all water users. The application of the methods developed in water management areas also rests on demonstrating their efficacy in test catchments, using these results to encourage the future CMAs to initiate implementation. Activities will be aimed at developing monitoring systems for measuring the impact of the process, particularly in terms of improved livelihoods for the rural poor, and for linking these to the monitoring systems.

This will require the inclusion of socioeconomic data into the national monitoring system. This form of monitoring is expensive, and the NWRS already indicates the need for considerable investment in water resources monitoring systems. This additional monitoring burden, if implemented as part of the routine monitoring program, may therefore prove unaffordable to the emerging CMAs.

Assistance to Emerging Users

One of the primary goals of this program is to ensure that the rural poor realize tangible benefits from using water. This is possible only if emerging users have the means, both financial and technical, to develop infrastructure to use the water productively. In this respect, Section 61 of the National Water Act makes provision to supply subsidies to emerging farmers who are members of water users' associations for the construction of communal waterworks. In addition, the NWRS indicates that water user charges for emerging farmers will be subsidized (decreasingly) over a period of 5 years.

Allocation schedules should accommodate the risk of possible bad debt from emerging farmers, who may initially struggle to afford water use charges even if they are subsidized. This may provide a basis to use water trading as a stopgap, where emerging users could trade some of their allocations to existing users, and to use the income from this to further establish infrastructure and for user charges. It may also provide an incentive for existing users to gradually implement water conservation and demand management measures.

Assistance to emerging farmers should also include the alignment of support from a number of government departments. In many cases, the Department of Land Affairs may need to accelerate the process of land reform, to make land available to emerging farmers, while the Department of Agriculture would have to provide agricultural extension assistance.

Conclusion

South Africa has embarked on one of the most ambitious redistributive water rights reform processes in the world. This summary and review indicates that such reforms must be seen as a process, not something that is accomplished all at once. Even after the lengthy but necessary process of public participation to develop the new laws, water resources managers in South Africa still face daunting challenges in putting this into practice.

Progress has been made in many quarters; however, the outcome of implementing all of the preparatory work in test catchments will be the next measure of success. An administration system, the Water Authorization Registration and

Management System, is currently being fine-tuned. It will include records for all registered and licensed water users on a national basis. At some point in time, this may also be incorporated into the national monitoring system. The concept of water trading also has to be developed and refined further, even though water trading currently is allowed between and among users.

Implementing water rights reforms requires improving the capacity of the government agency itself as well as of emerging and existing water users. Many changes have already taken place and much is currently happening, including restructuring and realignment of the national Department of Water Affairs and Forestry—all to support the new paradigm and approach toward Integrated Water Resources Management and improved rights and allocations to all in the country.

References

DWAF (Department of Water Affairs and Forestry). 1995. *You and your water rights—A call for public response.* Pretoria: Government of South Africa.

———. 1997a. *Fundamental principles and objectives for a new water law for South Africa.* Approved by the Cabinet in November 1996. Pretoria: Government of South Africa.

———. 1997b. *White paper for a new South African Water Law.* Approved by the Cabinet in April 1997. Pretoria: Government of South Africa. Web site: http://www.polity.org.za/html/govdocs/white_papers/water.html.

Chapter 7

Prior Appropriation and Water Rights Reform in the Western United States

Douglas S. Kenney

— This chapter reviews water allocation and management in the western United States. It first introduces the region, and then examines the legal and administrative framework for water management and needs for reform. In general, the water rights legislation in the region has favored those who arrived first or who have the economic power to acquire rights later, with little emphasis on community control and proportional sharing, and with large adverse impacts on instream flows and the environment.

Water is a tremendously important resource in the western United States. For approximately 150 years, water issues have been at the core of economic, cultural, and political life in the region. Yet, despite the regional importance of water allocation and management, and the enormous investments in infrastructure and technology, water resource management in the American West is generally based on laws and policies poorly suited to modern demands. To the outside observer looking in, the region offers a wealth of lessons—perhaps more negative than positive.

This chapter reviews water allocation and management in the American West. It begins with an overview of the region, which despite its aridity features extensive agricultural production and rapid population growth. Next, the legal and administrative framework for water management is examined, focusing primarily on the prior appropriation doctrine of water allocation. This leads to a discussion of the region's most pressing management issues, and the opportunities for, and constraints to, meaningful reform.

Regional Overview

As a nation, the United States traces its roots to European conquests of North America, in particular the establishment of English colonies along the Atlantic seaboard, and the subsequent revolutionary war of the late eighteenth century (DeVoto 1952). Soon after gaining independence and enacting a constitution in 1787, the young nation began to expand westward, winning new territories through war and negotiation with indigenous peoples (Native Americans) and those European powers, namely France and Spain, still clinging to a foothold in central North America. A variety of homesteading laws and related federal programs encouraged westward expansion and the establishment of farms, industries, and communities (Coggins, Wilkinson, and Leshy 1992). By the mid-1800s, the abundant land and other natural resources of the West, coupled with a transportation infrastructure of wagon trails and railroads, had pulled settlers to almost every corner of the region. As the nineteenth century wound down, territorial governments evolved into states, and the West began to emerge as a region with a distinct cultural identity.

The U.S. Census Bureau defines the West as including 13 states: Alaska, Arizona, California, Colorado, Hawaii, Idaho, Montana, Nevada, New Mexico, Oregon, Utah, Washington, and Wyoming. However, as a practical matter, most discussions of "the West" exclude Alaska and Hawaii, focusing instead on 11 contiguous states. With the notable exception of coastal regions in the Pacific Northwest, the defining characteristic of this region is its aridity. Annual precipitation totals throughout most cities of the American West average between 12 and 18 inches (30 to 46 centimeters), with many parts of the Southwest receiving considerably less. This is in stark contrast to the midwestern and eastern United States, and to England—the original source of most U.S. laws and customs. As discussed in the following section, this aridity has prompted the American West to pioneer unique water allocation and management strategies. Most water systems in the West rely on capturing heavy mountain snowfalls that melt each spring, rushing down canyons and mountain valleys to impoundments that store water for year-round use in low-altitude farms and cities. Figures compiled for the World Commission on Dams indicate that the United States is home to approximately 6,575 dams at least 15 meters in size, second globally to China's 22,000, and well more than twice as many as in the rest of North America, Central America, and South America combined (Gleick et al. 2002, Table 12). Over two-thirds of the storage capacity provided by these reservoirs is in the West (Guldin 1989). The 10 largest dams in the United States are in the West (Tarlock et al. 1998). The U.S. Bureau of Reclamation constructed much of the water-related infrastructure in the West, primarily to support irrigated agriculture and to generate electricity (often used to pump water).

Groundwater is also an important resource in the American West. As of 2000, groundwater pumping accounts for 25 percent of all withdrawals in the 11 western states, ranging from a high of 51 percent in Arizona to a low of 2 percent in Montana (Hutson et al. 2004). In many regions, the rate of groundwater pumping exceeds natural rates of renewal, leading to declining aquifers and increasing water stress. Many such problems now exist along the U.S. border with Mexico (Mumme 2000). Conjunctive management of surface water and groundwater is becoming increasingly sophisticated in the West; however, progress is slow in most regions outside of southern California (Blomquist, Schlager, and Heikkila 2004).

Total water withdrawals in the West (as of 2000) from streams and aquifers total 480 million cubic meters per day (or 175 billion cubic meters/year), a figure reflecting the whole spectrum of human water uses as well as the fact that most individual water molecules are reused several times by several users as streams travel downstream from the high mountains to the plains and, in most cases, the ocean (Hutson et al. 2004). Of this amount, irrigation is the major use of both surface and groundwaters, accounting for 75 percent of all withdrawals in the West compared to just 34 percent nationally. Other major demands include thermoelectric power generation (11 percent of withdrawals) and municipal (including domestic) needs (10 percent). Overall water use in the United States has stabilized in the past two decades, owing primarily to industrial efficiency improvements inspired by regulatory and pricing reforms. Still, total per capita withdrawals (for all purposes) in the West of 7,818 liters/day are still quite high by international standards and in comparison to other regions of the United States.

From a demographic standpoint, the West's most noteworthy quality is its rapid growth (U.S. Census Bureau 2001). From 1950 to 2000, the percentage of Americans living in the West climbed from 13 to 22 percent. During the 1990s alone, the region's population grew by almost 20 percent, with the fastest rates of growth found in the most arid states. Despite the traditional image of the rural westerner, the distribution of the region's 63 million people is highly concentrated in cities—particularly in the "sunbelt" cities of the Southwest (such as Los Angeles, San Diego, Phoenix, and Las Vegas)—making the West the most highly urbanized region of the United States (in percentage terms). This urbanization is expected to continue, with the West adding approximately 1 million new residents per year for the next two decades (U.S. Census Bureau 1997). Between these population centers lies almost 1.2 million square miles (304 million hectares) of land (excluding Alaska and Hawaii), supporting economies still based on irrigated agriculture, ranching, mining, forestry, and increasingly, tourism. Ownership of much of this land has been retained by the federal government as "public lands," managed by federal agencies for a variety of uses.

Legal and Administrative Framework for Water Allocation

The allocation of water among individual water users is governed primarily by laws and arrangements crafted by the states. The federal government has a strong presence in water issues because of its roles in water development, Indian and international treaty obligations, public lands management, and environmental protection. However, this body of federal law is essentially layered on top of state water law in a frequently awkward and problematic manner. While each western state has slightly different provisions and administrative arrangements, all have systems based on the doctrine of prior appropriation (e.g., see Corbridge and Rice 1999; Tarlock, Corbridge, and Getches 2002).

The prior appropriation doctrine emerged in California mining camps spawned by the 1849 gold rush. Mining required diverting water to extract and filter ore, but local streams often did not have sufficient flows to support all the potential mining operations. When newly arriving miners built diversion structures upstream of existing mining operations, flows downstream would be diminished or eliminated, rendering these older facilities useless. This practice was seen as inequitable, and discouraged investments in mines and other activities, namely agriculture, dependent on reliable water supplies. It also frequently resulted in violent conflicts, and slowed the settlement of the western territories—a strong national objective. Prior appropriation solved this problem by ensuring that waters, once diverted (or "appropriated") from a stream, would remain available to the original user and would be off-limits to potential future users.

The hallmark of the prior appropriations system is the concept of "first-in-time, first-in-right." This notion allows for the establishment of a priority system to determine the proper allocation of water among users on a stream when supplies are insufficient to satisfy all demands. Priority is based on seniority, meaning that senior rights-holders are those who first established a pattern of water use—as recognized in an administrative permit or judicial decree—as compared to more junior users. Seniority is important because, in a water-short year, senior water rights-holders receive all of their water before any junior water right-holders. Sharing is not a feature of western water allocation. When necessary, a senior water rights-holder may place a "call on the river" requiring upstream junior rights-holders to cease diversions until more senior users receive their full entitlements. This allocation regime normally applies to all recognized surface water rights.

The doctrine of prior appropriation also figures prominently in the groundwater law of most western states (e.g., Idaho, Nevada, New Mexico, Utah, Washington, and Wyoming) (Bryner and Purcell 2003). However, the laws are highly variable from state to state and from basin to basin within states, as special rules often apply to distinguish between tributary and nontributary groundwater, and to impose protections for aquifers under undue stress or of unusual importance. In many areas, the legal picture is clouded by the mixture of prior appropriation with the application of other doctrines, such as the common law (or absolute ownership) doctrine, which vests great rights to use groundwater to owners of overlying land. Modifications such as the correlative rights doctrine and the so-called American (or reasonable use) doctrine attempt to ensure that all rights-holders have equal opportunities to use water and that such use is limited to what is necessary for reasonable and beneficial purposes.

To administer and manage water rights, most states use systems based on permits issued by state agencies; Colorado is unique in using a system based on judicial decrees. In each system, legal protection is offered to water rights acquired through "appropriation." To obtain a water right through appropriation, a water user must identify unclaimed (that is unappropriated) water in a stream, must develop a structure or system to physically divert the water, and must apply these waters to a beneficial use. The diversion requirement is based on the historic assumption that all legitimate "beneficial uses" are off-stream. All appropriation states consider domestic, agricultural, municipal, and industrial uses to be beneficial, but the list is ever expanding. Recent additions are instream and minimum stream flows for environmental and recreational purposes. Once the diverted water is put to a beneficial use, the right becomes absolute and cannot be defeated by later uses even if they are considered to be more useful, more important, or more valuable.

Water rights acquired through appropriation and officially recognized by permit or decree specify the type and place of use, carry a seniority date corresponding to the date of first diversion and use, and are quantified based on the initial level of use calculated in either volumetric amounts (e.g., acre-feet), rate of flow amounts (e.g., cubic-feet-per-second), or, most helpfully, both.[1] Rights can also be obtained for water storage, with the understanding that water collected during wet periods will be released and consumed in dry seasons. The quantity of water in an appropriative right is the amount of water that is put to a beneficial use in a reasonable time with reasonable diligence. In this respect, diverting more water than reasonably necessary is considered wasteful and inefficient, and is thus not considered part of the water right. By denying rights to water used inefficiently, the legal intent is to remove the incentive for wasteful use. As a practical matter, however, this policy also discourages parties from improving efficiency, as any water saved (or "salvaged") is deducted from the original right. A similar outcome derives from policies calling for unused rights to be forfeited. To avoid loss of valuable water rights, this provision can encourage the perpetuation of some uses past their logical point of termination.

Should an existing or new user require additional water, new appropriations can be initiated only if the stream still contains unappropriated water. Often, finding physically and legally available water requires users to look to distant basins for water, which was not allowed under traditional "riparian" systems derived from the English common law found throughout the eastern and midwestern United States. Prior appropriation allows and thus encourages long-distance water transfers; without this provision, western settlement would be confined to a small number of stream corridors. Many of the West's largest cities, such as Los Angeles and Denver, became possible only because of long-distance water imports.

Once local and neighboring (intrastate) basins are devoid of unappropriated water, satisfying new demands requires purchasing preexisting water rights from willing sellers. In almost all cases, buyers are cities and sellers are farmers, as the vast majority of all water resources in the West are used in irrigated agriculture and, to a much lesser extent, other non-urban applications (Hutson et al. 2004). Despite the fact that water is a public resource, water rights are private property, and can be bought and sold much like any other commodity in a process known as water marketing. In some states and in some situations, land and water cannot be sold separately; but generally, water rights can be treated separately from land, an idea consistent with provisions that allow long-distance water transfers.[2] When market-based water transfers occur, the seniority date and quantity of the right is not changed, although the size of the transferred right is limited to the consumptive amount and not the diversion quantity.[3] This provision is essential to ensure that no other water rights-holders are potentially harmed by the transfer. In the marketplace, senior rights are much more valuable than junior rights, since senior rights can be relied on in dry years when junior rights prove worthless. Thus, in water marketing, the purchaser not only can choose the size of the right desired, but by considering the seniority of the right, can also choose the risk of shortage associated with the water supply.

Prior appropriation allows the movement of water between basins within states, but across state lines different rules apply. At this larger scale, allocation decisions can be made by the U.S. Supreme Court, which has devised a doctrine of "equitable apportionment" that calls on states to share water based on a variety of factors including existing use, physical and climatic conditions, availability of storage, economic efficiency, and so on.[4] As conditions change, the Court can reopen decisions and produce new water allocation formulas. Generally, in interstate water allocation disputes, states have sought a more predictable allocation, and have thus turned to interstate water allocation compacts, negotiated by state officials, and ratified by both the participating states and the U.S. Congress. Interstate compacts exist for the following western rivers: Arkansas, Bear, Belle Fourché, Big Blue, Canadian, Colorado, Klamath, La Plata, Pecos, Red, Republican Rio Grande, Sabine, Snake, South Platte, Upper Colorado, Upper Niobrara, and Yellowstone rivers, and on

Costilla Creek (McCormick 1994). Interestingly, at the interstate scale, the states have determined that water marketing is inappropriate and, consequently, it does not occur. A similar situation exists for international rivers in the West governed by treaties. Thus while water reallocation is a dominant trend in western water management, it is a trend confined to the interior of the western states where prior appropriation is paramount.

The prior appropriation doctrine is not only the dominant water allocation mechanism in the West, but it is also the region's de facto water policy, recognized in several state constitutions. The doctrine encourages removing water from streams and putting it to beneficial use as soon and as completely as possible, since late-comers are limited to, at best, junior rights, or are required to purchase rights from more senior users. One of several ways in which this is problematic regards the challenge of environmental protection and water quality management. These concerns are governed primarily by federal laws and programs that encourage leaving water in streams, layered on top of state water allocation regimes encouraging maximum diversion and consumptive use. This conflict is further complicated by the presence of federal water projects originally designed to serve state water rights-holders (mostly irrigators), but increasingly modified to serve other public uses. The net result is an uneasy coexistence of federal and state law.

This conflict is perhaps best illustrated by the concept of "federal reserved water rights." As explained by the U.S. Supreme Court,

> [W]hen the Federal Government withdraws its land from the public domain and reserves it for a federal purpose, the Government, by implication, reserves appurtenant water then unappropriated to the extent needed to accomplish the purpose of the reservation. In so doing the United States acquires a reserved right in unappropriated water which vests on the date of the reservation and is superior to the rights of future appropriators.[5]

Under this doctrine, the federal government acquired reserved water rights for the national forests, national grasslands, national parks, wilderness areas, wildlife refuges, Indian reservations, military installations, and a variety of other public lands. Collectively, these lands cover approximately half of the western states, including more than 80 percent of Nevada, and more than 72 percent of the Colorado River Basin, the major river of the arid and semi-arid West and the seventh longest river in the United States.[6]

It is a longstanding federal policy to try to incorporate federal reserved water rights into state prior appropriation systems.[7] However, few reserved water rights have been quantified, and there is great uncertainty regarding the amount of water necessary to fulfill the purposes of federal land reservations. Because reserved water rights can be quite old and may be quite large, they are difficult to incorporate into the administration of stream systems that are already fully appropriated under state law.

Overview of Major Issues

The American West is home to dozens of water issues—far too many to be fully discussed here. Nonetheless, most water issues in the region can be summarized by a single word: competition. Two types of competition are most salient: between the agricultural/rural and municipal/urban sectors, and between human/economic uses and environmental/nonmarket uses. In both variants, this competition for water is not merely about adequate supply, but about obtaining adequate supplies at desired levels of quality, cost, and reliability. To describe this competition in terms of allocation, therefore, is to ignore the richness of the conflicts; similarly, to distill this competition to matters of water rights is to miss the role of politics, culture, and economics.

At the root of the agricultural/rural and municipal/urban conflict are simple facts of economics and demography. While agriculture accounts for 80–90 percent of the water consumed in most western states, agriculture's relative contribution to Gross State Products continues to decline. In many cases, the value of water in agriculture is several orders of magnitude less valuable than in municipal/industrial applications (National Research Council 1992). In theory, this is a problem that prior appropriation is well adapted to handle, as water and water rights can be moved from user to user through market exchanges. Primarily in just the last two decades, water markets have sprung up throughout the West, particularly in arid regions featuring strong municipal growth (National Research Council 1992; Nichols, Murphy, and Kenney 2001).

These types of water transfers, however, create many problems. Of particular concern are the economic and social impacts on rural communities dependent on agricultural economies (National Research Council 1992). Since rights are held by individual farmers and not by the community at large, monies received in water marketing go directly to the farmers, while other members of the community receive no compensation. Thus, while farmers may receive a windfall, water exports can mean economic collapse for all businesses designed to support agricultural production, which in turn can undermine local tax revenues essential to support schools and other governmental services.

This highlights a real paradox in water allocation institutions: while allocations must be flexible to adapt to changing situations and reallocation mechanisms must feature low transaction costs to encourage maximum efficiency, some form of regulation and oversight is needed to minimize, or mitigate for, impacts suffered by various "third parties" outside of the decisionmaking chain. In its purest form, prior appropriation is concerned only with limiting impacts on other water rights-holders (which is done through the priority system); other interests are not considered. Every western state except Colorado has thus enacted some form of "public interest" standard for evaluating transfers. Presumably, such reforms would not be as necessary in allocation systems providing greater community input into water resources decisionmaking.

A more problematic type of competition for existing water allocation mechanisms is competition between human/economic uses and environmental/nonmarket uses. Not only does prior appropriation generally not recognize many values in, or societal obligations to, the environment, it can actively encourage environmental impacts by creating incentives for rapid and complete development of water supplies. This allocation scheme, combined with tremendous investments in water engineering, has had significant impacts on the natural environment.

Water development has fundamentally altered the quantity, quality, and timing of almost all the region's rivers, eliminating or modifying habitat faster than native species could possibility adapt. More than 20 western native fish species have gone extinct in the past century, while an additional 100 species may not be far behind (Tarlock et al. 1998). Salmon runs of the Pacific Northwest, for example, are perhaps one fifth of historic levels. Similarly, the loss of wetlands has, at times, been extreme—exceeding 90 percent in the Middle Rio Grande, the Colorado River delta (the terminus of the river in Mexico), and elsewhere (Tarlock et al. 1998; Pitt et al. 2000). The West's hardest working river, the Colorado, is, as author Philip Fradkin (1981) observed, *A River No More,* but rather a series of reservoirs holding roughly 4 years of flow. As mentioned earlier, part of the challenge in protecting and restoring environmental resources is embedded in jurisdictional conflicts, with prior appropriation based in state law and most environmental protection statutes being federal law. A related parallel is the conflict between private property rights and public rights. These complications ensure that discussions of environmental protection are often transformed into jurisdictional and constitutional debates, often emphasizing philosophical and symbolic content over a serious discussion of science and environmental values.

Reform of Water Allocation and Management Regimes

A rich literature exists identifying potential water law and policy reforms. There are three primary reform perspectives: economic, environmental, and equity.[8] Advocates of the economic perspective generally argue for the treatment of water as an economic commodity, subject to largely unconstrained market exchanges driven by private decisions. Historically, this position has been based primarily on the notion that subsidies—including taxpayer financed water developments and inappropriate pricing policies—and undue restrictions on transfers contribute to growing water scarcities (e.g., see Anderson 1983; Engelbert and Scheuring 1984). A different focus is characteristic of writings from the environmental perspective, which has at least two major threads (e.g., see Reisner 1986; Bates et al. 1993). One thread is the preservation ethic, with the corresponding concern over the ecological impacts of dams and development, and the lack of instream flow protections afforded under strict prior appropriation regimes. The other is the concern for pollution, also largely ignored under state water laws focused narrowly on issues of water allocation. The final perspective, equity, is somewhat less distinct or well defined than the previous two, but is equally pervasive in the literature. The equity perspective urges greater protections for excluded values and/or interests (e.g., non-rights-holders, tribes, rural communities, public interests, areas of origin) in traditional water laws and decisionmaking processes (e.g., see Brown and Ingram 1987; McCool 1987; Wilkinson 1989; Getches 1993).

As a practical matter, these lines of argument are not always compatible with each other, but where they are, they are most politically salient when melded together. For example, the greatest reform of the past quarter-century has arguably been the demise of the dam-building era. For several decades beginning in the 1950s, environmental protection advocates fought massive western water storage and diversion projects with little success, as virtually every major stream in the West was dammed. Only after environmentalists joined forces with fiscal conservatives offended by water development subsidies did meaningful reform take place, bringing dam-building excesses to an apparent end. However, these types of fundamental shifts in law, policy, and management have been exceedingly rare, with most reform being incremental rather than fundamental. Litigation and the expansion of markets, more so than true political leadership, have been at the heart of most progress, although several notable federal and state legal reforms have occurred. Most important at the federal level has been passage and enforcement of environmental legislation, while at the state level, incremental refinements to prior appropriation have brought a broadened definition of beneficial use, a commitment to considering the "public interest" as part of water transfers, and the establishment of modest programs for setting up water rights for instream flow protection (Bell 1997; Gillilan and Brown 1997).

A variety of additional reforms could potentially improve how the western United States allocates and uses its limited water resources. The lack of an explicit water policy is one obvious area of potential reform. Despite the importance of water to the West, it is often governed with an almost palpable lack of vision or meaningful deliberation, or any set of coordinated principles designed to achieve much more than the nineteenth century goal of western settlement. Integrated water resources planning at large (e.g., basinwide) scales is rare in the western states; most planning is confined to the scale of specific water systems owned and operated by individual water providers, and is often limited to the subject of water supply.

Looking forward, the obvious policy framework is one that emphasizes sustainability—admittedly a difficult concept to define and operationalize, but ultimately more practical than using prior appropriation as a de facto water policy. Recently, the western Water Policy Review Advisory Commission proposed sustainability as the primary principle for twenty-first century water management, arguing for arrangements within which "environmental, social, economic, and cultural values can be supported indefinitely" at "national, regional, and local levels" (Tarlock et al. 1998: xiv). Underlying this recommendation is the recognition that settlement is no longer the compelling regional objective, but rather, the need is to ensure the long-term viability of lands now occupied and developed. Infusing the sustainability objective into a system built around the priority system is admittedly difficult, but it is nonetheless the challenge currently facing reformers.

To the extent that prior appropriation can be limited to its function as an allocation mechanism, additional reforms are needed to deal with the interrelationships between surface water and groundwater, water quantity and quality, and connections between land use and water management. Several specific reforms are worth pursuing, but ultimately the overarching challenge is to better define the role that water allocation law plays within western water institutions.

The economics of western water are also in need of reform. In fact, no other area of reform is likely to produce as many societal and environmental benefits. Subsidies run rampant in western water, from project financing to water (and energy) pricing (Wahl 1989). Given that most water in the West is used in agriculture, the greatest room for improvement is in that sector. For example, it is not uncommon for taxpayers to subsidize both the construction and the operation of water projects that deliver water used to grow crops for which there is often insufficient market demand for farmers to recoup their (already subsidized) costs. This system is perpetuated by agricultural "price support" programs that use taxpayer funds to prop up these struggling farms, an action that not only perpetuates many inappropriate water uses, but also creates significant environmental impacts (and environmental remediation expenditures) and hinders international efforts to establish free trade in agricultural products.

Originally, this system may have been appropriate to encourage western settlement, and later could be viewed as a kind gesture to support struggling farmers. But promoting western settlement is no longer a national objective, and this system of chronic subsidies and bailouts has primarily served the interests of large corporate farms, rather than those of the small families presumably targeted for assistance. By ensuring that water costs reflect marginal costs of production as well as the opportunity costs of using water for other uses (including nonmarket uses such as environmental protection), it would be possible to significantly reduce water consumption while reducing the burden on taxpayers. To the extent that subsidies are retained or redirected, they should be used to correct environmental harms, to support farms located in appropriate areas and growing high-demand crops, and to cushion the impacts in areas transitioning from farming to other economic activities. In practice, none of these reforms is simple or painless and progress is slow. However, the logic of the overriding principle is undeniable: government should subsidize only those actions that are in the best interest of its people. In the world of western water, this rule is violated with regularity and at a grand scale. Further reforms are needed in water resources administration. One area of particular concern is the fragmentation of agency roles, responsibilities, and authorities based on political boundaries, functional areas of specialization, and a variety of related intergovernmental factors (Kenney 1997). With few exceptions, river basins and watersheds are foreign concepts in western water institutions. This fragmentation hinders the emergence of a holistic management perspective, discourages regional water planning, and impedes efforts to consider water and land-use decisions in an integrated fashion.

An even more central problem is the limited opportunities for public input into water decisions. Historically, western water decisions were made almost exclusively by political leaders, water engineers, and pro-development interest groups. In recent decades, many processes have been opened to greater public input, but additional progress is still needed. Limiting decisions to just those parties fortunate to have officially recognized water rights ignores the broad public importance of water.

Still additional reforms are needed in water management, defined here to mean those activities associated with the physical movement and control of water resources, and the actual servicing of customer demands. Here, the tradition is to focus primarily on supply-side management, unduly relegating conservation and other demand-management options to a secondary status. Water managers and political leaders have been hesitant to question water-using practices that are clearly inappropriate in arid and semiarid regions, such as the prolific use of landscaping crops adapted to humid areas and, thus, requiring huge amounts of irrigation. Economic subsidies further repress a more enlightened self-examination of how water is used and valued. Additionally, concern over drought has been taken to extremes in many regions, leading managers to overbuild systems far beyond what economic theory or environmental respect would dictate. Solutions for better management are varied, but typically emphasize limiting demands, strategically managing risk, and considering environmental and related public goods as part of water supply development.

Overall, the types of reforms needed in the American West are those that discourage excessive use, promote conservation and efficiency, and facilitate the reallocation of water from low-valued (mostly agricultural) to high-valued (mostly municipal) uses, all the while remedying past environmental abuses. While there are some opportunities for new development, an honest economic and social evaluation of management options will rarely support new projects as the best alternative. Ensuring that the best choices are made, however, means removing some of the distorted incentives provided by prior appropriation and by subsidies, and in turn, by administrative and management traditions shaped by these pillars of western water institutions. In addition, to the extent that reforms are able to "free up" more water, the West must be prepared to use some of this water to satisfy environmental and other public water demands currently underserved, rather than merely reallocating all saved water to support new growth that may undermine efforts to achieve sustainable water management.

Conclusion

The institutional arrangements controlling water resources in the western United States have been remarkably effective in promoting settlement, and in sustaining population and economic growth. Many nations look to the American West with envy, given the region's extensive network of water projects and its system of water rights that protects the interests of established rights-holders while permitting voluntary water reallocations through market-based exchanges. While these are significant accomplishments, the costs associated with this system—in economic, social, and environmental terms—have been significant, and both the equity and efficiency of the institutional arrangements remain a lingering concern. The story of water in the West continues to be one of winners and losers, and of decisionmaking systems designed, initially, to reward those who arrived first and, additionally, in modern times, those with the economic power to purchase preestablished rights. Arguably, neither principle is an ideal basis for a water allocation regime; other nations (and other parts of the United States) have chosen instead to emphasize principles such as community control and proportional sharing.

Notes

1. An acre-foot is approximately 325,900 gallons, or 1,233 cubic meters. One cubic foot per second is equivalent to 283 liters per second.

2. Much of the variability derives from different groundwater codes. Most commonly, groundwater believed to be tributary to surface water systems is subject to prior appropriation that does not link land and water ownership. The situation is more complicated when nontributary groundwater is involved, as control of those waters is often associated to some degree with land ownership.

3. Consumptive use is defined as diversions minus any flows that return to the stream and are subsequently used by other rights-holders.

4. For example, see *Nebraska v. Wyoming,* 325 U.S. 589, at 618 (1945).

5. *Cappaert v. United States,* 426 U.S. 128, at 138 (1976).

6. Statistics on federal land ownership are constantly changing, and are available from a variety of sources. For example, see U.S. General Services Administration (1996).

7. This policy is articulated in the so-called McCarran Act (43 U.S.C. § 666 [2000]), which calls for federal water rights to be quantified through state court processes.

8. This section draws heavily on Kenney (2001).

References

Anderson, T. L. 1983. *Water crisis: Ending the policy drought.* Baltimore: The Johns Hopkins University Press.

Bates, S. F., D. H. Getches, L. J. MacDonnell, and C. F. Wilkinson. 1993. *Searching out the headwaters.* Washington, D.C.: Island Press.

Bell, D. C. 1997. *Water in the West today: A states' perspective.* Report to the western Water Policy Review Advisory Commission. Denver.

Blomquist, W., E. Schlager, and T. Heikkila. 2004. *Common waters, diverging streams: Linking institutions to water management in Arizona, California, and Colorado.* Washington, D.C.: Resources for the Future.

Brown, F. L., and H. M. Ingram. 1987. *Water and poverty in the Southwest.* Tucson: University of Arizona Press.

Bryner, G., and E. Purcell. 2003. *Groundwater law sourcebook of the western United States.* Boulder: Natural Resources Law Center, University of Colorado School of Law.

Coggins, G. C., C. F. Wilkinson, and J. D. Leshy. 1992. *Federal public land and resources law.* New York: Foundation Press.

Corbridge J. N., Jr., and T. A. Rice. 1999. *Vranesh's Colorado water law: Revised edition.* Niwot: University Press of Colorado.

DeVoto, B. 1952. *The course of empire.* Boston: Houghton Mifflin.

Engelbert, E. A., and A. F. Scheuring. 1984. *Water scarcity: Impacts on western agriculture.* Berkeley: University of California Press.

Fradkin, P. L. 1981. *A river no more.* Tucson: University of Arizona Press.

Getches, D. H. 1993. From Askhadad, to Welton-Mohawk, to Los Angeles: The drought in water policy. *University of Colorado Law Review* 64: 523.

Gillilan, D. M., and T. C. Brown. 1997. *Instream flow protection: Seeking a balance in western water use.* Washington, D.C.: Island Press.

Gleick, P., W. C. G. Burns, E. L. Chalecki, M. Cohen, K. K. Cushing, A. Mann, R. Reyer, G. H. Wolff, and A. K. Wong. 2002. *The world's water, 2002–2003.* Washington, D.C.: Island Press.

Guldin, R. W. 1989. *An analysis of the water situation in the United States: 1989–2040.* Fort Collins, Colo.: U.S. Department of Agriculture, Forest Service.

Hutson, S., N. L. Barber, J. F. Kenny, K. S. Linsey, D. S. Lumia, and M. A. Maupin. 2004. *Estimated use of water in the United States in 2000.* U.S. Geological Survey Circular 1268. U.S. Department of the Interior.

Kenney, D. S. 1997. *Resource management at the watershed level.* Boulder: Natural Resources Law Center, University of Colorado School of Law.

———. 2001. *Two decades of water law and policy reform: Conference report.* Boulder: Natural Resources Law Center, University of Colorado School of Law.

McCool, D. 1987. *Command of the waters: Iron triangles, federal water development, and Indian water.* Berkeley: University of California Press.

McCormick, Z. L. 1994. Interstate water allocation compacts in the western United States—Some suggestions. *Water Resources Bulletin* 30 (3): 385–395, June.

Mumme, S. P. 2000. Minute 242 and beyond: Challenges and opportunities for managing transboundary groundwater on the Mexico-U.S. border. *Natural Resources Journal* 40: 341.

National Research Council. 1992. *Water transfers in the West.* Washington, D.C.: National Academy Press.

Nichols, P. D., M. K. Murphy, and D. S. Kenney. 2001. *Water and growth in Colorado.* Boulder: Natural Resources Law Center, University of Colorado School of Law.

Pitt, J., D. F. Luecke, M. J. Cohen, E. P. Glenn, and C. Valdes-Casillas. 2000. Two nations, one river: Managing ecosystem conservation in the Colorado River Delta. *Natural Resources Journal* 40: 819.

Reisner, M. 1986. *Cadillac desert.* New York: Viking Penguin.

Tarlock, D., S. Van de Wetering, L. MacDonnell, D. Kenney, J. Clark, C. Brown, C. Dougherty, and D. Glaser. 1998. *Water in the West: Challenge for the next century.* Denver: Report of the western Water Policy Review Advisory Commission.

Tarlock, A. D., J. N. Corbridge, and D. H. Getches. 2002. *Water resource management.* New York: Foundation Press.

U.S. Census Bureau. 1997. Population projections, states: 1995-2025. *Current Population Reports.* Washington, D.C.: U.S. Department of Commerce, Economic and Statistics Administration.

———. 2001. *Population change and distribution.* Washington, D.C.: U.S. Department of Commerce, Economics and Statistics Administration.

U.S. General Services Administration. 1996. *Summary report of real property owned by the United States throughout the world as of September 30, 1994.* Washington, D.C.: U.S. Government Printing Office.

Wahl, R. W. 1989. *Markets for federal water.* Washington, D.C.: Resources for the Future.

Wilkinson, C. F. 1989. Aldo Leopold and western water law: Thinking perpendicular to the prior appropriation doctrine. *Land and Water Law Review* 24: 1–38.

Chapter 8

Improving Water Allocation for User Communities and Platforms in the Andes

Rutgerd Boelens, Axel Dourojeanni, and Paul Hoogendam

— This chapter focuses on how to improve water allocation considering the water user majorities in Andean countries: the needs, capacities, opportunities, and obstacles of the peasant and indigenous communities, and local water management platforms. The water management context and policy debate are first briefly outlined, with a particular focus on watershed management and decentralization. The chapter then discusses the rights-based orientation of various water policy proposals for improving watershed management, defining four exemplary approaches. A brief overview presents their conceptual underpinning and their practical outcomes for water conflict resolution and integrated water management. The chapter concludes with the presentation of basic elements for analyzing and setting up consensus-oriented water management strategies, and recommendations and process guidelines for user-oriented water policies.

Farmer-managed water use and production systems form the backbone of local and national economies and food security in most Andean countries, but face increasing problems.[1] Growing demographic pressure contributes to the degeneration of natural resources and local livelihood systems, and the processes of migration, globalization, and urbanization of rural areas, among others, profoundly change the agrarian structure and living conditions. New interest groups enter the territories of local peasant and indigenous communities and often take over a substantive share of existing water resources, thereby neglecting local rules, rights, and agreements. The new water management context leads to increasing inequality, poverty, conflict, and ecological destruction. Consequently, rural communities particularly suffer from the current water crises. Together with other stakeholder groups who lack influence in water policymaking and implementation, they may be characterized as the tail-enders of current water society. Traditionally, water legislation and policies in the Andean countries have paid little attention to locally existing water rights frameworks, their problems, and their solutions. With rapidly growing pressure on water resources and increasing claims and conflicts among multiple use sectors, conventional bureaucratic and free market water allocation approaches seem to have worsened the crisis, instead of contributing to its solution.

As in other parts of the world, new policies for the regulation, intervention, and adaptation of water management are being developed as an answer to water crises. These often refer to participation, decentralization, and transferring management to local government. In principle, these could be major steps toward strengthening users' organizations, by granting them greater decisionmaking power and security in their water rights and respecting sufficient autonomy for water management according to their needs and potential. However, in these times of radical state downsizing in the Andean countries, the slogan of participation is often also a facade for the underlying intention to abandon essential public tasks and cut back on public spending in water management (Dourojeanni and Jouravlev 1999a; Boelens and Hoogendam 2002; Hendriks et al. 2003). Looking beneath participatory words and promising statements, one must ask whether transfer policies are also a strategy to maintain or even strengthen state control over water at the local level. Alternatively, as first evidence in many cases shows, the proposals may be questioned as being part of private-sector projects to accumulate water rights, gain control over water supply services, and multiply business profitability, free from governmental control and public regulation (Moreyra 2001; Bustamante 2002; Guevara et al. 2002).

Obviously, the challenge of making water laws and policies is strongly complicated by the multiple forms of water use and management systems in a context that is extremely diverse. All Andean countries have great differences in ecological and climatic regions as well as in institutional and technological environments, and also show impressive, historically grown diversities with respect to organizational and political structures, cultural backgrounds, and production rationalities.

Thus, the plural management forms and socioeconomic stratification make the problem of protecting natural resources even greater, since rules and regulatory mechanisms necessarily have to adjust to the issues and actors at stake. In the case of corporations and formal entities, governments can, to a certain extent, draw on the experience and environmental instruments, laws, administrative techniques, and institutions that already exist in other regions. However, with respect to the small-scale farming sector no easily replicable external models exist. Governments will need to rely strongly on the great variety of community institutions, and on the ethical standards and cooperation that govern local livelihoods, with management forms that sometimes may be supported by governmental or nongovernmental assistance. Compliance with environmental requirements in the rural and informal sector can be based only on the will and participation of the population itself, although central governments cannot escape the important role they have to play in, for example, education, promotion, financial support, and enabling legislation. Here, the technical challenge in the design phase of water management policies is not the major one. Much more difficult will be the tasks of consensus-oriented formulation of this policy and of ensuring its implementation in a democratic and equitable manner (Dourojeanni 1997).

This chapter explores the existing water rights frameworks and water policies in the Andean countries, and relates them to the diverse options and prevailing alternative proposals. It focuses particularly on the question of how to improve water allocation considering the needs, capacities, opportunities, and obstacles of the Andean countries' water user majorities: the peasant and indigenous communities and other local water management organizations and platforms. After the current water management context is presented, the water policy debate in the Andean countries is outlined, focusing particularly on watershed management. The next section explains how and why competition and conflicts among multiple users and uses in Andean watersheds generally take the shape of water rights arenas. The section that follows discusses the various water policy responses to the issue: the conceptual underpinning and the practical outcomes of approaches and frameworks for water rights conflict resolution and integrated water management. The subsequent section presents basic elements for analyzing and setting up consensus-oriented water rights strategies, and the last section elaborates recommendations, possible process guidelines, and the basic conclusions of the chapter.

Water Management Problems in the Andean Region

The Andean countries face enormous difficulties when trying to establish natural resource policies. Although there are many local-level community-based institutions, the countries lack adequate national-level systems and frameworks for the public or private management of natural resources. Institutional shortcomings are particularly pronounced in relation to management of river-basin water resources, forests, fauna, and soil conservation. User needs far outstrip the capacity of the public and private services providing support for these tasks.

Little is being done to institutionalize stable management systems. Apart from some bottom-up, interinstitutional, and nongovernmental initiatives, efforts have been mainly short-term investment projects that have failed to attain their objectives, for example, establishment of soil and forest conservation, river basin management bodies, and large-scale forestation programs with community participation (Dourojeanni 1997; ECLAC 1998). There is an absence of research and ongoing training programs. State intervention generally neglects the democratic involvement of user organizations.

One cause of regulatory gaps and errors has been that natural resource management ideas have been gaining ground in the region primarily because of outside influence, albeit with a time lag. This explains the tendency toward the hasty application of legislative and regulatory models imported from Western countries. These models were designed to regulate duly registered formal companies similar to those in the northern countries, and aimed at establishing comprehensive frameworks covering the entire range of environmental issues. In such situations, incentives, fines, and demands for compliance with the environmental legislation may be functional. Those countries also have the enforcement capacity that results from the greater administrative efficiency of the public sector. As a result, the initial steps toward environmental control in the Andean region erred on the utopian side in terms of their execution capacity, and overlooked the vast majority of users of the environment (Dourojeanni 1997).

In the Andean region there is increasing competition for water among different users and different uses, mainly as a result of increasing demands, both endogenous demands linked to irrigated agriculture and urban populations living in the basins and exogenous demands, especially from large urban centers and industrial, mining, and energy-sector businesses. Furthermore, water availability during times of need is declining compared to historical amounts, owing to climatic change and land management under great stress. Water retention and storage have been reduced and, during rainy seasons, peak flow rates have risen (ECLAC 1992a, 1998).

Competition, moreover, is not limited to the availability of water, the quantity, place, and timing of delivery, but is also strongly related to worsening quality. Increasingly, activities affecting water pollute it, rendering the resource useless for many or most purposes. The discharge of domestic and human wastes, solid residues, tailings from mining operations, industrial wastes, chemicals used in agriculture, and waste generated by livestock breeding has in many of the Andean river basins created a high-risk situation that also acts as a brake on development (ECLAC 1992b; Hoogendam 1999; Dourojeanni 2000a).

Burgeoning competition breeds conflict among upstream and downstream users within basins, and between those in different basins when water is transported outside the basin, as occurs more and more frequently. This competition is usually won by those with the greater economic, legal, or technological power. There are many examples of peasant and indigenous groups in the Andes whose water is diverted or withheld for hydropower projects or other such high-profit uses benefiting users outside the zone. This leaves the peasant population and other specific sectors and groups who are less able to apply political and economic pressure without access to their water resources, or it makes them suffer the consequences when their only water sources are polluted and they have no way to reverse the situation (ECLAC 1988; Bauer 1998; Boelens and Hoogendam 2002).

In general, water policies and practices in the Andean countries show little awareness of human dependence on water, of the limits to the availability of this resource, or of the opportunity or deprivation of others implied by every water use. Especially with respect to drinking water and water for industrial use, the emphasis is more on tapping new sources and on low-cost supply than on reducing waste or improving distribution.

The degradation of vegetation in catchment basins is another serious problem that has not yet received the necessary attention. This increases surface run-off, with consequent erosion and violent discharges in the rainy season, as well as decreasing the supply of subsurface groundwater that feeds springs and streams used in the dry season (Dourojeanni and Jouravlev 1999a). Furthermore, the accumulation of sediments shortens the working life of the dams built in the middle parts of the Andean river basins. The greatest problems, nevertheless, lie not on the physical or technical side, but in the policies, laws, and top-down organizational structures relating to water management.

Management of water resources has deteriorated over time, and has been unable to respond to the explosive growth of demand created by industry and the urbanization of recent decades. The ancient Andean civilizations, and later the predominantly rural and agricultural settlements, established hydraulic works and management rules and mechanisms for exploiting the resource in a relatively stable manner. Nevertheless, this physical and institutional heritage is incapable of meeting today's increased needs, nor has it been able to prevent conflicts over water from becoming more acute. The response of the Andean countries has consisted primarily of major investment in hydraulic works to expand urban and industrial supply. Opportunities for strengthening and adapting the institutions controlling distribution, physical maintenance, and the public attitudes toward the use of the resource have been neglected.

There has been an absence of national coordination, and of a comprehensive approach to water management. Conflicts between supply and demand have generally been resolved by each individual sector, whether public or private. Moreover, there has been very little investment in works to manage supply, such as facilities for measuring and monitoring water quality, controlling pollution and erosion, catchment basin management, land-use planning, and other investments to protect the population against extreme natural phenomena, and, generally speaking, to manage multiple uses of water (Dourojeanni 1997).

A consequence of the current rapid process of change is the coexistence in the region of various styles of water management, both traditional and recent. This may result from recent revisions to the water legislation (which, e.g., in the case of Chile have paved the way for establishing a water rights market), the enactment of environmental legislation, rethinking of the role of the state, privatization of water services, or, in some cases, the establishment of new institutions to manage the water in river basins. All these existing policies have been unable to address the dramatic situation of unequal distribution of water, of water-related development opportunities, and of public investment in the Andean countries, as several examples illustrate.

The Majes Project in Peru

In the Majes project in southern Peru, major investments were made, in the order of US$1.2 billion, to capture and conduct the water from the Colca Valley and irrigate the desert lowlands. The project irrigates only about 15,000 hectares, for 3,000 families who each obtained a 5-hectare parcel. This was an investment in the order of US$80,000 per hectare, or, what is even more appalling: US$400,000 *per family.* As Hendriks observes, these costs per hectare and per family could be reduced in the future only by significantly increasing the irrigation command area—which is nearly impossible (Hendriks 2002).[2]

The Majes project is known not just for its huge costs and technocratic, top-down execution but also for its severe ecological and social impacts. The original design excluded outright any provision of water for the upper basin where the indigenous communities live, and where the water comes from. Furthermore, to "recover" investments, those families who *did* acquire land and water rights in the lower basin, had to pay US$25,000 per parcel—by no means affordable for indigenous smallholder families, who basically live in subsistence conditions. Indigenous communities in the Andean catchment certainly were confronted with the project, however. They did get the largest share of the burdens, for example, the expropriation of land, strong price inflation, depredation of natural resources, destruction of terraces, and debilitation of existing patterns of organization and culture (Tipton 1988; Gelles 1998). The United Nations Economic Commission for Latin America and the Caribbean (ECLAC, in Spanish CEPAL, or Comisión Económica para América Latina y el Caribe de las Naciones Unidas) estimated that barely 0.2 percent of total project investment was allocated to the upper basin, where the poorest sectors were in great need for irrigation water. Moreover, comparing this budget with other options at that time, 750,000 hectares of abandoned terraces could have been recovered and brought back into production in peasant and indigenous communities (Manrique 1985; ECLAC 1988; Boelens 2003).

Unbalanced Investment in Ecuador

As in the previous Peruvian example, local community systems in Ecuador are largely forgotten when it comes to implementing national water policies. This becomes clear when, for example, we look at national statistics. Over the last decades basically all financial resources have been invested in state-managed systems that, overall, function extremely poorly. Out of a total of 850,000 hectares of irrigated lands, state irrigation systems represent only 220,000 hectares, of which 130,000 are actually irrigated. State irrigation systems benefit only around 60,000 user families, a figure that strongly contrasts with the millions of peasant and indigenous families who potentially could benefit from investments in locally managed irrigation systems (Hendriks et al. 2003).

The unbalanced investment policy not only is reflected in the type of systems benefiting from the financial resources, but it also shows the skewed distribution to different water user groups. According to Whitaker's (1992) study, peasant and indigenous farmers with less than 1 hectare—who are responsible for the major part of national food production—represent 60 percent of all farmers, but they received only 13 percent of the benefits of state spending in irrigation. At the same time, large landowners represent only 6 percent of all farmers, and they received 41 percent of the benefits of state spending in irrigation. The public financed all this: state irrigation investment in Ecuador at the time represented 11.6 percent of the total foreign debt (Whitaker 1992; Boelens 2003).

It is not unimportant to mention the water rights distribution that constitutes the background of these investment policies. Although no precise figures exist, it is estimated that 1–4 percent of the irrigator population concentrates 50–60 percent of all water rights concessions, where the large majority of users, almost 90 percent, constituted by smallholders, has access to only between 6 and 20 percent of all water rights (Galárraga-Sánchez 2000).

Water Rights Individualization in Chile

Indigenous peoples and peasant communities in Chile have faced the consequences of national water policy, which is based on one of the current and powerful global water policy models. Against their wishes and traditions, they have become included in the 1981 Water Code, dictating privatization of water rights. While some studies continue to praise the model,[3] empirical field studies indicate the disintegration of collective, indigenous systems. For most of the marginalized water use sectors, the individualization of water rights has increased insecurity and disorganization (Bauer 1997, 1998; Hendriks 1998; Dourojeanni and Jouravlev 1999b; Castro 2002). Moreover, according to the new legislation, decisionmaking rights on water management are now attached to economic buying power of individuals: rights-holders with more "water shares" (volumetric rights per time unit) have more decisionmaking power, contrary to indigenous management and collective interests. In many cases, an elite group owning water rights has been able to effectively deny the interests of the majority (the group of poorer users), and impose their own rules (Hendriks 1998; Gentes 2002).

Since individual water property owners can make use of the water entirely according to their personal interests, Chile faces the problem of strong increase in water contamination. Individual property owners are not sanctioned for polluting *their* property. Often, indigenous communities and downstream cities bear the consequences (Bauer 1998; Dourojeanni and Jouravlev 1999b). At the same time, the water market itself has not developed (or in some cases only very marginally), but extreme monopolization, speculation, and hoarding of water rights did. A few power generating and mining companies accumulated the vast majority of rights, but most of those rights are not used. The Water Code does not require water rights owners to actually make use of these rights, nor are they obliged to pay concession fees. This makes hoarding and speculation of water rights in a context of scarcity extremely attractive (Solanes and González-Villareal 1999). An important source for this accumulation and monopolization of water rights was the expropriation of the so-called "unregistered" indigenous community rights (Dourojeanni and Jouravlev 1999b; Castro 2002; Gentes 2002). In 2005, after years of legal struggle, several legal changes have been enacted to alleviate the harsh social and environmental impacts of Chilean water policy.

The Bolivian Water War and Protest against Privatization

The international consortium *Aguas del Tunari* was granted the concession to supply drinking water and a sewer system to the city of Cochabamba, Bolivia, in September 1999. A month and a half later, Act No. 2029 for the regulation of the sector was passed, containing a set of rules intended to regulate the use and exploitation of the water resources.

Both events caused reactions and mobilization of the population. In the urban areas people protested against the excessive increases of the rates. In the rural communities, farmers protested against the uncertain effects of the new law on their traditional rights. The social conflict blew up in February and in April 2000, with several days of intense clashes between the so-called *guerreros del agua* (water warriors) and the police, which culminated in the declaration of a national state of siege.

Social discontent finally led to the cancellation of the contract that had been agreed to with the *Consorcio Aguas del Tunari* and the modification of more than 30 articles of Act No. 2029, which became the new Act No. 2066. What happened in the *guerra del agua* (water war) in Cochabamba had a strong international impact as an example of resistance against the privatization of water and of water services, and has been recently repeated in the city of La Paz where another international consortium *Aguas de Illimani* has been forced to cease its services after years of discontent by its clients. At the same time, these protests lead to the opening of a process of wider participation for the formulation of regulations and policies concerning water resources. It is in this context that the *Consejo Interinstitucional del Agua* or CONIAG (Inter-institutional Water Council) has been recently created, as a forum where government representatives, social organizations, the private sector, academic institutions, and the municipalities take part. The mission of the forum is to reach a consensus in the formulation of a new policy and water legislation for Bolivia (Bustamante 2002). Furthermore, the government and international cooperation have plans to elaborate a *Programa Nacional de Cuencas,* which seeks to identify methods for solving critical problems in watersheds, such as conflicts over water use and pollution.

New Water Policies for a New Water Context

As outlined earlier, inhabitants of high-altitude Andean areas clearly suffer from the water management policies of the last decades, both centralist and neoliberal policies. Some government policies aim to provide technical assistance to peasant and indigenous communities to improve their irrigation, water supply, and small hydropower systems. However, other coexisting policies directly or indirectly clash with the former, opposing and often overriding them. For example, the Indigenous Law in Chile was enacted in 1993, among others, to protect and support development of indigenous territories, water resources, and management systems. In practice, however, the more influential Water Code and Mining Code overrule these intentional social and cultural policies when interests conflict. In the same way, petrol and mining companies in Peru, Bolivia, and Ecuador, backed by mining laws and investment policies, continue to destroy numerous catchment and watershed areas, neglecting the peasant and indigenous water use systems in these territories as well as the respective integrated development policies and environmental laws (Bauer 1998; Dourojeanni 2000a; Gelles 2002; Boelens 2003). The more powerful policies and intervention programs are often geared toward encouraging private and foreign investment, for example to tap natural resources or to generate energy for public services. These policies have granted decisive power to water use projects based on analyses from and benefits for "the outside."

The negative impacts and lack of functionality in national water management policy with regard to local situations is not a phenomenon limited to the Andean countries. Therefore there is a growing international interest in better coordination at the watershed level, by formulating framework laws that will grant greater decision-making leeway at the local level (ECLAC 1998; Solanes and González-Villareal 1999). In general, new water management policies consider it necessary to move toward greater decentralization and deconcentration of functions and powers, from national authorities toward the level of the river basin, catchment area, and watershed organizations. Here, the multiple interest groups must define how water will be apportioned, distributed, and managed, and take an active part in inter-sectoral water management.

The call for decentralization and deconcentration of water management in the Andean region is grounded in several arguments:

1. Conflicts over water among multiple, competitive uses and users will continue to increase due to growing demand for and scarcity of water, and increasing water pollution. These multisectoral conflicts materialize at the watershed level.

2. Jurisdictional limits now clash, but should coincide with the boundaries of the geographical unit where water accumulates and flows. This can involve one or more basins if they are interconnected by hydraulic works or underground water flow.

3. Water must be managed with participation from local governments and rural communities whose political and administrative jurisdictions overlap or belong to the watershed areas in question. "Platforms" of local interest groups have better capacity than national agencies to understand, analyze, and propose solutions to resolve local water management problems.

4. When decisions are made at the watershed level, it is easier to improve relationships of accountability among water regulators, water providers, and water users.

5. Economic losses can be reduced and public spending for water management can be cut back when conflicts among mutually dependent user groups are minimized and when direct relationships between investment and benefits in water management are established.

These proposals for change in water management policy have been taken up in discussions on the formulation of new water laws in the Andean region. Under titles such as decentralization, participation, privatization, and management transfer, processes are in motion to transfer some water management responsibility toward local or municipal government authorities, user groups, private enterprises, or combined public–private institutions (Bauer 1997; Hoogendam 1999; Dourojeanni 2000a; Bustamante 2002). The system level and water management aspects to be transferred vary with the circumstances. Management of the whole watershed may be involved—especially if it is small—or the operation of reservoirs, water distribution systems, or the secondary or tertiary units of large-scale irrigation systems. Policies and regulations may include only transferring the tasks of distributing water, the responsibilities for maintaining and operating certain facilities, or even privatizing infrastructure and the water itself, as in Chile.

However, new water policies are heavily contested in the Andean countries. Discussions hinge on such topics as the role of the state versus the private sector, and how suitably market forces can allocate water. The primary questions in these debates are: "Can and should water be treated as private commodity, or as a basic, nontradable human need, as a public, collective human right?" and "Must water allocation and/or water supply service be controlled by central public authorities, or can that control be decentralized or privatized?".

The effectiveness of top-down decentralization policies is questionable, especially since usually tasks but not decisionmaking powers are being transferred to lower management levels. Simultaneously, there is the fear that government actions to privatize water services and establish water markets will not be complemented by adequate frameworks or regulatory bodies to protect the collective interests and water rights of local communities (Solanes and González-Villareal 1999; Dourojeanni 2000a; Boelens and Zwarteveen 2003a).

Many countries in the Andean region, such as Peru and Ecuador, have attempted to copy Chile's Water Code verbatim, but then became enmeshed in interminable debates about its unsuitability, which continue to this day. There is a consensus among most stakeholders—powerful investor groups as well as marginalized sectors—on the need for a change toward decentralized water management. However, the motives, interests, and concrete proposals differ widely among them. Indigenous and peasant groups demand to take part in the policymaking process to offset their historical exclusion from these political arenas. Exclusionary policies have resulted in water policies that are not grounded in an in-depth analysis of the real problems and potentials of the different players in water management.

Where regulations and institutions have been implemented, they have often been only paperwork of good intentions but without sufficient backing in realistic strategies, means, or capacities (ECLAC 1992a, 1998). As a result, virtual or artificial water management bodies have been created that have no basis in a detailed analysis of local problems or practices, or in the effective involvement of local stakeholders. Moreover, these entities can easily deny and supplant local initiatives, organizations, and platforms that aim to coordinate among grassroots user organizations and enforce their own water management rules.

The Watershed as a Water Management Unit

In historical times, several river basins and catchment areas in the Andes were managed by the precolonial empires and polities in an integrated manner. Moreover, in general, human need for water resources provision did not surpass water availability in most areas. Very commonly, small and medium-scale watersheds were organized as systems of human-made production zones. "Vertical economies" were based on altitudinal zones and mutual collaboration and reciprocity between "high" and "low," with water as an important axis (Boelens et al. 2002; Mayer 2002).

Following from the preceding, as well as being a physical unit the watershed also has the characteristics of a social unit, although the boundaries are not so well defined. The watershed is a zone where groups of inhabitants are interrelated, sharing its water, and organizing around its reaches. In mountainous zones, rivers or mountain ridges between basins commonly define the pathways for transport, exchange, and communication. The hydrological characteristics and hydraulic works strongly influence the ways that people living in the basin interact and generate day-to-day interdependence.

Still, it was not until the 1970s that the concept of watershed management arose in policy discussions in the Andean countries. At first, it was highly slanted toward protecting the basins' more productive lowlands. In isolated highland areas, there was intervention only when these upper basins became problems or opportunities for exogenous economic development; when they were jeopardizing infrastructural works or settlements downstream, or when water could be gathered for urban and/or commercial purposes, such as mining, agribusiness, hydropower, or water supply for cities. This partial approach to watershed management, with a meaning that is reinterpreted according to the outlook and functions of each public agency in charge of pursuing its tasks under this banner, remains dominant to this day. Thus, there are "watershed management" programs that do only irrigation projects. Others only work on individual plots, only rehabilitate terraces, only control floodwaters, or only stabilize dunes.

Although watersheds and river basins are usually easily demarcated geographical units, it is difficult to establish coherent water management activities in basins. As previously mentioned, the boundaries of administrative entities (communities, municipalities, districts, provinces, regions, or countries) normally do not coincide with the natural limits of basins. In such cases, water management platforms require the collaboration of entities from different political and administrative zones, the coordination of which generates problems of competence and jurisdiction. There is often jurisdictional interference among local institutions, national agencies, and international assistance or investment programs. Many water use actions in basin areas are taken without consulting local authorities, especially if there are no visible basin-level water management bodies (Hoogendam 1999; Dourojeanni 2001).

Fundamentally, despite participatory discourse, and the presence of some institutional initiatives that seek to truly benefit the local Andean highland population, other reasons for undertaking watershed management have often prevailed over favoring sustainable development and enhanced value for high-altitude zones. Examples of these other reasons include controlling peasant and indigenous migration to the cities or trying to get them to return to their places of origin ("repeasantization" or "reruralization"); preventing city belts of poverty from swelling; preventing the erosion and sediments from affecting hydropower dams that supply energy to distant urban centers; mitigating the impact of flooding and drought in the lowlands; and averting the emergence of grassroots protests and violent resistance groups in the highlands.

Competition and Conflict among Multiple Uses and Users: A Water Rights Arena

Multiple-use water management at the level of basins and watersheds is a question concerning the societal distribution of water rights. Water rights do not just refer to the right to access and use water, but include the issues of control and authority (for an elaboration see Schlager and Ostrom 1992; Gerbrandy and Hoogendam 1998; Bruns and Meinzen-Dick 2000; Boelens and Hoogendam 2002). These include rights to access and use water (quantity, quality, timing, duration, and place of acquisition), rights to access and use infrastructure, rights to control and decisionmaking about management, rights to establish authority for sanctioning, legitimating, reinforcing normative frameworks, and, also important in the Andes, the rights to exercise local constructions of hydraulic identity and cultural water practices (Beccar, Boelens, and Hoogendam 2002). Over each issue, stakeholders confront each other, as do—at a more abstract level—ideologies and discourses.

In this arena, different rights-distribution interest groups can be distinguished. There are the stakeholders for whom water use represents benefits, whether by direct consumption or by generating products. Within abstract categories, such as farming, industry, mining, water supply, there is a variety of specific groups, normally in local, well-defined areas. There are also interest groups that are not necessarily direct users, such as basin inhabitants who are affected by flooding or pollution. Most watersheds have still other stakeholders who are not direct users, intervening or taking part in water management decisions, such as politicians, public officials and government agencies, nongovernmental organizations, development cooperation agencies, and research institutes. Definition of water management, water distribution, and water quality conservation takes place among representatives of such different groups and stakeholders that this management essentially becomes a process of ongoing confrontation and negotiation (Hoogendam 1995; Meinzen-Dick et al. 1997; Zwarteveen 1997; Meinzen-Dick and Zwarteveen 1998; Boelens and Zwarteveen 2003b). It is indispensable to analyze these interactions empirically and contextually to better understand the limitations and perspectives of processes to support and strengthen negotiation platforms, and to help generate consensus-building policies and strategies (Vincent 1996; Steins and Edwards 1999; Bruns and Meinzen-Dick 2000; Edmunds and Wollenberg 2001).

The difficulty in preventing conflicts, reaching consensus among different groups of rights-claimants, and establishing common usage rules and rights are not only political and normative issues. They also depend heavily on the characteristics of the Andean basins and their hydrology. Water availability and demand in the high mountain zones is unpredictable, irregular, and hard to measure. In addition, control of its use throughout the watershed is complex. Even if such control were possible for surface water, control and measurement are still more complicated for underground water, because withdrawals are almost invisible and difficult to control.

Water management by hydrological units is complicated further by the long distances in these basins (not only physical, but also sociocultural or economic distances). The scarcity of usable roadways makes it difficult for population groups along the basin to have exchanges. In general, users upstream care little about the problems of people downstream, but rather take full advantage of their strategic position, out of the control of those further down. However, in large river basins, major cities intervene in the upper reach and produce the opposite phenomenon so that those downstream take the water they need first from upstream. Without watershed agencies, valley authorities, or clear policies and rules adapted to each basin, water use generally boils down to seeking one's own advantage.

A general, outstanding feature of legislation on water resource management in Andean countries is either its slight influence in the Andean highlands (Gerbrandy and Hoogendam 1998) or its counterproductivity and the resistance that it provokes (Bustamante 2002; Gentes 2002; Guevara et al. 2002). In general, legal measures and norms to foster integrated water management are strongly modified by intermediary sectors and stakeholders with their own ideologies, rules, and interests (F. and K. von Benda-Beckmann and Spiertz 1998). In the day-to-day political arenas, they challenge the construction, application, and reproduction of rules and bring different socio–legal systems into interaction and confrontation. Legal pluralism, in the sense of the coexistence of different normative orders within one sociopolitical space (von Benda-Beckmann 1996), is broadly manifested in the water management field. It is reinforced not only by Andean peoples' diverse history and different physical and social contexts, but also by local resistance against the legislators' attitude itself. In most Andean countries, actual practices receive almost no consideration in the formulation of water laws, many of which are the result of copying foreign legal instruments. As Vidal mentions, "despite the society's diverse nature, legislation is always uniform, considering all of society as a homogenous reality, in which there is no room for different rights" (Vidal 1990). In countries such as Ecuador, Peru, and Chile, official regulations often very precisely define how water users must organize, how water must be distributed, how they must contribute to keeping up their irrigation system, and, sometimes, how they must set up their coordination body at the basin level (Moreyra 2001; Boelens 2005).

In the circles of Andean policymakers and legislators, the instrumental myth persists that the intended changes in water management can be made by just formulating and legislating official rules. The assumption is that bureaucratic implementation is an almost automatic consequence. However, changes require that the different parties involved—not just state agencies and officials—take action and apply normative instruments in social practice. These actions and social forces interact and generate different, particular normative frameworks. These mixtures vary from one watershed to another, and also from one users' group to another. The resulting diversity is an intrinsic consequence of the local processes of interaction and negotiations, within each specific region, and the adaptation of "macro" type organizational forms and regulatory norms to local circumstances.

In such a multilegal panorama, characterized by great heterogeneity of de facto authorities, legitimizing and being legitimized by divergent normative systems, it is not easy to achieve a consensus regarding water rights. It is not just a question of competition for use of the water and infrastructure, but also a conflict regarding the mechanisms that justify acquiring or claiming water rights. Different normative frameworks recognize different mechanisms. Furthermore, there is great heterogeneity regarding the contents or meaning of a "water right." This has very different features according to the normative framework that is deemed valid (Gerbrandy and Hoogendam 1998; Boelens and Doornbos 2001). Pluralism in systems of rights and authorities simultaneously present in Andean basins cannot be denied by official decrees, the imposition of a single positive normative system, or regulation by the market. Such imposition may seem quite appealing to legislators, politicians, project officials, and outside authorities, but it will never resolve the underlying conflicts. The search for platforms from which to negotiate, taking these divergences as starting points—although difficult to achieve—would seem to offer better opportunities.

Four Approaches to Accommodating Multiple Water Uses and Rights

In all efforts to build consensus on multiple uses and interests in watershed or river basin management, it is crucial to recognize that reconciling interests and decentralizing management fundamentally entails redistributing resources, authority, and power. This refers to the power of users, of involved nonusers and of the consensus-builders themselves. Hereby, societal relationships and power structures, manifested in the current unequal distribution of the means of production and wealth generated, decisively influence policy- and lawmaking regarding water resources and their enforcement. Therefore, when attempting to improve water resource management through a consensus-building policy, it is essential to analyze the different stakeholders, their knowledge, interests, and divergent powers, as well as their diverse strategies regarding water acquisition and use. This analysis must demystify all the official discourses based in terms of equity, democracy, or popular participation that fail to make clear how to achieve such goals.

In the Andean region (as a consequence of denying issues of power), explicit and in-depth discussion of existing interests and their influence in decisionmaking is often lacking in integrated watershed management programs. Instead, there are "established" intervention policies and "proven" rules and professional criteria. Thus, many programs are grounded in the implicit norms of professionals, institutions, and legal regulations, emphasizing above all "efficiency and productivity" in technical and economic terms. Also, in the socioorganizational field, there is the tendency to develop and impose the "most adequate" organizational structures and rules for consensus-building entities and negotiation platforms. So, many virtual organizations have emerged, often to channel institutions' interests and messages or to reinforce national legal regulations. In many cases, these external norms and artificial organizations have attempted to supplant the existing, local institutions of grassroots groups.

When analyzing the different discourses and action proposals that show up in the discussion on integrated water management, in the context of increasing water scarcity and competition, a number of marked differences stand out in their responses to the following questions:

- What water rights system (what regulation mechanism) can best allocate the water rights?

- What (kind of) regulatory entity should be responsible for this water allocation?

- How can conflicts about the resulting distribution of water and water rights be settled?

As a preliminary answer to these basic questions, four policy approaches may conceptually be distinguished in current debates, and with them proposals and strategies for intervening in watershed management (Boelens et al. 2002):

- the *"state" approach,* advocating governmental control over water management and over the allocation and adjustment of water rights;

- the *"market" approach,* seeking to decentralize management and to allocate or adjust water rights by means of market forces, using the "rational decisions of individual stakeholders";

- the *"consensus-based management" approach* (or *"concertation" approach),* seeking to decentralize management and to allocate or adjust water rights through regulation by consensus-based platform entities; and

- the *"empowerment" approach,* advocating the strengthening of local organizations (grassroots groups and marginalized sectors) to improve equitable resource distribution and to generate a balance between the power and opportunities of stakeholders involved in water management decentralization.

Below we briefly review some regulatory experiences that cover these approaches and analyze how the corresponding discourses are translated into practice. The focus of analysis is the actual capacity of these approaches to defend and find a consensus among different water uses and rights in the watershed, to resolve conflicts among stakeholders with criteria of equity, and to protect the ecological functions of the watershed or basin.

The State Approach

The first approach is grounded in granting the state a strong, decisive role in regulating and implementing multisectoral water management. The fundamental idea is to preserve and strengthen the public responsibility to ensure that all societal sectors and the environment have rights and access to this strategic resource. In practice, this often results in vertical imposition of the rules of play on users. In the case of decentralization of water management to the watershed or basin level, a government agency is commonly set up or appointed to be the agent responsible for local administration of water resources.

In Peru, for example, the Law to Promote Investments in the Agrarian Sector (1991) authorizes the creation of Autonomous Water Basin Authorities (IPROGA 1996). Article 55 establishes that "in basins with regulated irrigation and/or where there is intensive, multisectoral water use, Autonomous Water Basin Authorities will be set up, as the top decisionmaking body regarding water and soil resource use and conservation in that jurisdictional area." However, in most basins, these bodies have not been set up or they have remained paper institutions. In others they were established vertically and bureaucratically, without sectoral participation or intersectoral coordination or the capacity to gather stakeholders. Only in a very few cases have they attempted to bring the different sectors and grassroots user groups together, but even in those cases it has proved difficult to achieve democratic, effective management (Toledo 1999). In part, this is caused by the paternalistic history and still bureaucratic setting of water administration and the power of the dominant sectors preventing consensus and democracy. Moreover, the legislation itself vertically prescribes the organizational structures, functions, and forms of representation, and as such, gives little room to stakeholders' problems and potential in the contexts of particular watersheds.

In this way, great controlling power is maintained, paradoxically in a setting of decentralization and privatization. Apparently, the same medicine is prescribed for quite different ailments. These entities must operate "under the norms and supervision of the national-level water authority" (article 56) and strictly enforce the official water norms in the watershed. This ignores the tremendous variety in watersheds, especially considering the great difference among the coastal, highlands, and jungle regions, where users apply local normative systems that are quite different from positive law.

The Market Approach

As one of the options and instruments to decentralize water management and make water use more efficient, a model has arisen with universal pretensions. The model, grounded in a neo-institutional market approach, defends decentralization and privatization of water management services and privatization of water use rights, as in Chile. In Chile, water is formally a national good of public use. Nevertheless, individual property rights over water enjoy broad, strong protection. Article 24 of Chile's constitution states that: "Private water rights, recognized or constituted pursuant to law, shall grant their holders ownership over them." In legal practice, water rights in Chile function as private property objects, overriding other regulatory norms. The Water Code also grants total, permanent freedom of the way in which to use water that one has rights over, so water rights holders may use their rights or not, and may use them for any purposes or types of use that they wish; they may transfer them separately from the land, to use them anywhere else; and sell them like any other merchandise on the market.

The market approach is based on the idea that the free market—through competition among different users and among different water uses and allocations—will be able to choose and (re-)distribute water rights to the user or sector with the most profitable use for the water resource. By granting water rights to the economically most beneficial, valuable use, the regulatory function of the free market would increase the value and the efficiency of water use. By setting the real price of water on the free market and generally commoditizing the resource, multiple uses of water could be compared, determining the "optimal" uses and users (Bauer 1997; Dourojeanni and Jouravlev 1999b).

To enforce this approach in practice, water rights must be defined as private, exclusive, and transferable property. National legislation must defend the security of private ownership, to encourage investment in the best utilization of the resource, and must offer a framework promoting transactions among rights-holders, according to the opportunities and needs of any given moment. Government intervention would have to be limited to facilitating transactions among water users, enforcing contracts among players, and protecting private property (Bauer 1998).

In principle, economic instruments—for example, the "polluter pays" principle —can be useful in Andean watershed management. Under certain situations, even the market trading of water rights could be beneficial for users and the economy at large. It could, for instance, support reorganization of water management within a territory with productive and social relationships that are already highly market-oriented—providing there is a legal and administrative framework that effectively regulates protection and prioritization of certain environmental and collective interests. However, in the case of Andean communities, we see that commoditization and privatization of water rights entail tremendous environmental and social justice problems, and often have the opposite effect from what was intended. Especially when social usage priorities are not established, and effective, beneficial use of water rights is not prescribed, large mining and hydropower companies are quite free to accumulate and speculate with water rights (Solanes and González-Villarreal 1999). Therefore, water rights are often transferred or purchased by the economically most powerful entities at the expense of subsistence communities in the Andes (Castro 2002; Gentes 2002).

In the Andean countries, the neoliberal market approach was applied in Chile and, during the last few years, other countries in the region initially took this model as the guiding standard and tried to copy it. Then they had to back-pedal after extensive public protests, among other reasons, as Chile has tried to do in 2005 by making amendments for indigenous rights and for the protection of the environment. Although in theory the Water Code strengthens user organizations and grants them great autonomy over using their rights, it does not help with conflict resolution or collaboration among users. Especially in situations of insecurity and subsistence, for example, in the case of peasant and indigenous collective management systems, privatization produced very serious consequences. As Hendriks (1998) shows, in analyzing the effect of Chilean policy on concrete practice in peasant irrigation systems: "The more individual owners of water, the fewer owners of the system."

At the level of multisectoral water management in water basins, the approach does not seem to offer the generalized benefits that economic theory had predicted. The few in-depth studies that exist have shown, in practice, the great difficulty of the Chilean model in solving multisectoral problems, whereby it impedes integrated management at the watershed level. Economic development in the water sector based on market rights has multiplied water pollution problems, underground water management issues, problems in preserving ecological flows, in governing transfer of water between basins, and so forth—all problems left to be settled through ordinary civil law courts, between private and privatized players of unequal power. "In this context, creating new basin-wide organizations as they are currently discussed in Chile would almost certainly be ineffective. The private economic rights of their members, who may refuse to comply with new regulations, would handicap such organizations" (Bauer 1998:150; see also ECLAC 1998; Dourojeanni and Jouravlev 1999b). As Bauer (1998:112) notes, "the task of coordinating different water uses at the level of river basins is left mainly to voluntary bargaining among private rights holders and their organizations. Because state administrative intervention is so limited, when bargaining fails the conflicts are supposed to be settled by the ordinary civil courts, which have expanded powers." It even seems that the market-privatizing model itself, with great dependence on the highly legalistic judicial system, generates part of the fundamental problems. The dominant sectors, with formally established rights, are precisely the ones that benefit the most from the Chilean model (Hendriks 1998; Castro 2002; Gentes 2002).

Problems are illustrated by, for example, the case of irrigators and environmentalists in Bauer's studies. "Because private rights are so strong relative to the state's regulatory authority, the bigger and more powerful water users have little incentive to negotiate. [. . .] Irrigators, on the other hand, have less bargaining power, because they have less economic and political clout and face higher transaction costs in organizing themselves. Moreover, the electric companies are national political players while the irrigators' influence is more local and regional" (Bauer 1998:149). Although the democratic government has attempted to change the neoliberal legislation (with some first legal results in 2005) and, among other changes, has proposed setting up combined public and private multisectoral agencies for watershed management, nevertheless the resistance by economically powerful stakeholders and hegemonic sectors against state interference in their private property rights and the free market remains intense (ECLAC 1998; Castro 2002).

Access rights to water resources are not comparable to rights to other transferable goods, because of the great interdependence among multiple uses and users of a single source in a single watershed or river basin. Water use also affects nonusers and the environment. The private market policy does not recognize water's social and collective features of user communities and platforms. In the Andean countries' reality it fails to resolve multisectoral water rights conflicts, where there is no strong, effective legal and institutional framework to support it (Bauer 1997, 1998; Boelens and Dávila 1998; Dourojeanni 2000a; Moreyra 2001). In this situation, such a water policy not only encourages accumulation, monopolization, and speculation with water rights by the dominant sectors, but it also tends to foster disorganization, by individualizing water management and externalizing conflict resolution.

The Consensus-Based Management Approach

A third group of institutional strategies and proposals to address intersectoral conflicts over water in the Andes and foster beneficial use and equitable water rights with environmental preservation, is grounded in a consensus-building or "concertation" approach (ECLAC 1992b, 1998; Dourojeanni 1997; IPROGA 1996; IMAR 1997). It is not the all-powerful state, or free-market rules, but negotiation and collaboration among different players, often with diverging interests but mutually dependent on each other, who have to reach a consensus that is beneficial for all. These strategies and proposals include, as a core element, generating or strengthening platforms (*mesas de concertación*) and mechanisms for consensus-building, for integrated water management at the watershed level, coordinated and comprised by combined entities: governmental and nongovernmental organizations, multisectoral, endogenous and exogenous bodies, representing the wishes of different interest groups.

This proposal to improve quality of life and satisfy the interests of all users and parties involved in the basin or microregion, for mutual or equitable benefit, makes it compulsory to consider participation by representatives of all of them. It is necessary to seek consensus among all interest groups regarding their water rights and their divergent normative systems, bearing in mind the possible transactions among participants and strategies and means to carry them out. At present, many legal, political, and institutional proposals, both governmental and nongovernmental, mention the importance of working on a consensus basis at the watershed and river basin level. This management by consensus does require an adequate information system, transparent, and broadly accessible. It generally has an outlook that is not limited to multisectoral water management but also involves other resources and activities. However, there are very few cases in the Andes that have materialized management platforms that are genuinely multisectoral and democratic. They often exist only on paper or have been institutionalized from the top down by state agencies or development organizations.

The approach's strong point is also its weakness. "For negotiation on activities to lead to sustainable development with equity, it has to happen within a framework of democratic consensus-building in which all players are aware of the proposed aims, their responsibilities and the future consequences for managing the watershed's resources. The overarching objective that is posed . . . is to organize water use in a harmonious, win-win manner among all water users" (IPROGA 1996). However, administration or redistribution of water rights at the territorial level is no easy matter for such a platform, precisely because it runs against vested interests, often quite powerful ones. In addition, few interest groups are aware of their responsibilities. Theoretically, they are based on "general" consensus and can work well when there are possibilities for transactions among stakeholders. Such transactions can be achieved only with awareness of proposed solutions and analysis of social, environmental, and economic costs and benefits, and with political interest in true social change. If mutual benefits cannot be found, the process of transferring or redistributing rights can easily be blocked by powerful players or sectors already holding rights. The latter will find ways to dominate platforms and otherwise will turn to other ways to satisfy their interests.

The Empowerment Approach

The empowerment approach is grounded in two basic concepts regarding the dynamics of watershed management. First, that many changes in water management do not result from the planning of an integrated strategy for water resource use, but from collective initiatives by users in terms of a shared interest or need. Most of the time, such local platforms are not organized to address the entire integrated water management situation, nor do they intend to; rather, they come together to address specific water supply problems. They generally do not gather (or want to invite) all stakeholders and water users within their platform, because some nonparticipating players do not share in their interests, or because the platform's objectives may be based precisely on mobilizing against the actions of a certain group of stakeholders.

The second concept is that distribution and adjustment of water uses and rights are processes entailing harsh confrontations among individual users and among collective sectors, which are not based on harmonious, consensual negotiation. The less powerful groups, although also facing internal conflicts among themselves, have almost always suffered the consequences of "reorganization of rights and uses" by other, stronger players. Many recent studies have shown the destruction of habitats and extraction of water resources from rural communities to benefit mining, hydropower, and agroindustrial companies or modern irrigation systems with economically and politically powerful users (e.g., see ECLAC 1998; Gelles 1998). Other studies have shown how certain interest groups, such as women, and indigenous and poor users are denied access to decisionmaking positions and negotiation platforms (Gerbrandy and Hoogendam 1998; Moreyra 2001; Boelens and Hoogendam 2002).

The empowerment approach seeks to empower groups with less voting and advocacy power, so they can gain the capacity to defend their interests regarding water management and related issues. One way to empower people is through sectoral organization or joining forces among groups with similar problems and proposals. These mobilization platforms are often oriented toward demanding the creation or restitution of rights to which they feel they are entitled. This approach generally feels that self-valuing, organization-building, internal democratic participation, and enhancing negotiating capacity are strategic elements, along with the capacity to build alliances with other grassroots groups and assistance institutions. According to the problems deemed most important, platforms can—when the situation calls for it—seek alliances with other users and inhabitants of the basin or microregion, especially when their mutual dependence on water gives rise to possibilities for win–win reciprocal transactions. Within this approach, possibilities for multisectoral management appear, for example, when environmental groups, peasant organizations, and nongovernmental organizations, sometimes with local government agencies, join and manage to consolidate fronts that force other players to respect "responsible water management."

Elements for Analysis of Consensus-Building and Empowerment Strategies

Only a combination of the main elements from the different approaches can generate a perspective for working on an equitable and sustainable water rights approach. The issue is how to strike a balance among the different water allocation mechanisms and to select and build regulation and conflict resolution systems. This balance is site specific and depends, among other things, on the hydrological situation, competition for use, power relationships, and the political and administrative structure in force in the basin where coordinated management action is to be taken. Variations in Andean watersheds have led, over time, to the creation of various local institutions. New policies must be based on contextual needs and potential in particular territories. Therefore, water management policies cannot be simply copied from one country to another, or from one basin to the other. They require great creativity and knowledge of the local setting's current status and historical development.

Accordingly, no single recipe can be prescribed for watershed entities, for river basin committees, or for a water rights policy, beyond setting general criteria as to regulatory mechanisms and bodies. Key elements for analysis can help to define strategies geared to improving multisectoral watershed management. As for regulatory mechanisms and bodies, it is important to establish decentralized entities, that have—within an overall legal framework—sufficient flexibility to adjust their norms to the specific reality of their own watershed.

The most important regulatory elements of water legislation involve the need to: (1) ensure effective and beneficial use, prevent speculation, and guarantee the social and production functions of water; (2) protect the ecological base in terms of water quality and quantity; (3) prevent passing negative externalities on to other users; (4) avoid accumulation and distribute water usage rights according to criteria of equity; and (5) make water management decisions based on active stakeholder involvement and political democracy. Regulatory bodies must be of the "negotiation and consensus-building platform" type, because it is only through direct participation by different user groups that the greatest degree of reconciliation may be assured among interests and conflicts in the planning and ordering process.

To make an impact beyond the micro level, avoiding the pitfall of only setting up macro entities that have nothing to do with local management, it is indispensable to work toward simultaneously combining organization-building in the Andean highlands watersheds on a relatively large scale, with empowering management initiatives in sub-basins and microbasins. Only the establishment of relations among major basin organizations and platforms organized by sub-basins and microbasins will make it possible to resolve conflicts among multiple users, and to work for shared water management with a multisectoral vision.

Consensus-building processes cannot be planned in an easy, linear fashion, since they are not limited to official settings and timing—often they are informal and unplanned. However, support institutions can accompany the consensus-building processes. Platforms for collaboration are strengthened insofar as their participants have access to alternative actions, in order to decide on the most suitable action. Moreover, an approach seeking to combine consensus-based management and water rights with an empowerment approach must be oriented toward the generation of platforms that include the interests articulated and advocated not only by formal negotiators ("the ones who always show up") but also by those from lower-profile, marginalized, and less-organized groups. Focusing on these groups' interests and outlooks entails the need to accompany these groups explicitly and concretely in water rights negotiation forums. It will also be necessary to find ways to organize bargaining and consensus processes such that they really enable the introduction of ideas and proposals from all groups, and to give them genuine authority to implement the agreed policies.

Here, the potential role of the state is undeniably important. It has the power to contribute to more equitable, sustainable water management. For example, the state can supply information on the water balance and on diverse users and uses; enact fair regulations on water provision and other benefits; provide legal and operational backing for users' self-management of water systems and for multisectoral platforms; serve as the arbiter for conflicts that cannot be settled locally; cofinance and comanage larger-scale systems; seek consensus and coordinate an operational strategic plan for water resources and concessions; and provide interactive training with and for users. If all Andean highlands basins are to be addressed, it is vital to have a logistics, research, debate, and exchange center, to support local initiatives and also generate technical, organizational, legal, political–administrative, and financial proposals that can be flexibly adapted to site-specific characteristics.

Among the elements of analysis to be considered in drafting policies and strategies for watershed management, we suggest to focus particularly on the analysis of

1. *The stakeholders or interest groups* (including individuals, groups, and institutions). They may be classified by motivations and interests, living standards, historical backgrounds, position in the basin or elsewhere, knowledge, capacity for participation and organization, degree of and potential for development, investment capacity, and political, economic, and social power.

2. *The setting* within which stakeholders are located, including their livelihoods, production systems, institutional environments, frameworks of activities, and the potential for the resources sustaining their local (water use) economies. This includes the geographical and political-administrative dimensions of the water management unit and concerns especially the physical and social hydrology of the basin.

3. *The normative frameworks,* which include national legislation and local norms of customary law; their contents, power, and interaction with each other; and their recognition by interest groups in the watershed.

4. *The objectives and criteria* of stakeholders, explicit and implicit, which differ according to their particular water management needs and aspirations.

5. *The problems and conflicts* that relate to single and multisectoral water management, ecological and human problems, and their hydrological, hydraulic, and institutional backgrounds. This includes divergent problem perceptions by different interest groups.

6. *The restrictions* that limit attaining stakeholders' goals and aspirations, and achieving consensus-based, equitable development in a setting. Constraints may be "endogenous" or "exogenous" and may be technical, political, legal, economic, financial, organizational, or cultural. They generally involve a mixture of these factors that impede reaching actors' objectives.

7. The different *solutions* that are expected by or for interest groups, whether on a particular basis (to meet individual interests) or collectively (to satisfy the interests of multiple players).

8. *The multisectoral water management processes* that have existed or still exist. This requires the analysis of negotiation processes among interest groups to accommodate different water uses and rights: consensus-building and conflict-resolution strategies, decisionmaking, objective-prioritizing, development of rights and management rules, training and consciousness-raising, resource mobilization, activity planning and implementation, and monitoring of outcomes and adjustment of goals.

9. *The institutional entities for multisectoral water management* that are in place. They are the materialization (or not) of negotiation processes in watershed organizations or platforms for negotiation and collaboration, and consist of both formal and informal institutions, with their geographic and administrative coverage.

The above elements are functional for the *analysis* or *assessment* of local water use problems in watershed areas. They can also be useful in processes of *building alternatives* for multisectoral watershed management when making strategies based on consensus-building and/or organizational empowerment approaches. In that case, collective analysis with the groups involved, considering the elements outlined earlier, is complemented by prioritizing problems and elaborating objectives, strategies, methodologies, and programmatic activities to achieve alternatives. These elements may be considered as the building blocks for "iterative processes"—not necessarily in any sequential order—within a process approach.

For Andean watersheds, the methodologies prepared by ECLAC (Dourojeanni 2000b), IMAR (1997), and IPROGA (1996) are useful. Watershed analysis, formulation of participatory intervention proposals and programs, with actual *concertation* management, would be based on an analysis of environmental perception ("space as lived"), analysis of the environmental profile ("space as a given"), and an analysis of the confrontation and correlation between these two, in different consensus-building cycles. In process approaches, it is often necessary to divide the basin's territories into small enough parts to be able to identify direct transactions and operational linkages among stakeholders, optimizing the realistic possibilities of local management without losing sight of basin-level perspectives and interrelationships.

Conclusion

The current water use situation in most Andean watersheds is characterized by deregulation and boundless competition among different types of uses and user groups. The players who usually win are those with the greatest economic, political, or technological power. Their utilization often threatens the availability of water for people with less power and, even worse, can take away the water that the latter have used for centuries for their livelihood and survival. Internal conflicts over water, within and among local organizations, further worsen the crisis situation. Another effect of the lack of effective regulation is an increase in water pollution, with no accountability for polluters.

To keep unfair competition for water use and pollution from generating greater injustices and imbalances, it is necessary to develop water use regulation policies, focusing on concrete implementation of basin management strategies, with a user-oriented bottom-up approach and, simultaneously, implementation all the way down to the micro level. In discussions on such regulations, there are four approaches with different proposals regarding the mechanisms for water use regulation, the type and functioning of regulatory bodies, and the establishment of platforms for conflict resolution among users. We have labeled these approaches as based on the central state, the market, consensus, and empowerment.

Recently, global, market-oriented policies aiming at water rights privatization have been strongly promoted through official proposals but encountered strong resistance among the Andean peasant and indigenous population, and many other sectors. Where the multiple use of water is concerned, the greatest sustainability is obtained by reconciling the economic, social, and environmental interests among the user sectors, not by pure competition among multiple uses. The water management bodies in the river basins will have to give attention to ways of facilitating this task. If, on the contrary, allocation of water is conducted by means of competition in an unregulated free market, reconciliation will rarely be achieved. If the use of water by sectors is defined only in terms of its short-term economic profitability, extreme conflict situations can be created.

The empowerment approach offers several important insights that can contribute to improving existing water management. More accurately than conventional approaches, it focuses the analysis on what happens in policymaking and implementation, identifying them as the outgrowth of negotiation processes among different interest groups. It also explicitly seeks greater social justice in water management and in the emancipation of the less well-to-do groups with less negotiating power. A weakness of the approach is that it is not proactively geared to work for an integrated water management policy, so in instrumental terms it must be combined with the consensus-based solution approach and with certain ideas from the other two approaches.

From this standpoint, planning and implementing an integrated water management policy calls for generating "regulatory entities," with watershed or basin bodies that may be classified into at least three levels: the macrobasin, the sub-basin or mesobasin, and the microbasin. At each of these hydrological, organizational, and political levels the different user groups need to be represented. These organs have to coordinate their activities, whenever required, with the existing administrative institutions. Obviously, such bodies or platforms must include in their focus the issue of underground water uses and users. The multisector, participatory water management responsibilities of these platform organizations relate to regulating the basin-level rules, resolving conflicts, reinforcing collaboration, coordination, and consensus-building, rather than free-market competition or vertical, top-down bureaucratic regulation.

Since social relationships and existing power structures are the backdrop for consensus-building, consensus-based solutions do not automatically lead to more appropriate or equitable results. The Andean cases show how the great majority of public investments in irrigation are made to benefit areas and stakeholders that are already well off and better organized. This also shows how public action and governmental institutions are not neutral. Above all, they seek the guarantee of being able to invest public monies in ways that will yield economic and political returns, and access to resources generally reflects the interests of the groups that can influence local and national rule-setting for distribution. Consequently, it is necessary for negotiation platforms to be based on processes of empowering groups with lesser capacity for representation, knowledge, and economic resources, so they can genuinely take part in watershed organizations, with their own proposals and greater decisionmaking power. Tacitly excluding them from negotiations would seem expedient for the other stakeholders, but often even for them it helps only in the short term, because exclusion arrangements generate, in the long run, more protests and social and economic losses, than those based on criteria of equity and relative sufficiency for all.

Last, but not least, water resources legislation must support this effort. An appropriate legal framework must be provided that will consider the social, productive, and economic functions of water. On the basis of public domain considerations, not private ownership, the state has the duty of regulating water supply for all societal sectors, with justice and preventing concentration of water in the hands of a few. In the national setting of multiple uses for water, it is fundamental to establish social, economic, and environmental priorities that guarantee livelihoods and food-supply security for all members of society.

Notes

1. This chapter is based on Boelens et al. (2002).

2. Hendriks (2002) elaborates how phase one of the Majes project involved developing 23,000 hectares under irrigation. Increasing the irrigation area is virtually impossible, since there are strong indications that the availability of water has reached its limit. The water requirements scheduled by the project were far too optimistic. Although the Majes project has resulted in a national scandal because of its outrageous costs, this type of project is certainly not exceptional to the Andean region.

3. For an overview of the debate, see Dourojeanni and Jouravlev (1999b) and Gentes (2002, 2003).

References

Bauer, C. 1997. Bringing water markets down to earth: The political economy of water rights in Chile, 1976–95. *World Development* 25 (5): 639–656.

———. 1998. Slippery property rights: Multiple water uses and the neoliberal model in Chile, 1981–95. *Natural Resources Journal* 38: 110–155.

Beccar, L., R. Boelens, and P. Hoogendam. 2002. Water rights and collective action in community irrigation. In *Water rights and empowerment,* eds. R. Boelens and P. Hoogendam. Assen, the Netherlands: Van Gorcum.

Benda-Beckmann, F. von. 1996. Citizens, strangers and indigenous peoples: Conceptual politics and legal pluralism. *Law and Anthropology* 9: 1–42.

Benda-Beckmann, F. von, K. von Benda-Beckmann, and J. Spiertz. 1998. Equity and legal pluralism: Taking customary law into account in natural resource policies. In *Searching for equity. Conceptions of justice and equity in peasant irrigation,* eds. R. Boelens and G. Dávila. Assen, the Netherlands: Van Gorcum.

Boelens, R. 2003. Local rights and legal recognition. The struggle for indigenous water rights and the cultural politics of participation. Paper presented at the Third World Water Forum, March 2003, Kyoto, Japan.

———. 2005. Rules, rights and resistance. Water rights and property creation as a local empowerment strategy of peasant and indigenous communities in the Ecuadorian Andes. *Law and Anthropology,* forthcoming.

Boelens, R., and G. Dávila, eds. 1998. *Searching for equity: Conceptions of justice and equity in peasant irrigation.* Assen, the Netherlands: Van Gorcum.

Boelens, R., and B. Doornbos. 2001. The battlefield of water rights. Rule making amidst conflicting normative frameworks in the Ecuadorian Highlands. *Human Organization* 60 (4): 343–355.

Boelens, R., and P. Hoogendam, eds. 2002. *Water rights and empowerment.* Assen, the Netherlands: Van Gorcum.

Boelens, R., and M. Zwarteveen. 2003a. The politics of Andean water policy reforms: Local and indigenous rights in the context of privatization policies. *Austrian Journal of Development Studies* 19 (4): 56–76.

———. 2003b. Water, gender and "Andeanity": Conflict or harmony? Gender dimensions of water rights in diverging regimes of representation. In *Imaging the Andes: Shifting margins of a marginal world,* eds. T. Salman and A. Zoomers. CEDLA Latin America Studies 91. Amsterdam: Aksant Publishers.

Boelens, R., A. Dourojeanni, A. Durán, and P. Hoogendam. 2002. Water rights and watersheds: Managing multiple water uses and strengthening stakeholder platforms. In *Water rights and empowerment,* eds. R. Boelens and P. Hoogendam. Assen, the Netherlands: Van Gorcum.

Bruns, B. R., and R. S. Meinzen-Dick, eds. 2000. *Negotiating water rights.* New Delhi: Vistaar Publications and London: Intermediate Technology Publications.

Bustamante, R. 2002. *Legislación del agua en Bolivia.* Working Paper WALIR/Water Law and Indigenous Rights. ECLAC/United Nations Economic Commission for Latin America and the Caribbean and Wageningen University. Cochabamba, Bolivia.

Castro, M. 2002. Local norms and competition for water in Aymara and Atacama communities, Northern Chile. In *Water rights and empowerment,* eds. R. Boelens and P. Hoogendam. Assen, the Netherlands: Van Gorcum.

Dourojeanni, A. 1997. *Dawn in the Andes,* ed. ECLAC/United Nations, Santiago, Chile.

———. 2000a. *Water allocation among competing uses with a basin perspective.* Paper presented at the Second World Water Forum, March 2000, The Hague, the Netherlands.

———. 2000b. *Procedimientos de gestión para el desarrollo sustentable.* ECLAC, United Nations, Santiago, Chile.

———. 2001. Desafíos para la gestión integrada de los recursos hídricos, In *Policy and institutions for integrated water resources management,* Carbondale, Ill.: International Water Resources Association.

Dourojeanni, A., and A. Jouravlev. 1999a. *Gestión de cuencas y ríos vinculados con centros urbanos,* LC/R.1948, ECLAC/United Nations, Santiago, Chile.

———. 1999b. El código de aguas en Chile: Entre la ideología y la realidad. *Serie Recursos Naturales e Infraestructura,* no. 3, ECLAC/United Nations, Santiago, Chile.

ECLAC (United Nations Economic Commission for Latin America and the Caribbean). 1988. *Gestión para el desarrollo de cuencas de alta montaña en la zona andina.* ECLAC/United Nations Economic Commission for Latin America and the Caribbean, Santiago, Chile.

———. 1992a. *Políticas de gestión integral de aguas y políticas económicas.* ECLAC/United Nations, Santiago, Chile.

———. 1992b. *Bases conceptuales para la formulación de programas de manejo de cuencas hidrográficas.* ECLAC/United Nations, Santiago, Chile.

———. 1998. *Ordenamiento político-institucional para la gestión del agua.* ECLAC/United Nations, Santiago, Chile.

Edmunds, D., and E. Wollenberg. 2001. A strategic approach to multistakeholder negotiations. *Development and Change* 32: 231–253.

Galárraga-Sánchez. 2000. *Informe Nacional sobre la gestión de los recursos hídricos.* Quito, Ecuador.

Gelles, P. 1998. Competing cultural logics: State and "indigenous" models in conflict. In *Searching for equity: Conceptions of justice and equity in peasant irrigation,* eds. R. Boelens and G. Dávila. Assen, the Netherlands: Van Gorcum.

———. 2002. *Andean culture, peasant communities, and indigenous identity.* Working Paper WALIR/ Water Law and Indigenous Rights. ECLAC/United Nations Economic Commission for Latin America and the Caribbean and Wageningen University. Riverside, California.

Gentes, I. 2002. *Estudio de la legislación oficial chilena y del derecho indígena a los recursos hídricos.* Working Paper WALIR/Water Law and Indigenous Rights. ECLAC/United Nations Economic Commission for Latin America and the Caribbean and Wageningen University. Santiago, Chile.

———. 2003. *Estudio sobre marcos normativos indígenas y consuetudinarios referente a la gestión del agua en Chile.* Working Paper WALIR/Water Law and Indigenous Rights. ECLAC/United

Nations Economic Commission for Latin America and the Caribbean and Wageningen University. Santiago, Chile.

Gerbrandy, G., and P. Hoogendam. 1998. *Aguas y acequias.* Cochabamba, Bolivia: PEIRAV/Plural Editores.

Guevara, A., I. Vera, P. Urteaga, and G. Zambrano. 2002. *Estudio de la legislación oficial peruana sobre la gestión indígena de los recursos hídricos.* Working Paper WALIR/Water Law and Indigenous Rights. ECLAC/United Nations Economic Commission for Latin America and the Caribbean and Wageningen University, Lima, Peru.

Hendriks, J. 1998. Water as private property: Notes on the case of Chile. In *Searching for equity: Conceptions of justice and equity in peasant irrigation,* eds. R. Boelens and G. Dávila. Assen, the Netherlands: Van Gorcum.

———. 2002. Water rights and strengthening users' organizations: The art of negotiating. In *Water rights and empowerment,* eds. R. Boelens and P. Hoogendam. Assen, the Netherlands: Van Gorcum.

Hendriks, J., R. Mejía, H. Olázaval, L. Cremers, M. Ooijevaar, and P. Palacios. 2003. *Análisis de la situación del riego en la República del Ecuador.* Mission Report, Consejo Nacional de Modernización—ATN/SF-7743-EC, Quito, Ecuador.

Hoogendam, P. 1995. Water rights: Interaction in a normative domain. Department of Irrigation and Water Engineering, Wageningen University. Photocopy.

———, ed. 1999. *Aguas y municipios. Retos para la gestión municipal del agua.* La Paz, Bolivia: PEIRAV/Plural Editores.

IMAR. 1997. *Plan maestro para la cuenca hidrográfica Chancay Lambayeque. Avances metodológicos.* Instituto de Apoyo al Manejo de Agua de Riego/IMAR Costa Norte, Chiclayo, Peru.

IPROGA. 1996. *Metodología para la elaboración de planes maestros de cuencas,* Instituto para la Promoción de la Gestion del Agua/IPROGA, Lima, Peru.

Manrique, N. 1985. *Colonialismo y pobreza campesina: Caylloma y el Valle del Colca siglos XVI–XX.* Lima, Peru: DESCO.

Mayer, E. 2002. *The articulated peasant. Household economies in the Andes.* Boulder, Colo.: Westview Press.

Meinzen-Dick, R., and M. Zwarteveen. 1998. Gendered participation in water management: Issues and illustrations from water users' associations in South Asia. *Agriculture and Human Values* 15: 337–345.

Meinzen-Dick, R., L. Brown, H. Feldstein, and A. Quisumbing. 1997. Gender, property rights and natural resources. *World Development* 25 (8): 1303–1316.

Moreyra, A. 2001. The emergence and functioning of multiple stakeholder platforms for watershed management in Latin America. Working Paper of the Collaborative Work Program.

Department of Irrigation and Water Engineering, Wageningen University and World Bank, Wageningen/Washington.

Schlager, E., and E. Ostrom. 1992. Property-rights regimes and natural resources: A conceptual analysis. *Land Economics* 68 (3): 249–262.

Solanes, M., and F. González-Villareal. 1999. The Dublin principles for water as reflected in a comparative assessment of institutional and legal arrangements for integrated water resources management. TAC Background Paper 3. Stockholm: Global Water Partnership.

Steins, N. A., and V. M. Edwards. 1999. Platforms for collective action in multiple-use common-pool resources, *Agriculture and Human Values* 16: 241–255.

Tipton, J. 1988. Institutional factors influencing public sector decisionmaking on the management of Andean river basins. In *Management for the development of high-mountain river basins in the Andean region.* Santiago, Chile: ECLAC, United Nations.

Toledo, A. 1999. *Diagnóstico de la legislación y las políticas de gestión del agua al nivel de las cuencas hidrográficas en el Perú.* Photocopy. Lima, Peru: SNV.

Vidal, A. 1990. Derecho oficial y derecho campesino en el mundo andino. In *Entre la ley y la costumbre,* eds. R. Stavenhagen and D. Iturralde. Mexico City: Instituto Interamericano de Derechos Humanos.

Vincent, L. 1996. Communities and catchments: Perspectives on intersectoral water management and use at different scales. In *Strategies for intersectoral water management in developing countries: Challenges and consequences for agriculture,* eds. J. Richter, P. Wolff, H. Franzen, and F. Heim. Feldafing, Germany: DSE.

Whitaker, M. D. 1992. *El rol de la agricultura en el desarrollo económico del Ecuador.* Quito, Ecuador: IDEA.

Zwarteveen, M. 1997. Water: From basic need to commodity: A discussion on gender and water rights in the context of irrigation. *World Development* 28 (8): 1335–1349.

Part 4

New Water Laws: Assessing Implications

Chapter 9

Analysis of Spanish Water Law Reform

Alberto Garrido

— Spain's 1999 Water Law attempts to overcome many of the challenges in Spanish water resources management, including reallocation, environmental impacts, and financing needs. This chapter analyzes potential implications of the law, particularly for water rights transfers, and the planning and construction of hydraulic works. Issues that may affect the development of water rights trading and water markets include restrictions on transfers between rights with different priorities, determination of amounts of water eligible for transfer, and potential for water banking. While the water law introduces new provisions regarding environmental protection and financing of hydraulic infrastructure, further changes will be needed to address the objectives established by the Water Framework Directive of the European Union.

Only 14 years transpired between the passage of the water law in 1985 and its amendment in 1999. This is a short period, considering that the previous water law dated back to 1879. The 1999 Water Law alluded to the problems Spain has to solve regarding water policy management in an attempt to overcome them in the near future. This in itself is a sign of certain weaknesses in the text of the 1985 Law. The new law appears to make three specific diagnoses of the water situation in Spain.

First, although water could be used more efficiently, the 1985 Law failed to encourage entitlement holders to do so. Water authorities would not venture into water rights reallocation, disregarding the ample room granted through article 55 of the old law. The excessive rigidity of the entitlement system made it almost impossible to introduce changes in the use of water, since a new entitlement could be requested only when another one expired. Thus, the new text supports the thesis that rents and welfare were being lost due to law that lags behind market forces.

Second, the 1985 Law was not very successful in environmental matters. There are large rivers with no life in the riverbeds, and many reservoirs with medium or high levels of eutrophication. There is also evidence that the timid fiscal measures regarding the environment have been a complete failure, and there has been little enforcement of the law concerning the discharge of effluents.

The third problem was the incapacity to finance construction of hydraulic works without burdening state budgets, or increasing public debt beyond the figure established by the economic-financial system of the 1985 Law. This system had decreased the financial costs borne by the beneficiaries of the water works. The new law hands over the construction and management aspects of hydraulic works to the new public water companies, three at least having already been established. These companies are also responsible for the collection of taxes and rates from their users.

The precepts of the 1999 Law regulate a range of matters:

- to make the entitlement system more flexible so as to increase water use efficiency;
- to further the regulation of reuse and desalination;
- to achieve measurement of consumption levels of all water users;
- to promote coordination between different sectoral policies and government bodies;
- to tighten control measures regarding waste and improve water quality;
- to regulate and redefine hydraulic works and explore new management and financing models; and
- to foster the performance and responsibility of user associations in matters of water management, and reinforce cooperation with the government agencies.

The 1999 Law was later consolidated into Law 62 of December 20, 2003, which modified the Revised Text of the Water Law passed by Executive Order 1/2001 of July 20, 2001. It also incorporates the European Parliament and Commission Directive 2000/60/EC of October 23, 2000, which establishes a community framework for action in the area of water, in short the Water Framework Directive (WFD) (European Union 2000). Law 62 of 2003 is the legal text in force, and article citations in this chapter refer to the 2003 Law. However, the reforms of the 1999 Law were entirely maintained in the consolidation. Therefore, this chapter refers to the 1999 reform, as this enacted the major changes with respect to the 1985 Law, on which this chapter will focus.

The second section analyzes several provisions in the law that regulate water rights transfers. The third section then discusses some implications for the development of hydraulic infrastructure, including finance, environmental impacts, and coordination. The fourth section outlines other significant aspects of the new law, including management transfer, measurement, and desalination. The concluding section summarizes the main results from the analysis.

Water Transfers

The new law introduces various precepts aimed at improving the economic efficiency of water use. Articles 67 through 72 regulate water rights transfer contracts, and deserve detailed analysis. We analyze only those that clearly intend to modify the future water market from a political and social stance.

Transfers between Priorities

Article 67 states that only entitlement holders can enter into contracts and that the water buyer must be of similar or greater priority than the water seller. Let us consider an entrepreneur who wishes to set up an industry to transform agricultural products. In a region or basin lacking in water resources, an entrepreneur has few options to acquire the volume of water for the production process, so it is unlikely that the entrepreneur will be able to obtain an entitlement. Furthermore, the law prevents reaching an agreement with an irrigator for an entitlement transfer contract, because this would violate the precept that states that all transfers should respect the order of priority established in article 60 or by the Water Board Plan. Large consumption industries that are not linked to urban networks are of lower priority than agricultural uses. This situation reduces the possibilities for improving efficiency of water uses.

The restriction on transfers from senior to junior rights-holders also poses other problems. Using experimental economics data collected in a laboratory setting, Garrido and Rassenti (2003) found that senior users are better off if they can sell water to junior ones. Restricting this kind of trade harms senior users without making junior ones better off. In addition, the restricted market favors lower reservoir levels than would be the case with an unrestricted market. A liberalized environment, in which all subjects freely trade among themselves, increases water prices and expands the consumption of senior users at the cost of junior users, who are compensated by higher sale prices. A liberalized environment would also make continuous accounting (carrying over unused water between years) especially useful for larger seniors' consumption and benefits, and would result in higher reservoir levels. Such a market institution would provide more efficient allocation across sectors and periods. Thus, the new law still restricts transfers in ways that impair the welfare of the holders of both senior and junior rights.

Transparency in Exchange Procedures

Article 68 seeks to enhance the transparency in exchanges by requiring that exchanges be requested in writing and sent to the corresponding water authority. The request must be sent to the user associations to which both parties in the exchange may belong. Once the request has been made, the corresponding water authority may reject it within one of two time periods, either one month, if the exchange is between users of the same association, or two months for other cases.

Within this time limit, the water authority must carry out the important task of verifying whether third parties or the public in general will be affected and make sure that a water seller transfers a volume to which they hold transferable rights. The Ministry of Agriculture and the autonomous communities (as regions are called in the Spanish constitution of 1978) are urged to present a preliminary report within ten days. However, the article does not state whether this is binding. It is difficult to establish whether these time periods are sufficient. However, experience in recent years has shown that the public hydraulic domain has not been particularly well looked after by the authority that holds responsibility for doing so (Embid Irujo 2000; Garrido 2000), which raises questions about how well these responsibilities for reviewing proposed transactions will be executed.

This provision also poses issues in relation to the argument repeatedly maintained by agrarian officials to defend social interests linked to irrigated areas, who state that irrigated areas secure population levels in fringe zones and generate wealth that otherwise would not be assured. Given this social benefit it would seem contradictory to allow an irrigator to transfer all or part of his water supply, driven by strictly private calculations. His function as an irrigator supposedly entails more than production activities or generation of income in order to support other social benefits. If the corresponding agrarian authority were to extend an unfavorable report on a transfer request based on this argument, then it would be up to the president of the water authority to decide whether or not to grant the request.

To prevent damage to rural economies, other countries have imposed limits on the water volumes that can be reallocated from irrigators and it is surprising that this has not been done in Spain. For instance, water sales out of the irrigation sector are limited in California and similar restrictions were proposed in the Province of Alberta, Canada (Easter, Rosegrant, and Dinar 1998).

Transferable Quantities from Water Savings

Article 68, in point 2, states that if a seller is an irrigator, then the land that he will no longer water, or will irrigate with a smaller volume of water, must be put on record. A water seller will be able to transfer only the volume resulting from a productive strategy requiring less water than the seller's corresponding quota for that particular year. Let us take another likely example in which there is a moderate drought situation in a water basin area and the irrigators do not have access to the corresponding volume of water that they would have in normal years. If in a normal year the irrigator receives 6,500 m^3 of water per hectare then in a year of drought the quota might be established at 4,500 m^3. In that case, the volume of water eligible for transfer would correspond only to the amount saved by changing the crops that would be grown with 4,500 m^3, for example to consume only 2,000 m^3 and transfer 2,500 m^3 to a water buyer.

If the saving in water is due to technical changes in the irrigation system of the land then it may be more difficult to quantify the exact volume of water the irrigator is releasing for transfer. It may also be difficult for the water authority to verify this, let alone supervise and monitor the situation. The market will have an effect only in such circumstances as water shortages or moderate drought, since in years of abundance there will be no need for entitlement holders to seek additional water. It is for these years that it is hoped the market will improve economic efficiency, but to realize these benefits, the amounts available for transfer because of savings need to be clearly defined.

Government Acquisition

The third point of article 68 contemplates the motives for denial of a request for transfer rights. It states that the authorities may exercise, in the stated time period, their right to preferential acquisition of water volumes that are the object of exchange. This is convenient because

- transfers at fictitiously low prices may be prevented;
- it provides a mechanism for the water authorities to obtain supplies for the ends and purposes they deem necessary; and
- it grants flexibility to the water authorities to manage hydrological resources.

If the authority needs water volumes, for whatever purpose, then it may interrupt the agreement process between the interested parties and in this way avoid the need for separate expropriation proceedings. However, if the water authority does this too often, then the users will think that the time they devote to examining and negotiating agreements and obtaining information on the necessary requirements is in vain, thus discouraging the process of reallocation among users.

Surplus Water Volumes

Article 69 establishes that users may hand over the rights only to the supply or volume of water really used, or, if necessary, as corrected according to the best practice criteria established by the Water Board Plan. From an economic aspect, this has negative effects. It prevents an irrigator from handing over surplus water volumes, probably as a result of having an old and overgenerous license. Furthermore, this may deter many irrigators with generous quotas from offering part of their entitlement to other water buyers. An immediate source of improvement would arise if these irrigators decrease the amount of water they use in order to offer the rest to other parties. The question is whether they should be financially rewarded for being careful with an already scarce resource. Lack of such an incentive is likely to mean that less water is saved and less water is made available for transfer.

Reference Quotas

Certain signs in the new law show the aim of the legislature is to encourage more efficient use of water. Point 6 of article 114 introduces the idea of reference quotas. Rates or taxes may be multiplied by a factor oscillating between 2 and 0.5 when the consumption of a water rights-holder is respectively greater or lower than the reference quota established by the water basin hydrological plan or by the regulations of the respective sector planning body. This attempt is praiseworthy, but given the small number of payments resulting from the application of the economic financial system to irrigated areas already in operation, it is unlikely it will have much impact on water uses in such areas. The reference quotas will logically take into account the natural and technical conditions and the consumption levels of the usual crops in each area. Therefore, it can be expected that the real consumption levels will not deviate much from the reference quotas. It is thus unlikely that this readjustment of taxes will introduce important changes in the use of water, particularly in the matter of irrigated areas. However, this is a sign that the government has taken a stake in stimulating a pattern of uses according to the reasoned needs for each area and activity. At the same time, expressing disagreement with the bad use of water by penalizing the user with even a small fine is of considerable significance.

Price Ceilings

Article 69 states that the agreed price is free of restrictions but adds that, according to regulation, maximum amounts may be established. Variation in prices may be attributable to many causes, but this is not necessarily a bad thing. If there was evidence of abusive behavior, monopolistic practice, or extortion, then the water authority should prevent the transaction from taking place, resorting to antitrust legislation. Price ceilings can also be evaded. If the water seller demands a compensation amount that exceeds the established level and the water buyer accepts it, then they may find a subterfuge in order to avoid the "maximum amount established by regulation." Nevertheless, such complications would increase transaction costs. Therefore the imposition of price ceilings may act to reduce the efficiency of water transfers, without yielding corresponding benefits.

Rights over the Transferred Volume

The second point of Article 69 states that the transferred volume should be used effectively and adds that the transfer does not imply expiry of the entitlement. The lack of such a clause could arouse suspicion among potential water sellers. However, there may be a slight potential for friction between this point and article 67, which states that the water buyer must be of similar or greater priority than the water seller. Let us consider the case in which an irrigator could challenge an entitlement transfer from an industrial water rights-holder to an urban one. If the farmer can prove that he does not have enough water to irrigate his land, then by law he would be entitled to use the surplus volume. In a situation like this, the authorities would have few legal arguments for denying the irrigator's claim to the resources of which the industrial entitlement holder apparently has "too much." This shows another way in which the priority system may affect the potential for transfers, despite the attempt in this case to confirm the continuity in entitlement.

Water Banks

Article 71 outlines the idea of creating water banks or exchange centers for water rights. The water authorities may create such initiatives by way of agreements with the Council of Ministers, as long as a severe drought prevails, aquifers are overexploited, or the need to regulate uses and resources is taken into consideration. The purpose of this initiative is for the water authority to be able to launch a bid for the acquisition of water rights and then offer them according to the price it establishes. The same point sets out that hydrological and accounting or financial operations incurred by such initiatives should be registered separately from those of a different nature. This law may make it possible for the water authorities to carry out water banking aimed at releasing volumes of water that entitlement holders volunteer for transfer. The authority will then be able to make these volumes available for those parties who are able and willing to pay the price. This option requires a degree of audacity and determination on behalf of the water authority and a considerable number of preliminary studies. (The famous water bank that came into being in 1991 in California began its conception in 1974.) It could reap remarkable benefits for a water basin area that is in a moderately critical situation. In addition, Gomez Ramos and Garrido (2004) show that, in many cases, transferring the option to use water under particular circumstances (such as drought) would be valuable to further increase intertemporal economic efficiency.

In this transfer of resources, it may not be possible to identify who is transferring water to whom. The transaction will be similar to that of a financial market in which, from the buyer's point of view, the identity of the seller is irrelevant and vice versa. Furthermore, the water authority will be in a position to allocate the water volumes according to general interest, or to the regulations and rates for water use, in order to partly compensate the government for the financial cost of the works carried out and cover their running and maintenance costs. However, only those water authorities that have an expert information system in real time would be able to manage their basin areas properly and transfer water rights accordingly. If a water authority creates a water exchange center, it would be able to obtain quantities of water, and offer them at the preestablished price, resolving some of the difficulties that otherwise might impede transfers. Thus, water banking could reduce risks and overcome the obstacle of order of priority that may obstruct bilateral transfer contracts between entitlement holders.

Transfers in Time

The approach chosen by the legislature, aimed at facilitating the exchanges of entitlements between rights-holders, makes it possible to improve the economic efficiency at least in space, but not in time. An improvement in space takes place when exchanges occur that allow scarce resources to be used by those parties that value them most, or that can generate most profit from them. However, this possibility does not create clear incentives to moderate use before the drought cycle reaches its worst moments. The chosen option makes it possible to resolve a problem of scarcity, produced under certain specific circumstances, but does not contribute optimally to relieving its intensity or decreasing its damage.

An element that has been maintained after the water reform is the notion that any unit left in the reservoir on a season's termination is considered common property. This is what is called discontinuous accounting, or the "use-it-or-lose-it" doctrine. All users are thus encouraged to use or sell the water to which they are entitled before the season is over. In practice, this implies that no water rights can be claimed over saved units beyond a season, either intentionally or unintentionally. While not explicitly forbidden in the law, there is no guarantee over the rights associated with the units kept in the reservoir. This removes any incentive to save water in abundant seasons in order to have it available for sale or use during drought ones.

An improvement in efficiency in time occurs when the parties currently holding entitlements and available water anticipate future periods of drought or scarcity and decide to ration their use of water so as to have some available in the future. The new law completely ignores the creation of water banks that allow a certain degree of speculation, so that those parties holding rights can defer the consumption of part of the water to which they are entitled, in order to use it or sell it in the following period. Water entitlements in Spain do not respect the possibility that irrigators may decide not to use their water rights in the current season and to do so in the next one. If the new law aims at improving the economic efficiency of the use of water in periods of drought, then the purpose of the water banks should be to reduce the probability and intensity of droughts, through making it possible to accumulate water by deferring its consumption.

The new law goes into great detail regarding aspects that regulate transfer contracts but is very sparse regarding the basic precepts that should regulate water banks, or "exchange centers" as the law calls them, for water exchanges in time before periods of drought. This is a serious defect, because exchange centers offer greater possibilities than transfer contracts for mobilizing resources and minimizing environmental risks and damage to third parties.

Findings from Experimental Economics

Garrido and Rassenti (2003), based on their experimental economics results, formulated a few conclusions related to designing principles for water markets in Spain. In general terms, the 1999 water sector reform in Spain represents a timid step to let markets dictate the allocation of scarce water resources. However, the reform is based on exactly the same definition of water rights and priorities that existed before the 1999 water law amendment. Two critical elements are still present in the way water rights are defined in Spain.

First, the complex and detailed system of priorities in which senior users have preferential access to scarce resources over junior ones has been kept in place in the 1999 reform. With these provisions, legislators intended to protect urban consumers, placed at the top of the priority system, and reduce their exposure to drought periods. This has two major implications for market functioning: first, senior users will receive a biased and larger proportion of the resources that natural supply makes available, and second, senior users will not be allowed to sell water to junior ones. The second element that has been perpetuated is the inability to carry over water into a subsequent year, which reduces incentives for conservation and storage.

Based on the findings from an experimental economics laboratory study, Garrido and Rassenti (2003) identified two policy implications. First, they found that incentives to reserve water when it is abundant in order to have it available during shortages are needed to reduce society's vulnerability to droughts. This implies that rights-holders must be allowed to trade (speculate) with water savings, the drawback being that society may abhor such practices, especially during extreme drought circumstances. Second, a water sector reform that implements trading strategies for the first time requires that water rights definition also be amended. For instance, priority mechanisms and other market restrictions may hurt the group of users that market regulations are trying to protect, and should be adjusted.

Analysis of the likely implications of various provisions of the law, supported by laboratory findings from experimental economics, indicates that while the new water law does allow transfers, the potential for voluntary water transfers and development of water markets is still restricted in many ways. This offers a basis for considering revisions to the law and its implementation that would more effectively achieve the objectives of the law, with increased benefits for water users and society.

Hydraulic Works

Coordination and Impact Assessment

The main objective of article 128, and the following ones, is to coordinate the planning of hydraulic works (and other actions in the public water domain) with the autonomous and local governments and with other ministries. This will reinforce the reciprocal commitment to coordinate all actions and plans affecting various fields, such as town and country planning, or development of nonhydraulic infrastructure.

The new law explicitly requires compulsory studies on the environmental impact for hydraulic works projects of general interest. The new text also redefines the procedure for declaration of general interest. This should bear the implicit approval of public utility as well as stating as in point 130.4 that, if "hydraulic works of general interest affect the socio-economic equilibrium of the municipality where they are located, a territorial restitution project will be drawn up and carried out so as to compensate for the said problem." What is not explicitly indicated is exactly which authority or governing body is expected to take on such a commitment and how it will be financed.

Works of general interest should not interfere with environmental requirements, should be projected and planned in coordination with the involved authorities, and should be coherent with any sectoral plans of the economy, especially in matters of irrigated land. There should be a proposal for the financing of such works and a study should be carried out on the taxes and rates to be charged to the beneficiaries. The Ministry of Economy and Finance should be informed accordingly. The references to coordination at sector level and between authorities are notable and should be valued accordingly. Such coordination concerns all actions or plans carried out by water authorities or by other governing bodies, where there may be competitive friction or reciprocal problems.

This examination of the new law is necessarily focused on considering how it might be put into practice. The law hardly changes the structure of the hydraulic authorities in comparison with the initial structure introduced in the 1985 text. Nevertheless, it does stress, on several occasions, the need for coordination between the various authorities and sectoral plans of the economy, and town and country planning. Thus, it is likely that future actions in water matters will be more coherent and be better interwoven with other public actions.

The problems most difficult to solve, such as environmental deterioration of the public domain and water contamination, are tackled by the new law with measures that reinforce control and tighten up sanctions for practices that damage the natural environment. However, all this will be in vain unless the water authorities apply the law in a rigorous way. The basin authorities are autonomous entities that, with regard to water, are an interested party. They regulate uses, monitor and protect the public domain, and at the same time are the only party fully aware of the real environmental state of the basins. Thus, it is difficult to expect them to carry out forceful actions in favor of the quality of the environment if this were to go against the interests of water rights-holders and only benefit society at large, via provision of public goods that are less tangible than rights-holders' benefits.

Some countries have created agencies for the protection of the environment, such as the United States, Sweden, or the United Kingdom, granting them the same independence from the executive power that other regulating bodies of the economy enjoy. In this way, the actions of these agencies in favor of the environment, or rather of the fulfillment of the environmental regulations, are independent from the authorities carrying out actions that could cause possible damage to the environment. In Spain, this independence is not possible because of the way in which the attributes of the basin authorities are defined. In short, we cannot expect substantial environmental benefits from the new law. Much more can be expected from the enforcement of the WFD and the strict surveillance that European Union's institutions perform on EU member states.

Significance for Civil Works Construction

Evaluation of the significance of the new law for construction of civil works must wait until the National Hydrological Plan presents a new project. The new law seems to tighten the criteria that projected hydraulic works should fulfill to obtain approval. Projects for new works should show ex ante that they will have no notable impacts on the environment, and that they will be financed by a plan that does not allow for unforeseen deviations from the public expenditure nor debt. However, the creation of public companies to take over the construction or management of hydraulic infrastructures is based only on the general assumption that a company would do better than the hydraulic authority. The latter is not very efficient in the management of its works or in the collection of its rates. Other advantages, such as projects being better constructed or applied technologies being more advanced, may be nonexistent because the same consulting agencies and construction companies will design the projects and build the works, whatever the purpose or ownership of the works under the project.

Finance

In water basin areas belonging to more than one autonomous community, the responsibility of collecting charges and rates as well as the effluent discharge tax is transferred to the National Tax Agency. The corresponding water authorities sign an agreement with the National Tax Agency for this purpose. This should be interpreted as implicit recognition that, first, the water authorities have not been very successful in collecting charges, taxes, or rates, and second, they should orient their resources to carrying out more important tasks of water management. They should leave tax collection responsibilities to the authority that has the best available means of doing so.

The new law still disregards the problems and omissions of an economic–financial system that has become obsolete. The law reduces its objectives to recovering part of the construction costs of the works as well as their operation and conservation costs. The minor changes in the economic–financial aspects introduced by the new law are no more than a mere prelude to what Water Framework Directive will bring about in many areas, particularly regarding rates for water use and cost recovery objectives. The approval of the EU Water Policy Framework Directive in 2000 (European Union 2000) for water policies has exonerated the legislature from assuming the political and social cost of modernizing an obsolete and paternalistic economic–financial system. The WFD must be enforced by all European member states (EU-25), including ambitious water pricing and environmental objectives. The legislature is leaving the increase in the cost of water for users to come into force with the future application of the Directive in Spain. This could be considered an example of good political judgment since this is a very unpopular policy in Spanish agriculture.

However, the transition period established for European regulations to come into full force is rather long. This means a considerable delay before the new directive is applied in Spain and the economic–financial system is modernized, an aspect that is necessary for better overall management of water basins and resources. Livingston and Garrido (2004) argue that tariffs are less important than institutions, because water resources are highly complex and very prone to all sources of externalities.

The poor state of Spain's basins and their deterioration is partly attributable to the water authorities' lack of human, material, and economic resources with which to take on all the functions that the legislation confers to them. The draft of the Water White Paper devoted considerable detail to this same diagnosis (Ministerio de Medio Ambiente 1998). For example, there is a certain paradox in the fact that the Regional Government of Madrid suggests that the customers of the Canal de Isabel II water company should be charged an environmental tax in order to finance the costs of restoring the environmental quality of the rivers, riverbeds, and riverbanks of the regional territory, since this task should really be carried out by the Hydrographic Confederation of the Tajo River. The budgets that the basin authorities have available for environmental improvements are meager or practically nonexistent, since the current financial system only contemplates costs related to financing or operating works, and the experience of collecting waste taxes is very unsatisfactory, which is not adequately resolved by the new water law.

Other Topics: Management Transfer, Measurement, and Desalination

Management Transfer

The new law foresees the possibility that user associations, whether they be communities or central boards, take on the responsibility for operation and maintenance of their hydraulic works. A formal proposal on behalf of the water authority and of the Ministry of the Environment is required in order to carry this out, as well as drawing up and signing an agreement defining the management and, more importantly, the economic–financial aspects. The government could exploit this option so that users will be prepared to take on the responsibility for the technical and economic management of infrastructure specifically linked with the use of water for each defined user group.

This option for management transfer, which has hardly been discussed in debates and discussion groups in Spain, constitutes a priority program in many countries with large areas of irrigable land. Depending on the country, it has been developed according to different legal formulas. For example, in the case of New Zealand all infrastructure has been privatized. In Mexico, the responsibility of all the important irrigation projects has been transferred to the irrigator communities with considerable success. The experiences that have been documented do have one common conclusion: users do not want to take on the management of the more deteriorated infrastructure unless a considerable budget is allocated for their repair and modernization, whereas well conserved infrastructures are usually transferred without any difficulty.

Measurement

The water rights transfer contracts and the exchange centers defined in articles 67–71 will constitute technical challenges. The possibility of increasing or reducing the available water volumes by way of these techniques requires greater rigor in matters of the measurement and control of uses. In the Spanish water basins in which there is more responsibility regarding water, the return flows generated by one user feed the available supply for another located downstream from the first. Therefore, any change produced in the level of use upstream, whether as a result of an entitlement transfer contract or of improvement in the technical efficiency of a water rights-holder, may alter the available volumes for third parties or affect the public domain. The water authorities will need to control the levels of use in detail, identifying the specific place and time in which they take place and updating their records and expert systems with any changes that occur between water entitlement holders, and between these parties and the water basin authority.

A positive aspect of the new law that has passed more or less unnoticed is the clear intention of the law to promote the control and measurement of water consumption levels. The compulsory requirement to obtain an entitlement shows that the legislature recognizes the importance of the returns generated in each use process. The law establishes the need to distinguish between the water volumes that enter a production process, the real amounts consumed, and the difference between these, as a subproduct of recognized economic value that needs to be regulated and protected.

The best way to be able to value something is to be able to count it. Compulsory measurement is a substantial step toward manifesting, in an effective and rigorous way, what all the studies guess at, but cannot demonstrate with exact figures; namely, that the use of water is very inefficient in a notable proportion of the total consumption of water in Spain. The measurement of consumption levels, added to the slight effect of increasing or decreasing coefficients of taxes and rates according to upward or downward deviations of real consumption levels from preferred levels, as well as transfer contracts and exchange centers, are three positive aspects of the new law. Such aspects contribute to the essential objective of defining uses and rights, of appreciating the value of water, and of changing the popular notion that resources are inexhaustible.

Desalination and Reuse

The law recognizes the freedom to install seawater desalination plants, as long as the necessary authorization is obtained regarding effluent discharge and occupation of land or coastlines. The desalted waters that are integrated into the public hydraulic domain will be regulated in the same way as other waters. The reuse of waters resulting from an exploitation process such as desalination requires a legal entitlement. The law authorizes contracts between the holder of an effluent discharge license and another party that obtains an entitlement to reuse the waters. In this way, purified or reclaimed waters gain importance.

Conclusions

The new law aims to improve the economy and environmental quality of water, promote hydraulic works with sounder finance, foster coordination between the various governmental departments and different authorities, and further the participation of user associations in management tasks and operation of infrastructures, as well as in the planning of resources. Table 9.1 summarizes a number of outstanding issues and evaluates the main weaknesses and strengths of the 1985 Law, the 1999 Law amendment, and the European Union's Water Framework Directive.

The attempt to make the water rights regime more flexible to improve efficiency and rationality of water use is praiseworthy. However, the way in which it has been carried out has technical defects. Chief among these are that only holders of an entitlement can participate in a water rights transfer contract; transfers should be necessarily made according to the order of priority; and the nature of the rights has not been modified to clarify exactly what can be exchanged and thus facilitate the transparency of the process. While transfers under the law allow spatial shifts in use, the inability to carry over unused water inhibits adjustments in time of use, failing to realize the full potential for conservation and storage to reduce shortages and increase the productivity of water.

In matters of coordination of policies, actions, and authorities, the law offers interesting pillars on which to construct a coherent hydraulic policy with a more environmental and less agrarian future. It is risky to venture any hypothesis as to

Table 9.1 Comparison of the 1985 law, 1999 amendment, and EU Water Framework Directive

Identified problem	1985 Law	1999 Amendment	EU WFD
Economic/allocation efficiency	• Rigid rights system • Large governmental role • Poor intertemporal allocation	• Timid liberalization • Foresees the role of water banks • Maintains exact 1985 rights definition • Unreasonable expectations for water markets	• Left to the member states' own policies and institutions
Environmental deterioration	• Very poor performance • Clear deterioration	• More relevant role to environmental reports • No substantial change from 1985	• Strong emphasis on targets and enforcement • Spain accountable to EU institutions on performance
Finance	• Strong reliance on subsidies • Poor cost recovery rates	• Little changes from 1985	• Mandatory implementation of full cost recovery prices and polluter-pays principle • Spain accountable to EU institutions
Institutional framework	• Well established • Legitimate	• Little change from 1985 • Promotes "water corporations" for new projects	• Mandatory public participation • Not too different from Spanish water boards
New water technologies: desalinization and water reutilization	• Clearly obsolete • Almost complete disregard	• New provisions • New rights over reused water • Regulation for desalinized water	• Left to the member states' own policies and institutions
Hydro works and infrastructure	• Obsolete definition • Government-led policies	• Complete redefinition • Sounder project finance • Stricter environmental evaluation	• Strict environmental evaluation and decision processes • Mandatory economic and financial evaluation • Emphasis on projects for water quality restoration
Policy coordination: national, regional, and municipal governments	• Poor/inadequate	• New provisions enhancing deeper coordination	• Left to the member states' own policies and institutions

Source: Author's elaboration.

possible improvements in the environment, without considering the determination of the water authorities to apply the law to matters such as effluent discharge and control and monitoring of the public hydraulic domain, especially those authorities that administer water basins in a permanent state of stress as with regard to water resources.

The new law contemplates mechanisms that, if administered well, can complete the work of the authorities and generate valuable data to provide information on their planning tasks. It offers opportunities for the users to reveal the essential uses for which resources should be made available, at a reasonable cost, and those that are redundant and could be well used to foster alternative uses, contribute to the increase in strategic reserves, and improve the environment.

References

Easter, K. W., M. W. Rosegrant, and A. Dinar, eds. 1998. *Markets for water: Potential and performance.* New York: Kluwer.

Embid Irujo, A. 2000. *La reforma de la Ley de Aguas (Ley 46/1999 de 13 de diciembre).* Madrid: Civitas.

European Union. 2000. Directive 2000/60/EC of the European Parliament and of the Council establishing a framework for community action in the field of water policy. *Official Journal (OJ L 327)* December 22, 2000.

Garrido, A. 2000. La reforma de la Ley de Aguas. *Iuris* 39 (May): 44–51.

Garrido, A., and S. Rassenti. 2003. Water markets design and experimental economics evidence. Paper presented at the 12th Annual Conference of the European Association of Environmental and Resource Economists, June 28–30, 2003, Bilbao, Spain.

Gómez Ramos, A., and A. Garrido. 2004. Formal risk-sharing mechanisms to allocate uncertain water resources: The case of option contracts. *Water Resources Research* 40: W12302.doi:10.1029/2004ER003340.

Livingston, M. L., and A. Garrido. 2004. Entering the policy debate: An economic evaluation of groundwater policy in flux. *Water Resources Research* 40: WS12502.doi:10.1029/2003WR002737.

Ministerio de Medio Ambiente. 1998. El libro blanco del agua. Madrid.

Chapter 10

Development of Water Rights in Indonesia

Suharto Sarwan, Tjoek Walujo Subijanto, and Charles Rodgers

— One objective of Indonesia's 2004 Water Law is to establish a uniform system of water use rights. The law distinguishes between water usage for basic needs and noncommercial purposes, including domestic uses and small-scale "people's" agriculture; and exploitation, including industrial, municipal, hydropower, and commercial agriculture. The former uses are entitlements requiring no formal permit, and the latter require formal licensing for specific uses of water. This chapter outlines the legal and conceptual framework for water use rights in Indonesia; describes key aspects of rights enacted in the new water law, including differences between usage and exploitation rights and prohibition of transfers of water use rights; presents an illustrative example of water allocation management in the Brantas Basin; and then looks at water use rights as property rights and human rights.

Recent social and economic developments in Indonesia have induced a paradigm shift in water resources management. Historically regarded as a social good, water has been transformed into an economic good with a social and environmental function. These developments have also affected the roles and management strategies of the law concerning water: from provider toward enabler, from centralized toward decentralized authority, from single purpose toward a multisector approach, and from narrow toward broader stakeholder participation (DGWR 2003).

Table 10.1 Indonesian total availability of surface water and groundwater

Island(s)	Area (million km²)	Population (million)	Water potential (MCM/yr)	Water demand (MCM/yr)	Water potential: Per km² (MCM/yr)	Water potential: Per capita (1,000 m³/yr)
Java	0.133	121.4	187,000	83,378	1.411	1.54
Lesser Sunda Islands	0.071	11.1	60,000	13,827	0.839	5.40
Sulawesi	0.186	15.0	247,000	25,555	1.327	16.53
Sumatra	0.475	43.3	738,000	25,298	1.553	17.04
Borneo	0.536	11.3	1,008,000	8,204	1.881	88.96
Mollucas + Papua	0.493	4.2	981,000	589	1.991	232.93
Indonesia	1.894	206.3	3,221,000	156,850	1.700	15.62

Source: Machbub (2000); WRI (2003).

Adequacy of water availability, both in quantity and in quality, greatly influences many aspects of social well-being and prosperity, including health, food security, industrial development, and environmental sustainability. Industrialization and population growth in Indonesia have caused significant impacts, and place increasing pressure on available water resources, which leads to further competition between beneficiaries and between uses. Industrialization and population growth have also caused declines in water quality and decreases in dependable flow as a result of the degradation of catchment areas. These pressures are responsible for a relative decrease in water availability over time, leading ultimately to water scarcity.

Indonesia is a tropical archipelago of more than 17,500 islands, with a total land area of 19.2 million square kilometers. Rainfall variability reflects the extreme geographical diversity, which is further reflected in surface and groundwater potentials (LRI 1990; WRI 2003). Table 10.1 summarizes statistics on Indonesia's water resources situation. World average water availability is close to 7,600 cubic meters per capita; Asia has the smallest continental average at 4,000. Indonesia as a whole has 15,600 cubic meters per person but this masks great differences within the archipelago (Machbub 2000; WRI 2003). Java, which contains 121 million of Indonesia's 206 million inhabitants, has the lowest availability, 1,500 cubic meters per capita, extremely low relative to West Papua and the Mollucas at 233,000.

The extent of water scarcity in Indonesia can be appreciated by considering the ratio of potential water availability to demand. It is predicted that by the year 2015, on some islands, this ratio will be less than one during many periods. A study conducted by the Ministry of Public Works and the Ministry of Forestry in 1995 identified a number of critical basins, including Cisedane, Ciliwung, Citarum, Cimanuk, Citanduy, Jratunseluna, Bengawan Solo, and Brantas. In these basins, the water use potential index, the ratio of demand to dependable flow generally equals or exceeds 0.5.

Water resources are a national resource that must be managed wisely and sustainably to secure the greatest benefit for the welfare of existing and future generations. However, water scarcity has the potential to create conflict among beneficiaries and between communities of users. Therefore, sustainable water management is considered a strategic task, essential in sustaining national development and requiring a national commitment. In the past, water resource development strategies tended to emphasize the supply side. Water was treated as a free good, and stakeholder participation was quite limited. In many basins, the current strategy for the development and management of water resources is now focusing on the demand side. To achieve efficient water allocation, it is understood that it is now necessary to establish a water use rights system.

Water allocation is perhaps the most important element of water resources management. Allocation must be implemented to achieve national objectives, as guided by clear principles of rights and priorities, of which the water use rights system is of central importance. Effective management policies require a system for water allocation and water rights administration that recognizes the legitimate private uses of a public resource. As demand increases relative to an essentially fixed, limited supply, leading to intersectoral competition, public regulation based on recognized water rights will be required to achieve societal goals.

In light of a series of factors including the natural characteristics of water; increasing demand; the paradigm shift from water as a social good to water as an economic good with social function; and the tide of opinion within the water resources community, a consensus has emerged among stakeholders and policymakers that the substance of water rights in Indonesia must be clarified. Determination of water rights in this context includes rights, duties, impacts on allocation, affected parties, jurisdiction (boundary), and responsibilities to the environment. The process of developing a water rights system was included in the Water Resources Reform Program that began in 1999.

In this chapter, we first present the legal and conceptual framework for water resources management in Indonesia. We next discuss water rights reform as part of Indonesia's ambitious water sector reform agenda, including some key aspects of the 2004 Water Law, brief descriptions of the planned program of pilot implementation, and anticipated outcomes of water rights reform. A description of the Brantas Basin in East Java illustrates the context of water allocation reform. We then discuss some aspects of water use rights in Indonesia as property rights and human rights.

Legal and Conceptual Framework for Water Rights

Legal Framework for Water Management

The Constitution of 1945 established the fundamental principles of water resources management in Indonesia. Article 33 of the constitution states that the earth, water, and any wealth therein are governed by the state and utilized as far as possible for the welfare of the people. The basic national law governing water resources management has been Law No. 11 of 1974 on Water Resources, supported by Government Regulation No. 22 of 1982 on Water Resources Management, Government Regulation No. 23 of 1982 on Irrigation and Drainage, and the Basic Agrarian Law No. 5 of 1960. According to Law No. 11 (1974) article 5 paragraph (1), intersectoral water uses were to be coordinated by the minister responsible for water resources. Government Regulation No. 22 of 1982 provided detail on the basis for management at the river basin level, including planning and coordination activities.

A 1989 Decree of the Minister of Public Works on the Determination of 90 River Territories in Indonesia divided Indonesia into 90 river territories (*Wilayah Sungai*) that in turn encompass 5,590 river basins. Most river basins are small, about 87 percent cover less than 500 square kilometers (Amron 1998). River basins in Indonesia, and particularly in Java, are usually short, steep, and rainfed, with 94 percent of rivers less than 50 kilometers long. Only 15 rivers are longer than 400 kilometers. According to the 1989 decree, and a related 1990 Decree on Management of Water Resources in River Territories, regional governments manage 72 river basins, with responsibilities delegated under the concept of comanagement. Fifteen river basins are managed directly by the Minister of Public Works, because their boundaries cross provincial boundaries. Public corporations currently manage three basins: Jasa Tirta I (PJT-I) manages the Brantas river basin in East Java and the Bengawan Solo river basin in East and Central Java, and Jasa Tirta II (PJT-II) manages the Citarum river basin in West Java. Some other river basins on Java, Sulawesi, and Sumatra have already begun developing public river basin management institutions. Under the current reform agenda, new public corporations or branches of Jasa Tirta I will manage the basins of Jratunseluna, Serayu-Bogowonto, and Jeneberang.

Water distribution within each basin is supposed to be based on a water allocation plan. The plan should be agreed on by the representatives of the water users and the water manager in a coordination forum called the Water Resources Management Committee, or *Panitia Tata Pengaturan Air* for the provincial level and *Panitia Pelaksana Tata Pengaturan Air* for the basin level.

The kernel of Indonesian water use rights is found in the Basic Constitution of 1945, stipulating that water resources, although governed by the state, must be utilized for the welfare of the people. Water use rights per se were first mentioned in the Basic Agrarian Law No. 5/1960. Water was identified as a gift of the Almighty and everyone has a right to its use, although certain uses require permission and others do not. The 1974 Water Law required corporations, associations, and individuals to obtain government approval (a license) and assigned the primary responsibility to the central and local governments to ensure that water and water resources are used beneficially. The water law also required that water allocation be subject to established priorities.

Government Regulation No. 22/1982 established the principles and the basis for water management. In water management regulations, the principles of public utility, harmony, and conservation should be applied. A water right was interpreted as water use right. Moreover, the regulation stated that everyone has a right to use water for their basic needs in daily life, for domestic purposes, and for domestic livestock. This government regulation established the basis for water use permits, but did not address the process by which water rights are formally established.

Indonesia has had a water licensing system applied to some specific economic uses, including urban water supply, hydropower, industry, mining, and commercial agriculture. Licensing was intended primarily as a strategic planning instrument, a guide to the allocation of water use for the purposes of meeting development goals, as distinct from short-term operational decisionmaking. In contrast to commercial uses, users could obtain water for domestic, household, and other basic, non-commercial uses without prior permission from the designated authority, subject to certain limitations. The earlier licensing was applied selectively to help regulate water use to meet development goals, but this partial system fell short of fulfilling the basic principles of fair and effective water allocation. To illustrate, during drought, water supplied for irrigation and river maintenance flow, which were not governed by licenses, might be reduced in order to secure the required quantities of water for those other beneficiaries who did have licenses to use the water.

Conceptual Principles

Ideally, in terms of economic theory, a structure of property rights in water that would facilitate the efficient allocation of water should include several characteristics. Universality means that all water resources are subject to some claim status, and property rights claims to water resources, including the nature and contents of these rights, are clearly identified, consistently applied, and universally respected. With exclusivity, all benefits and costs (setting aside externalities) arising from the rights are exclusively owned; and exclusively borne, respectively, by the rights-holder. Transferability allows specific components of the right to be transferred through freely negotiated, legally transparent transactions. Enforceability secures all rights from unlawful takeover or violation, via a well-defined process of grievances and remedies.

In establishing the structure of water rights, a clear justification must be provided for the initial distribution of claims. On this matter, there is no universal consensus along either historical or ethical lines. Muslim water law establishes a fundamental right of human access to water, as a gift from God, and imposes an equally fundamental duty to conserve, and to share based on priority of need (*chafa:* the right of thirst) beginning with water for domestic uses, followed by water for animals, then water for irrigation. Water is viewed, together with pasture and fire (fuel) as a common entitlement (*waqf,* usufruct or collective property) (see Faruqui, Biswas, and Bino 2001).

Other systems of water rights based on notions of community or common property are also prevalent in Indonesia. An often-cited example of a community-based water rights system in Indonesia is the Balinese *subak* (e.g., see Sutawan 2000). Such common property water rights systems are often characterized by relatively clear boundaries and flexible rules. However, this flexibility, potentially valuable during changing or uncertain conditions, is often difficult to realize through formal or statutory law.

Broadly speaking, the evolved legal structures of property rights in water in the West tend to follow either riparian doctrine, appropriation doctrine, or some combination. Under the riparian doctrine, the landowners have the right to divert (but typically not to store) a portion of the natural flow of water through or adjacent to their land, for reasonable and beneficial use. Under an appropriation doctrine, a person may acquire a right to divert, store, and use water simply by being the first to develop a previously unallocated source of water. In some places, this right is sometimes not tied to land ownership, and may be transferred, even outside of the watershed. In contemporary Indonesian water resources management systems, many farmers (and others) typically share water that is often stored at and delivered from remote locations via public infrastructure, and use it for a wide variety of purposes. Adoption of undiluted versions of either riparian or prior appropriation-type doctrines is neither practical nor appropriate, particularly when fairness and efficiency are paramount objectives. Indonesian farmers, who traditionally were more likely to use water for basic needs and subsistence farming than for commercial purposes, typically receive water allocations that reflect the outcome of discussion and agreement with others. This suggests that allocation and issuance of water rights must apply principles of justice and fairness. Ideally, the water right will guarantee the rights-holder access to water of the proper volume and at the proper time, and as appropriate to their investment.

There are three basic principles guiding Indonesia's efforts to implement water use rights. These are general use, efficiency, and sustainable supply. General use refers to an understanding that a clear, complete, and detailed water right arrangement will secure the right of parties to use the water as appropriate to their basic needs, received on time in sufficient quantity. Efficiency refers to an understanding that a clear, complete, and detailed water right arrangement will create an obligation of the water user to use the water (1) for beneficial purposes; (2) as efficiently as possible; (3) without endangering the environment, the water resources quantity and quality; and (4) without unnecessarily impairing or disturbing other users' ability to use water. A sustainable supply refers to an understanding that a clear, complete, and detailed water right arrangement will reflect conditions specific to each basin and locality in the resulting water allocation system, including both long-term and real-time aspects of water allocation, as well as the national social and economic perspective on water resources.

Reforming the Indonesian Water Rights System

The Government of Indonesia is currently undertaking a program of broad reform of water resources policy to improve the national institutional framework for water resources development and management; the organizational and financial framework for river basin management; regional water quality management, regulatory institutions, and implementation; and national irrigation management policy, institutions, and regulations (DGWR 2003). Water rights play an important role in these reforms. An essential first phase of this process is the revision of the enabling legal framework for water resources management.

To secure equitable and efficient water allocation, the government will establish a national framework for an enforceable water rights system for surface and groundwater. Indicators of progress toward this goal are issuance of a new Government Regulation for Water Rights and issuance of guidelines for the revised provincial water licensing regulations and allocation of water use rights. Water rights for irrigation schemes will be explicitly addressed, and prevailing customary water right concepts will be considered. The water user rights system will be supported by appropriate national regulations as well as a uniform provincial framework of water licensing for abstraction and discharges that covers all water sectors.

A formal water use rights system is also essential in order to document and to protect the historical claims of existing water users within a basin, as well as to accommodate new users. Three broad roles emerge for water use rights. They should enable the government to manage the nation's water resources more effectively and efficiently. Water use rights provide the community, and individuals within the community, a degree of certainty concerning the availability of the water resource, so that they can invest with confidence. Rights serve as a basis for resource accounting, which is necessary both for long-term planning and for real-time water allocation decisionmaking in the basin. A formal water use rights system is currently intended as a tool for effective basin-wide bulk water allocation at all times and, in particular, during times of water scarcity, especially in the dry season.

A water use rights system is a formal procedure to confer, from public ownership as managed by the government to the user, the right to use surface or groundwater in a particular basin or location. It carries out specific policy objectives of the government with regard to water use. In this process, historical water diversion and use are documented, users and uses are identified, water use is quantified, water available for allocation is determined (quantified), and the water that has been allocated is monitored with respect to its use(s). When the system is in place, clear legal and administrative procedures establish the priorities of respective rights, providing for transparent water allocation and water administration. The system also helps identify those users and uses that would be affected by proposed actions or activities that would alter or modify the quantity and quality of the water resources in the basin.

Usage and Commercial Rights in the 2004 Water Law

In February 2004, a new National Water Law, intended to replace Law No. 11 of 1974 on Water Resources, was passed by the Indonesian House of Representatives. The law defines a water use right as "the right to get and use or exploit water for various purposes." The law then defines more specific categories of use rights, *Hak Guna Pakai Air* (usage for basic needs and noncommercial uses) and *Hak Guna Usaha Air* (commercial exploitation).

Usage rights are "acquired without permit to fulfill daily basic needs for individuals and people's agriculture located in irrigation systems." Daily basic needs encompass what is required "to achieve healthy, clean and productive life" and include water used in religious services, drinking, cooking, bathing, and washing. Irrigated agriculture requires a permit if it involves changing the condition of the water resource, takes large volumes of water, or occurs outside of existing irrigation systems. The Elucidation to the water law states that permits are required if water use exceeds 2 liters per second per household head, and that pumping requires a permit even if for people's agriculture.

Throughout much of Java, 2 liters per second of continuous flow would service an irrigated area of one hectare or more, assuming wet transplanted paddy as is commonly grown during the first dry season. A single volumetric standard may not be appropriate for all regions, as conditions governing evapotranspiration and soil percolation vary extensively throughout the archipelago. Although this is certainly the case, it is clearly possible to regionalize this standard based on soils and climatic data. Moreover, a rule based on flow volume, as distinct from cultivated area, appears preferable for many reasons, not the least of which is the incentive it provides for water conservation. In establishing this threshold, the government has taken an important step toward protecting smallholder and subsistence agriculturalists' priority right of access to irrigation water.

Commercial rights can be granted to individuals or corporations via permit, and are provisional rights to exploit water resources for specified commercial purposes. These purposes include, among others, electric power generation, municipal water supply, industrial production, and agribusiness. Licenses are highly restrictive with respect to the type of use permitted—they are not broad volumetric commercial abstraction licenses.

As in the previous water law, water rights of traditional legal communities are to be accepted, as long as they are not in conflict with national interests, laws, and regulations, and as long as they actually continue to exist. The new law also states that customary rights must have been confirmed by regional government regulations. The means of resolving conflicts between traditional users and/or laws and "national interests and laws and regulations" are not made clear, however, and this suggests an interesting arena in which many issues raised in the new water law may be tested.

Subsequent government regulations will specify explicit details of the implementation of water use rights, which may include the duration of rights, conditions for terminating rights, and procedures for dealing with droughts or other extreme situations.

Prohibition of Transfers

The question as to whether or not water user rights as specified in the new National Water Law could be transferable generated considerable debate. In the course of preparing the reform program, a right to transfer water under the framework of established use rights was envisioned. This would have enabled the transfer of water use rights from the original permit holder to a third party on the basis of a legitimate agreement that could be endorsed by responsible authorities. A transfer of a water use right might apply to all, or to only a part of the original owner's water use rights. In case of a temporary transfer, the formal "splitting" of the water use right would not be necessary. Transfers of water rights might have occurred through private trading, or through regulated transactions established by agreement between water users in which the appropriate government authority would play a central role.

There was concern that the permissibility of water use rights transfer would introduce a potential for abuse. A negative impact of such arrangements could occur in the event that a water right were (temporarily) transferred to, and subsequently not relinquished by a *pengusaha kuat* (literally "strong company") resulting in the original right holder (presumably less powerful) being deprived of their right to water.

In the Water Law passed by the Parliament in February 2004, no allowance is made for the transfer of water use rights. The Law states "Water utilization right . . . cannot be leased out or transferred, partially or wholly." The Elucidation adds: "If water utilization right is not used by the holder of water utilization right, Government or regional government can revoke the related water utilization right." The law prohibits transfers and specifies penalties, fines, and imprisonment for violators.

This would appear to settle the issue for the time being, at least with respect to private transactions. Key to understanding the proscription on water markets is the fact that under the new law, water use rights and commercial licenses are *purpose-specific.* In Western water law, rights typically adhere either to individuals (doctrine of appropriation) or to land (riparian doctrine), each framework providing a basis for transfers as private transactions. According to the new Indonesian Water Law, however, a farmer (irrigator) is *not* free to transfer his water use right, for example, to an industry, since his right was derived from the use of the water in irrigation and not from his ownership of the land, riparian or otherwise.

If water rights were transferable, then a clear water rights arrangement could improve the efficiency of water resources allocation by directly facilitating water right transfers. An example is the transfer of water out of irrigation to industrial and domestic uses. A transferable water right would provide farmers with an incentive to use water more efficiently, if the water saved could be transferred (sold or leased). It would provide one more alternative solution to the problem of increasing water scarcity, at a time when the construction of new dams is increasingly expensive and attended by many serious problems including resettlement and land compensation. Within the framework of the new water law, arrangements by which government reallocates water, with compensation for those whose rights are reduced (e.g., a functional equivalent of water banking, or coordinated agreements for retirement of an existing right and issuance of a new right) might be developed, but processes for reallocation are not explicitly specified.

Preliminary Implementation of Water Use Rights

The Government of Indonesia intends to conduct an exploratory, pilot program introducing water use rights to specific regions. The pilot program will be implemented in three locations, the Citarum River Basin in West Java, the Jratunseluna

River Basin in Central Java, and the Brantas River Basin in East Java. These river basins have been chosen because their water resources have been extensively developed over long periods, each contains various categories of water users, and each possesses the potential for intersectoral conflict. The decision to conduct a pilot implementation program is motivated by the fact that the Government of Indonesia's experience in implementing water use rights is limited to commercial licensing, so the information gathered during these trial programs will be invaluable in improving the legal framework for water use rights.

The preliminary programs will focus on groups that use water primarily for commercial and irrigation purposes. The number and composition of these groups will be chosen to be representative, so that results from pilot programs can be generalized to regions outside the target basins. The experience gained through the pilot basin programs will be used to strengthen implementation of water use rights. This should be the starting point for Indonesia to adopt a uniform licensing system procedure within the framework of a national water use rights system. In consideration of the macrocharacteristics of water availability, of increasing demand due to growing population, and the increasing variety of competing water uses, and of forces of economic globalization and the liberalization of trade, all of which impact on the management of water resources, the rapid implementation of effective water use rights in Indonesia is a high priority.

Anticipated Outcomes from Water Use Rights Reforms

The intended outcomes include assignment of rights, improvements in water use security and efficiency, and increases in the level of responsibility of water users. The implementation of water use rights could be evaluated as successful on the basis of consistency of water rights implementation and all related laws and regulations at all stages, and improved allocation and productive efficiency achieved through the implementation of water use rights.

The creation of water use rights creates a legal channel by which rights-holders can fulfill all basic needs with respect to water, while fulfilling all responsibilities corresponding with these rights. This could help avoid some conflicts related to water use, since each rights-holder will acquire an understanding of both the extent and limits to their rights. In the process, the government will have a control instrument for determining policies and decisions. Water rights-holders who understand their rights should also understand the demarcation of their rights, so that they will make efficient use of water, making more water available for use by others in support of their rights and interests.

Water availability depends on many other elements beyond the structure of rights, such as the presence of reservoirs, other water resources infrastructure, and the requirements of the environment. Water rights-holders, while exercising their rights, should also assume greater responsibilities for safeguarding and protecting the water resources system to which they are connected in order to sustain the integrity of the system. If rights-holders fail to meet these duties, they will be subject to claims by any other users harmed by their action.

Case Study in the Brantas River Basin

The Brantas River Basin is located in the Province of East Java. The watershed covers 11,800 square kilometers and the main channel stretches 320 kilometers from its source on Mount Arjuna to New Lengkong, where it branches into two rivers, Surabaya River and Porong River, each of which discharges into the Madura Strait. Along its main stem, many tributaries join the Brantas, including the Lesti, Ngrowo, Konto, and Widas rivers. Figure 10.1 depicts the Brantas Basin, including important water resources management features.

Average precipitation in the basin is close to 2,000 millimeters/year, about 80 percent of which occurs during the rainy season from December to May. Annual surface discharge is around 12,000 million cubic meters (MCM) on average. About 3,000 MCM is subject to regulation by storage dams, a quantity constrained primarily by the limited surface storage, which currently totals only 297 MCM.

Beginning in 1961, the Brantas River Basin Development Project carried out river basin development, under the authority of the Directorate General of Water Resources Development. In that year, the first Master Plan was established, with primary emphasis on flood control. Large reservoirs constructed in the upper reaches for flood control also provided water supply for irrigation and hydropower generation.

In 1973, the Master Plan was reviewed and Master Plan II prepared, with a primary orientation toward supplying water for irrigation, in line with government policy that emphasized self-sufficiency in rice production. During this period, some additional reservoirs and barrages were built. Work on flood control projects continued.

Having achieved relative success with rice production, the government then turned to strengthening the industrial sector in the 1980s. Consequently, the river basin development plan was reviewed again in 1985. Master Plan III emerged with the main purpose of supplying water for industry and municipalities. The need was later felt to review the master plan, to improve water resources conservation and management. The Master Plan IV, reflecting these priorities, was completed in 1998.

The benefits of development under the Master Plans can be summarized as follows:

- flood control for events up to a 50-year return period;
- water supply for 83,000 hectares of paddy fields that directly abstract water from Brantas main stem (out of a total 345,000 hectares of irrigated area within the basin) supplying up to 2,500 million cubic meters of irrigation water per year;
- energy production of about 1,000 million kilowatt-hours per year;
- bulk water supply for industries and municipal drinking water of about 380 MCM/year;
- maintenance flow of 204 MCM/year; and
- flows supporting fisheries of 41 MCM/year (PJT-I 2002).

During preparation of the fourth Master Plan, it was anticipated that the Brantas River Basin would face diverse problems due to population growth and industrial development. Water demand is projected to increase significantly, while the supply will remain limited. Previous assessments of water balance in the growing urban areas of Gresik, Bangkalan, Mojokerto, Surabaya, and Sidoarjo highlighted the importance of developing new sources of surface water (such as the proposed Genteng, Kedungwarak, and Beng dams) to cope with the growing demand. Although these dams are classified as "promising" projects based on benefit-cost analysis, the unit water costs are still considered too expensive given current abilities to recover costs. The costs for the proposed Genteng, Kedungwarak, and Beng dams were 1,119; 1,090; and 889 Rp/cubic meter (US$1 = 11,300 Rp in June 2001), respectively: by comparison, the unit water cost of Wonorejo Dam (2001) was only 520 Rp/cubic meter (JICA 1998:V-32). These projects (or their equivalent) will almost certainly be required in the near future.

However, water supply and demand projections within the Brantas to the year 2020 under a range of assumptions concerning supply indicate that supply augmentation alone will not provide a comprehensive solution to the pending water shortage. Demand management therefore will also be important. Supply augmentation together with improvements in irrigation efficiency, water reuse, and recycling are currently anticipated to allow the basin to accommodate growing urban demand up to the year 2020. Based on these projections and assumptions, implementation of water use rights, and possibly water right transfers, might make an important contribution toward coping with future water deficits.

Figure 10.1 The Brantas Basin

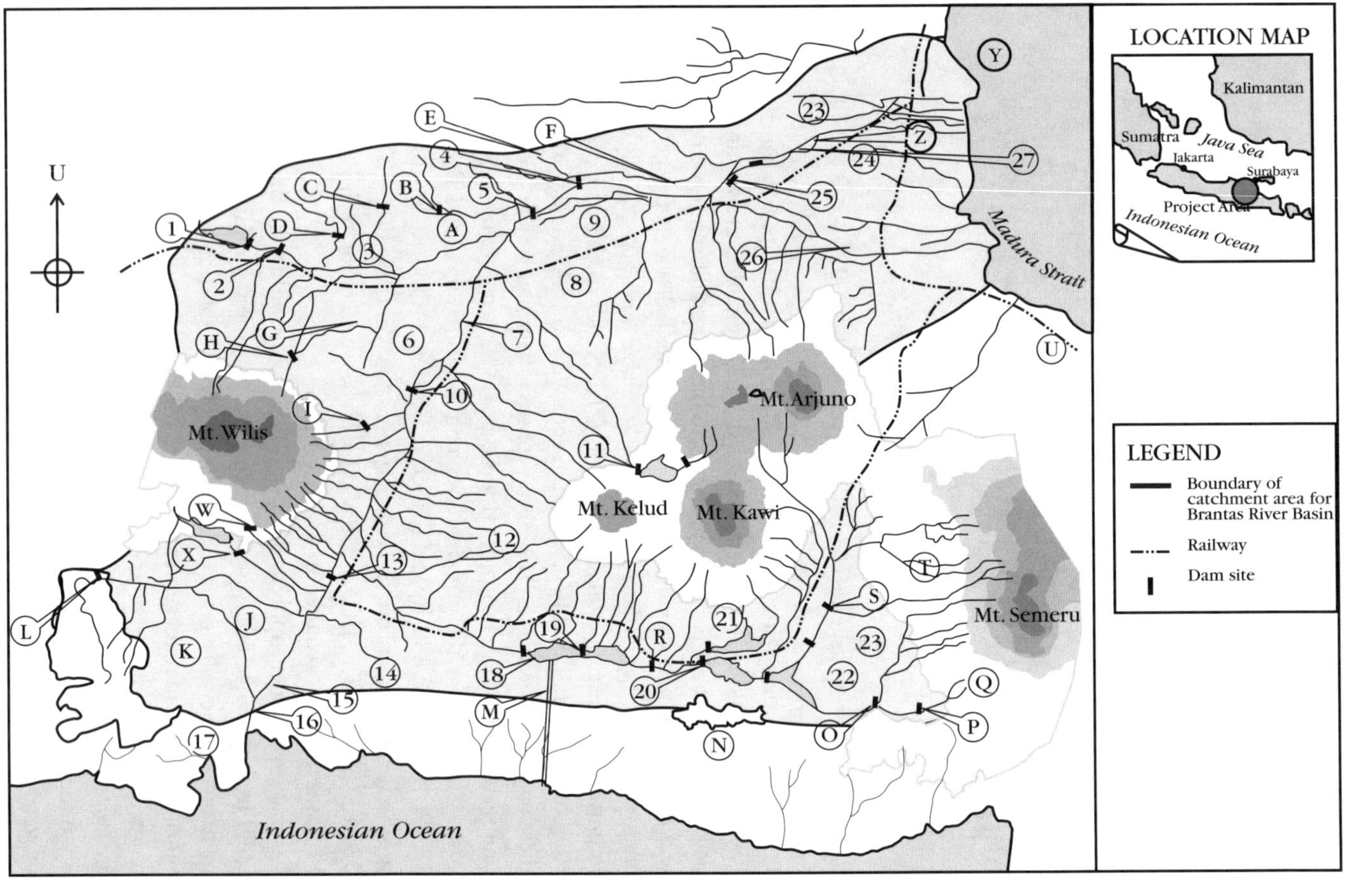

Source: Based on map provided by Jasa Tirta I Public Corporation.

Completed projects

1. Bening Dam
2. Glatik Dam
3. Widas irrigation 3200 HA
4. Mentupus rubber dam
5. Jatimlerek rubber dam
6. Warujayeng irrigation area
7. Middle Reach River improvement
8. Paparpeterongan irrigation area
9. Turi Tunggorono irrigation area
10. Mrican Barrage
11. Selorejo multipurpose dam
12. Mt. Kelud debris control
13. Tulungagung Gate
14. Lodoyo Tulungagung irrigation area
15. Parit Agung Canal
16. South Tulungagung Tunnel
17. Gulungagung Hepp
18. Lodoyo Aftgerbay
19. Wlingi multipurpose dam
20. Sutami multipurpose dam
21. Lahor Dam
22. Sengguruh Dam
23. Kepanjen Dam
24. Brantas Delta irrigation area
25. New Lengkong Dam
26. Kaliporong River improvement
27. Karangpilang Treatments Work

Proposed projects

A. Widas extension area 3200 HA
B. Beng Dam
C. Kedungwarak Dam
D. Semantok Dam
E. Beng irrigation area 3200 HA
F. Gottan Losare irrigation area 4300 HA
G. Widas South irrigation area 5500 HA
H. Kuncir Dam
I. Babadan Dam
J. Wonorejo irrigation area
K. Trenggalek irrigation area
L. Tugu Dam
M. Flood diversion
N. Lestileft irrigation area 2300 HA
O. Lesti Dam
P. Genteng Dam
Q. Upper West watershed management
R. Sutami multipurpose dam
S. Lumbangsari Dam
T. Upper Brantas watershed management
U. Umbulan Spring

Under-construction projects

W. Segawe Weir
X. Wonorejo Dam
Y. Suragaya Urban Development Project
Z. Karangpilang Treatments Work

Industrial water recycling, such as recirculation of cooling water, can be a major source of water savings. Domestic water use can be made more efficient by steps ranging from repairing leaks in municipal systems to installing low-flow showerheads. Efficiency in irrigation water use can be enhanced by technologies including drip irrigation and microsprinklers; management changes such as the adoption of demand-based irrigation scheduling systems and conjunctive use of surface and groundwater; and institutional improvements including the creation of effective water users' associations.

Water allocation in the Brantas Basin is based on a water allocation plan, which is discussed and agreed on by representatives of various categories of water users, as well as by Jasa Tirta I Public Corporation (PJT-I), in a coordinated forum called the Provincial Water Resources Management Committee. The water allocation system currently practiced in the Brantas Basin is based on decrees issued by the governor of East Java. As described earlier, the water licensing is a form of acknowledging water use rights as well as an instrument for regulating use. The content of the water licensing system can be summarized as follows:

1. All water users shall have a license from the governor of East Java.

2. PJT-I (the river basin authority) will guarantee the supply of water, to the extent feasible considering available discharge.

3. The license will be issued following issuance of technical recommendations from PJT-I, a recommendation from chief of regency as chief of the Irrigation Committee and consideration from the Consideration Group on Surface Water Licensing.

4. Other relevant rules and regulations are fulfilled.

5. The beneficiaries shall pay a fee for operation and maintenance of water resources infrastructure.

Regulation of the implementation of licenses is the responsibility of the agencies involved, including the East Java Provincial Government, Provincial Water Resources Services, PJT-I, and others. Control over the implementation of licenses is by designated agencies, which in the Brantas Basin include the Government of East Java, Water Resources Services, and PJT-I.

Modeling Transferable Rights

To illustrate the potential of trading of licensed water to improve the economic productivity of water resources, we present some results from modeling studies

Figure 10.2 Allocation scenarios with and without transfers

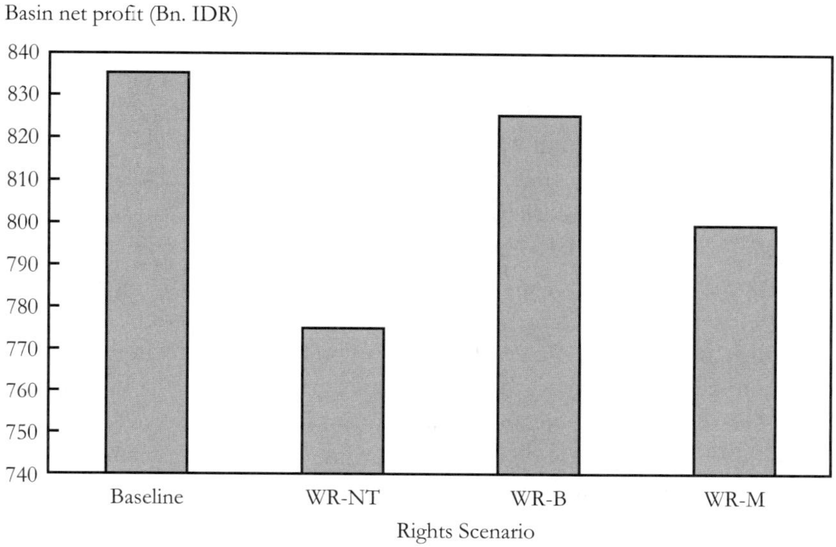

Source: Rodgers and Zaafrano 2002.

recently conducted in the Brantas Basin, East Java. An integrated economic-hydrologic basin simulation model (Rodgers and Zaafrano 2002) was used to compare four water rights scenarios.

The first, economically idealized, scenario allocated water purely according to its highest economic return, without regard to water use rights and subject only to hydrologic and infrastructure constraints and minimum supply constraints for domestic uses and environmental flows. In the second scenario (WR-NT), with water rights and no trading, each irrigation system was assigned a volumetric right, by period, which corresponded to efficient cultivation along historical cropping patterns. In this scenario, any water not used productively at a site is simply forfeited, and flows downstream. In the third scenario (WR-B), irrigation systems could either buy additional water from or sell unused water to the river basin management authority ("the broker") at a flat price per cubic meter, subject only to supply constraints. (This constitutes a form of water banking, in which so long as the basin authority has water to sell, it must sell it, and it must purchase whatever is offered without regard for whether or not it can be resold.) The fourth scenario (WR-M), water rights market clearing, was similar to the third, but industries and water utilities were excluded from water trading, and sales were private transactions —a buyer had to be found for every unit sold.

Figure 10.2 shows that the use of a simple system of volumetric rights, based on historical cropping patterns, with no trading, has lower aggregate basin output by comparison with the first scenario where economic returns were optimized. This occurs because at least some water resources do not move to the locations and uses where marginal net value is highest. However, if a simple water brokerage system is present (scenario three), virtually the same level of output (and implied water economic productivity) is achieved as under the first scenario. In the fourth scenario, allocation efficiency is also improved as compared to the fixed right (second) scenario, although not to the same extent as in scenario three because the rules governing transfers are more restrictive. In the third and fourth scenarios, the welfare of irrigators at any particular location would be improved through such voluntary trades, if we assume that they would never agree to trade unless trading made them better off.

Models and scenarios such as these provide one tool for evaluating the impact of different rules for water use rights on the economic efficiency of water allocation. They indicate the potential economic gains from institutional arrangements that would facilitate reallocation between water uses, such as transferable water use rights, or, under the current law, arrangements that would compensate users for giving up rights that the government could then reallocate to others.

Human Rights and Property Rights

In moving from principle to statute and on to implementation, it is necessary to acknowledge that the intentions behind efforts to establish or to strengthen water rights simultaneously reflect two distinct sets of social objectives. On one hand, water rights may be promoted as the legal manifestation of the concept of basic human rights, in the sense of natural entitlements, as defined in documents such as the United Nations Covenant on Economic, Social and Cultural Rights (UNESCO 2002). From this perspective of distributive justice, embedded in sources as diverse as the arguments of Rawls (1971) and Moslem water law, one essentially views water rights as desirable and necessary in order to protect the interests (and perhaps the survival) of society's least powerful against coercion and dispossession by the strong or the wealthy. On the other hand, water rights may be understood explicitly as property rights in water, reflecting a utilitarian perspective. Water rights are desirable in this context for reducing the friction in economic transactions and for reducing the risks associated with investments that enhance water productivity.

Ownership is often described as a "bundle" of distinct rights. Table 10.2 compares usage and commercial rights in the new law with the framework of property rights proposed by Honore (1961). It is somewhat difficult to characterize water rights within this framework, since, among other factors, water has no stable boundaries. Honore's system also strongly reflects Western European concepts of ownership.

Table 10.2 Comparison of water use rights as property rights

Characteristic	Description	Basic water usage rights	Commercial water use rights
(1) Right to possess	The right to exclusive physical control of the thing owned (includes right to exclude)	Yes, within confines of use allotment	Yes, within confines of licensed quantities
(2) Right to use	The right to personal enjoyment and use of the thing (as distinct from 3 and 4)	Yes, although qualified by type of use	Yes, although qualified by license conditions
(3) Right to manage	The right to decide how and by whom a thing shall be used	Unclear (limited)	Yes, although qualified by license conditions
(4) Right to income	The right to the benefits derived from forgoing personal use of a thing and allowing others to use it	No (formally prohibited)	From products; but not through transfer of water use rights
(5) Right to capital	The right to alienate the thing and to consume, waste, modify, or destroy it. To alienate is to convey or transfer as a matter of an owner's choice and not in the course of the state's legal activities	Right to consume, obligation to conserve	Right to consume as specified in license, obligation to conserve
(6) Right to security	Immunity from expropriation	Yes, subject to priorities	Subject to allocation plans and priorities
(7) Power of transmissibility	The power to devise or bequeath the thing	Implicit	No, transfers prohibited
(8) Absence of term	Indeterminate length of one's ownership right	Yes, for uses not requiring license	No, may be limited by term of license and renewal conditions
(9) Prohibition of harmful use	Duty to forbear from using the thing in certain ways harmful to others	Yes	Yes
10) Liability to execution	Liability to having the thing taken away for repayment of debt	No	Unclear, but (probably) effectively yes
11) Residuary character	The existence of rules governing the reversion of lapsed ownership rights. Reversion is the right of succession or future possession or enjoyment.	Government holds	Government holds

Source: Characteristics and descriptions of rights are from Honore (1961).

In many societies, an absolute "right to exclude" others would be viewed as an intolerable defect in the framework of rights, especially with respect to resources essential for life, or commonly shared or managed resources. It is thus important to recognize that a rights framework that is "incomplete" with respect to full ownership does not indicate a deficiency or flaw in that framework.

Neither usage rights nor commercial rights fulfill the requirements of full ownership. This follows primarily (but not exclusively) from the "right to capital," which corresponds most closely to the core concept of ownership, at least in the Western tradition (Becker 1977:20). To grant individuals, groups, or other institutions this right would undermine the intent of Indonesia's constitution, which clearly establishes the state's authority to govern water resources.[1] In both categories of water use right, specific rights characteristics are qualified, sometimes heavily. Usage rights are categorically qualified in terms of what meets the definition of a basic use. Specific conditions of the license qualify commercial rights.

Usage rights lie closer to the root concept of "rights" as widely understood. This follows from the conditions under which water user rights can be denied: for basic uses, the right is presumed, and such water use is assigned a high priority by law, except under unusual intervening circumstances. By contrast, the state is (evidently) not compelled to issue commercial use licenses upon request, but retains an element of discretion beyond the statutory requirements. There is clear merit in both arguments, for water rights as human rights and property rights, as well as the potential for conflicting objectives. The ambitious task faced by Indonesian lawmakers and regulators is simultaneously to protect the legitimate historical claims of current water users, to make explicit the hierarchy of claims on scarce water, and to permit and facilitate investment and the economic transactions that lead to greater efficiency in water use. In addition, the process of specifying and formalizing water use rights presents Indonesian policymakers with a unique opportunity to address longstanding problems associated with the maldistribution of wealth and productive resources. The process of allocating claims to increasingly scarce water could be employed as a tool for promoting the health and economic welfare of the nation's poorest citizens. Legislation implicitly acknowledges these distinct objectives through the conceptual, as well as legal distinctions provided between basic or noncommercial users and uses (addressing arguments from natural rights and religious duty) and commercial uses (addressing arguments for economic efficiency).

Some uses of water, however, do not fall neatly into either category. The irrigation of small family-owned plots, typically for paddy and *polowijo* (irrigated, dry-footed crop) production, is seldom either purely subsistence, or purely commercial. To illustrate, in a recent field study conducted in the Brantas Basin, East Java, where irrigated plots are on average less than 0.4 hectare, it was found that an average of around 40 percent of paddy produced was consumed within the producer's household. Much of the income derived from marketed paddy paid for basic necessities (Rodgers and Zaafrano 2002). The importance of this category of water use in Indonesia cannot be overemphasized. Surface irrigation schemes divert more than 70 percent of current water abstractions in the Brantas, the majority to large gravity schemes serving numerous smallholders (most of whom would be well below the threshold of 2 liters per second for which permits would not be required).

It has been persuasively argued (e.g., Gleick 1999) that rights of access to and use of water for basic purposes are clearly and fully implicit in internationally recognized human rights to life, and to adequate food, clothing, and shelter. Indeed, it is hard to imagine how these baseline conditions could possibly be guaranteed absent a corresponding and no-less-fundamental right to water, particularly if we interpret these rights as including an acceptable level of human dignity. The case for derived rights for irrigation water use is, unfortunately, less self-evident. The U.N. Economic and Social Council (UNESCO 2002) is prepared to argue for a derived water right for food production (irrigation implicit) through "right to adequate food," "right to health," and "right to gain a living by work." However, they acknowledge a distinction based on priority of right: "(Nevertheless) priority in the allocation of water must be given to the right to water for personal and domestic uses. Priority should also be given to the water resources required to prevent starvation and disease, as well as water required to meet the core obligations of each of the Covenant rights" (UNESCO 2002:2). In a similar vein, Gleick (1999) argues for the existence of derived rights to water arising from provisions of basic human rights covenants, but notes that rights to adequate health and nutrition can, technically, be satisfied through the direct provision of food. This argument is possibly more problematic when applied to rights to livelihood by work.

But note that none of these technicalities preclude arguments for establishing formal priorities of allocation that favor irrigation over, for example, industrial use, particularly where irrigation is clearly not a purely commercial enterprise, but rather enables the primary means to livelihood for established communities of smallholders. Under Indonesia's water law, basic uses, including noncommercial irrigation, are granted highest priority, but priorities in allocation of water for commercial uses are established at the discretion of government at the appropriate level.

Conclusions

As an important component of Indonesia's comprehensive water sector reforms, the government passed a new National Water Law in February 2004. One objective is to establish a uniform system of water use rights. The law distinguishes between basic usage rights (*Hak Guna Pakai Air*) and commercial or exploitation use rights (*Hak Guna Usaha Air*). Basic usage rights are entitlements requiring no formal permit, while exploitation rights require formal licensing for specific uses of water. The law specifically precludes transfers of water rights. Experience from the pilot basin programs will be used to strengthen national implementation of water use rights.

The Brantas Basin offers an example of relatively effective institutions for river basin management, which have been developed over many decades. However, analysis using a hydrologic–economic model indicates that transfers could yield substantial additional benefits, compared to establishing only nontradable rights.

Under the new law, transfers between sectors could occur, but only through the agency of the government, which would reacquire water use rights when, for example, land is converted out of irrigated agriculture, commercial permits expire, license conditions are violated, or if the right is not exercised. The government would then be able to reallocate this water to different parties or sectors, subject to priority and availability. Given the interest of numerous international institutions in seeing water use rights made transferable, it is likely that the issue of water use transfers will be revisited in Indonesia's future.

It is entirely reasonable, however, to insist that the basic framework of use rights be established, clarified, and legally secure before allowing market-type transfers. The government will necessarily have an ongoing role in supervising water sector transactions whatever the form they ultimately take, in order to perform its constitutionally mandated functions, to ensure that water allocation decisions are consistent with local custom and regional development goals, and to protect the welfare and economic security of all of Indonesian citizens, particularly the weak and vulnerable.

Notes

1. The equivalence of "to govern" and "to own" is not completely self-evident, although the state's power to alienate is an important aspect of the right to capital. State ownership is qualified, however, by its duty to utilize water resources for the welfare of the people, thus negating rights to waste or destroy, which Honore included (1961) under the right to capital.

References

Amron, M. 1998. Basin water resources management policy in Indonesia. Jakarta: Directorate General of Water Resources Development, Ministry of Settlements and Regional Infrastructure.

Becker, L. 1977. *Property rights: Philosophic foundations.* London: Routledge and Kegan Paul.

DGWR (Directorate General of Water Resources, Ministry of Settlements and Regional Infrastructure, Republic of Indonesia). 2003. Republic of Indonesia: Water resources management—

Toward enhancement of effective water governance in Indonesia. Country report prepared for the Third World Water Forum. March 2003, Kyoto, Japan.

Faruqui, N. I., A. K. Biswas, and M. J. Bino, eds. 2001. *Water management in Islam.* Tokyo: United Nations University Press, International Development Research Centre.

Gleick, P. 1999. The human right to water. *Water Policy* 1 (15): 487–503.

Government of Indonesia, Minister of State for Public Planning, Chairman of National Development Planning Agency. Letter to Mr. James D. Wolfensohn, President, The World Bank, April 29, 1999 concerning water resources and irrigation sector: Policy, institutional legislative and regulatory reform program.

Government of Indonesia. 2002. Draft Law of the Republic of Indonesia about water resources, October 24, 2002, version, English translation.

———. 2004a. Draft of Law of the Republic of Indonesia about water resources, March 2004 version. English translation by N. Arifin, No. 05/03/04—Jakarta, March 17, 2004.

———. 2004b. Explanation (Elucidation) of Draft of Law of the Republic of Indonesia about water resources, March 2004 version. English translation by N. Arifin, No. 05/03/04—Jakarta, March 17, 2004.

Honore, A. M. 1961. Ownership. In *Oxford essays in jurisprudence,* ed. A.G. Guest. Oxford: Clarendon Press. Quoted in Becker, Lawrence. 1977. *Property rights: Philosophic foundations.* London: Routledge and Kegan Paul.

JICA (Japanese International Cooperation Agency). 1998. The study on comprehensive management plan for the water resources of the Brantas River Basin in the Republic of Indonesia. Final report, Main report. Jakarta: Indonesia, Ministry of Public Works, Directorate General of Water Resources Development.

LRI (Land Resources of Indonesia). 1990. The land resources of Indonesia: A national overview. Regional Physical Planning Programme for Transmigration. London: Overseas Development Administration. Jakarta: Departemen Transmigrasi.

Machbub, D. 2000. *Pengelolaan sumberdaya air berwawasan lingkungan pada pengembangan wilayah.* Jakarta: Badan Penelitian dan Pengembangan Departemen Permukiman dan Pengembangan Wilayah.

PJT-I (Perusahaan Jasa Tirta I). 2002. *Company profile.* Malang, East Java: PJT I.

Rawls, J. 1971. *A theory of justice.* Cambridge, Mass.: Harvard University Press.

Rodgers, C., and R. Zaafrano. 2002. A water resources management policy simulation model of the Brantas Basin, East Java, Indonesia. Paper prepared for the final policy workshop "Irrigation Investment, Fiscal Policy and Water Resources Allocation in Indonesia and Vietnam," November 21–23, 2002, Ho Chi Minh City, Vietnam.

Sutawan, N. 2000. Negotiation of water allocation among irrigators' associations in Bali, Indonesia. In *Negotiating water rights,* eds. B. R. Bruns and R. S. Meinzen-Dick. London: Intermediate Technology Publications.

UNESCO (United Nations Economic and Social Council). 2002. Substantive issues arising in the implementation of the international covenant on economic, social and cultural rights. General comment No. 15: The right to water (Articles 11 and 12 of the international covenant on economic, social and cultural rights.) Committee on Economic, Social and Cultural Rights, Twenty-ninth Session, November 11–29, 2002, Geneva.

WRI (World Resources Institute). 2003. *Water resources and freshwater ecosystems—Indonesia.* Washington, D.C.: WRI.

Chapter 11

Institutional Design Considerations for Water Rights Development in China

Bin Liu

— Under the water law that was approved in 1988 and amended in 2002, China plans to introduce a water rights system to replace the water use permit system. This chapter documents the need for a water rights system, based on several case studies that describe water-related problems including water shortages, water pollution, and environmental degradation, and describes an example of recent water transfer among Chinese cities. The chapter also provides ideas and suggestions on where such a system should be placed from an administrative point of view, and what issues would need to be considered during the implementation of a water rights system.

China is a developing country that faces both substantial water resource shortages and environmental degradation of the resource base. Annual water demand continues to increase because of a growing population and rapid economic growth. In some districts with serious water shortages, the development and use of freshwater resources has reached or surpassed existing sustainable capacity limits. In 1998, the water used in the Haihe River Basin, the Huanghe (Yellow) River Basin, and the Huaihe River Basin was equal to 88 percent, 68 percent, and 56 percent of total average annual availability, respectively. These levels surpass a suggested sustainable use ratio of 40 percent (UNCSD 1997).

Furthermore, water pollution in China is becoming increasingly serious. Water pollution directly decreases the amount of water available for productive uses and can render entire water bodies unusable, adding to growing water shortages. In 1998, an assessment of 100,000 kilometers of river reaches found that 46.5 percent were polluted. For the Haihe basin, the ratio of the polluted river reaches to total river reaches amounts to 62.3 percent. Ninety percent of municipal water resources are polluted to some degree (MWR 1998).

Under the present system for water resource management in China, the cost of using water is nearly zero. This gives water resources a status similar to a public pasture, an open access commons. As a result, it is difficult to avoid injudicious development and overuse of water, which result in highly visible external diseconomies, such as rivers drying up, ecosystem degradation, and environmental deterioration. These adverse environmental impacts in turn have negatively affected the sustainable development of the society and, in some regions, have slowed down economic development. Moreover, these diseconomies to the society are becoming increasingly recognized and widespread.

Water scarcity and shortages do not prevail everywhere in China, so interbasin transfers from abundant regions into water-short regions could alleviate some of the problems. However, uncertainty regarding water rights, and the high costs of water transfers, pose obstacles to such plans and actions. Similar to the case of public pasture, it would be difficult to recoup investments into such transfer schemes, and so such schemes are carried out only by the government. Moreover, the property rights of even completed transfer schemes may be uncertain. Therefore, increased certainty and security in the form of property rights to water should be a priority issue to improve water resource allocation in China, and should be based on a sound legal framework.

The next section presents background information on water rights development in China, shortcomings of the current system, and cases that illustrate issues in water rights development. The third section analyzes some key conditions for developing a water rights system: basic concepts for rights, public and private character of rights, who holds rights, priority in use, transfers, and initial definition of rights. The fourth section compares strategic options for organizing water rights administration. The fifth section addresses key issues of fairness and expropriation in the management of water rights. The concluding section discusses water rights in the context of water resources allocation and the prospects of water rights development in China.

Water Rights Development in China

The present water resources management system in China is based on the Water Law approved in 1988 and amended in 2002. The Implementation Measures for a Water Use Permit System, issued by the State Council in 1993, sets out major rules for water resources administration. In recent years, several regulations concerning water allocation have been issued by the State Council for regions and river basins facing serious water shortages. They include important legal documents for water resource allocation and control in the Yellow River Basin, titled the Plan for the Annual Available Water Supply Allocation and the Mainstream Water Operation in the Yellow River and the Water Operation Management Measures for the Yellow River. Other acts regularize water sharing among provinces and districts, including the Water Allocation Plan for the Heihe River, the Water Allocation Plan for the Zhanghe River, and the Water Resources Management Code for Talimu River in Xinjiang Autonomous Region.

In addition, regulations at the ministry level, such as the Regulation for Procedures to Examine and Approve Water Use Permit Applications, the Regulation for Supervision and Management of Water Use Permits, and the Regulation for the Management of Water Quality for Water Use Permits, translate general stipulations into practical water resource management. In addition, most provinces develop provincial-level Water Resources Management Codes that reflect regional-level water resource management issues and supplement national legislation. Water resource management in China has been strengthened and clarified based on this legislative framework.

Shortcomings of the Water Resources Management System

A number of shortcomings and limitations constrain the performance of the water resources management system. The management role of government administration is overemphasized. The water resources management system concerns mainly administrative issues, with the government being responsible or taking charge of almost all of the tasks. Under purely administrative control, it is difficult to avoid uneconomic resource allocations, creating a form of "government failure." At the same time, without the participation of water users, it is difficult to counterbalance the administrative power exerted by the government and to guarantee equity in water resources management. Not all practical issues arising from water resource management are clarified.

Although the constitution states that water resources belong to the whole nation, and it is further stated in the Water Law that the state exercises ownership over water resources on behalf of the nation, problems remain between central and lower level water management. Because of the characteristics of water resources, practical management is usually implemented by governments at the province, city, and county levels. For example, the provincial government charges a resource fee for water usage. However, inconsistencies between the higher and lower levels in management of water resources continue to make it hard to control water use and promote optimal management of the resource.

Integrated management, particularly joint water quality and quantity management, has so far not been realized. Water management is segmented among different government departments and interests. As a result, water quality is not an integral part of water use and management. An important issue here is how to provide rights to water that meet water quality standards, in addition to providing a certain quantity.

There is a general paucity of data and information on the quantity of water available and allocated by period, spatial location, and user. As a result, water resource management plans might not be practical in nature or feasible to implement, even after their formulation, as in the case of the Yellow and Heihe (Black) river basins, with adverse consequences for water resources management. Moreover, there remain de facto uncertainties in authority between river basin commissions, provincial governments, and local districts regarding water resource management, leading to further obstacles to practical water management.

There is insufficient supervision of water use permits. There is too little scrutiny during permit examination and approval. River reach surveys on water management mostly cover only sections between provinces, which, however, are far from actual water users. This further reduces supervision for the water use permit system.

In the present water resources management system, transfer of water use permits is forbidden. Although this regulation ensures some continuity in resource allocation for the overall economy, it is not proper for the further optimal allocation on the microeconomic level, and blocks any role for the market in resource reallocation.

Case Studies for Water Rights Development in China

Water Conflict in the Zhanghe River Basin. The Zhanghe River passes through three provinces. Its upper reach is located in Shanxi Province, while the lower reach forms the border between Hebei and Henan Province. It flows through Pingshun County of Shanxi Province, Linzhou City and Anyang County of Henan Province, and Shexian County and Cixian County of Hebei Province. Many small-scale water transfer projects have been built along the river, such as Hongqi Canal and Yuejin Canal of Henan Province, Dayuefeng Canal and Xiaoyuefeng Canal of Hebei Province, among others.

The river channel is not long, but lies in a forbidding mountain area with a dearth of cultivated land. The living standard along the river is very low, with the population depending on a limited amount of farmland. An increasing population coupled with continuing deterioration of the ecosystem in the basin has created enormous tension between the people living on the two opposite river banks, who have been fighting for the limited water resources and meager arable farmland since the 1950s. The level of conflicts accelerated after 1980, resulting in criminal actions such as explosions, mass fights, and the destruction of hydraulic infrastructure. During the drought season, some villagers construct unauthorized dams to divert limited water resources to their own side, without considering the resulting damage on the other side.

Along the river, authorized water intake projects compete to take water. Thus, the total intake capacity reaches 100 cubic meters per second during the irrigation season, leaving no more than 10 cubic meters per second in the river channel. Moreover, in recent years, the natural flow of the Zhanghe River has gradually decreased, owing to excessive water development and the continuous deterioration of the ecosystem. The water-related strife has greatly undermined the social stability and economic development of the local area.

On June 3, 1989, the State Council adopted the Water Distribution Scheme for the Zhanghe River drafted by the Department of Water Resources. In 1992, under the coordination of the Department of Water Resources, Henan and Hebei Province jointly endorsed the Agreement to Solve the Water-Related Conflicts in the Zhanghe River. Meanwhile, a special administration bureau was established to take care of the overall management for the 108-kilometer-long river channel located along the borders of the three provinces. This bureau has strengthened the planning and management capacity for the river and has put more emphasis on the reasonable distribution of limited water resources. Moreover, based on the plan adopted by the Department of Water Resources, some water distribution projects have been implemented to satisfy the demands stipulated in the Water Allocation Plan of the Zhanghe River.

One example for the operation of the administration bureau relates to the 2002–03 winter/spring season. During that irrigation season, the minimum flow of the river channel was only 2.7 cubic meters per second, which threatened normal agricultural cultivation and escalated the existing tensions among water users along the river. Under the coordination of the administration bureau, the local governments in the lower reach provided US$90,000 to transfer a total amount of 30 million cubic meters of water from five reservoirs located in the upper reaches to the Hongqi Canal and Yuejin Canal irrigation zones of Henan Province and to the villages of the two provinces along the river. This additional water supply mitigated the water resource conflicts during the peak irrigation period and ensured the irrigation of 25,000 hectares of farmland. As a result, corn yields increased by 1,500 kilograms per hectare, and a rapport could be achieved among water users on both sides of the river.

In this case, the water distribution scheme was clearly defined by legal documents, in which key factors, such as the quantity of water to be used, were explicitly stated. This improved the status of the water right. The predictability of where water would be used was advantageous for the maintenance and management of the water in the system. Moreover, the unified management of the water resources in the whole river basin was favorable to achieving a more optimal resource utilization and distribution from upper to lower reaches, particularly in extreme climate events, such as the recent drought.

Water Supply Contract between Yiwu City and Dongyang City in Zhejiang Province. Dongyang City and Yiwu City border each other, and are located along the upper reach of the Jinhua River, an important tributary stream of the Qiantang River. Before the recent reform and opening of the economy and policies, those two cities represented minor economies within Zhejiang Province. With the implementation of reform and the opening policy, the market economy boomed in the two cities, which then assumed leading positions in the province.

Yiwu City has relatively scarce water resources, with per capita usable water of 1,132 cubic meters per year. However, its residential population exploded from 30,000 to 350,000 people during the 1980s and today the city's population totals more than 500,000 people. The water supply capacity of Yiwu City could not keep up with rapid population growth. Most of the urban water is delivered from Badu reservoir, which was completed 2 years ago, located about 60 kilometers away. Water is beginning to constrain the further development of the city.

Dongyang City has a more favorable water supply, with per capita usable water of 2,126 cubic meters. Dongyang City owns two large reservoirs, Hengjin and Nanjiang. Hengjin Reservoir is located at the upper reach of Dongyang River, with a total reservoir volume of 280 million cubic meters and a designed reservoir volume of 173.2 million cubic meters. The reservoir was completed in 1964, but the spillway control was not installed initially, which resulted in a total reservoir capacity of only 142.7 million cubic meters. In 1998, the irrigation zone of Hengjin Reservoir was selected as one of the nation's main hydraulic projects for comprehensive agricultural development. After project implementation, an annual supplementary water supply capacity of 53 million cubic meters per year could be achieved, and canal efficiency levels for the main and tributary canals have been raised to 0.90 and 0.65, respectively. A total of 29.81 million cubic meters of irrigation water has been saved while the total irrigation area has been enlarged. After deliberate considerations about the long-term water resource situation, Dongyang City decided to transfer 50 million cubic meters per year of their former irrigation water to Yiwu for urban water supply.

According to water demand projections, new water sources for Yiwu City were needed within the next 2–3 years. Consequently, some preliminary plans were put forward. After undertaking a scientific feasibility study and technological and economic comparisons for both short- and long-term plans, the municipal government decided to provide a total of US$24 million as construction funds in exchange for a right to water supply of 50 million cubic meters per year from the Hengjin Reservoir owned by Dongyang City. On November 24, 2000, Yiwu City and Dongyang City signed a joint agreement to transfer part of the water use right of Hengjin Reservoir from Dongyang City to Yiwu City. This was seen as a pioneering agreement, signaling a reform in water use rights in the country, with the possibility of transferring these rights.

According to the agreement, Yiwu City pays for the water use right of 50 million cubic meters per year of water in Hengjin Reservoir with 200 million RMB (US$24 million). The water quality should reach Class I as stipulated by the national standard. After the water use right is transferred, ownership of the water resource does not change. Dongyang City is still responsible for the management and maintenance of Hengjin Reservoir. Yiwu City will be charged at a rate of US$0.012/cubic meter as an integrated management fee (including a water resource fee).

Yiwu City will be responsible for the design and investment of an aqueduct system that will transfer the water from the reservoir to the city. The construction component located within Dongyang City will be carried out by Dongyang City, but financed by Yiwu City. The total amount to purchase the water use right will be paid as installments along with the project construction. Thus, the transfer of the water use right of a water surplus of 50 million cubic meters and the ensuing compensation for water usage could satisfy the growing water demand of Yiwu City. Meanwhile, the hydraulic infrastructure of Dongyang City has begun to serve Yiwu City, and the 200 million RMB hydraulic construction fund of Yiwu City has been reallocated to Dongyang City to be employed for the long-term development of water resources.

The surplus water transfer from Dongyang to Yiwu has some characteristics of a water use right transfer, especially regarding the regulation related to the transfer and the actual transfer. The transfer satisfies the demand of Yiwu City while improving water supply conditions for existing users, thus producing both social and economic efficiency in terms of resource optimization. However, although this agreement is considered the first water use rights transfer in China, both buyer and seller do not have a legal right to surplus water usage. There is also no legal support for the apparently permanent duration of this transfer, which could undermine the transaction later on. As such, this transfer could only be considered a water supply contract (until the permit to use water was transferred, and thus the most fundamental prerequisite of a water right transfer was fulfilled).

Water Rights Transfer in Inner Mongolia and Ningxia. The areas along the Yellow River in the Inner Mongolia Autonomous Region and Ningxia Hui Autonomous Region are short of water resources, and total water usage has reached its allocated quota within the basin. At the same time, the water use structure of the two regions is unbalanced, with industrial water usage only 3 percent of total water usage, much lower than the national average of 20 percent. Agriculture uses more than 95 percent of the water, with the aged irrigation infrastructure resulting in lower water use efficiency. There is thus great potential for agricultural water saving. In the recent years, the economy has developed quickly in the two regions, with increased industrial and urban water requirements along the Yellow River. Thus, water has become a key constraint on economic transformation and development.

Since it is difficult to increase total water availability, the Yellow River Water Resources Commission, together with the water administration departments in the two regions, conducted water rights transfers in 2003 to solve the industrial and urban development water requirements. Through adapting water use structure and implementing water saving in irrigation districts, and under the condition of guaranteeing the domestic, food-security, and basic ecological water requirements, some agricultural water was transferred to the industrial sector, with compensation based on mutual benefits. This realized the optimal allocation of water resources. Through May 2004, eight large industrial projects in the two regions have signed agreements of intent for water rights transfer, with a total compensation of 360 million RMB.

To guide, formalize, and promote water rights transfer, the Ministry of Water Resources issued The Guiding Opinions of the Ministry of Water Resources on the Yellow River Main Stream Water Rights Transfer Tentative Work in Inner Mongolia Autonomous Region and Ningxia Hui Autonomous Region. This document defined the procedures and pricing considerations in water rights transfer. Based on the Opinion, the Yellow River Water Resources Commission formulated the "Yellow River Water Rights Transfer Management Method (Tentative)," for the Inner Mongolia Autonomous Region and Ningxia Hui Autonomous Region.

In this case, through the government's guidance to realize the partial transfer of agricultural water to the industrial sector, with compensation, the process functions as a form of water rights transfer under government regulation. This is a sign of how water rights practices in China are gradually being formalized and supported by legislation.

Water Allocation under the South-to-North Water Transfer Project. The northern part of China suffers extreme water shortages. The South to North Water Transfer

Scheme plans to transfer water along three different routes—the eastern, middle, and western routes—from the abundant Yangtze River to ameliorate the water shortages in the Huanghe, Huaihe, and Haihe plains and the nation's arid northwestern territory. To implement a unified planning and allocation system of the water resources in those five regions will be key to ameliorating the water shortages experienced in northern China.

To implement the South-to-North Transfer project, as a first step, source areas should be mapped with destination areas and compensation rules for the source areas should be established. The benefits to the various destination areas should be coordinated to avoid the phenomenon of "more water, more waste" which might be caused by the ambiguity between the right and obligations related to the planned water transfer. Real water demands in the destination areas should be determined based on careful analysis.

The allocation of the benefits produced by the water transfer is correlated with the construction. Several matters need to be established at the onset of construction, including the obligation to construct the transfer infrastructure and the right to use the transferred water during the operation period, the respective roles of local and central governments, as well as operation rules and water distribution criteria during the construction and operation periods. Moreover, the obligations, rights, and benefits of the water supply management companies and the water users need to be detailed.

Appropriate water quality levels (as a mixture of new and existing water resources), efficient usage, and economic prices for water need to be determined in this great opportunity that would dramatically change the water supply structure for large populations. Improved water use efficiency should be a major component of this water transfer project. Moreover, the cheaper water that had been illegally appropriated by industrial, agricultural, domestic, and municipal users should be returned to the original agricultural users. In the process, the water belonging to the ecosystem, which has been absorbed by farmers, could be released to the environment again. For these and other reasons, in the feasibility study of this huge water transfer project introduction of water rights issues is very important, as is the distribution of costs and benefits of this investment (Liu and Zhu 2002).

The implementation of this large water transfer project calls for the utilization of water use rights to distribute the water appropriately and to manage the water transferred from south to north adequately. However, there is a dearth of necessary lawful support from the nation's current law enforcement and water administrative system and thus it is imperative to accelerate the implementation of a comprehensive water rights legal framework.

Conditions for a Future Water Rights System in China

The Basic Concept of Water Rights

A water right is a kind of usufruct right that is clearly defined by law. It is also an exclusive right for water use related to the nation's ownership to water resources, which can be considered as a property right (Liu, Yang, and Wang 2001). There is as yet no formal definition for a usufruct right in China. However, the concept has been included in the draft of the *China Property Right Law*. In this draft, the water right is described as a usufruct right.

Generally, the characteristics that define the water right include purpose of use, quantity, quality, run-off, location, and period of water intake, as well as the priority level of the water right. There are multiple ways to categorize a water right: by origin, divided into customary and formal rights; disaggregated by purpose of use, including industrial, agricultural, domestic, municipal, ecological, and fishing rights; by frequency of water intake; by water availability, for example, by season; and by duration, that is, whether temporary or permanent.

The acquisition of new water rights should take account of and respect existing or old water rights. Before obtaining permission from the authority for the water right, the applicant should confirm consent from the owners of related existing water rights.

Water rights management is generally based on a basin-level management system, which can be divided into several subsystems with different levels. For each level, every water rights authority can manage only those water rights within this level of the system and should act so as to not damage existing water rights. The management of water rights systems includes registration and dissemination in a bulletin of established rights, the determination of priorities, and the coordination among water use rights, as well as the adjudication of water rights.

The Character of the Water Right

A water right has both a private and a public character. Whether a water right is a private right or a public right is subject to constant debate.[1] As a private right, the water right entitles the owner of the right to the benefit from water use, and this right can be inherited, enforced, or transferred. The public character of the water right relates to the need to distribute water rights to the benefit of the environment and social justice. Ideally, a water right should foremost be private, but regulated by the government to also attain benefits for the general public and the environment. As such, the government can restrict the acquisition, utilization, and transfer of water rights, and will carry out the management of water rights. If deemed necessary, the government can expropriate water rights or authorize competing water rights that have a higher priority in use level based on the needs of the public, without approval by existing water rights-holders.

Although the government retains certain rights to intervene in the water rights system, the main objective of the system will be to make the water right as stable and transparent as possible to serve the interests of the water rights-holders. Thus, a balance needs to be established between a stable and efficient water rights system and the achievement of public interests related to water rights.

Generally, the property right is more beneficial to the rights-holder than a contractual obligation would be. However, if there is too much administrative intervention regarding water rights allocation, uncertainty regarding the rights associated with the property right for water might increase, and water users might prefer contractual obligations rather than water rights. Therefore, it will be important that the water rights system strictly restricts government interventions into water allocation, to ensure the stability of water rights.

Analysis of the Holder of the Water Right

The holder of the water right could be an enterprise, a social organization, a legal person (such as a corporation), or a natural person. As public manager, the government implements the authorization and regulation of the water right, and plays a managerial role in the water right system. As such, the government, with the exception of the central government (based on ultimate ownership by the state), should not become an owner of water rights. Otherwise, the equality of the water rights system cannot be ensured.

In practice, there will often be issues related to water allocation that need to be negotiated among government authorities operating at the same level. Sometimes, higher-level government authorities can help achieve cooperation among lower-level authorities regarding water allocation. The Plan for the Annual Available Water Supply Allocation for the Yellow River defines the management purview of each government authority involved in the process, in particular as it relates to its role to defend the public interest.

For environmental and ecological water rights, although they concern the public interest, this could be represented by a government agency, acting as manager (trustee) of the right. Alternatively, the right could be licensed directly to certain organizations such as nongovernmental organizations or societal juridical persons, which are authorized to act as an agent for the public interest.

Water rights are particularly important in agriculture, as this sector accounts for about 70 percent of water consumption in China. In most countries, farmers obtain water rights as individuals, as do some societal juridical persons such as water users' associations, or service delivery companies. These water rights are typically related to the private ownership of land.

According to the present land management system in China, farmland is collectively owned by peasants. Each farmer's land share is relatively small. As a result, the adjudication of water rights directly to farmers might be uneconomical, in terms of water resource development and irrigation works, and would result in high costs for administration and management of the water rights system.

Therefore, agricultural water rights in China should not be issued directly to farmers, but instead to water users' associations set up by farmers and the society, or to enterprises or other juridical persons originating from the reform of the present irrigation administrative agencies. Water users' associations are mainly service agencies for the water use of farmers, whereas the irrigation management agency has the role not only of a service agency but also of a water supply enterprise with government authorization. In some special areas, water rights could be authorized directly to farmers, when it is deemed necessary and beneficial to water resources management.

If the water right is authorized to a juridical person such as a water users' association or the irrigation management agency, it will be crucial to ensure that individual farmers are treated fairly by these organizations. In practice, that means that a set of control measures must be established. For example, to control a water users' association, farmers can participate in election of officers and in democratic management, and establish related organizations to safeguard their interests. Regarding the irrigation management agency, there are three ways to exert control: first, to relate the permit for the management agency to the performance regarding water rights; second, through management of contracts to supply agricultural water; and third, to have farmers participate in and supervise the juridical person.

Priority in Use of Water Rights in China

Priority is a key element of water rights. First, water rights should be acquired based on the priority; and second, the priority of related rights can be used to solve some conflicts among water rights. As in the water systems of other countries, there are mainly two kinds of principles regarding the priority of the water right: one is an appropriation principle, based on historic usage; the other is a riparian principle, which is based on the ownership of the land adjoining a stream or other water body. The riparian right is generally used in Europe and the eastern United States, in areas characterized by sufficient water resources. One form of an appropriation right was mainly adopted in the western United States when water resources were scarce, with new water rights allowed only for surplus water in excess of the appropriation rights of older users, often summarized as "first in time, first in right."[2]

Forms of the riparian and appropriation doctrine are both accepted in Japan; for example, specific rights may be issued for new reservoir storage based on the availability of extra water. The adoption of allocation principles depends on the history and the object of water rights management as well as on the condition of the water resources. The specific principles need to be adjusted to local conditions in practice, to realize a reasonable and efficient usage of water resources (Liu, Yang, and Wang 2001).

The appropriation doctrine embodies respect for the history of water development and usage. The application of this principle could consider more varied water interests more appropriately than the riparian principle. Finally, it should be relatively easy to issue water rights based on the historic appropriation. Therefore, an appropriation doctrine should be adopted as the basic principle in China for water rights initialization and management.

In addition, the interest of the area of origin of the water source should be considered as a supplementary factor. Run-off and groundwater resources stemming from rainfall vary by region and with different land use. Areas where water originates should obtain some level of priority in using the water. This applies to riparian areas or areas above groundwater sources as well. However, these interests should remain secondary to the appropriation doctrine and should come into play only when the appropriation doctrine is not affected, for example, in allocating new rights where extra water is available.

During the initial definition and adjudication of water rights, the interests of the area of origin should be considered as a supplementary factor to the prior appropriation doctrine. Once the water rights system has been set up, the new water rights authorization should be strictly based on the appropriation doctrine, which will add to the transparency and stability of the water right. The water use purpose could be a point of reference as well and could be used as a secondary, affiliated principle.

Water Rights Transfers

In recent years, particularly in the face of rapid economic development, some types of water trades that have characteristics similar to water rights trading could be observed, particularly in areas facing severe water shortages. The most well known example is the Dongyang-Yiwu water purchase discussed earlier, which has broken new ground in the Chinese water management system and has given some impetus for the establishment of a water rights system in the country. The goal of a water transfer should support public water rights management through reallocation of water rights, and through development of new water rights, without significant adverse impacts on water rights in the area of origin.

Water rights can be divided into three categories according to the origin of the water resources: current water rights, which have been set up following the development of the water resources; rights to surplus water, which could be granted for developing surplus water resources; and incoming water rights, which can be added based on an interbasin water transfer. In general, water rights are closely related to the configuration of the macroeconomy, which can be described using terms such as achieving food security, growing urbanization, and industrial development. The configuration of the macroeconomy changes gradually. Therefore, restrictions need to be in place regarding the transfer of present water rights to ensure stability and to further development of the economy as a whole.

Incremental water rights stemming from water rights transfers, on the other hand, can be achieved only following large-scale investment. They should be related to the investment itself in order to protect the interests of the investors. The prerequisites of such water rights, for example, future users and purposes of usage, should be defined at the outset of the investment. More recently, drainage water rights, which refer to the right to polluted drainage water (including contaminated water), have come to the forefront, and could be a pilot area for water rights transfers. Cases here include the wastewater from Shanghai City and Jiaxing City in Zhejiang Province. To carry out water rights transfers in an appropriate manner and to deal adequately with all parties involved in the transfer, it is important to adjust measures to local conditions. As a result, an optimal configuration of water resources can be promoted and benefits to the economy, society, and ecology can be realized in an integrated and comprehensive manner.

To enable water rights transfers, a series of steps need to be carried out. Data collection and analysis of water resources, including standards, methods, and organization of inspections and evaluations, should be established or strengthened. Water usage should be supervised more closely, and water rights need to be clearly defined and measured.

A registration system for water rights should be established. Laws and policies related to water rights should be adopted and implemented. Water allocation should be optimized and guided through economic incentives, such as water resource fees, taxes, and water prices. The boundaries of water rights should be specified and clearly defined including quantity and duration of specific water rights. The system should protect water rights, particularly guaranteeing the stability of agricultural water rights.

The rules, organizations involved, and methods of trading, as well as the quantity of water traded and the procedures involved in trading should be stipulated.

Laws and regulations involved in supervising the water rights trade should be formulated that clearly define the role of the government, administrative procedures, and mechanisms for accountability and recourse for rights-holders.

The Initialization of the Water Right

At present, China is attempting to develop a water rights system. The initialization of the water right should be the first step in setting up such a system. To do this, historical and present water rights should be clarified and authorized as formal water rights in order to be brought into the new water rights system.

The definition of initial water rights should respect historic water usage and the water allocations under the current water permit system to avoid unnecessary confusion, panic, and potential conflicts that might result from trying to establish a completely new assignment of water rights. Customary rights, and stipulations of the water law, should be adhered to. They include a right to access water for domestic use and for small irrigation uses along rivers in areas that are not part of irrigation management areas. The initial water rights formulation should be, at the same time, simple, clear, and transparent to reduce management costs and uncertainties. As discussed earlier, priority should be accorded following the appropriation principle with secondary consideration of the riparian principle as well as the purpose of the water use. The three major rules to adjudicate initial rights could be to (1) respect historic and present water use, (2) avoid large adjustments, and (3) consider the water use purpose as a reference.

The priority of water rights can be expressed in different ways, depending on the condition of the water resource. For example, in an area with abundant water resources, priority can be based on the duration of the water use permission. In areas with water shortage and potential conflicts during the dry season, rights could be divided into stable wet season rights and temporary wet season rights, similar to the Japanese rights implementation, as it is easier to change levels of priority than the water right itself.

Organizational Options for the Water Rights System

Generally, there are two types of organizational systems for water resource management, unitary and federal systems. A unitary system would be appropriate for the analysis of the historic legal water management system in China. This system is also reflected in contemporary water resource management practices, and recent adaptations to water shortages.

Regarding the specific structure of the unitary water rights management system, three kinds of options need to be taken into consideration: (1) to keep and fully utilize the present water management system; (2) to reform the present water management system and enforce river basin commissions as agencies of the State Council; and (3) to set up water resources committees for water rights management at the national, river basin, and local levels.

The third option addresses the concern that the present water resource management authority might not be powerful enough to manage a water rights system. This weakness, in fact, relates mostly to the existing confusion regarding the definition of the rights and obligations associated with water rights among the government, society, and enterprises, and between the central and local government, and among various departments within the central government. Therefore, the existing weakness relates not to the present water management itself, but to the speed of accepting innovations and new mechanisms by the government.

The second option would involve upgrading some river basin commissions to a level directly below the State Council. This would, on the one hand, reduce the number of administrative levels and thus facilitate management; on the other hand, it would add to the workload of the State Council. Therefore, it is difficult to judge the full benefits of such a structure. Moreover, even if placed at this level, the river basin commission would still be at a lower level in the government hierarchy than provincial governments.

Water resource committees for water rights management—at the national or river basin level—are not authorized by the law. Furthermore, the new committee for water resources management may incur juridical conflicts with the water resources ownership authority of the State Council, which acts on behalf of the nation. It would be difficult to sort out the respective administrative roles between the committee and the government, and between committees at different levels. Moreover, a legal basis would need to be established first.

The first option suggests that the water right management should be based mainly on the present water resource management system, which would allow for a smooth continuation from present into future water administration. This appears to be a suitable solution for the initial development of the water rights system. This type of management could also be suitable for innovative measures, especially regarding the definition of the administrative authority of the government. The current management and administration system is also conducive to a certain efficiency. It will be helpful to separate the administrative authority properly by appropriate levels and to encourage the management and participation of water users.

Key Issues in Water Rights Management

Fairness of the Water Rights Permitting Procedure

Fairness is an important element in adjudicating water rights to exclude improper uses and users, and will lead to a more stable and respected water right. The foundation of a fair procedure lies in its transparency to the public. A fair procedure should ensure that every party related to the water rights permission could fully state their claim. The procedure should also allow for a reasonable predictability of the outcome of the water rights permit procedure.

The principle of fairness does not exclude an acknowledgement of the economic nature of water rights. Instead, fairness is the underlying principle for economic use and efficiency of the water right. Only after fairness is guaranteed can economic indicators and principles, such as water and cost savings, be pursued.

Expropriation of the Water Right

Expropriation of water rights can lead to uncertainty regarding the security of the water right. Only transparent and strengthened legal procedures can guarantee that expropriation and its procedures are open to the public and occur in a predictable manner. As the water rights-holder may consider expropriation as a type of administrative invasion, it must be strictly limited. The possible conditions that can lead to the expropriation of water rights need to be strictly regulated and carefully stated, in order to ensure stable and truly beneficial water rights.

Since the expropriation of water rights is a deprivation to the rights-holder, which invades the legal interest of the water rights-holder, the holder should be compensated for the expropriation. In the present legal system of China, compensation can be obtained only if the expropriation by the government was not legal. Compensation for legal takeover by the government, on the other hand, is specified only in some policies, which are associated with differing levels of uncertainty. Thus, the compensation for the water rights expropriation should be regulated in the water rights system, to improve the security of the water right to the rights-holder.

If water expropriation occurs, the power of the rights-holder will be very small compared to the power of the government. Thus, there must be efficient administrative relief to safeguard the interest of the rights-holder in case of expropriation. For example, a right to lodge an administrative complaint in case of expropriation should be included in the legislative framework.

Conclusions

Water Rights System and Water Resources Allocation

The water rights system falls under the general system of water resources management as defined by the law. Establishing a water rights system does not automatically translate into optimal water resource allocation. However, a properly specified and reasonably allocated water right can benefit overall water resource allocation.

There are many ways to achieve a more optimal allocation of water resources, through legal, economic, or technical means. However, an appropriate water rights system forms the basis for any optimal water resources allocation. Only under the legal management for water rights can a stable, predictable, and reasonable water resources allocation be realized, and then the economic adjustment measures can become more efficient. The establishment of a water rights system should be based on the theory of optimal water resource allocation and serve an improved allocation of water resources.

The Prospect for Developing Water Rights in China

The process for setting up a water rights system will be long and gradual, moving from theory to practice in a step-by-step approach. Basic activities that need to be carried out at the outset include an agreement on the quantity and quality of the water that will be subject to water rights, the definition of the water right and the respective roles of water manager and user, and the formulation of an operational plan with related procedures. Then, a water rights permit procedure will be developed, implemented, and standardized, including related documentation. The priority system will be implemented, and the legal framework will be completed. Once the legal system is complete, water rights markets could be contemplated. Within this process, the definition of the initial water right, and the continuing regulation and gradual introduction of the system are considered the key steps.

The water rights system needs to take full account of the history of water use. In a first step, the water rights system could regulate the present water resource management system, without reallocating rights. The currently existing water permit system in China, in some cases and in recent years, has realized activities that are similar to those that would take place in a fully established water rights system, particularly in relation to permit management, water allocation, and quantity and quality control. The advantages of the water use permit system should not be forgotten, especially unified management for both surface and groundwater resources, and the powerful administration, especially in relation to intermediation.

The process of water rights system development should be adjusted to local conditions, in particular local water resource characteristics. For example, in the Yellow and the Haihe river basins, attention should focus on initial water rights determination with an emphasis on improved water use efficiency and environment, and on the allocation of incremental (out-of-basin) water rights. In the Huaihe River Basin and the Taihu River Basin, key water rights issues will relate to pollution prevention, water quality improvements, and the definition of clean water rights. In the Changjiang (Yangtze) and Zhujiang (Pearl) river basins, water rights registration and management, as well as water pollution control will be important (Liu 2001).

Education and raising awareness concerning water rights in the entire country will be key for a successful water rights system. Only when all water users—wherever they may be located and whatever sectors they belong to—recognize the economic interest of water resources properly and have their water rights protected through a strong legal framework will there be sufficient support for a water rights system. As water rights affect everybody in the society, we can foresee that their development will also promote future innovation in the legal and economic system of China.

Notes

1. For examples of how public authority limits private use of water rights in some western states in the United States see *City & County of Denver v. Sherif,* 193,96 P.2d 836,840 (Colorado 1939); and *Pratt v. Department of Natural Resources,* 309 N.W.2d 767,771 (Minnesota 1981).

2. [Editor's note: As used here, an appropriation principle covers not only individually sequential rules for prior rights, as in the western United States (see Kenney, this volume), where each senior (prior) rights-holder should receive their full entitlement, in order of historic usage associated with their right, before the next rights-holder is allowed any water; but also proportional systems where all holders of water rights (or holders of a particular class of rights), share equal rights to the available water, as in Australia (see Haisman, this volume).]

References

Liu, B. 2001. Advice on water right in China water information net. December 24, 2001.

Liu, B., and E. Zhu. 2002. On the south-to-north water transfer project and water rights system. *China Water Resources* 2002: 1.

Liu, B., G. Yang, and L. Wang. 2001. Water right system and water resource management in China. *China Water Resources* 2001: 4.

MWR (Ministry of Water Resources, China). 1998. *China water resources bulletin.* Beijing: MWR.

UNCSD (United Nations Commission for Sustainable Development, Report of the Secretary General). 1997. *Comprehensive assessment of the freshwater resources of the world.* Preparation coordinated by Stockholm Environment Institute (SEI) for UN/UNDP/UNEP/FAO/UNESCO/WMO/World Bank/WHO/UNIDO.

Part 5

Conclusions

Chapter 12

Reforming Water Rights: Governance, Tenure, and Transfers

Bryan Randolph Bruns, Claudia Ringler, and Ruth Meinzen-Dick

— Water rights can be useful tools for protecting availability of water for basic needs, securing irrigation deliveries, increasing urban water supplies, and enhancing environmental flows. The water rights reforms reviewed in this book show some common patterns in performance problems that induce institutional change, initiative by government, increases in stakeholder consultation, concern with transferability of water rights, and continuing challenges in implementing new policies and responding to environmental needs. As a whole, reform experience suggests that institutional design should pay much more attention to the time dimension of water rights reforms. A phased approach offers a practical pathway to making reforms more effective in (1) redesigning water governance, (2) resolving water tenure, and (3) regulating transfers of water rights. To help guide future reform efforts, research priorities include improving understanding of existing forms of rights to water, analyzing critical factors for institutional design, advance testing of alternative rules, and empirical assessment of institutional alternatives.

As competition for water grows across the globe, water users and water management organizations seek better institutional arrangements for coordinating use and resolving conflicts. Done right, water rights reform can secure access to water for existing users and offer equitable ways to meet additional water needs, including urban expansion, economic growth, and environmental protection. However, reforming water allocation institutions also faces many risks. Change may bog down in policy debate or be stalemated while problems worsen. Even if new laws and regulations are enacted, they may remain unimplemented, opposed by powerful stakeholders, constrained by lack of institutional capacity, or crippled by unworkable stipulations. Reforms may consume great effort but yield little impact, or even backfire, engendering confusion, conflict, and insecurity about access to water. Registration procedures may make it difficult or impossible for some existing users to have their rights recognized. Security for some users may come at a cost of reinforcing inequities and institutional rigidity that excludes others. Reforms may achieve economic gains, but leave environmental demands unmet. These are just some of the many ways in which well-intentioned reforms may be frustrated or fall short of their objectives in improving water management. The chapters in this book have illuminated options for designing reforms and navigating the sometimes treacherous institutional landscape of water rights reform.[1]

The next section of this chapter looks at common patterns across different cases of water rights reform. The third section reviews the role of water rights as tools for achieving water management objectives. Many of the most important practical lessons from this book concern carefully considering time as an essential dimension in the institutional design of water rights reforms, and so the fourth section discusses crucial aspects of timing reforms. The fifth section outlines a phased approach to more effective reform of water rights: redesigning governance, resolving tenure, and regulating transfers. The sixth section then identifies priority issues for further improving research and practice in water rights reform.

Comparing Cases

The cases of water rights reform discussed in the earlier chapters of this book cover countries on six continents, describing changes in resource tenure rules governing access, use, management, and transfer of water. The case studies show some commonalities in performance problems that prompted the reforms, sources of initiative, changes in allocation principles, forms of public participation in water governance, and challenges for future development of water allocation institutions. Table 12.1 briefly recapitulates characteristics of the cases under these headings.

Problems Prompting Reforms

Almost all the authors noted increasing competition and conflict accompanying water shortages. Water rights systems in Australia, Spain, and the western United States promoted relatively secure access for irrigators, but these systems have faced growing challenges from urban growth and environmental concerns. Social inequities in access to water were a key issue in South Africa and the three Andean countries, and the risk that poor farmers would lose access to water vital to their livelihoods was voiced as a major concern in water law debates in the Andes and Indonesia. Water pollution affected basins in Mexico, while salinization was a major problem in the Murray-Darling Basin in Australia. Transboundary allocation and reallocation between states and provinces posed problems in Australia, the United States, and China.[2] Growing demand, water shortages, and environmental concerns stand out as major factors that helped impel or induce reform in water rights.

Initiators

Governments at the national and state (province) level were the primary initiators of reforms in all the cases discussed in the book. Federal governments in the United States and Australia provided some impetus for reform at the state level, as did the European Union Framework Directive on Water for Spain. The World Bank and other multilateral and bilateral development agencies have encouraged reforms in Indonesia, South Africa, Vietnam, and in Andean countries.

Social movements played a major role in opposing proposed reforms in the Andean countries, and in some other countries such as Thailand and Sri Lanka (Gunatilake and Gopalakrishnan 2002). However, civil society groups so far have generally not moved from opposing proposed water law revisions to initiating or achieving enactment of their own policy proposals. None of the reforms seemed to arise directly from popular demands and pressures. Reforms may have sought to accommodate stakeholder organizations concerned with watershed management, which have emerged or been promoted in many countries. However, such watershed-oriented groups do not seem to have played major roles in defining reforms and their implementation, although this may have started to change in some places (Boelens, Dourojeanni, and Hoogendam, this volume, and see Warner and Moreyra 2004; Warner and Verhallen 2004).

The reforms focused on surface water, managed through established technologies of canals and reservoirs, and paid less attention to the regulation of private pumping (despite its proliferation in recent decades).[3] Reform proposals were framed in the language (discourse) of concepts prevailing with elite communities of water bureaucrats and experts.[4] Although water agencies could draft laws, these were subject to significant revisions resulting from political pressures as they passed through the legislative process, and political dynamics could also delay or stall legislative changes.

Reforms in Mexico, China, and Australia were strongly linked with major shifts by national governments toward pro-market policies (as had also occurred in Chile, for example), intended to reduce burdens of agricultural and water-related subsidies and make agriculture and the overall economy more internationally

Table 12.1 Comparison of water rights reform cases

Country/ region	Key dates	Performance deficiencies	Initiators and initiatives	Allocation before reforms	Allocation after reforms	Performance impacts	Public Involvement	Challenges
Mexico	1992 Water Law 1994 Regulations	Scarcity, pollution, conflicts	Government, market policy	Agency administration	Registration. Tradable rights, 10-year renewal, IMT	User pays Some trading Control in some basins	Public education, representatives on basin bodies	Overallocation. Long time needed
Australia, New South Wales (NSW)	1994 policy by Council of Australian Governments (COAG)	Salinity, shortages, river health, trans-boundary conflicts, overallocation	State and federal governments. Market policy, environmental values	Usufruct rights, tied to land	Cap, water rights untied from land, access and use rights split, proportional, reliability levels, 10-year renewal, continuous accounting, IMT	Trading and economic gains Environmental flows	Extensive public consultation on reforms	Reallocation to environment, interstate trade
South Africa	1994 Water Law	Racial inequities in access to water	National government. Regime change	Rights for commercial farmers	Reserve prioritizes basic needs and environment, redistribution mechanisms, WUAs	Planned	Extensive consultation, representatives on catchment boards	Implementation, consultative process
Western United States	1980s–1990s	Environmental impacts	Federal and state governments, competition, environmental values	Prior rights, local user governance	Tradable rights, instream flows. Mix: prior rights, markets, environmental priorities	Urban supplies, environment still lacks	Mainly elite control	Reallocation for environment. Equity

Andes	1990s–draft Water Laws	Poor communities lose water. Inequitable projects	Donors, national governments. Neoliberal policies	National laws, local user governance	Proposals for tradable rights in Chilean-type laws opposed. Still tension of state and communities. Some IMT	Few changes—inequitable reallocation persists	Participation, but limited and biased	Combining consensus-building and empowerment
Spain	1985 and 1999 Water Laws	Environmental shortages	National government, European Union Water Directive	Rights, not tradable, local user governance	Tradability relatively restricted. Legal provision for IMT	1985 reforms little impact, trying again	Policy for more user participation	Restrictions on tradability
Indonesia	2002 Water Law	Shortages, uncompensated reallocation	Donors, national government. Regime change	Agency administration, some domestic and industrial users licensed, local user governance	Usage and commercial rights, not transferable, WUAs and federations, IMT pilots	Law passed, not yet implemented	Stakeholder representatives in water councils	Implementing law, protecting rural rights to water
China	1988 and 2002 Water Laws	Shortages, environmental and agricultural losses	National government. Market policies	Agency administration, some licensing, local user governance	Caps in interprovincial basins, environmental allocations. Transferable rights proposed, WUA programs	Security Environmental flows. Some transfers	Little so far. Hearings planned for water rights issuance	Environmental flows, protecting rural rights to water

Source: Compiled from previous chapters.

Notes: IMT = Irrigation management transfer; WUA = water user associations.

competitive. Regime change helped precipitate reform in water policy and law in Indonesia, and even more so in the case of South Africa's efforts to redress racial inequities in access to water. Societal shifts in environmental values and policies, reflected in changes in leaders' priorities, had a strong influence in Australia and the western United States, and also played a role in other countries including China, Indonesia, Spain, and South Africa. Overall, initiatives for change in water rights seem to have been triggered primarily by influences outside of the water sector, and were then shaped through elite perceptions and politics within the sector.

Allocation before Reform

In most cases, water was initially controlled through agency administration. Even where formal user rights existed, these were usually tied to land and not transferable. Thus, water rights in Australia had been linked to land, as they also were in most western states of the United States until the last few decades. In China, Mexico, and Spain, rights were not tradable. Rights to use water for irrigation were generally unregistered in China, Indonesia, and Mexico. At local levels, water allocation embedded in community institutions for user governance continued to play significant roles in the Andes, Indonesia, and elsewhere. Irrigators' organizations have historically played a strong role in governing local water allocation in Spain and the western United States.

Allocation after Reform

Enabling at least some transferability has been the major change, allowing exchanges among rights-holders to begin to play a greater role in water allocation. Reforms in Australia untied water from land, with substantial trading appearing within states, and pilot efforts begun for trading between states. In recent decades, many states in the western United States increased the options for water trading, although still limited to trades within individual states. China, Mexico, Spain, and South Africa enacted legal changes establishing a framework for transferable water rights. In Mexico, some trading has occurred in limited areas, while transfers are more limited in Spain and implementation procedures are still under development in China and South Africa. Transferability of rights was a key point of contention for Indonesia's draft water law, whose final version prohibits transfers of water use rights. Proposed laws including tradable rights (as had been earlier enacted in Chile) met strong opposition in Andean countries. With the exception of some specific areas of Australia and the western United States, highly developed water market systems have not yet appeared in the cases discussed here.[5]

In many cases, attention to registering rights and enabling transfers seems to have overshadowed the more basic issue of security of tenure, and the consequent need to strengthen institutions for conflict resolution. This is an issue not just in countries seeking to incorporate irrigation water use into formal water rights systems, but also for areas with long histories of formal rights for agricultural water. Thus, for example, Australia, Spain, and the western United States are still grappling with questions of how to integrate environmental allocation into basin water governance, dealing with the implications of competing claims and reallocation for long-established users such as irrigators.

Reforms in Australia and Mexico transferred irrigation management responsibilities to irrigators' associations, thus strengthening user governance of local water allocation. China, Indonesia, and South Africa also had significant initiatives to transfer irrigation management to water users' associations (WUAs), with some positive impacts on local equity in water distribution, but so far without major changes in rights, authority, or outcomes concerning water allocation above the level of individual irrigation systems.

Participation

Extensive public consultation was a major part of reforms in Australia and South Africa, countries that have undertaken some of the most ambitious reforms. Substantial public education was carried out as part of introducing reforms in Mexico. Most of the countries discussed in this book have moved to increase stakeholder participation in basin or sub-basin boards, councils, committees, or similar bodies. In China, the United States, and elsewhere, participatory innovations have been increasingly applied to improve management of water quality (Wheeler 2000, and see Schlager, this volume; Rose 2002; and Tietenberg 2002). In most countries, stakeholder bodies have been assigned policy and advisory roles, rather than directly wielding authority over budgets and basin management agencies. In other words, reforms have increased consultation, but not actually shifted power to make final decisions. Weak representation of poor farmers has been raised as criticism of participatory bodies in the Andes, Mexico, and South Africa (Boelens, Dourojeanni, and Hoogendam, this volume; Wester, Merrey, and de Lange 2003), and the chapter on the United States also criticizes elite dominance of policymaking.

Challenges

Most of the challenges for future development of water rights institutions are posed by implementing laws that have been enacted, and by demands to increase environmental flows. In Australia, New South Wales and other states are seeking ways to provide more water for environmental needs, as well as developing interstate water trading. South Africa still faces challenges of putting into practice the new principles enacted in its water law, including quantifying the reserve allocated for basic human needs and the environment. The legacy of the prior rights system in Colorado and other western states in the United States strengthens the position of existing rights-holders, and constrains the options for responding to demands to increase allocations for the environment. Spain will need to find ways to address the environmental objectives in the EU Water Framework Directive, as well as possibly developing more effective ways to facilitate trading. Mexico is still working on reconciling overallocation of registered rights with the quantities of water actually available. Indonesia also faces challenges in figuring out ways to implement its new water law (if the law survives recent constitutional challenges). China is developing implementing arrangements to apply the principles promulgated in the 2002 Water Law. For Peru and other Andean countries, better methods for involving stakeholders might help generate consensus about how to reform water allocation in ways that will help rural communities.

In sum, water rights reform has mainly been driven from outside the water resources sector, including by regime change, by reforms intended to strengthen markets and economic productivity, and by shifts in environmental concerns. Basin-level water allocation is primarily governed by bureaucratic agencies, with widespread initiatives to increase stakeholder voice, and some localized examples where trading plays a significant role in reallocation. Water rights institutions play an increasing role in controlling surface water, but so far have had less impact on aquifer management.

The Right Tools

Water rights are not a panacea, and may or may not be the "right tool for the job." The preceding chapters illustrate some of the achievements and limitations of water rights in relation to specific goals in water management. This section reviews some of the issues and outcomes related to ensuring water for basic needs, securing reliable rights for irrigation, accommodating customary rights, supplying water to cities, and increasing environmental flows.

Basic Needs

South Africa's "reserve" will prioritize water for basic domestic use and environmental needs. Almost all countries exempt minor water use for drinking, bathing, sanitation, and watering of household livestock from licensing requirements. Such exemptions provide priority, but only if supplies are actually available and not consumed upstream. In other words, their effectiveness depends on whether water governance institutions can regulate excessive abstraction by competing users.

Under Indonesia's new water law, "people's agriculture" is allowed access to water without requiring a license, and may be defined in a way that covers the majority of small cultivators. Such household water use may provide a vital resource, not just for home consumption but also to grow crops for sale. Many rural, periurban, and even urban water systems support small-scale irrigation, and so affect the demand for and use of water. However, including home gardens and other small-scale irrigation substantially expands the volumes of water covered under such basic needs, particularly during the dry season and dry years, and so could affect the priority and security of water supply for more narrowly defined domestic uses.

In the case of South Africa's reserve, the water rights system will act as a tool to deliberately prioritize domestic and environmental needs, and restrict irrigation and other uses to the remaining amounts. In general, water rights systems may regulate the amounts abstracted for urban and rural water supply systems, and, as discussed later, may facilitate reallocation to such systems. Thus, water rights may help secure supplies for basic needs by restricting competing uses. However, actual delivery of water for basic needs depends on developing water supply systems and the institutions that manage and finance service provision.

Secure Irrigation

In areas such as Australia and the western United States, formal water rights systems were developed to ensure reliable access for irrigators. In some parts of Mexico, new water rights institutions have been used as a basis for addressing conflicts where demand and claims exceed available supplies of surface- and groundwater. Systems such as these have reduced conflicts and uncertainty for irrigators. On the other hand, effective water rights systems may act to lock in the access of irrigators, providing them with security and incentives for investment in improving their irrigated agriculture, but possibly making it more difficult to shift water to other users and uses.

In the Andes, and many other parts of the world, community institutions regulate access to water for agriculture, but their access to water is vulnerable to being lost to stronger outside groups. Lack of clear water rights in China, Indonesia, and elsewhere leaves farmers with access to water that is insecure and uncertain. However, changes such as codification of rights might create new insecurities, especially if the arrangements for enforcing rights and for review and compensation of transfers are unclear or ineffective. Thus, proposals to develop formal rights create both threats and opportunities for the security of local access to irrigation water.

Customary Rights

Programs to reform rights to water may threaten to disrupt or destroy local institutions that regulate access to water. The formulation of new water laws without understanding of existing systems is particularly problematic, but even codification itself can rigidify and distort customary systems (Sengupta 2000). Mexico required registration within a deadline, or else rights would not receive legal protection. Such deadlines may be included in laws without much thought about their implications for customary rights, and without consideration of alternatives that better protect existing uses and avoid disrupting local institutions for water management. Indonesia's new water law takes a different approach, recognizing basic rights for small-scale use, without requiring registration.

In practice, countries may accept most existing rights, even when these had not been fully documented, and it would be desirable to formulate statutes in ways that are compatible with such practices. Reforms in China propose to clarify rights primarily by recognizing existing use. A goal for management platforms in the Andes would be to allow regional communities to protect their rights to water, in ways that would provide such broader communities with autonomy to manage water, without necessitating fragmentation into separate rights for individual householders or villages (Boelens and Bustamante 2005). As part of new policies to implement a more just allocation and increase welfare, South Africa now seeks to redistribute water rights, and develop capacity to make productive use of the water, for communities that were previously dispossessed and denied their customary rights to land and water.

Urban Water

Growing cities and industry generate increasing demands for water. In almost all countries, irrigation consumes the lion's share of water use. In theory, relatively modest reductions in water use by irrigated agriculture would be more than enough to supply the needs of cities and industries. Changes in technology and cropping practices have the potential to allow such reductions without necessarily reducing yields. However, a more common pattern is for farmers to lose water with little or no compensation and assistance in adjusting to increased water scarcity. China, Indonesia, and many other countries are still struggling to develop mechanisms by which water transfers out of agriculture could occur without harming the welfare of farmers. This is one reason for the interest in developing tradable water rights and water markets, which might allow such transfers to occur through voluntary "win–win" transactions between farmers and cities. Australia and the United States offer examples of water rights systems that have allowed such voluntary transfers in some cases. Water rights in Mexico are transferable, and some trades have begun between industry and agriculture, primarily for groundwater.

The chapter on Australia offered some estimates of the economic value of water transfers, which occurred primarily within the agricultural sector, once these were enabled and facilitated by water rights reforms. However, experience in Latin

America and elsewhere indicates that developing water markets is more complicated than sometimes expected or assumed. Clarifying existing rights is problematic. Regulation of transfers usually must take into account consumptive use and return flows, and consider impacts on local communities and the broader environment. Attempting to leap directly to a tradable rights system may be a recipe for frustration and failure. Instead, as discussed later, a phased approach to water rights development may be more effective. Nevertheless, many of the cases in this volume illustrate the potential role of water rights for establishing a better institutional framework for equitable shifts of water from agriculture to municipal and industrial use.

Environmental Flows

Reallocating water to meet environmental priorities continues to be a major challenge in the western United States, despite or even because of the long history of water rights and complex institutional development. In Australia, license renewal provides an occasion for adjusting allocations in order to reclaim more water for environmental needs. However, since this is not sufficient to provide the amounts sought for the environment, debate continues about how to meet these needs, and to what extent such transfers may require compensation. After China's Yellow River began to repeatedly dry up, not reaching the sea for months at a time, the State Council intervened successfully to set limits on total abstraction, determine provincial allocations, and ensure flows to the sea. These principles are embodied in the 2002 Water Law. However, comprehensive implementation of the principles in other basins, and at lower levels within provinces and sub-basins is a task for the future. Indonesia's new water law declares the importance of environmental objectives, although it provides little detail on how such objectives will be realized. As mentioned earlier, the specific mechanisms for implementing South Africa's reserve have gone through a long process of formulation, but are still not yet fully specified. (However, it is worth noting that South Africa differs from most countries in requiring water licenses for commercial forestry that would increase water consumption.) In the western United States, some examples exist of water rights trading being used to augment environmental flows, which has sometimes required amending legal requirements for beneficial use and determining what entity would hold rights on behalf of the environment.

More commonly, increased environmental flows have been sought through mechanisms that would not require payment or other compensation, based on principles of national sovereignty over water (such as the public trust doctrine), which assert an overriding national priority. Pressures to reallocate water for environmental needs will continue to be a major challenge in many countries. Although environmental allocations are usually not embodied in formal water rights, water rights systems structure the context within which contests over water play themselves out, and determine feasibility of regulating competing uses.

Water rights systems have been relatively effective in securing access to water for irrigators, and in some cases tradable water rights have facilitated transfers within agriculture and from agriculture to municipal and industrial use. Reallocating water for environmental demand poses a continuing challenge, with current usage levels still leaving many basins overallocated when compared to environmental objectives.

Water rights are one type of tool for water management, which can be effective only in combination with other supportive institutional arrangements. Tradable water rights are an even more specialized tool, suitable for use under specific conditions, but not the only or best tool for dealing with every problem. Decisions about when and how to modify and apply water rights need to consider objectives and conditions, to analyze whether water rights are one of the right tools, and if so, what modifications in water allocation institutions may be most useful, feasible, and timely.

Time for Reform

A central lesson from the preceding chapters is that water rights reform takes time, and that timing should be carefully considered in reforming water allocation institutions. Efforts to reform water rights may yield little benefit if pushed too soon, too quickly, or without appropriate synchronization between different components of institutional change. Conversely, reforms may be more effective if applied with realistic patience, timing that matches local priorities, and schedules that allow continuous learning and integration among changes in policy, regulation, and practice.

Time Scale

Experience in Mexico and elsewhere indicates that the relevant time scale for reform may be better measured not in a few months or a few years, but in decades (Garduño 2001 and in this volume). Many years of discussion and debate usually precede passage of legislation. Attempting to avoid this debate will, at a minimum, reduce the effectiveness of reforms, and may generate opposition that stalls the entire process. Compiling comprehensive information on water use within a large basin is a large task, as is developing effective institutional capacity for dealing with overallocation and other conflicts. Formal rules only become effective as they are applied within a matrix of local practices and understandings (e.g., see Guillet 1998). Such local ideas and norms tend to evolve much more slowly than formal regulations (North 1990). Expectations and schedules for institutional change and outcomes from water rights reform need to be matched to suitably long time scales, while still delivering more immediate benefits along the way.

Prioritizing Basins

Basins differ in the demand for and potential benefits from changes in water allocation institutions. South Africa is an example of a country that has set clear priorities for implementing changes in some basins before others. Prioritizing areas with the greatest needs and opportunities, rather than forcing all areas to move at the same pace, helps to make institutional change more efficient, effective, and productive. Rather than attempting to impose nationwide changes simultaneously, an enabling institutional framework that allows the timing of changes to respond to local conditions could be more effective. While the need for such local flexibility may seem obvious, laws and regulations continue to be passed that assume uniform and simultaneous implementation, rather than enabling prioritization and local initiative.

Time for Participation

Public involvement takes time and resources, but yields benefits in developing reforms that can be implemented with understanding and support of those involved. Extensive stakeholder consultation was central to the preparation of South Africa's water law in the face of severe inequities in access to water and profound societal transformation. A similar approach is being applied to working out how the water rights reforms will be put into practice. Lack of participation and lack of consideration about how proposed water rights reforms would impact rural communities has generated opposition to the reforms in Andean countries such as Peru, Ecuador, and Bolivia, as well as other countries such as Sri Lanka and Thailand (Abernethy, this volume; Boelens, Dourojeanni, and Hoogendam, this volume; Gunatilake and Gopalakrishnan 2002; Trawick 2003).

Development of empowered platforms for negotiation offers one way to formulate reforms that may command broader social support, but requires investing time and other resources (Boelens, Dourojeanni, and Hoogendam, this volume). Public consultation also played a major role in reforming water rights in Australia, with some of those initially most opposed later becoming strong proponents of change (Haisman, this volume and personal communication). China has recently issued guidelines on a framework for water rights development that explicitly includes improving negotiation procedures, as well as use of public hearings (MWR 2005).

The cases described in this volume illustrate the space that exists for water users and agency officials to shape how water rights reform occurs. Rather than simply being imposed, institutional change can be heavily influenced by the perceptions and interests of those involved. Investing in consultation early in the process can bear fruit in smoother reforms later on. Although administrative agencies typically continue to be the principal actors in water rights reforms, there is much scope for making reform more effective by allowing adequate time for involvement of stakeholders.

Parallel Schedules

It may seem logical to first develop policy, then revise laws and regulations accordingly, and subsequently devise ways to implement the new rules. However, a parallel-track approach to water rights reform is likely to prove faster and more effective (Garduño, this volume). Policies need to be framed in terms of achievable objectives. Laws and regulations that cannot be implemented become at best irrelevant and at worst may foment confusion and conflict. Experience suggests that water rights reform can work better if it builds on experimentation, on paper and in the field, to understand what will actually be required to put changes into place. It can even be useful for planners or implementers to identify bottlenecks by practicing all the procedures themselves, particularly to identify the difficulties that women or other marginalized users might face in securing their water rights through the proposed procedures. If regulations are developed in parallel with drafting of laws, then both can be adjusted to ensure there is adequate legal backing for regulations and that new laws support changes that can be put into practice.

Adaptive Management

Over time, the challenges facing water management change. The prior rights systems in Colorado and other states of the western United States were developed to support irrigated agriculture. In recent decades, these states have modified water rights in various ways to facilitate transfer of water among farmers and to growing urban areas. However, many aspects of the prior rights system still fit poorly with contemporary demands for environmental water quality and ecological preservation (Kenney, this volume). The Murray-Darling Basin in Australia now faces major challenges in trying to reclaim a greater share of water for environmental needs, in a climate prone to drastic variations in water availability. One of the arguments for limited duration for water licenses is that periodic renewal or reissuance provides a useful opportunity for adjustment in response to changing conditions and lessons learned (Haisman, this volume). Long-term climatic cycles and global climate change can be expected to pose continuing challenges for water allocation, along with other processes such as urbanization, and problems such as water pollution. Thus, there is a need for water rights systems that can adjust over time, not freezing into a single equilibrium pattern of allocation, but adaptively responding to continuing shifts in water availability, demand, and societal priorities.

Redesigning Governance, Resolving Tenure, and Regulating Transfers

Many water conflicts may be resolved by strengthening governance institutions for settling disputes and making rules. Formal rights are unlikely to make much difference unless rules on water tenure are accepted as legitimate and effectively enforceable. This implies a priority on forming forums, dealing with specific conflicts and developing general rules, rather than rushing to register rights. Steenbergen and Shah (2003) call for "rules before rights," pointing out how in some situations, relatively simple rules, such as timing of irrigation turns or spacing between well locations, may enable effective water management without requiring specification of individualized volumetric rights to water. In the broad definition of water rights used in this book, it can be said that "rules are rights," regulating who has rights to access, use, manage, or transfer water.

Rushing to formally register rights may generate "cadastre disasters" (Meinzen-Dick and Nkonya 2005) of expensive paper rights that are meaningless, or that disrupt existing institutions for water allocation, resulting in confusion and regress rather than in progress toward secure and equitable rights. Time is needed to build understanding and some degree of consensus on rules about access to water.

Premature emphasis on transfers and particularly on tradable rights before ensuring security for existing rights is a high-risk option, and quite possibly a recipe for resistance and failure. Areas known as examples of tradable rights, such as Australia (Haisman, this volume), the western United States (Kenney, this volume), and Chile (Bauer 2004), have each built on over a century of experience with formal water rights systems. Attempts to leap directly to tradable water rights have resulted in debate and rejection of water law reforms in countries such as Ecuador, Indonesia, Peru, Sri Lanka, and Thailand (see Abernethy, this volume; Gunatilake and Gopalakrishnan 2002; Trawick 2003). Development of systems of tradable rights takes time and experience. In the development of markets for tradable rights, transactions may initially require detailed negotiation and then become more routine and standardized over time (Colby 2000).

If rights are vested in users, then they gain an incentive to consider voluntary transfers, opening a politically feasible path to water rights reform. By contrast, attempting to dispossess water users from use they have enjoyed sets the stage for conflict. Attempts to impose administered prices paid to government (i.e., treating water purely as state property) may be resisted by users as expropriation of their rights to water and the value of such use that has been capitalized into land rights (Rosegrant and Binswanger 1994; Mohanty and Gupta 2002). A phased approach, vesting rights in existing users, and focusing on clarifying rights before developing mechanisms for transfers may be far more politically feasible. Unbundling water markets from other aspects of a water rights system may be crucial to allowing water rights to develop as a management tool to protect access to water, resolve conflicts, and facilitate equitable transfers.

Water rights transfers require well-defined rights (secure tenure). Effective governance institutions are needed to clarify rights and settle conflicts. Forums that establish simple rules may be sufficient to deal with many problems of basin water management, without requiring formalized rights. Water allocation can be arranged in accordance with various rules regulating water tenure, without requiring that such rights be transferable. Voluntary trading of water rights between users is only one of several forms for shifting rights to water, which also include intermediated exchanges (as in water banking), and compensation for involuntary reallocation. Given the institutional dependence of formal water rights and rights transfers on more basic governance arrangements, it may be helpful to distinguish three aspects of institutional change in reforming water rights:

1. *Redesigning governance*—forming more inclusive forums to negotiate agreements and rules;

2. *Resolving tenure*—establishing rules and other institutional arrangements to clarify rights and provide recourse for settling disputes; and

3. *Regulating transfers*—implementing routine mechanisms for temporary and permanent transfers, including relevant safeguards.

This should not be taken to mean that every water rights reform will or must deal with all three aspects. As mentioned above, in some cases, particularly where decisions are infrequent, it may be sufficient to focus on improving governance institutions that can deal with management problems on an occasional and ad hoc basis. In other cases, even if rights are clarified more comprehensively, but there are few pressures for reallocation, there may be no urgency to develop systematic mechanisms for dealing with transfers. If transfers are important, but relatively infrequent and unique, then they might be individually negotiated, with little need or advantage for developing specialized institutional arrangements, let alone the elaborate arrangements for registration and regulatory review that would be needed for sophisticated water markets. Therefore, these three aspects need not be found

Table 12.2 Characteristics of redesigning governance, resolving tenure, and regulating transfers

	Redesigning governance	Resolving tenure	Regulating transfers
Activities	Form forums for negotiating agreements and rules	Clarify rights, and ensure recourse for conflict resolution	Implement mechanisms for transfers
Allocation institution	User management: forming forums for participatory governance	Legislation and administration: define and recognize rights	Markets: trade/ compensation
Collective action level	Constitutional: stakeholders and scope, rules for making rules	Collective choice: rulemaking	Operational: applying rules, practice
Institutional design problems	Representation, decision costs, legitimacy	Monitoring, commitment, measurement	Enforcement, agency, recourse
Management challenges	Authority: arranging jurisdiction	Control: setting limits, caps, licenses	Accounting for transfers and impacts (externalities)
Transaction frequency	Low: ad hoc, complex negotiation	Medium: standardize framework for rights	High, enabling many exchanges
Performance criteria	Encompassing multiple interests, sustainability	Equity in allocation, security, reliability	Efficiency: water productivity
Dispute resolution	Who is at the table? Who can veto?	Choose rules and referees	Win-win agreements, safeguards
Common property and game theory	Overuse: tragedy of commons, free riding (negative sum)	Allocation: coordination, assurance (zero sum)	Mutual gains: cooperation (positive sum)

Note: Issue locations show relative emphasis, and are not intended as exclusive categories but as heuristic clustering of more closely related issues.

in every water rights reform, and some reforms may pay relatively little attention to transfers. However, we suggest that distinguishing between reforms in governance, tenure, and transfers, and ensuring that reforms place adequate priority on the first two before focusing on development of mechanisms for transfers, would contribute to more effective water rights reforms.

As shown in Table 12.2, these three aspects emphasize different clusters of activities, types of water allocation institutions, levels of collective action, institutional design challenges, management tasks, transaction frequencies, performance criteria, dispute resolution issues, and problems in terms of common property resource management and game theory.

Reform revises how administrative allocation, user governance, and market exchange are combined in water management (Bruns and Meinzen-Dick, this volume). Redesigning governance is often about introducing additional elements of user management into water allocation institutions, especially at the level of setting goals and policies. Administrative agencies usually play a major role in formulating rules, formally recognizing tenure rights, and resolving conflicts. Market exchange relationships become more prominent with transfers, as voluntary trading forms prices, or in negotiating possible compensation for losing access to water (involuntary water reallocation).

Redesigning basin water governance often requires a "constitutional" level (Ostrom 1990) process of collective action to include new stakeholders and a wider scope for water management (both geographically and across sectors), restructuring who will be involved and how decisions will be made. In such a process, stakeholder participation may be an essential means to incorporate different views and interests. Integrating environmental considerations into water allocation illustrates some of the constitutional-level complications of including different stakeholders and issues. There are technical complications in revising rules to include additional resource attributes and management objectives, such as environmental concerns with water quality and low flows, and in putting such rules into operation. However, the changes involved in redesigning governance to accommodate additional agencies and interest groups may well be even more challenging.

At the collective choice level of making rules, resolving water tenure requires determining the scope of rights to access, withdraw, manage, exclude, and transfer (Schlager, this volume). Key questions concern whose claims will be recognized, criteria that define rights, and arranging institutions to resolve conflicts. At the operational level, rules are then put into practice: recognizing rights, allocating water, and dealing with disputes. One subset of rules may well concern transfers, in which case reallocation could become primarily an operational-level process of transactions among users, or between users and those agencies mediating voluntary or involuntary transfers.

Reform must deal with institutional design problems of decision costs, principal–agent relationships, and commitment (Schlager, this volume). Decision costs are a major challenge for forums where stakeholders come together, delineate the scope of issues to be addressed, and seek agreement on rules for making rules. Resolving tenure usually relies on delegating duties to agencies to formulate more detailed regulations and put them into operation, so the problems of aligning agents' incentives and monitoring their behavior are crucial. Transfers can only occur where rights-holders can make credible commitments, based on rights that can be defended against infringement, and enforceable agreements for temporary or permanent transfers between users. Similarly, compensation for involuntary reallocation depends upon the state's commitment to respect existing rights. For governance, consensus about legitimacy and norms is an objective, while resolving tenure requires effective enforcement, and transfers need more detailed monitoring and accounting.

In redesigning or "reconstituting" water governance, institutional development tasks require arranging and coordinating authority among various entities, including the vertical and horizontal linkages through which they will interact. For basin water allocation, this typically requires combined efforts by multiple agencies and jurisdictions. Resolving tenure can apply such authority to set limits on abstraction or discharge, for example through determining overall caps and limits associated with specific licenses. In most places, transferability brings a need to deal with externalities, ways in which transfers may affect other users and the environment.

If resource conflicts are relatively rare, then infrequent, ad hoc solutions may be sufficient to deal with allocation and reallocation. Examples can be dealing with drought or specific projects to expand urban water supplies. Clarifying tenure requires some intensive effort to establish rules about who has what rights, but then may proceed with more minor adjustments. Water markets or water banking institutions can support more frequent transactions, by decentralizing decisionmaking to those engaging in specific transactions, subject to regulatory review according to standard criteria.

Satisfactory performance in establishing institutions for basin management requires addressing shared societal interests in effective governance institutions, encompassing multiple interests of different groups (Olson 2000), including intergenerational issues of environmental sustainability. Resolving tenure focuses on distributional issues of who gets what, security of access to resources, with major implications for social equity. Transfers can contribute to economic gains from greater efficiency, so that the productivity of water increases in value, while safeguards may help mitigate adverse impacts on equity and the environment.

In the terminology of dispute resolution, redesigning governance is about who has a seat at the table, and who has some degree of veto power over an agreement. Such veto power may be explicit, or implicit in the potential for noncompliance. Some practical examples of those with potential veto power, unless they consent to and comply with rules, include dispersed rural water users, groundwater pumpers, and hydropower operators. Resolving tenure is a matter of agreeing on the rules of the game, and who will act as mediator, arbitrator, or referee, to manage disputes and determine penalties for violators. In contrast to sports games with winners and losers, transfers offer the potential for "win–win" agreements, but also the need to protect against affected third parties ending up as losers.

In the analytical language of research on common property institutions and game theory, the basic challenge in redesigning governance is to overcome problems of overuse and underprovision, particularly free riding, which make everyone worse off, that is, a negative-sum game where noncooperation yields much lower payoffs for everyone. Clear allocation of rights emphasizes creating conditions that assure coordinated action by multiple users, although they may sharpen contention over dividing a fixed amount, that is, shifting to a zero-sum game where one person's gain is another's loss. Transfers open up the opportunity for mutual gains, cooperation that does not just divide a fixed pie but yields a bigger pie to share, that is, positive-sum games.

In some cases, reforms may progress sequentially through the three aspects of redesigning governance, resolving tenure, and regulating transfers. In other cases, forums alone, or in combination with more careful delineation of rights, may be sufficient. As in Mexico and South Africa, it may be feasible to enact a legal framework enabling support for new governance arrangements, redefined rights, and tradability, but in other cases political circumstances may suggest a phased approach to revising legislation. However, at a more practical level, changes need to be clearly sequenced. Attempts to institute transferability without well-defined rights are unlikely to succeed. Trying to redefine rights without ways to gain acceptance and support from major stakeholders is also unlikely to be fruitful. This analysis suggests that institutional design for water rights reform will be more effective if it takes account of how transfers and rights depend on more basic governance institutions, and suitably sequences emphasis on redesigning governance, resolving tenure, and regulating transfers.

Priorities for Applied Research

The chapters in this book not only offer insights from practice and analysis, but also provide a basis for identifying priorities for further study. As shown in Figure 12.1, a learning cycle can flow through understanding existing systems, discussing issues, developing reforms, studying reforms, and then repeating the process. Applied research can examine ongoing reforms, contributing to the process in an individual country and also distilling broader lessons for policymakers, stakeholders, and wider publics.

Research should look at both successes and failures, and should use research designs capable of understanding the complexity of the systems under study. Key areas of concern include further detailed research to understand existing systems, deeper analysis of critical factors for institutional design, using simulations to com-

Figure 12.1 Water rights learning cycle

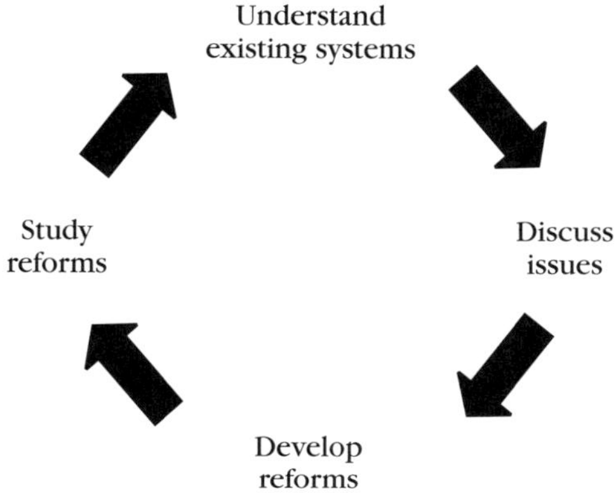

pare alternative rules for water allocation, and empirical assessment of institutional alternatives in water allocation.

Understanding Existing Systems

As noted in Chapter 2 and seen in many of the case studies, no country starts with a blank slate in water rights reform, even when water rights have not been codified in statutory law. Yet the existing range of water rights are insufficiently understood in many countries embarking on this process. For example, participants at the African Water Laws Workshop (2005) called for research and capacity building to record and understand local community-based water arrangements and the interface with other legal frameworks, including the gender dynamics of how water is used for multiple purposes. This "baseline" is critical for identifying the range of stakeholders and assessing how different types of reforms are likely to affect each group, with particular emphasis on poor and marginalized groups.

Institutional Analysis

Research on common property institutions for the management of natural resources including water, forests, pastures, and fisheries has developed a substantial body of concepts and research findings, some of which were introduced in the first two chapters of this book. Much more can be done to apply these concepts, and ideas from related research such as on collective action, game theory, and new institutional economics, to particular factors that play a crucial role in water rights reform (see Ostrom et al. 2002).

Research has identified the feasibility and cost of monitoring resource use, and related enforcement actions as a key factor, and one open to change through technological innovation. The potential impact of advancing information and communication technologies on measuring water flows and making hydrological information easily accessible thus offers very fertile ground for further study, from conceptual and practical perspectives.

Surface water abstraction, groundwater abstraction, and water pollution all affect common-pool resources, but have major differences, not only in the cost and feasibility of monitoring (Schlager, this volume, and see Rose 2002), but also in the differences between regulating extraction from a common pool versus regulating discharge into a common "sink" (Dietz et al. 2002). These merit further analysis to better understand how to fit management institutions to relevant resource characteristics.

Basin water governance can benefit from combining multiple institutions at different levels. However, in many cases horizontal linkages are underdeveloped, and vertical linkages primarily perceived in terms of competition (e.g., centralization versus decentralization), rather than consciously designing arrangements to optimally align complementary advantages of different institutions (Schlager, this volume; Young 2002). Therefore, much more needs to be done to understand the potential for deliberately designing improved institutional architectures and better-structured combinations of allocation institutions.

Research has led to better understanding and acceptance that neither state administration, nor user governance, nor water markets, provides the sole solution for every water management situation. As illustrated by some of the chapters in this book, there may be a general relationship between water scarcity and the need for detailed rights and institutional arrangements to regulate transfers of rights to resources. However, much remains to be learned about movement along a spectrum from rare negotiations to sophisticated markets (Colby 2000; Tietenberg 2002), and the factors that shape whether and how institutions evolve along such a pathway.

Empirical Assessment of Institutional Alternatives

Much policy debate concerning water rights is driven by fears of adverse impacts that may result from disruption of customary water rights, excessive abstraction, and unregulated water rights transfers. However, there is a shortage of empirical evaluation on the actual impacts of such problems and, more importantly, the differences in performance between alternative regulatory regimes, in terms of transaction costs, equity, productivity, sustainability, and other criteria.

Alternatives for accommodating existing rights without necessarily requiring registration do exist, including delegating authority to community organizations and authorizing agency recognition without registration. More should be done to understand the potential for further institutional innovation along these lines, and how such alternatives may affect outcomes for customary water users and others. This includes the impact of exemptions from licensing requirements, especially where the exemptions may include smallholder irrigation. Furthermore, the overall costs and benefits of formal licensing versus other institutional arrangements for regulating water need to be better analyzed.

Overallocation produces practical problems of limiting resource use, as well as potential constitutional questions of government jurisdiction, and eligibility for compensation for those affected by changes. While the full ecological costs of excessive abstraction may be difficult to determine, measures to partially restore flows may have more specific and measurable impacts. Mechanisms for dealing with overallocation, including issues of speculative claims and distributional equity, deserve more detailed examination.

The community impacts of allowing water transfers are a key point of concern and debate concerning changes in water rights institutions. More detailed analysis would provide useful insights for policy and practice. Relevant topics include economic multiplier effects, lumpiness and specificity of water assets, third-party effects on rural society, and the incidence of benefits and costs, particularly for the poor, that result from allowing or prohibiting flexibility in reallocation. As noted by Abernethy (this volume), in many countries these need to be considered in the context of rural–urban migration, rapid urbanization, and contested claims to water. Different forms of regulation can be expected to vary in their costs, vulnerability to corruption and manipulation, and effectiveness in preventing or mitigating adverse impacts of transfers, and so deserve further comparative study.

Testing Allocation Rules

Trying out different approaches to water allocation in the field, even on a pilot basis, is a long and uncertain process. However, several methods offer faster feedback on the implications of alternative rules. Institutional analysis can pinpoint crucial issues, such as incentives, monitoring, and enforcement, and problems of commitment, agency, and decision costs (Schlager, this volume). A great deal can be learned by walking through the process, particularly doing so with selected communities or individuals who have less education or access to other resources. Laboratory experiments can test rules, for example, whether restrictions on certain types of transfers, or limits on carrying over rights between seasons, have desirable effects, or may inadvertently worsen equity and productivity in water management

(Garrido, this volume). Integrated hydrologic–economic models provide another systematic way to identify the potential effects of changing rules, for example, the potential gains from allowing transfers and the opportunity costs of prohibiting transfers among users (Sarwan, Subijanto, and Rodgers, this volume). Models and other planning methods can be used with panels of stakeholders to look at different scenarios for water management, including use with participatory platforms for negotiating basin water allocation (such as those discussed by Boelens, Dourojeanni, and Hoogendam, this volume). While the relevant methodologies are relatively well developed as research techniques, there is much scope for participatory application of such methods in action research and practical implementation as part of reforms in water allocation. Better insights on existing rights, and on ways to adjust institutional designs, quick tests of alternative allocation rules, and improved empirical outcomes of regulatory arrangements would be particularly useful priorities for institutional learning about water rights reform.

Conclusions

The most crucial lessons for institutional design from the studies in this volume concern carefully considering the time dimension of water rights reform, particularly the importance of closely linking legal and regulatory changes with learning from past practices and pilot implementation, allowing enough time for stakeholder participation and for institutional change, and establishing enabling institutional frameworks adaptable to evolving basin priorities. Finding practical pathways to apply water rights as tools for more equitable, sustainable, and efficient water management requires better sequencing of reforms, successively emphasizing redesigning institutions for participatory water governance, resolving tenure rights, and developing equitable arrangements for regulating transfers.

Notes

1. The discussion here is based on the earlier chapters and other cited works. This chapter also draws on discussions and group presentations from the International Working Conference on Water Rights: Institutional Options for Improving Water Allocation held February 12–15, 2003, in Hanoi, Vietnam. For a synthesis of the main conclusions from the workshop process, see Bruns (2003).

2. Selection of cases for the Hanoi conference, and this book, deliberately focused on water reforms within countries, and not on international institutions for transboundary management.

3. On challenges of regulating pumping, see, among others, Shah (2005). For a comparative study of evolution in groundwater management institutions in three U.S. states, see Blomquist, Schlager, and Heikkila (2004). For development of groundwater rights, see Garduño et al. (2002).

4. These groups of water experts, officials, and researchers can be seen as part of an international "epistemic community" (Haas 1993) engaged in discussing problems and solutions. See Saleth and Dinar (2004) for an extensive analysis of expert perceptions of interrelationships among institutional arrangements and performance in water management.

5. In the case of Chile there is also commentary about the extent to which significant water trading has been concentrated in a few areas, particularly outside the intensively studied case of the Limari Valley (Bauer 2004).

References

African Water Laws Workshop participants. 2005. Plenary statement of participants. International workshop on African Water Laws: Plural Legislative Frameworks for Rural Water Management in Africa, January 26–28, 2005, Johannesburg, South Africa.

Bauer, C. J. 2004. *Siren song: Chilean water law as a model for international reform.* Washington, D.C.: Resources for the Future.

Blomquist, W., E. Schlager, and T. Heikkila. 2004. *Common waters, diverging streams: Linking institutions to water management in Arizona, California, and Colorado.* Washington, D.C.: Resources for the Future.

Boelens, R., and R. Bustamante. 2005. Formal law and local water control in the Andean region: A field of fierce contestation. Paper presented at the African Water Laws Workshop: Plural Legislative Frameworks for Rural Water Management in Africa, January 26–28, 2005, Johannesburg, South Africa.

Bruns, B. R. 2003. Water rights: A synthesis paper on institutional options for improving water allocation. Synthesis paper based on the International Working Conference on Water Rights, February 12–15, 2003, Hanoi, Vietnam. Mimeo.

Colby, B. G. 2000. Cap-and-trade policy challenges: A tale of three markets. *Land Economics* 76 (4): 638–658.

Dietz, T., N. Dolsak, E. Ostrom, and P. C. Stern. 2002. Introduction: The drama of the commons. In *The drama of the commons,* eds. E. Ostrom, T. Dietz, N. Dolsak, P. C. Stern, S. Stonich, and E. U. Weber. Washington, D.C.: National Academy Press.

Garduño, H. 2001. *Water rights administration: Experience, issues and guidelines.* FAO Legislative Study 70. Rome: FAO.

Garduño, H., S. Foster, C. Dumars, K. Kemper, A. Tuinhof, and M. Nanni. 2002. Groundwater abstraction rights: From theory to practice. *GW-MATE Briefing Note 5.* Washington, D.C.: World Bank Group and Global Water Partnership.

Guillet, D. 1998. Rethinking legal pluralism: Local law and state law in the evolution of water property rights in northwestern Spain. *Comparative Studies in Society and History* 40 (1): 42–70.

Gunatilake, H. M., and C. Gopalakrishnan. 2002. Proposed water policy for Sri Lanka. The policy versus the policy process. *Water Resources Development* 18 (4): 545–562.

Haas, P. M. 1993. Epistemic communities and the dynamics of international environmental co-operations. In *Regime theory and international relations,* eds. V. Ritterberg with P. Mayer. Oxford: Clarendon Press.

Meinzen-Dick, R. S., and L. Nkonya. 2005. Understanding legal pluralism in water rights: Lessons from Africa and Asia. Paper presented at the African Water Laws Workshop: Plural Legislative Frameworks for Rural Water Management in Africa, January 26–28, 2005, Johannesburg, South Africa,

Mohanty, N., and S. Gupta. 2002. *Breaking the gridlock in water reforms through water markets: International experience and implementation issues for India.* Delhi: Liberty Institute.

MWR (Ministry of Water Resources, China). 2005. *Framework for water rights system development.* January 11, 2005. Beijing: MWR.

North, D. C. 1990. *Institutions, institutional change and economic performance.* New York: Cambridge University Press.

Olson, M. 2000. *Power and prosperity: Outgrowing communist and capitalist dictatorships.* New York: Basic Books.

Ostrom, E. 1990. *Governing the commons: The evolution of institutions for collective action.* New York: Cambridge University Press.

Ostrom, E., T. Dietz, N. Dolsak, P. C. Stern, S. Stonich, and E. U. Weber, eds. 2002. *The drama of the commons.* Washington, D.C.: National Academy Press.

Rose, C. M. 2002. Common property, regulatory property, and environmental protection: Comparing community-based management to tradable environmental allowances. In *The drama of the commons,* eds. E. Ostrom, T. Dietz, N. Dolsak, P. C. Stern, S. Stonich, and E. U. Weber. Washington, D.C.: National Academy Press.

Rosegrant, M. W., and H. P. Binswanger. 1994. Markets in tradable water rights: Potential for efficiency gains in developing country resource allocation. *World Development* 22 (11): 1613–1625.

Saleth, R. M., and A. Dinar. 2004. *The institutional economics of water: A cross-country analysis of institutions and performance.* Northhampton, Mass.: Edward Elgar and the World Bank.

Sengupta, N. 2000. Negotiation with an under-informed bureaucracy: Water rights on system tanks in Bihar. In *Negotiating water rights,* eds. B. R. Bruns and R. S. Meinzen-Dick. New Delhi and London: Vistaar and Intermediate Technology Press.

Shah, T. 2005. The new institutional economics of India's water policy. Paper presented at the African Water Laws: Plural Legislative Frameworks for Rural Water Management in Africa, January 26–28, 2005, Johannesburg, South Africa.

Steenbergen, F. van, and T. Shah. 2003. Rules rather than rights: Self-regulation in intensively used groundwater systems. In *Intensive use of groundwater. Challenges and opportunities,* ed. M. Llamas and E. Custodio. Lisse, The Netherlands: Balkema.

Tietenberg, T. 2002. The tradable permits approach to protecting the commons: What have we learned? In *The drama of the commons,* eds. E. Ostrom, T. Dietz, N. Dolsak, P. C. Stern, S. Stonich, and E. U. Weber. Washington, D.C.: National Academy Press.

Trawick, P. 2003. Against the privatization of water: An indigenous model for improving existing laws and successfully governing the commons. *World Development* 31 (6): 977–996.

Warner, J., and A. Moreyra, eds. 2004. *Conflictos y participación. Uso múltiple del agua.* Montevideo. Editorial Nordan (Ecoteca No. 35).

Warner, J., and A. Verhallen. 2004. Multi-stakeholder platforms for integrated catchment management: Towards a comparative typology. Paper presented at the 11th International Conference on Multi-Organizational Partnerships, Alliances and Networks (MOPAN), "Coalitions and Collisions," June 23–26, 2004, Tilburg, the Netherlands.

Wester, P., D. J. Merrey, and M. de Lange. 2003. Boundaries of consent: Stakeholder representation in river basin management in Mexico and South Africa. *World Development* 31 (5): 797–812.

Wheeler, D. 2000. *Greening industry: New roles for communities, markets, and governments.* New York: Oxford University Press.

Young, O. R. 2002. *The institutional dimensions of environmental change.* Cambridge, Mass.: MIT Press.

Acronyms and Abbreviations

ADB	Asian Development Bank
BCM	billion cubic meters; see table below for conversions
CAPRI	Collective Action and Property Rights Initiative (a system-wide program of the CGIAR)
CGIAR	Consultative Group on International Agricultural Research
CMA	Catchment Management Agency (South Africa)
COAG	Council of Australian Governments (state and federal)
DFID	Department for International Development (UK)
DG	Director General
DLWC	Department of Land and Water Conservation (Australia)
DWAF	Department of Water Affairs and Forestry (South Africa)
EU	European Union
FWL	Federal Waters Law (Mexico)
FWLL	Federal Water, Levy Law (Mexico)
GIS	Geographic Information System
ha	hectare
IFPRI	International Food Policy Research Institute
IMT	irrigation management transfer
IWRM	integrated water resources management
km	kilometer
MCM	million cubic meters, see table below for conversions

mm	millimeter(s)
MWR	Ministry of Water Resources (China)
NGO	nongovernmental organization
NSW	State of New South Wales, Australia
NWC	National Water Commission (Mexico)
NWL	National Waters Law (Mexico)
NWRS	National Water Resources Strategy (South Africa)
O&M	operation and maintenance
PIM	participatory irrigation management
PJT-I	Perusahaan Umum Jasa Tirta I, state corporation responsible for management in Brantas Basin, East Java, and the Bengawan Solo Basin, Central and East Java, Indonesia
PJT-II	Perusahaan Umum Jasa Tirta II, state corporation responsible for management in Citarum Basin in West Java, Indonesia
PPP	public–private partnerships
WFD	European Union Water Framework Directive of 2000
WUA	water users' association

Units for water volumes

10^{12} liters	teraliter (TL)	billion cubic meters (BCM)	cubic kilometer (km^3)
10^9 liters	gigaliter (GL)	million cubic meters (MCM)	810.7 acre-feet
10^6 liters	megaliter (ML)	thousand cubic meters	0.8107 acre-feet
10^3 liters	kiloliter	cubic meter (m^3)	1 metric ton

Contributors

Charles L. Abernethy (abernethy@itmin.com) is a civil engineer and works as a consultant on management of irrigation and water resources, focusing mainly on developing countries. He resides in Colombo, Sri Lanka. He was connected with the International Water Management Institute in its initial years, as director of research and as senior technical advisor. Prior to that, he headed the Overseas Development Unit of Hydraulics Research, Wallingford, England, and he has developed master's degree courses in management of irrigation systems and in management of erosion and sedimentation. His main professional interest is integration of the technologies of water management with their social, institutional, and economic dimensions, with particular emphasis on our need to prepare better for a future that will be very different from the past.

Rutgerd Boelens (rutgerd.boelens@wur.nl) is a lecturer and researcher with the Irrigation and Water Engineering Group at Wageningen University, the Netherlands. His research focuses on water rights, peasant and indigenous water control, legal pluralism, and interactive irrigation development, particularly in the Andean countries. Currently, he coordinates the program for Water Law and Indigenous Rights (WALIR) on official and local water rights frameworks in Peru, Bolivia, Chile, Ecuador, and Mexico (with a comparative case in the United States). His books include *Searching for equity: Conceptions of justice and equity in peasant irrigation* (with Gloria Dávila, Van Gorcum, 1998); *Water rights and empowerment* (with Paul Hoogendam, IEP/Van Gorcum, 2002); and *Liquid relations: Contested water rights and legal complexity* (with Dik Roth and Margreet Zwarteveen, Rutgers University Press, 2005).

Bryan Randolph Bruns (bryanbruns@bryanbruns.com) is a consulting sociologist with an independent practice specializing in participatory management of irrigation and water resources. He holds a Ph.D. in development sociology from Cornell University. He co-edited *Negotiating water rights* with Ruth Meinzen-Dick. His areas of interest include the role of technological change in international development, infrastructure governance, and dynamics of property rights institutions. Additional information and papers are available at his Web site, www.BryanBruns.com.

Axel Dourojeanni (adourojeanni@eclac.cl) is a natural resources management specialist who now works as a private consultant. He graduated as an agricultural engineer from the National Agrarian University in Peru, and received a master's degree in watershed management from Colorado State University at Fort Collins. He became a principal professor at the National Agrarian University and later headed the Natural Resources and Energy Division of the United Nations Economic Commission for Latin America and the Caribbean (UN/ECLAC) in Santiago, Chile. He has advised on the formulation of water and natural resource laws and on river basin management in Peru, Brazil, Mexico, Chile, and many other countries. His publications include *Management for high mountain river basin development in the Andean zone* and, as editor and primary author, *Dawn in the Andes,* a vision of sustainable development for the Andean region.

Héctor Garduño (hgarduno@mexis.com) is an international consultant on water resources policy, planning, and management. He holds civil engineering and master in hydraulic engineering degrees from the National University of Mexico. Some of his experiences in the Mexican civil service and in assisting other countries were published by FAO in *Water rights administration: Experiences, issues and guidelines.* Since 2000 he has been a core member of the World Bank/Global Water Partnership GW-MATE (Groundwater Management Advisory Team).

Alberto Garrido (alberto.garrido@upm.es) is an associate professor of agricultural and resource economics at the Universidad Politécnica de Madrid (UPM). He holds a degree in agricultural engineering from UPM, a master of science in agricultural and resource economics from the University of California at Davis, and a Ph.D. in agricultural economics from UPM. He has consulted internationally for the Organization for Economic Co-operation and Development (OECD), the Inter-American Development Bank (IADB), World Bank, Food and Agriculture Organization of the United Nations (FAO), European Parliament, and European Commission, and in Spain for the Ministry of Environment, Ministry of Agriculture, Parliament, and the autonomous communities of Aragon and Navarre. He has authored more than 55 publications in the area of natural resource and water economics. He is presently editing a book on water policy in Spain.

Brian Haisman (brianhev@optusnet.com.au) is a consulting water resources manager with an independent practice specializing in all aspects of applied water policy, particularly water rights, asset management, operations, and organizational development. He holds a master of engineering science degree from the University of New South Wales, Australia. He has lengthy experience with integrated water management, has held senior positions in the Murray-Darling Basin Commission, and was director of water resource management for New South Wales. He has been awarded the Order of Australia for outstanding services to water conservation and natural resource management.

Paul Hoogendam (siric@supernet.com.bo) is an irrigation engineer, holding a master of science degree in agricultural engineering from Wageningen University, the Netherlands. He currently heads a consultant team responsible for an investment program in intercommunal irrigation projects in Bolivia. His research results and experiences on water rights and irrigation design have been published in *Aguas y acequias: Derechos de agua y gestión campesina de riego en los Andes bolivianos* (with Gerben Gerbrandy), *Water rights and empowerment* (with Rutgerd Boelens), and *Obras de riego para zonas montañosas* (with Alfonso Bottega).

Douglas S. Kenney (douglas.kenney@colorado.edu) is a senior research associate at the Natural Resources Law Center, University of Colorado School of Law, Boulder, Colorado. He holds a Ph.D. in natural resources from the University of Arizona, specializing in water policy, law, and management in the western United States. He has served in a variety of water-related research and advisory capacities, including work for the Western Water Policy Review Advisory Commission, and is editor of *In search of sustainable water management: International lessons for the American West and Beyond* (Edward Elgar, 2005).

Bin Liu (liubin@mwr.gov.cn) is a senior engineer in the Ministry of Water Resources of China. He holds a master of science degree in water resources from Tsinghua University. His major areas of interest are water resources, water rights, and integrated river basin management. He has published numerous research papers in leading journals in China.

Ruth Meinzen-Dick (r.meinzen-dick@cgiar.org) is a senior research fellow in the Environment and Production Technology Division of the International Food Policy Research Institute. She holds a Ph.D. in development sociology from Cornell University. She coordinates the CGIAR System-wide Program on Collective Action and Property Rights and conducts research on various aspects of water and natural resource management, gender issues, and poverty reduction. Her publications include *Negotiating water rights* (co-edited with Bryan R. Bruns), *Institutional reforms in Indian irrigation* (co-authored with Ashok Gulati and K. V. Raju), and *Innovations in natural resource management* (co-edited with Anna Knox, Frank Place, and Brent Swallow).

Gavin Quibell (quibellg@dwaf.gov.za, gavinq@netactive.co.za) is a freelance consultant with some 20 years of experience in water resource management, water quality, and water environmental management. Most recently he has been acting as the DFID technical advisor to the Water Allocation Reform program in South Africa. This involves developing the methodologies around the reallocation of water from the "haves" to the "have-nots," to address poverty while still supporting continued growth and investment in the country's economy.

Claudia Ringler (c.ringler@cgiar.org) is a research fellow in the Environment and Production Technology Division of the International Food Policy Research Institute, where she co-leads IFPRI's water research program. She holds a Ph.D. in agricultural economics from the Center for Development Research, Bonn University, Germany. Her research interests are in water resources management (in particular, river basin management) and agricultural and natural resource policies for developing countries.

Charles Rodgers (crodgers@uni-bonn.de) is a senior research fellow at the Center for Development Research (ZEF), Bonn University, Germany, and scientific coordinator of the GLOWA Volta Project, a nine-year study of the physical and socioeconomic determinants of the hydrologic cycle within a major transnational West African basin. He is a civil engineer, hydrologist, and applied economist specializing in integrated river basin planning and management, irrigation and agricultural water management, the economics of irrigated agriculture, hydrologic and biophysical modeling, and operations research. He received a Ph.D. in civil engineering–hydrology from the University of Wisconsin at Madison and an M.S. in agricultural and natural resources economics from the University of Minnesota. Prior to joining ZEF, he was a postdoctoral scientist at the International Food Policy Research Institute, Washington, D.C., and an independent consultant in hydrology and hydrometeorology.

Suharto Sarwan formerly headed the section for West Indonesia, Sub-Directorate for Basin Water Resources Management, in the Directorate of Water Resources Utilization and Management, Directorate General of Water Resources, Ministry for Human Settlements and Regional Infrastructure, Indonesia, and now heads the subdirectorate of Water Resources Institutions.

Edella Schlager (eschlager@eller.arizona.edu) is an associate professor in the School of Public Administration and Policy at the University of Arizona. She holds a Ph.D. in political science from Indiana University. She co-authored *Common waters, diverging streams* with William Blomquist and Tanya Heikkila. The book focuses on the conjunctive management of surface- and groundwater in the western United States. Her areas of interest include local-level governance of common-pool resources, water policy and administration, and the emergence and change of institutional arrangements for governing natural resources.

Ashwin R. Seetal (seetala@dwaf.gov.za) is a director with the Department of Water Affairs and Forestry, South Africa, and leading the Directorate for Water Allocation. He has worked in the department for 15 years in various disciplines, including water quality management and legal enforcement, stakeholder engagement and capacity building, institutional transformation and establishment, policy development, and water allocation planning and reform. His expertise extends from strategy formulation through to systems development and program implementation. Prior to joining the department he spent 10 years as a researcher and academic, with a strong emphasis on the aquatic environment in the fields of botany, microbiology, and ecology. He has wide and varied interests in the environment, politics and social science, law, finance, business and management, health, and personal development. His passion for holistic thinking, practicality, and integration forms the essence of his professional credo.

Tjoek Walujo Subijanto (tjoekws@yahoo.com) is director of operations for the Brantas River at Jasa Tirta I Public Corporation (the Brantas and Bengawan Solo River Basin Management Agency), based in Malang, Indonesia. He received a degree in mechanical engineering from Brawijaya University. He has worked on various development projects in the Brantas River Basin for over 18 years. After the establishment of the Jasa Tirta I Public Corporation, he was appointed chief of the research and development bureau. He was a member of the working team for the Indonesian Water Resources Policy Reform. He was also an active participant in the establishment of the Asian Network of River Basin Organizations (NARBO) at Batu, Malang, Indonesia, in February 2004 and now serves as the vice executive director of the Indonesian NARBO Secretariat, responsible for international co-operation and communication.

Index

Page numbers for entries occurring in boxes are suffixed by a *b;* those for entries in figures by an *f;* those for entries in notes by an *n,* with the number of the note following; and those for entries in tables by a *t.*

Water Rights Reform